AF734614

PHARMACOLOGY – RESEARCH, SAFETY TESTING AND REGULATION

THE COST OF PRESCRIPTION DRUGS

PHARMACOLOGY – RESEARCH, SAFETY TESTING AND REGULATION

Additional books and e-books in this series can be found on Nova's website under the Series tab.

PHARMACOLOGY – RESEARCH, SAFETY TESTING AND REGULATION

THE COST OF PRESCRIPTION DRUGS

ALFRED BONSAINT
EDITOR

snova
New York

Copyright © 2020 by Nova Science Publishers, Inc.

All rights reserved. No part of this book may be reproduced, stored in a retrieval system or transmitted in any form or by any means: electronic, electrostatic, magnetic, tape, mechanical photocopying, recording or otherwise without the written permission of the Publisher.

We have partnered with Copyright Clearance Center to make it easy for you to obtain permissions to reuse content from this publication. Simply navigate to this publication's page on Nova's website and locate the "Get Permission" button below the title description. This button is linked directly to the title's permission page on copyright.com. Alternatively, you can visit copyright.com and search by title, ISBN, or ISSN.

For further questions about using the service on copyright.com, please contact:
Copyright Clearance Center
Phone: +1-(978) 750-8400 Fax: +1-(978) 750-4470 E-mail: info@copyright.com.

NOTICE TO THE READER

The Publisher has taken reasonable care in the preparation of this book, but makes no expressed or implied warranty of any kind and assumes no responsibility for any errors or omissions. No liability is assumed for incidental or consequential damages in connection with or arising out of information contained in this book. The Publisher shall not be liable for any special, consequential, or exemplary damages resulting, in whole or in part, from the readers' use of, or reliance upon, this material. Any parts of this book based on government reports are so indicated and copyright is claimed for those parts to the extent applicable to compilations of such works.

Independent verification should be sought for any data, advice or recommendations contained in this book. In addition, no responsibility is assumed by the Publisher for any injury and/or damage to persons or property arising from any methods, products, instructions, ideas or otherwise contained in this publication.

This publication is designed to provide accurate and authoritative information with regard to the subject matter covered herein. It is sold with the clear understanding that the Publisher is not engaged in rendering legal or any other professional services. If legal or any other expert assistance is required, the services of a competent person should be sought. FROM A DECLARATION OF PARTICIPANTS JOINTLY ADOPTED BY A COMMITTEE OF THE AMERICAN BAR ASSOCIATION AND A COMMITTEE OF PUBLISHERS.

Additional color graphics may be available in the e-book version of this book.

Library of Congress Cataloging-in-Publication Data

ISBN: 978-1-53617-540-0

Published by Nova Science Publishers, Inc. † New York

CONTENTS

PREFACE

The prescription drug delivery system—how a drug gets from the manufacturer to the patient—is complicated. More than 4.4 billion prescriptions are written for drugs each year for Americans who then pick up these prescriptions at 60,000 drugstores or receive them from doctors or hospitals or online pharmacies.

Chapter 1 is about how Americans pay for prescription drugs and where that money goes.

Chapter 2 is about the process, beginning with the manufacturer's development of a drug, the different steps through which the drug travels before arriving in a patient's hands, how this is paid for, and what the costs are at each step along the way.

In: The Cost of Prescription Drugs
Editor: Alfred Bonsaint

ISBN: 978-1-53617-540-0
© 2020 Nova Science Publishers, Inc.

Chapter 1

THE COST OF PRESCRIPTION DRUGS: HOW THE DRUG DELIVERY SYSTEM AFFECTS WHAT PATIENTS PAY*

Committee on Health, Education, Labor, and Pensions

Present: Senators Alexander, Collins, Cassidy, Young, Murkowski, Scott, Murray, Sanders, Casey, Franken, Bennet, Whitehouse, Baldwin, Murphy, Warren, Kaine, and Hassan.

OPENING STATEMENT OF SENATOR ALEXANDER

The CHAIRMAN. Good morning.

The Senate Committee on Health, Education, Labor, and Pensions will please come to order.

Today's hearing is about how Americans pay for prescription drugs and where that money goes. This is a bipartisan hearing, which means Senator Murray and I have agreed on the topic, and we have agreed on the witnesses.

Senator Murray and I will each have an opening statement, and then we will introduce the witnesses. We hope you will summarize your remarks in about 5 minutes each, which will leave Senators time to engage in a conversation with you. Senators will have about 5 minutes of questions as we go around.

---

* This is an edited, reformatted and augmented version of Hearing of the Committee on Health, Education, Labor, and Pensions, United States Senate, One Hundred Fifteenth Congress, First Session, on the Cost of Prescription Drugs: Focusing on How the Drug Delivery System Affects What Patients Pay, Publication No. S. HRG. 115–355, dated June 13, 2017.

The committee is having this hearing in response to a bipartisan request from a number of members of the committee. That request was led by Senator Cassidy and Senator Franken, but it included Senators Collins, Baldwin, Murkowski, Whitehouse, Capito, Sanders, Enzi, and Warren. All suggested we should have this hearing.

This will be the first of three hearings we plan to hold on prescription drug costs. The purpose of this first hearing is to see if we can better understand a complex subject and agree on some basic facts. Americans want to know who pays for prescription drugs and where that money goes.

Next month, the committee will hold a second hearing to hear about the process, beginning with the manufacturer's development of a drug, the different steps through which the drug travels before arriving in a patient's hands, how this is paid for, and what the costs are at each step along the way.

In the fall, we will hold a third hearing to hear from Norm Augustine and consider a report that he is leading from the National Academy of Sciences. The report is the outcome of a project called, "Ensuring Patient Access to Affordable Drug Therapies."

The United States leads the world in innovative biomedical and pharmaceutical research and development, and American patients benefit from having access to most lifesaving drugs first.

Our country produces more than 20 percent of the world's wealth, and it is well known that we spend a large share of that wealth on our health, a much larger share than many other advanced countries.

In 2015, according to the Centers for Medicare and Medicaid Services, healthcare spending totaled nearly 18 percent of our country's Gross Domestic Product. Prescription drugs were about 10 percent of that spending and closer to 15 percent when you consider prescription drugs administered in hospitals and doctors' offices.

At around the same time in 2014, the World Bank showed the United Kingdom was spending 9.8 percent of its domestic product on health care, Germany 11.1 percent, and Finland 9.6 percent.

More than 4 billion prescriptions are written for drugs each year for Americans who then receive these drugs at 60,000 drug stores, from doctors or hospitals, or from online pharmacies. The total cost to the overall health system of these prescriptions each year is $450 billion to be paid by taxpayers, by patients, by hospitals, and insurers, among others.

Many of these are truly miracle drugs. They cure Hepatitis C, keep cancer at bay, stop a stroke, and prevent heart attacks.

According to the Centers for Disease Control and Prevention, Americans are living on average 10 years longer than their life expectancy in the 1950s. Access to innovative drugs is a major reason why.

In 2003, Congress passed the Medicare Part D Prescription Drug program, which provides drugs to about 41 million Americans over 65 years of age. The Congressional

Budget Office estimates that prescription drugs from those on Medicare will cost taxpayers and patients about $94 billion this year.

While safe prescription drugs have become an integral part of American family lives today, all of this is relativity new.

In 1906, Congress passed the Federal Food and Drug Act, which added regulatory responsibilities to the Food and Drug Administration's scientific mission by prohibiting interstate commerce in misbranded and adulterated food, drugs, and drinks.

In 1938, this was updated to require a manufacturer to show that each new drug must be safe before it comes to the market, starting a new system of drug regulation.

It was only in 1941 that the Food and Drug Administration, in response to the Insulin Amendment, first began to require that a drug be tested and certified for purity and potency, the first being insulin for the treatment of diabetes. During the next decade and beyond came approval of mass produced penicillin, other antibiotics, and a broader range of drugs.

Developing and approving a drug today is a lengthy and costly process. According to the Tufts Center, from the beginning of the research and development phase through FDA approval, developing a new drug takes, on average, 10 to 15 years and can cost close to $2.6 billion. Let me say that again. According to the Tufts Center, from beginning the research and development phase through FDA approval, developing a new drug takes, on average, 10 to 15 years and can cost close to $2.6 billion.

Success is far from guaranteed. Fewer than 12 percent of drugs that make it to Phase I clinical trials are finally approved by the FDA.

According to Research! America, the United States spent $159 billion on medical health and medical research and development in 2015. The National Institutes of Health funded roughly 19 percent of that; 8 percent was funded by universities and independent research institutes; 5 percent came from other Federal and State governmental entities; 4 percent from foundations and professional societies; 15 percent, or $24 billion, was funded by the medical device industry and other non-biopharma private industry. The largest share of this research, 49 percent or $78 billion, was funded by the biopharmaceutical industry.

It is from these investments that we can expect to see the medical miracles that NIH Director Francis Collins has predicted will occur during the next decade: Artificial pancreas for those with diabetes; new cancer cures; a vaccine for Zika; a vaccine for HIV/AIDS; and a universal flu vaccine; medicines to identify individuals at risk for Alzheimer's before symptoms as well as provide effective therapies to slow or even prevent the disease.

Over the years, this committee in a bipartisan way has produced important laws to reduce the cost of drugs before they are approved by the FDA.

For example, last year's 21st Century Cures legislation; the Hatch-Waxman Act, which created the generic drug industry; and multiple FDA User Fee Agreements, which have helped fund the FDA and modernize our drug and device approval process.

Our focus today is different. It is on what happens to the cost of the drug after it is approved by the FDA. We will examine the path an approved drug takes from the manufacturer to patient, and how this affects what the patient pays.

We hope to agree on some basic facts such as whether prescription drug prices are going up or down, and by how much?

We want to know as prescription drugs move from FDA approval through a complex process and into the hands of patients, where does the money go?

What are rebates and what is their impact on consumers? Who actually pays the cost of prescription drugs?

This is a discussion that affects the well-being of every American family. It is important that we work together to conduct this fact finding in a bipartisan way.

Senator Murray.

OPENING STATEMENT OF SENATOR MURRAY

Senator MURRAY. Well, thank you, Chairman Alexander.

As I have made clear, the burden of prescription drug costs is a huge problem. I hear about it from far too many families in my home State and across the country.

I am glad we are having this discussion today. It is something Democrats on this committee have wanted to do for a very long time, and I am pleased that we are working on some additional hearings. I am hopeful this work can lead to some real bipartisan progress.

I want to express my appreciation, in particular, to Senator Franken, who has been underscoring the importance of hearing from actual patients about the struggle they face in affording the medication they need. Our work on this committee is strongest when patients' and families' voices are part of this process. I agree, we should make sure that that happens as our discussion on this continues.

I also want to note that today's hearing, on a topic central to families' experience with our healthcare system, takes place in the midst of a pivotal and deeply concerning moment for our healthcare system as a whole.

My colleagues on the other side of the aisle appear to be dead set on jamming their version of Trumpcare through the Senate in a matter of days. They have held no hearings, engaged in no public debate, and provided no information for people across the country to understand what this all-male, Republican working group has in store for their health and financial security.

For comparison, during the debate on the Affordable Care Act, we held 57 bipartisan meetings, hearings, roundtables, and walkthroughs on the text in this committee alone, and another 53 in the Finance Committee. There were 25 consecutive days of debate on the Senate floor.

Mr. Chairman, I just have to say this morning, I cannot say how strongly enough, how unacceptable this is, and I will be very loud and vocal about this, and continue to push for hearings and open debate on the Senate version of the Trumpcare bill.

In fact, given this committee's long track record of bipartisan successes, I have to say I am really surprised and disappointed that we are allowing this to happen. I know you are part of the process that is going on in secret.

I just have to tell you, people deserve public debate about the future of our healthcare system especially since all Senate Republicans' promises to the contrary, it unfortunately sounds like this legislation is based on the very same principles as the disastrous House Trumpcare bill, including higher costs for families, especially seniors and people with pre-existing conditions.

Millions of people will be kicked off Medicaid. Insurance companies, once again, will be allowed to charge people more for basic healthcare like maternity care or mental health services, or as we are talking about today, the expensive, but essential prescription drugs they need. All to give a massive tax break to special interests in the health industry and hand President Trump a hollow political win.

Let us be clear, as many of my democratic colleagues have said, this is not a healthcare bill. It is an attack on families, and health, and financial security.

What I really do hope is over the next several weeks as Republicans hear from many people across the country who would be devastated by this bill that they choose to change course.

I will say again, Democrats are ready, like we always have been, to work together on continuing to fix our healthcare system in ways that make our healthcare system more affordable while preserving quality of care and getting more people covered.

We cannot begin that conversation until Republicans reverse course and stop trying to take our healthcare system backward with a reckless repeal effort and politically motivated sabotage that is creating damaging uncertainty in our markets and driving up our families' costs.

I sincerely hope that this effort is backed off because there are urgent challenges like the one we are talking about today that really deserve our attention.

Today's astronomically high prescription drug prices are an unsustainable burden on our healthcare system as a whole and especially on the patients and families that we represent. I have heard from far too many families who are forced to choose between high-priced medication, paying the bills, or putting food on the table. That really is no choice at all. So as I said before, it is well past time for this conversation and for progress on this issue.

As we discuss the reality of the high prices too many of our constituents are paying for prescription drugs, I do think it is important to note that President Trump is wrong to point the finger at the FDA.

Over two-thirds of new drugs are now launched in the United States, more than triple the rate in the early 1990s, when the first user fee programs were enacted. The Agency has reduced the backlog of generic applications to help get competitive, cheaper drugs to patients.

I am pleased this committee took steps in the FDA Reauthorization Act to increase transparency and foster more competition in the generic market, thanks to the work of Senators McCaskill, Collins, and Franken.

We should always look for ways to get more safe, effective treatments to patients as quickly as possible. The FDA approval process is the wrong place to look if we really want to tackle high drug prices.

I am proud that a number of Democrats on this committee have put forward a number of ideas to get at the root of the problem, which are the high prices set by drug manufacturers.

Democrats have introduced legislation, including bipartisan legislation, to demand more transparency from pharmaceutical companies about what is behind the soaring drug prices, allow Medicare to negotiate fair prices for prescription drugs, and to prevent manufacturers from engaging in price gouging and more.

I am grateful to all the members of this committee who have worked together, and across the aisle, to advance these polices, which would make a real difference to the patients and families we serve.

Mr. Chairman, I am glad to hear that today's conversation on the burden of prescription drug prices will not be the last on this committee, but there is a lot more we can do and should do together to tackle this issue.

Again, it is deeply disappointing that instead of working with Democrats to bring down the price of prescription drugs for families, and the other challenges that so many people face in the healthcare system, my Republican colleagues are very focused on a partisan, political, and damaging effort to enact Trumpcare within the next few weeks without any public scrutiny.

I really hope that instead of working to jam Trumpcare legislation through, according to an independent CBO analysis, is a direct threat to the lives, and health, and financial security of millions of people. That you all will reconsider, reverse course, and work with us on solving problems.

If you do, if you drop your efforts to sabotage the healthcare system and enact Trumpcare, and if you are ready to tackle the challenges by bringing down the healthcare costs for families, we are at the table. We are ready to work and we want to do that.

Thank you very much, Mr. Chair.

The CHAIRMAN. Thank you, Senator Murray.

I will repeat. This is a hearing requested by Democrats as well as Republicans on drug prices. It is a bipartisan hearing and it is one in which Senator Murray and I have agreed on the witnesses.

We welcome the witnesses. I will introduce you now. Each witness will have up to 5 minutes to give his testimony. We are going to go from left to right, but let me introduce them this way.

Dan Mendelson is the first witness we will hear from. He is the president of Avalere Health, a leading healthcare consulting firm specializing in strategy, policy, and data analysis for life sciences, health plans, and providers. Prior to founding Avalere in 2000, he served as Associate Director for Health at the White House Office of Management and Budget.

Next, we will hear from Allan Coukell, senior director of health programs at The Pew Charitable Trusts. The Trusts is an independent, nongovernmental organization that conducts analysis to provide useful data on issues and trends in public policy. Mr. Coukell oversees initiatives at The Pew related to drug and medical device innovation and safety, the pharmaceutical supply chain, FDA, specialty drugs, as well as other efforts related to health costs and delivery.

Third, Dr. Paul Howard is senior fellow and director of health policy at the Manhattan Institute. Dr. Howard has written on a wide variety of medical policy issues including FDA reform, bio-pharmaceutical innovation, consumer-driven healthcare, Medicare and Medicaid reform.

Last, we will hear from Dr. Gerard Anderson, professor of health policy and management at the Johns Hopkins University Bloomberg School of Public Health and Medicine. Dr. Anderson is also director of the Johns Hopkins Center for Hospital Finance and Management. He is currently conducting research on drug pricing, chronic conditions, comparative insurance systems in developing countries, medical education, and healthcare payment reform.

Mr. Mendelson, let us start with you and go down the line.

Welcome.

STATEMENT OF DAN MENDELSON, PRESIDENT, AVALERE HEALTH, WASHINGTON, DC

Mr. MENDELSON. Thank you very much.

Chairman Alexander, Ranking Member Murray, members of the committee, thank you for the invitation to discuss how the healthcare delivery system affects what consumers pay for prescription drugs.

I also want to thank the incredible team at Avalere Health whose passion to be the essential voice improving healthcare is being realized today. Of course, my comments are my own and do not reflect the views of my organization or our parent company, Inovalon.

My full testimony has plenty of detail about the current system, including trends in pricing that address a lot of the initial questions that you asked, Senator Alexander.

I have chosen to focus my comments today on three items—aspects of the delivery system that are within the purview of this committee. First, let us focus on benefit design.

In recent years, payers have been under increasing pressure to meet consumer demand for constrained premium growth. Deductibles and cost sharing for medications have increased substantially across both commercial and Government payment systems.

Growth and exposure to cost by consumers is seen across traditional employer plans, Government plans, as well as high deductible plans. Cost sharing for drugs is typically higher on a percentage basis from that for hospital or other medical care. It is not uncommon that you will see a patient paying more for a chronic medication than they would for a surgery, even though the surgery costs the healthcare system more.

One other thing to consider is that cost sharing is typically calculated on the basis of the full price of the drug before accounting for rebates or discounts offered by the manufacturer. There are some exceptions to this. For example, CVS Health can adjudicate rebates at the point of sale and give the consumer a net price.

There is a question, why should an individual with a chronic illness, who needs a high cost medication, not benefit from the price concessions given by a pharmaceutical company on that particular product in the competitive class?

We also need to think carefully about the incentives that benefit designs give patients. For example, if a patient with Multiple Sclerosis, rheumatoid arthritis, or anemia has to use a drug in its class and the only drugs available have a 35 percent co-pay, why should they have to pay that percentage co-pay even though the only reason that they are doing it is because they have this particular condition? Why should a patient have to pay more than the cost of a generic drug for a generic drug in a design?

These are all questions that, I think, are important.

My second area of focus is competition. Speeding the approval of second and third branded drugs to market would dramatically expedite competition and result in price concessions from manufacturers.

You saw this with the second drug in the Hepatitis C category when it was approved. The net prices of these products were reduced dramatically.

A second area, that I know is a strong interest and within the purview of this committee, is generic pharmaceuticals where approving generics on an expedited basis in various places does create dramatic consumer surplus. Then finally, biosimilar competition and expediting these drugs to market.

All of these are really very important and an important facet of the delivery system because it is in this competition that drug prices actually come down over a period of time.

My final area of focus is value-based contracting. We are in the midst of a very dramatic transformation in healthcare from pay for volume to pay for value. This is of direct relevance, I believe, to the cost of pharmaceuticals. We see this in Medicare Advantage.

For example, Medicare Advantage plans have to do well on their quality metrics in order to have a viable business. A lot of these quality metrics are being driven by things like the prescription of generic cholesterol lowering medications.

In fact, we see many plans actually paying substantial amounts of money to create programs to get patients to take these medications. That is the kind of design that, benefits the program and the kind of design that is important in the future.

One other aspect that I would like to mention is data. Using the patient's data to identify gaps in care, doing analytics on that basis, and then ensuring that the patient that actually needs the medication is getting what they need, also has tremendous promise to reduce total health system costs, and merits the focus of this committee.

There are many regulations right now that actually prevent manufacturers and health plans from entering into the kinds of arrangements that can actually reduce cost for consumers, and they do merit the focus of the committee.

I want to close with one comment about process. Underlying all of our work is the view that collaboration is absolutely critical to fashioning good policy. So in the work that we do, we are always looking for solutions that will be embraced by a broad array of policies. We are a nonpartisan, nonpolitical organization and try to focus in that way as well.

I am excited to continue supporting this discussion as it evolves over the course of the three hearings.

Thank you very much.

[The prepared statement of Mr. Mendelson follows:]

PREPARED STATEMENT OF DAN MENDELSON

Summary

The focus of this testimony is how the healthcare delivery system affects what consumers pay for prescription drugs. Consumer exposure to drug costs is determined by benefit design, the competitiveness of drug classes, and approaches to provider payment, among other factors. Health system change, including outcome-based payment and value-based contracting, has potential to incent better alignment between consumers and providers.

Benefit Design

In recent years, payers have been under increasing pressure to meet consumer demand for constrained premium growth through changes to benefit design. Deductibles and cost sharing for medications have increased substantially across government and commercial payers, leading many consumers to pay more out-of-pocket for drugs.[1] For medications subject to the deductible or coinsurance, consumer cost sharing is typically calculated on the full cost of the drug before accounting for rebates or discounts offered by the manufacturer to the health plan or pharmacy benefit manager. Of course, consumer costs are also importantly determined by the pricing decisions made by pharmaceutical companies prior to entry of product into the supply chain.

Market Competition

Increased competition in the pharmaceutical markets holds promise for substantially reducing costs. Speeding the approval of the second- and third-branded drugs in a therapeutic class would expedite competition and lead to more rapid price concessions. Ensuring a continued robust market for generic pharmaceutics is vital for effective cost management and improvement of population health outcomes. Finally, there is much promise for consumers in effective biosimilar competition as patents on key biologics expire.[2]

Market Driven Solutions

As payers strive to link payment to value, healthcare stakeholders must agree on how to define and measure the value of any given product or service. Importantly, in addition to reflecting patient perspectives on what constitutes value, assessments of value should consider not only cost of the medication but also total cost of care, including pharmacy and medical spending.

Outcomes-based contracts also represent a significant opportunity to shift away from prescription drug list pricing toward value-based reimbursement models. Avalere recently

---

[1] Avalere Health, "Consumer Costs Continue to Increase in 2017 Exchanges," January 18, 2017, http://avalere.com/expertise/life-sciences/insights/consumer-costs-continue-to-increase-in-2017-exchanges.

[2] Avalere Health, "Five Obstacles to Competition in the United States Biologics Market," http://avalere.com/expertise/life-sciences/insights/five-obstacles-to-competition-in-the-united-states-biologics-market.

found that 70 percent of health plans have favorable attitudes toward outcomes-based contracts, and one-half of health plans indicate they have outcomes-based contracts already in place or are actively negotiating them.[3] Existing regulatory barriers, including standards related to government price reporting and the Anti-Kickback Statute, presently hamper further development of this trend.[4]

Health system change is increasingly assigning value to improvements in population outcomes for common medical conditions, and many of these outcomes can be effectively achieved through better use of medication. Further alignment of stakeholder interests around the use of pharmaceuticals holds promise to benefit consumers as payment systems evolve toward value-based designs.

Ensuring Access, Innovation, and Affordability of Prescription Drugs in Our Delivery System, Dan Mendelson President, Avalere June 13, 2017, Statement before the Senate Committee on Health, Education, Labor and Pensions

Introduction

The prices that consumers pay for drugs are determined jointly by health system design, pharmaceutical company pricing, and decisions by health plans, pharmacy benefit management (PBM) practices, and other transactions involving distributors and pharmacies along the supply chain. As the healthcare system moves from volume- to value-based payments, the incentives underlying many of these market-based pricing decisions are also changing rapidly. The purpose of this testimony is to elucidate how these factors ultimately determine the prices paid by the consumer for drugs.

How Net Prices to the Consumer Are Determined

The pharmaceutical supply chain is the means through which prescription medicines are delivered to patients (Figure 1).[5] Drugs typically originate in manufacturing sites; are

---

[3] Avalere Health, "Health Plans are Actively Exploring Outcomes-Based Contracts," May 30, 2017, http://avalere.com/expertise/life-sciences/insights/health-plans-are-actively-exploring-outcomes-based-contracts.

[4] Eli Lilly and Company and Anthem, "Promoting Value-Based Contracting Arrangements," January 2016. https://lillypad.lilly.com/WP/wp-content/uploads/LillyAnthemWP2.pdf.

[5] Avalere Health (formerly The Health Strategies Consultancy), "Follow the Pill: Understanding the US Commercial Pharmaceutical Supply Chain," Kaiser Family Foundation, March 2005.

transferred to wholesale distributors; stocked at retail, mail-order, and other types of pharmacies; subject to price negotiations and processed through quality and utilization management screens by PBMs; dispensed by pharmacies; and ultimately delivered to and taken by patients. There are many variations on this basic structure, as the players in the supply chain are constantly evolving, and commercial relationships vary considerably by geography, type of medication, and other factors. The pharmaceutical supply system is complex and results in price variability across different payers and consumers.

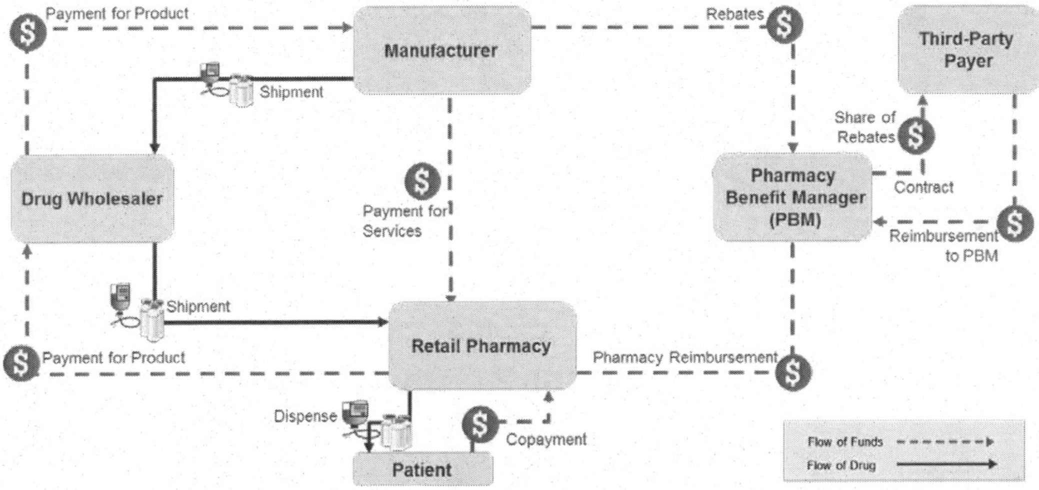

Figure 1. Retail, Pharmacy Benefit Product and Reimbursement Flow.

Drug Spending Trends

Drugs dispensed in the pharmacy and medical benefit account for approximately 13% of total US healthcare costs.[6] This frequently-cited figure uses total national health expenditures as a basis for calculating the percentage. Other experts sometimes use a subset of national health expenditures or total medical claims as the denominator, which accounts for the range of percentages often cited in this context. In recent years, new innovations have increased spending on specialty medications, which now account for $384 of the $895 per person per year spent on drugs.[7] These trends particularly impact

[6] Centers for Medicare & Medicaid Services, National Health Expenditure Data. NHE Tables. December 2016. https://www.cms.gov/Research-Statistics-Data-and-Systems/Statistics-Trends-and-Reports/NationalHealthExpendData/NationalHealthAccountsHistorical.html; Altarum Institute Center for Sustainable Health Spending, "A Ten Year Projection of the Prescription Drug Share of National Health Expenditures Including Non-Retail," May 2017 (Addendum II).

[7] Quintiles IMS Institute. "Medicines Use and Spending in the US," May 2017. http://www.imshealth.com/en/thought-leadership/quintilesims-institute/reports/medicines-use-and-spending-in-the-us-review-of-2016-outlook-to-2021#form.

the Medicare program, in which the Medicare Trustees project that Part D spending will grow at an average annual rate of 9.2% from 2016-2025.[8]

Over the past five years, list prices for protected pharmacy benefit drugs have increased 11.5%, while net prices have increased 6.1% (Figure 2).[9] The difference is the result of rebates and other discounts from manufacturers to public and private payers. These considerable differences between list and net pricing trends show the power that competition and payer negotiation have on drug prices. As multiple products for a given indication come to market, plans and PBMs may negotiate rebates and other price concessions from manufacturers in exchange for preferred formulary placement and improved access. Typically, payers use these price concessions to reduce overall premiums, but the rebates are not shared directly with patients at the point of sale. As a result, most patients who fill a prescription are paying cost-sharing based on a price that is generally not reflective of rebates negotiated by a health plan or PBM.

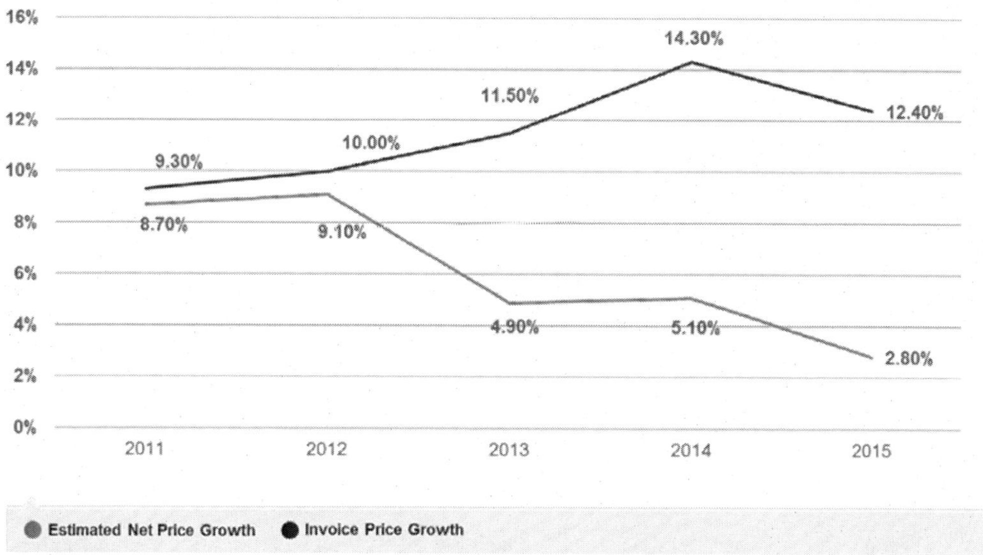

Figure 2. List vs. Net Price Growth, Protected Pharmacy Benefit Drugs, 2011-2015.

Benefit Design

Insurance benefit designs increasingly expose consumers to the full cost of their medicines through percentage co-payments for drugs. Further, consumer exposure to out-of-pocket costs has increased as deductibles have grown across benefit programs.

---

[8] Medicare Trustees. "2016 Annual Report," June 2016. https://www.cms.gov/research-statistics-data-and-systems/statistics- trends-and-reports/reportstrustfunds/downloads/tr2016.pdf.

[9] Quintiles IMS Institute. "Medicines Use and Spending in the US," April 2016, http://www.imshealth.com/en/thought-leadership/quintilesims-institute/reports/medicines-use-and-spending-in-the-us-a-review-of-2015-and-outlook-to-2020.

In recent years, payers have been under increasing pressure to meet consumer demand for constrained premium growth through changes to benefit design. In particular, the financial crisis accelerated adoption of high deductible health plans (HDHPs) among employers.[10] In addition, the patient protections put in place under the Affordable Care Act (ACA) required payers to focus on benefit design as a way to offer competitive premiums in an environment where price-sensitive consumers focus on monthly costs. Consumers are therefore paying more out-of-pocket for prescription drugs as deductibles increase and use of coinsurance for drugs becomes more common. Of course, other factors unrelated to the delivery system effects that are the focus of this hearing are also responsible for increased payment by consumers – such as the cost of newly launched products and the increases in list prices over time referenced in cost sharing.

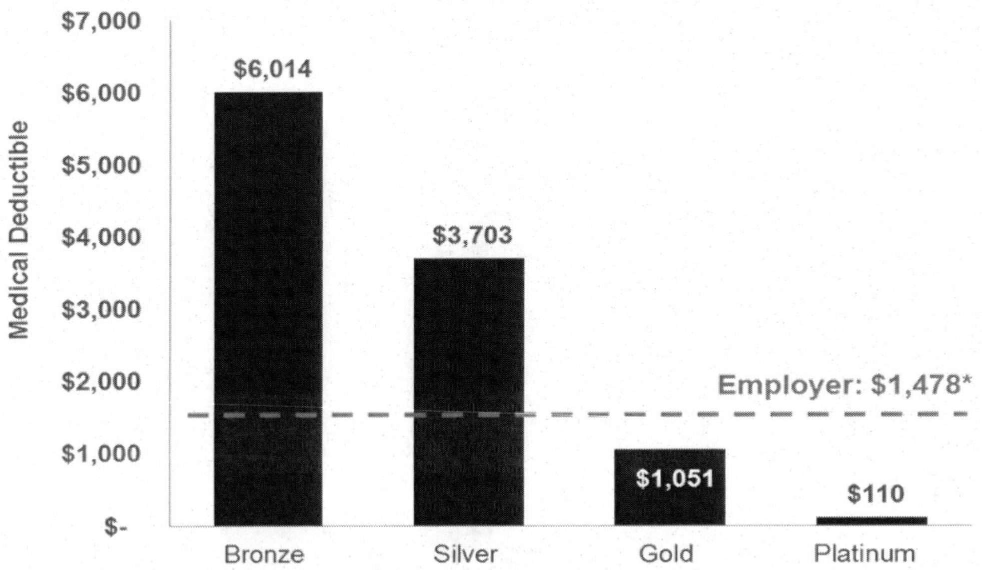

Figure 3. Average Combined Deductibles for Exchange Plans by Metal Level in 2017 Compared to Employer Plans in 2016.[11]

Health plan deductibles have grown steadily over time. Among individuals with employer coverage, average deductibles increased 49% over the last five years, rising to $1,478 in 2016.[12] For individuals enrolled in coverage through exchanges, 2017 unsubsidized silver plans had average deductibles of $3,703—a 20% increase from 2016

[10] Bureau of Labor Statistics. "Consumer-Driven Health Care: What Is It, and What Does It Mean for Employees and Employers?" October 2010. https://www.bls.gov/opub/mlr/cwc/consumer-driven-health-care-what-is-it-and-what-does-it-mean-for-employees-and-employers.pdf.

[11] Avalere PlanScape®, a proprietary analysis of exchange plan features, December 2016 and Kaiser-HRET, "2016 Employer Health Benefits Survey." Avalere analyzed data from the FFE Individual Landscape File released October 2016 and the California and New York state exchange websites.

[12] Kaiser-HRET. "2016 Employer Health Benefits Survey," September 2016. http://www.kff.org/health-costs/press-release/average-annual-workplace-family-health-premiums-rise-modest-3-to-18142-in-2016-more-workers-enroll-in-high-deductible-plans-with-savings-option-over-past-two-years/.

and a 49% increase from 2014 levels.[13] Importantly, 56% of exchange consumers receive cost sharing reduction subsidies (CSRs), which lower deductibles to between $243 and $3,070 on average based on consumer income. The American Health Care Act (AHCA) would repeal the CSRs.[14]

For drugs dispensed in the deductible, consumers pay the full cost of the drug based on the price negotiated by the pharmacy or provider. This price generally does not reflect rebates or other post point-of-sale price concessions offered by the manufacturer to the health plan or PBM. As a result, patients who choose plans with significant deductibles and also use specialty and high-cost medications can face large bills for these drugs early in the calendar year, which may cause them to forego care or prevent them from complying with prescribed drug regimens. Research shows that high out-of-pocket costs reduce medication adherence and use.[15] Indeed, only 9% of patients without a deductible abandon prescriptions, while patients with a deductible abandon medications at a rate of 23% and 27% for brand and specialty drugs respectively.[16]

Once consumers spend through the deductible, they continue to pay cost-sharing as they access products and services. Increasingly for prescription drugs, this cost sharing takes the form of coinsurance, in which individuals pay a percentage of the cost of the drug rather than a fixed dollar copayment. Coinsurance is calculated based on a price that is not reflective of most discounts or rebates negotiated by the health plan or PBM.

As the number of specialty medications on the market has increased, so too has the use of specialty drug tiers. In 2016, 43% of employer plans had separate tiers for these products. Among those plans, 46% charge coinsurance averaging 26%.[17] This trend is more pronounced in the exchange markets where 84% of all 2017 silver plans charge coinsurance for specialty drugs with average coinsurance amounts of 37% of the drug cost (Figure 4).[18]

---

[13] Avalere Health, "Consumer Costs Continue to Increase in 2017 Exchanges," January 18, 2017, http://avalere.com/expertise/life-sciences/insights/consumer-costs-continue-to-increase-in-2017-exchanges.

[14] Avalere Health, "AHCA Will Remove Low-Cost Sharing Guarantees for Low-Income Individuals," May 16, 2017. http://avalere.com/expertise/managed-care/insights/ahca-will-remove-low-cost-sharing-guarantees-for-low-income-individuals.

[15] Goldman DP, Joyce GF, Zheng Y. Prescription drug cost sharing: associations with medication and medical utilization and spending and health. *Jama.* 2007;298(1):61-69. Kirkman MS, Rowan-Martin MT, Levin R, et al. Determinants of adherence to diabetes medications: findings from a large pharmacy claims database. *Diabetes care.* 2015;38(4):604-609. Li P, Schwartz JS, Doshi JA. Impact of Cost Sharing on Therapeutic Substitution: The Story of Statins in 2006. *Journal of the American Heart Association.* 2016;5(11).

[16] Quintiles IMS Institute. "Medicines Use and Spending in the US," May 2017. http://www.imshealth.com/en/thought-leadership/quintilesims-institute/reports/medicines-use-and-spending-in-the-us-review-of-2016-outlook-to-2021#form.

[17] Kaiser-HRET. "2016 Employer Health Benefits Survey," September 2016. http://www.kff.org/health-costs/report/2016- employer-health-benefits-survey/.

[18] Avalere PlanScape®, a proprietary analysis of exchange plan features, December 2016. Avalere analyzed data from the FFE Individual Landscape File released October 2016 and the California and New York state exchange websites.

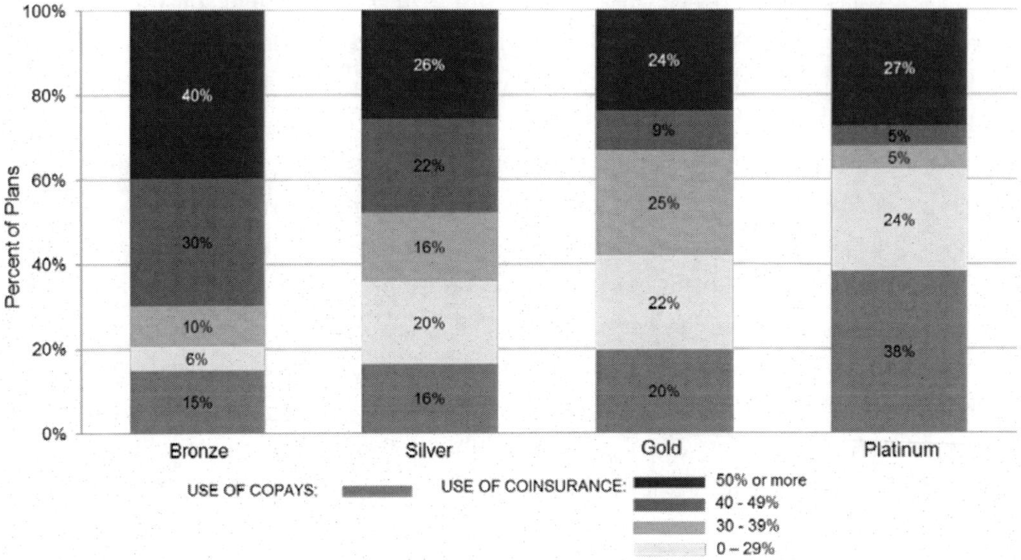

Figure 4. Prescription Drug Cost Sharing on Specialty Tier in Exchange Plans.

Notably, the ACA implemented a maximum out-of-pocket limit that caps consumer costs across all healthcare services. This limit offers important protection for chronically ill individuals against catastrophic healthcare costs, but does not extend to Medicare beneficiaries. In addition, as benefits expose consumers to increasing costs, use of copay assistance has also risen. IMS reports that 19% of commercial brand drug claims in 2016 included the use of a copay coupon to reduce out-of-pocket costs, with significant variation across therapeutic classes.[19] Across all forms of insurance, consumer out-of-pocket burden is not evenly distributed among covered benefits. Outpatient prescription drugs are covered at lower percentage rates than some other services. One study, using data from 2014, showed that for all drugs covered by insurance in the US, consumers paid 13% of every dollar compared to 3% for hospital stays, 7% for emergency care, and 14% for physician office visits.[20] These data demonstrate the role of benefit design in shaping consumer perception of cost.

Market Competition

Consumer experience with drug costs is importantly determined by the competitiveness of drug classes. Increased competition in a class–whether through the

---

[19] Quintiles IMS Institute. "Medicines Use and Spending in the US," May 2017. http://www.imshealth.com/en/thought-leadership/quintilesims-institute/reports/medicines-use-and-spending-in-the-us-review-of-2016-outlook-to-2021#form.

[20] Avalere analysis of Medical Expenditure Panel Survey, 2014, from the US Department of Health and Human Services, Agency for Healthcare Research and Quality. https://meps.ahrq.gov/mepsweb/. Accessed February 2017. Analysis includes all individuals with any source of health care coverage, including public and private.

introduction of a generic or a competitive branded product–typically results in substantial net price reductions, particularly for legacy products.

Health plans and PBMs play an important role in negotiating drug rebates and discounts on behalf of employees, individual market consumers, and government programs. This role is exemplified when a second-to-market brand medication enters the market. While underlying data is proprietary, recent experience associated with the Hepatitis C market suggests competition among brands led to significant reductions in net prices for innovative medicines.[21] In addition, managed care entities incent use of lower-cost alternatives, including generics. Health plans and self-insured employers expect that their PBMs will effectively manage cost–and often compensate on that basis.

In addition to managed care stakeholders, drug approval and exclusivity processes introduce competition into the marketplace. For traditional, small-molecule drugs, the generic approval system created under the Drug Price Competition and Patent Term Restoration Act of 1984 (known as the Hatch-Waxman Act) has been effective at maintaining commercial incentives for drug development through market exclusivity, while creating strong pricing pressure through generic competition later in the product lifecycle. Despite concerns during the passage of Hatch-Waxman, the number of approved New Drug Applications (NDAs) has remained relatively constant in over three decades since its enactment, and generic drugs now comprise 89% of all drugs dispensed in the US.[22] On average, drug prices decrease by 51% within 12 months of generic competition and decrease by nearly 80% within 6 years. In the past 10 years, cost savings from generics are estimated at $1.68T.[23]

There are a few exceptions where competition does not produce dramatic cost savings for patients in today's environment. First, is the case of generics with limited or no competition, in which the traditional competitive pricing pressures do not always apply.[24] FDA Commissioner Scott Gottlieb has already indicated his support of initiatives to focus on speeding entry of second-to-market generics.[25] For products that have not yet reached the end of their exclusivity, the FDA may also be able to accelerate approval of the second product to market to encourage more rapid competition and price concessions from branded drugs.

---

21 Humer, Caroline, "HCV price war will save an estimated $4 billion," Reuters, January 2015. http://www.reuters.com/article/us-express-scr-hepatitisc-idUSKBN0KV26X20150122.

22 FDA. "Summary of NDA Approvals & Receipts, 1938 to the present." 2011. https://www.fda.gov/aboutfda/whatwedo/history/productregulation/summaryofndaapprovalsreceipts1938tothepresent/default. htm. Last accessed 2 May 2017.

23 Ostroff, Stephen. "Building a Modern Generic Review Process." Food and Drug Administration. FDA, 4 Feb 2016. Web. 28. April. 2017. https://blogs.fda.gov/fdavoice/index.php/2016/02/building-a-modern-generic-drug-review-process/.

24 Government Accountability Office. "Generic Drugs under Medicare," August 2016. http://www.gao.gov/assets/680/679022.pdf.

25 Edney, Anna, "Drug Prices Become Target for FDA as Chief Expands Purview," Bloomberg, June 2017. https://www.bloomberg.com/news/articles/2017-06-05/drug-prices-become-target-for-fda-as-chief-expands-agency-s-view.

Biologics are another area of focus for improved competition. Biologics have grown to represent 79% ($11.5B) of Medicare Part B (Figure 5) and 21% ($8.7B) of Medicare Part D spending for the top 20 drugs in each program.[26]

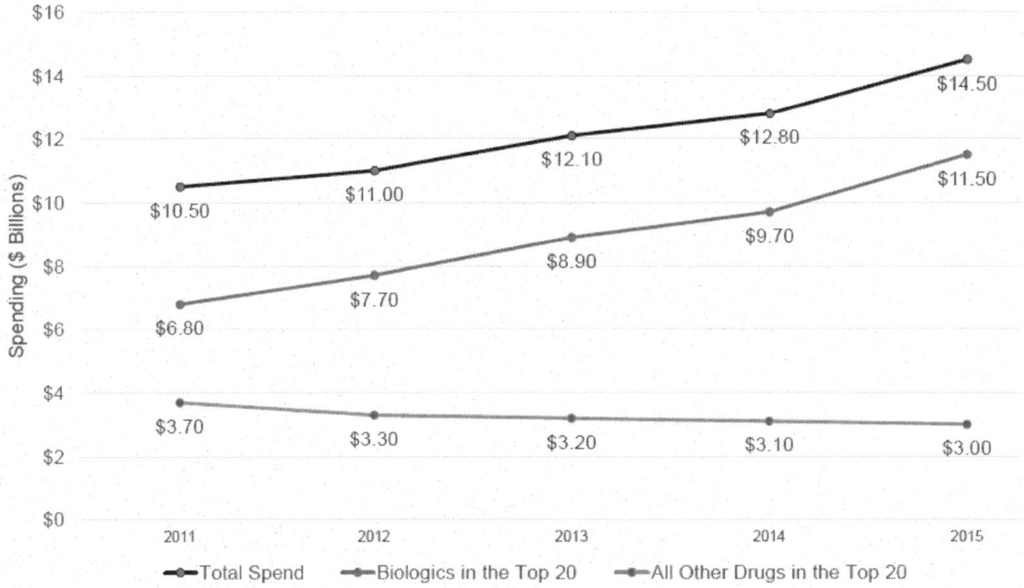

Figure 5. Medicare Top 20 Part B Spending Trends.

In 2010, a biosimilar approval pathway was created with an expectation that a multi-source competitive market could offer potential savings for the US health system.[27] However, obstacles remain that may limit the pricing benefits of a truly competitive biologics market—including both innovator and biosimilar products:

1) Complexity of Development: While generics typically experience a 3-5 year development timeline and a cost of $1-5M dollars, biosimilar development requires 8-10 years and potentially costs $200M or more due to the complexity of the molecules involved.[28] As a result, it is unlikely that biosimilars pricing will ever match the level of savings in the generic pharmaceutical market.

---

[26] Avalere Health, "Five Obstacles to Competition in the United States Biologics Market," http://avalere.com/expertise/life-sciences/insights/five-obstacles-to-competition-in-the-united-states-biologics-market.

[27] The biosimilar pathway was created by the Biologics Price Competition and Innovation Act (BPCIA) as Title VII of the Patient Protection and Affordable Care Act in 2010. Available at: http://www.fda.gov/downloads/Drugs/GuidanceComplianceRegulatoryInformation/UCM216146.pdf.

[28] DiMasi, Joseph A., Henry G. Grabowski, and Ronald W. Hansen. "Innovation in the pharmaceutical industry: new estimates of R&D costs." Journal of Health Economics 47 (2016): 20-33. Federal Trade Commission. Emerging health care issues: follow-on biologic drug competition. June 2009 Report. Available at: http://www.ftc.gov/os/2009/06/P083901biologicsreport.pdf.

2) Prescribing Patterns: Patient and provider reticence to switch from a reference biologic to a biosimilar may also hamper market competition, though this manifests itself differently in different therapeutic areas.
3) Interchangability: As of yet, the FDA has not issued final guidance on how products would be designated as interchangeable, which limits the potential for automatic substitution and associated cost savings.
4) Physician Reimbursement Model: Within Medicare Fee-For-Service, the Average Sales Price (ASP) payment methodology may limit competition by paying physicians the same plus 6% add-on payment for either the innovator or the biosimilar product, which does not encourage providers to prescribe the biosimilar.
5) Consumer Out-of-Pocket Costs: Within Medicare Part D, the current benefit structure results in beneficiaries paying substantially more out-of-pocket for biosimilars relative to the innovator product.[29]

Market-Driven Interventions

As payers strive to link payment to value, healthcare stakeholders must agree on how to define and measure the value of any given product or service. In 2015, a series of new public-facing value frameworks emerged to address this question—attempting to balance clinical benefits of a given product against the system-wide costs. Many of these frameworks failed to adequately consider patient preferences in their assessments.

In 2017, Avalere and *FasterCures* launched the Patient-Perspective Value Framework that assesses the benefits and costs of different healthcare options in the context of patients' personal goals and preferences, including things like symptom relief, complexity of regimen, and cost to the patient's family. This sort of holistic assessment of value that is broader than clinical outcomes and customized to reflect individual patient perspectives will be crucial for continuing to evolve our drug payment and delivery system to reward value.

Importantly, assessments of value should consider not only cost of the medication but total cost of care, including pharmacy and medical spending. Unfortunately, in many instances, public program structures, contractual relationships, and data limitations prevent effective assessments of value based on total cost of care. For instance, the Medicare Part D program is inherently structured to encourage lower, more competitive

[29] Avalere Health. "Patient Out-of-Pocket Costs for Biosimilars in Medicare Part D." Avalere Health, April 2016. Web. 19 May 2017. Available at: http://go.avalere.com/acton/attachment/12909/f-02c0/1/-/-/-/-/20160412_Patient%20OOP%20for%20Biosimilars%20in%20Part%20D.pdf.

premiums for drugs by reducing pharmacy benefit spending—even if higher spending on medications could reduce costs in Medicare Parts A and B.

Outcomes-based contracts also represent a significant opportunity to shift away from prescription drug list prices toward value-based reimbursement models. A recent survey conducted by Avalere found that 70% of health plans have favorable attitudes toward outcomes-based contracts, and one-half of health plans indicate they have outcomes-based contracts already in place or are actively negotiating them.[30] Unfortunately, existing regulatory barriers, including standards related to government price reporting and the Anti-Kickback Statute, presently hamper further development of this trend.[31]

Effective outcomes-based contracts require next-generation data analysis and interventions that enable payers and manufacturers to identify patients eligible for treatment, target outreach to ensure appropriate adherence and quality improvement, and measure product performance against pre-agreed-upon outcomes on an ongoing basis. Consumer benefit can be substantially enhanced through data-based engagement around pharmaceuticals, including:

1) Data Aggregation and Management: Facilitating data sharing between a health plan and manufacturer to enable real-time contract management and ongoing evaluation of results.
2) Patient Identification: Designing algorithms to proactively identify patients most likely to benefit from a given therapy based on their demographics, geography, treatment type, and insurance coverage. Conducting statistical modeling to predict patient outcomes and potential benefit from the product.
3) Patient and Provider Engagement: Conduct targeted outreach to providers and directly to patients with interventions intended to improve adherence and achieve desired outcomes.

As more manufacturers and health plans embark on these data-driven partnerships, the market will evolve away from historical pricing models and toward new, innovative ways to reward outcomes.

Conclusion

The focus of this testimony is how the healthcare delivery system affects the pharmaceutical prices faced by consumers. Consumer exposure to drug costs is

---

[30] Avalere Health, "Health Plans are Actively Exploring Outcomes-Based Contracts," May 30, 2017, http://avalere.com/expertise/life-sciences/insights/health-plans-are-actively-exploring-outcomes-based-contracts.

[31] Eli Lilly and Company and Anthem, "Promoting Value-Based Contracting Arrangements," January 2016, https://lillypad.lilly.com/WP/wp-content/uploads/LillyAnthemWP2.pdf.

determined by benefit design, the competitiveness of drug classes, and approaches to provider payment. As benefit design evolves, deductibles and cost sharing for medications have increased across government and commercial payers, increasing out-of-pocket spending. Of course, consumer costs are also importantly determined by the pricing decisions made by pharmaceutical companies prior to entry of product into the supply chain, and the level and type of rebates and discounts granted.

Active management of the pharmaceutical benefit is vital to establishing a competitive pricing dynamic and achieving optimal patient outcomes. However, it is critical to ensure that benefit designs are achieving their promise, and not effectively serving as barriers to good medical and cost management. The value of pharmaceuticals should always be assessed in the context of total medical costs, and unfortunately, many government programs and employer benefit strategies fail to integrate the pharmaceutical expense line into the context of overall medical management.

Increased competition in the pharmaceutical markets holds promise for substantially reducing costs. Speeding the approval of the second- and third-branded drugs in a therapeutic class would expedite competition and lead to more rapid price concessions. Ensuring a continued robust market for generic pharmaceutics is vital for effective cost management and improvement of population health outcomes. Finally, there is strong potential for consumers in growing biosimilar competition.

Health system change is increasingly assigning value to improvements in population outcomes for common medical conditions, and many of these outcomes can be effectively achieved through better use of medication. A patient-oriented perspective on value is key to ensuring that the American healthcare system continues to evolve toward the consumer. Further alignment of stakeholder interests around the use of pharmaceuticals holds promise to benefit consumers as payment systems evolve towards value-based design.

THE CHAIRMAN. Thank you, Mr. Mendelson. Mr. Coukell, welcome.

STATEMENT OF ALLAN COUKELL, SENIOR DIRECTOR, HEALTH PROGRAMS, THE PEW CHARITABLE TRUSTS, WASHINGTON, DC

Mr. COUKELL. Thank you, Chairman Alexander, Senator Murray, and members of the committee, for holding this important hearing.

Drugs are the fastest growing segment of healthcare spending and are projected to remain so. Indeed, net spending on pharmaceuticals increased 42 percent over the past decade and more than two-thirds of that was in the last 3 years.

This creates a challenge for individual patients who face high out-of-pocket costs and three-quarters of Americans say that drug prices are unreasonable. It also represents a challenge for any individual or business that pays taxes or insurance premiums which cover most of the cost of drugs.

The best way to establish prices is usually a free and competitive market, but the market for drugs is complex and deeply influenced by public policy. Effective competition is limited in a number of ways.

For example, new drugs and some older drugs have monopoly pricing power or lack competition. There are misaligned incentives at many points in the system and historically, we have paid for new therapies, whatever the cost and however modest the benefit.

Before I get to policy options, I would like to spend a moment on the main drivers of drug spending.

The upward trend is largely the result of the rising cost of new medicines, especially high-cost biologics or specialty drugs. These are used by only 1 or 2 percent of the population, but account for more than 40 percent of costs.

Launch prices for new drugs are at unprecedented levels and year-on-year increases in brand drug prices fuel further growth. In contrast, generic drugs create significant savings despite sharp increases in the price of some individual generic products.

Generic competition has long been the main tool used to manage drug spending in the United States. When there is no competing product, the FDA prioritizes its review of new generics, but there are factors that delay generic entry in some cases, including the misuse of REMS programs and reverse payment or pay-for-delay agreements, both factors that Congress could address.

As I have noted, the main driver of spending growth is biologic drugs where Congress has granted 12 years of monopoly protection. That is more than double the 5 years of protection typical for a small molecule drug.

Another consideration is the increasing share of high-priced drugs that come to market with taxpayer subsidies and other benefits through the Orphan Drug Act. It is important to support the development of products for rare diseases, but Congress may wish to ensure that the program does not have unintended costs when the drugs are used in larger populations than the Act originally considered.

For drugs that do not have generic competition, but where there are multiple competing products that meet a similar clinical need, here there are tools that are widely used in commercial insurance, but are absent from some public programs, especially Medicare Part B.

For example, Part B lacks a formulary and any process for utilization management or prior authorization. Indeed, Part B is designed in such a way that physicians and other providers receive greater reimbursement when they choose higher priced drugs over lower cost alternatives.

Similarly, in Medicare Part D, there are a number of situations where plans are required to cover every drug in a class, such as antidepressants, and this reduces the Plan's leverage to negotiate prices.

Most of our national drug spend accrues to drug manufacturers. Estimates vary and we do not have great numbers, but at least 70 percent. Several other entities including pharmacy benefits managers, pharmacies, and wholesalers also each retain a share.

The crucial question for a self-insured employer or a plan sponsor is whether they could possibly obtain lower cost if the PBM's cut were smaller. This is a matter that largely sits in the negotiations between private parties, but it is a question that Congress could address as it pertains to public programs such as Part D.

Finally, let me turn to the issue of value. Fundamentally, the debate about drug prices is a debate about value. Is the cost of the drug justified by the clinical outcomes that it produces? Value-based or outcomes-based contracts between manufacturers and purchasers are an attempt to formalize this understanding and sometimes to tie the level of payment directly to the results achieved.

Such agreements may play an important role for some products, though to date, they remain relatively rare and their effect on healthcare costs has been limited. They are unlikely to become ubiquitous in the future, not least because they are costly to negotiate and monitor.

In the larger sense, however, better alignment around value is needed. We should take into account health benefits that do not show up in the drug budget, but also recognize that the market only works when the potential purchaser has the ability to decide not to cover drugs when the cost is not justified.

We live at a time of exciting biomedical innovation. We owe it to patients and taxpayers to ensure that the cost of drugs is sustainable into the future.

Thank you and I welcome your questions.

[The prepared statement of Mr. Coukell follows:]

Testimony before the Committee on Health, Education Labor and Pensions, June 13, 2017, Allan Coukell, Senior Director of Health Programs, The Pew Charitable Trusts

Chairman Alexander, Ranking Member Murray, members of the committee, thank you for holding this hearing and for the opportunity to present testimony.

I direct health programs at The Pew Charitable Trusts, a nonprofit, nonpartisan research and policy organization. One of our focus areas is the challenge of rising drug spending.

Net spending on pharmaceuticals has increased 42 percent since 2006, with more than two-thirds of that growth occurring since 2013.[32] Indeed, prescription drug spending is now the fastest growing share of health spending, and projected to remain so.[33] Currently pharmaceuticals account for 16.7 percent of total expenditures.[34] This creates challenges for:

- Individual patients, who face high out-of-pocket costs. Surveys show that three-quarters of Americans think drug prices are unreasonable.[35]
- American taxpayers and businesses, which pay the bulk of the cost of drugs through taxes and insurance premiums.

Rising drug spending is a challenge for policymakers, too, because while a competitive market is generally the best way to establish prices, the market for drugs is complex and deeply influenced by public policy, and effective competition is limited in a number of ways. These include:

- Monopoly pricing for new drugs,
- Lack of competition for some older drugs,
- Misaligned incentives and incomplete information for stakeholders, including payers, providers and patients at many points in the system, and
- A historical willingness to cover new therapies without ensuring that their clinical benefits justify the price.

In discussing potential policy options, it is important to understand the main drivers of increased drug spending. This trend is largely the result of the rising cost of new medicines, particularly high-cost specialty products (including biologics),[36] which are only used by a small share of the population, but account for more than 40% of drug spending.[37] Today, fewer than two percent of prescriptions account for over one-third of

[32] QuintilesIMS Institute, "Medicines Use and Spending in the U.S.: Review of 2016 and Outlook to 2021," May 2017, Available at: http://www.imshealth.com/en/thought-leadership/quintilesims-institute/reports/medicines-use-and-spending-in-the-us-review-of-2016-outlook-to-2021.

[33] The Centers for Medicare & Medicaid Services projects that prescription drug spending growth will continue to outpace overall health care cost increases over the next decade. Source: Centers for Medicare & Medicaid Services, "National Health Expenditure Projections 2016-2025," Available at: https://www.cms.gov/Research-Statistics-Data-and-Systems/Statistics-Trends-and-Reports/NationalHealthExpendData/Downloads/proj2016.pdf.

[34] Health and Human Services Assistant Secretary for Planning and Evaluation, "Observations on Trends in Prescription Drug Spending," March, 2016, Available at: https://aspe.hhs.gov/system/files/pdf/187586/Drugspending.pdf.

[35] Kaiser Family Foundation, "Kaiser Health Tracking Poll: September 2016," September 2016, Available at: http://kff.org/health-costs/report/kaiser-health-tracking-poll-september-2016/.

[36] Examples include medicines for cancer, multiple sclerosis, and autoimmune conditions.

[37] QuintilesIMS Institute, "Medicines Use and Spending in the U.S.: Review of 2016 and Outlook to 2021," May 2017, Available at: http://www.imshealth.com/en/thought-leadership/quintilesims-institute/reports/medicines-use-and-spending-in-the-us-review-of-2016-outlook-to-2021.

retail drug spending.[38] Some of these products are exciting therapeutic advances – true breakthroughs – but some are not. And they are reaching market at ever-higher launch prices. Net prices (i.e., prices after rebates) are also increasing. These products will typically not face generic competition for years. Increased volume of sales and year-on-year price increases for brand drugs that don't face competition are also a driver of spending. As more and more innovative medicines come to market, the growth in launch prices and the growing share of the population that could potentially rely on these products looks unsustainable.

While new brand drugs drive spending growth, generic drugs create significant savings. In 2016, about 90% of prescriptions dispensed were for generics, but total spending on these medications actually fell,[39] despite sharp increases in the prices of some individual products.

Net pharmaceutical manufacturer revenue from U.S. sales reached $323 billion in 2016.[40] This represents the large majority, but not the total of U.S. drug spending, because other entities, including pharmacy benefit managers, wholesalers and pharmacies, also each retain a portion of total spending on drugs.

Potential Policy Responses

Increased Competition from Generic and Biosimilar Products

Competition from generic drugs has long been the main tool used to manage drug spending in the United States.[41] Currently, the FDA prioritizes the review of first generics, as well as generic applications for drugs for which there is only one manufacturer;[42] however, other policy responses could facilitate generic entry, including:

---

[38] QuintilesIMS Institute, "Medicines Use and Spending in the U.S.: Review of 2016 and Outlook to 2021," May 2017, Available at: http://www.imshealth.com/en/thought-leadership/quintilesims-institute/reports/medicines-use-and-spending-in-the-us-review-of-2016-outlook-to-2021.

[39] QuintilesIMS Institute, "Medicines Use and Spending in the U.S.: Review of 2016 and Outlook to 2021," May 2017, Available at: http://www.imshealth.com/en/thought-leadership/quintilesims-institute/reports/medicines-use-and-spending-in-the-us-review-of-2016-outlook-to-2021.

[40] QuintilesIMS Institute, "Medicines Use and Spending in the U.S.: Review of 2016 and Outlook to 2021," May 2017, Available at: http://www.imshealth.com/en/thought-leadership/quintilesims-institute/reports/medicines-use-and-spending-in-the-us-review-of-2016-outlook-to-2021.

[41] Generics are now nearly 90 percent of all prescriptions filled, but less than 30 percent of drug spending. QuintilesIMS Institute, "Medicines Use and Spending in the U.S.: Review of 2016 and Outlook to 2021," May 2017, Available at: http://www.imshealth.com/en/thought-leadership/quintilesims-institute/reports/medicines-use-and-spending-in-the-us-review-of-2016-outlook-to-2021.

[42] FDA Center for Drug Evaluation and Research, Manual of Policies and Procedures 5240.3. Rev 2. Prioritization of the Review of Original ANDAs, Amendments, and Supplements, 2016, http://www.fda.gov/downloads/AboutFDA/CentersOffices/OfficeofMedicalProductsandTobacco/CDER/ManualofPoliciesProcedures/UCM407849.pdf.

- Policies to ensure that manufacturers of brand name drugs cannot block generic developers' access to sample products required for bioequivalence testing,[43] and
- Policies to limit so-called "reverse payment" settlements that can, in some cases, be anti-competitive by delaying generic market entry.[44]

However, the agency alone cannot address the challenge of escalating drug costs. In particular, it should be noted that biologic drugs are one of the most significant drivers of increased spending and they represent nine of the 10 highest expenditure products in Medicare Part B.[45] Any policy that hastens access to biosimilars and increases competition among these pew products would reduce spending.[46] This includes better aligning biologic and small-molecule exclusivity periods. Congress gave new biologics 12 years of monopoly, free of competition from biosimilars, which is more than double the five years of protection typically granted to new small molecule drugs.

In addition, an increasing share of drugs comes to market with the benefit of taxpayer subsidies and other benefits established through the Orphan Drug Act (ODA). While important to incentivize the development of products for rare diseases, in some circumstances, these products are used much more widely than the ODA intended.[47]

---

[43] Barriers to generic entry exist when brand drug manufacturers prevent generic companies from obtaining their products in order to carry out the testing necessary to develop a generic version of a drug. In some cases, FDA orders a manufacturer to develop a program to ensure safe use of a high-risk product, such as a requirement that a drug can only be acquired through select providers, or the manufacturer may independently opt for a restricted distribution network. However, some generic manufacturers allege that these provisions are used to restrict generic company access. Litigation to obtain samples for comparative testing often takes years to conclude. Source: The Pew Charitable Trusts, "Policy Proposal: Improving Generic and Biosimilar Developer Access to Brand Pharmaceutical Samples, May 2017, Available at: http://www.pewtrusts.org/en/research-and-analysis/fact-sheets/2017/05/policy-proposal-improving-generic-and-biosimilar-developer-access-to-brand-pharmaceutical- samples.

[44] Brand and generic companies frequently strike "reverse payment" or "pay-for-delay" settlements that involve a brand pharmaceutical manufacturer paying one or more potential generic competitors to resolve patent infringement lawsuits and agree upon a date by which the generic product can come to market. Both the brand and generic company benefit under such agreements, while the public pays higher prices than it would if the generic available sooner. In 2015, for example, the Federal Trade Commission (FTC) reached a $1.2 billion settlement with Cephalon, Inc. for illegally blocking generic competition to its blockbuster sleep-disorder drug Provigil, driving up costs for consumers, insurers, and pharmacies. FTC and the Congressional Budget Office have estimated that banning or otherwise limiting these agreements would generate significant savings for consumers and taxpayers. However, any policy should also consider that some such settlements may be pro-competitive.

[45] Medicare Payment Advisory Commission, "Report to the Congress, Medicare and the Health Care Delivery System," , June 2016, Available at: http://www.medpac.gov/docs/default-source/reports/june-2016-report-to-the-congress-medicare-and-the-health-care-delivery-system.pdf?sfvrsn=0.

[46] There is a substantial difference in the duration of market protection provided to makers of biological drugs, which are derived from living cells, and that given traditional pharmaceuticals. Reducing the period of guaranteed exclusivity for biologics from the current 12 years to seven years would bring them more in line with traditional drugs. Such a change could generate more than $4 billion in savings to Medicare and other federal health care programs over 10 years. Source: Kaiser Family Foundation, "Summary of Medicare Provisions in the President's Budget for Fiscal Year 2016," February 2015, Available at: http://kff.org/medicare/issue-brief/summary-of-medicare-provisions-in-the-presidents-budget-for-fiscal-year-2016/.

[47] Daniel MG, Pawlik TM, Fader AN, *et al.* The Orphan Drug Act: Restoring the Mission to Rare Diseases. *Am J Clin Oncol.* 2016 Apr;39(2):210-3.

Congress may wish to evaluate a number of policy options to ensure the appropriate balance, including:

- Limiting the 340B carve-out for products with an orphan designation, and
- Considering the potential to cap the value of public subsidies.

Increased Competition among Existing Drugs

In cases where there are multiple competing, but non-identical brand drugs on the market, there are a range of tools that payers can use to manage spending while protecting patient access. These include formulary placement, prior authorization, and step therapy. While these approaches are well established in commercial insurance, they are absent or limited in parts of the Medicare program. For example, reimbursement policies in Medicare Part B, which pays for the use of physician administered drugs, creates a financial incentive for clinicians to choose high-priced drugs over lower cost alternatives of similar effectiveness.[48] In Medicare Part D, the private plans that administer the outpatient prescription drug benefit are required to cover all drugs on the market in six protected classes.[49] This mandate limits the ability of Part D plans to negotiate discounts for drugs in these classes. To increase competition among existing drugs in Medicare, consideration could be given to policies that would:

- Increase competition within the Medicare Part B program,[50]
- Increase competition within Medicare Part D,[51] and
- Shift some drugs from the medical to the pharmacy benefit.

---

[48] Health and Human Services Assistant Secretary for Planning and Evaluation, "Medicare Part B Drugs: Pricing and Incentives," March 2016, Available at: https://aspe.hhs.gov/system/files/pdf/187581/ PartBDrug.pdf.

[49] Current law requires Medicare drug plans to cover every medication within six broad classes, including antidepressants and antipsychotics. Giving greater flexibility to private Part D plans in how they design their drug benefits could improve their ability to negotiate lower drug prices on behalf of Medicare beneficiaries and the federal government. Source: Lee T, Gluck A, Curfman G, "The Politics Of Medicare And Drug-Price Negotiation (Updated)," *Health Affairs Blog*, September 19, 2016, Available at: http://healthaffairs.org/blog/2016/09/19/the-politics-of-medicare-and-drug-price-negotiation/.

[50] The Medicare Part B program spends some $25 billion each year for drugs administered in clinics and physician offices. Policies to manage biosimilar drugs similar to the current approach for generics could create greater competition. Source: The Pew Charitable Trusts, "Can Biosimilar Drugs Lower Medicare Part B Drug Spending?" January 2017, Available at: http://www.pewtrusts.org/en/research-and-analysis/issue-briefs/2017/01/can-biosimilar- drugs-lower-medicare-part-b-drug-spending.

[51] Medicare price negotiation (which is currently prohibited by statute) would achieve savings only if combined with new authority for Medicare to design its own formulary or preferred drug list, similar to how private plans prioritize certain drugs among equally effective therapies. Source: Shih C, Schwartz J, Coukell A, "How Would Government Negotiation Of Medicare Part B Drug Prices Work?," *Health Affairs Blog*, February 1, 2016, http://healthaffairs.org/blog/2016/02/01/how-would-government-negotiation-of-medicare-part-d-drug-prices-work/.

An Increased Focus on Value

Value-based or outcomes-based contracts (OBCs) between manufacturers and purchasers – contracts that tie the price of a drug to specified outcomes – may play an important role for some products, though their impact on health care costs has been limited to date. A recent survey of 45 health plans found that 24 percent of them have an outcomes-based contract in place today, and an additional 30 percent are in negotiations to enter into one.[52] However, just one-third of plans with an OBC in place reported cost savings. There are numerous challenges in setting up these contracts, and their utility may be limited by their cost to negotiate and the need for sophisticated data systems to monitor success.[53] However, policymakers could examine to what extent federal law or regulations pose potential barriers for establishing OBCs. For example, the Centers for Medicare & Medicaid Services could consider whether Medicaid Best Price rules may impede these agreements and develop additional guidance, if warranted.

Nevertheless, policymakers should consider additional strategies to incorporate the value of a drug into coverage and payment decisions. Factoring value into coverage decisions – including the choice not to cover drugs whose cost isn't justified – would help reduce overpayment for marginal clinical gains. Alternatively, policies to limit the price of drugs based on assessments of their value when comparable alternative therapies exist are strategies that have the potential to lower spending on pharmaceuticals in public programs.

Opportunities to Improve Transparency in Drug Benefit Contracting

Pharmacy benefits managers – the intermediaries that insurers and employers pay to both administer prescription drug benefits and negotiate discounts from drug companies – play a crucial role, using their large sales volumes and their ability to create formularies to spur drug manufacturers to offer price concessions. However, a share of the savings accrues to the pharmacy benefit managers themselves, and their contracts can be extremely complex, making it difficult even for sophisticated benefits administrators to determine whether they've achieved optimal savings.

Congress could consider requiring greater transparency of contract terminology and definitions between payers and pharmacy benefit managers,[54] as well as mandating the

---

52 Avalere, "Health Plans Are Actively Exploring Outcomes-Based Contracts," Available at: http://avalere.com/expertise/life-sciences/insights/health-plans-are-actively-exploring-outcomes-based-contracts.

53 Garrison LP, Carlson JJ, Bajaj PS, et al. "Private Sector Risk-Sharing Agreements in the United States: Trends, Barriers, and Prospects." *American Journal of Managed* Care, September 2015, Available at: http://www.ajmc.com/journals/issue/2015/2015-vol21-n9/Private-Sector-Risk-Sharing-Agreements-in-the-United-States-Trends-Barriers-and-Prospects.

54 More than two dozen of the largest U.S. corporations, including American Express, Coca-Cola, IBM, Marriott, and Verizon, have proposed greater transparency in these contracts. Source: Silverman E, "The 'gouge factor': Big companies want transparency in drug price negotiations," *STAT News*, August 2, 2016. Available at: https://www.statnews.com/pharmalot/2016/08/02/drug-price-transparency-pharmacy-benefits-manager/.

ability for payers to audit these deals, and ensuring that entities that advise purchasers on PBM contracts do not also have financial relationships with the PBMs themselves.

Conclusion

As Congress seeks to manage the challenge of rising drug spending, it should look at the range of challenges and policy solutions to achieve a balance between access to innovative medicines and the equally important need to constrain cost-growth in health care. I thank you for holding this hearing, and welcome your questions.

The CHAIRMAN. Thank you, Mr. Coukell. Dr. Howard, welcome.

STATEMENT OF PAUL HOWARD, PH.D., DIRECTOR AND SENIOR FELLOW, HEALTH POLICY, MANHATTAN INSTITUTE, NEW YORK, NY

Mr. HOWARD. Thank you.

Chairman Alexander, Ranking Member Murray, members of the committee.

I would like to thank you for the opportunity to testify today about, "The Cost of Prescription Drugs: How the Drug Delivery System Affects What Patients Pay."

I am truly honored to be speaking to you as part of such a distinguished panel.

My testimony today is derived from my research and experience as director of health policy and a member of the Manhattan Institute's Project FDA.

I believe our focus in this area should try to achieve three goals. To broadly promote innovation for the American patient; to reduce rent-seeking in the drug delivery system, and realign provider incentives to match the best treatment to the most appropriate patient; and finally, to continue our broad shift of reimbursement away from volume and toward value.

The United States has become the unquestioned global leader in medical innovation over the last several decades thanks to a virtual cycle of innovation where older generic drugs compete very effectively with branded drugs once those patents expire.

Inexpensive generic competition—accounting for close to 90 percent of retail drugs sold in the United States—forces branded companies to press the frontiers of science and innovation, and develop new medicines that can offset other components of healthcare spending including unnecessary hospitalizations, physician visits, and nursing home use.

Innovation benefits patients by extending and improving health, but it also benefits the economy by creating more jobs and attracting more investment to the United States.

This is a social and economic contract that has worked remarkably well for the most part. In fact, it is no exaggeration to say that we stand on the precipice of a Golden Age of medicine.

New treatments could allow us to attack diseases at the molecular and genetic roots. We can finally begin to speak of lasting remissions, sharply reduced disability, and even true cures for once dreaded diseases like cancer. Even more powerful approaches, like regenerative medicine and gene therapy will undoubtedly be approved by the FDA over the next 5 to 10 years.

The outlook for innovation has never been brighter even as the industry is embroiled in a wave of product pricing controversies.

However, while most prescriptions in the United States are broadly affordable—in fact about 30 percent of all prescriptions have $0 co-pays—there are real challenges facing patients, particularly patients with serious, chronic illnesses who are facing too much cost sharing from benefit designs through high co-insurance and deductibles, largely for what are called specialty medicines.

This is a serious challenge that must be addressed. High out-of-pocket costs can lead to lower patient compliance, increased financial stress, worse health outcomes, and even higher costs overall.

Without abandoning the current market-based paradigm, we do need to update it to meet the challenges of the 21st century and to take full advantage of new technological tools that can enable us to more rapidly match the right patient to the right medicine at the right time and at an affordable price for both patients and society.

I have three specific recommendations for Congress today.

First, reduce renting-seeking in the drug delivery system. This effort should begin with fixing the 340B Drug Discount Program. 340B drug sales have become a major source of hospital revenues and account for as much as 50 percent of infused oncology products.

The shift of treatments into the 340B environment has increased the cost of cancer medicines, increased the cost of treatment for patients with both commercial insurance and Medicare Part B coinsurance, and has changed the mix of treatments toward more expensive therapies.

Congress should reform 340B and return it to its original intent to assist hospitals that largely serve indigent and uninsured populations, and ensure that its rebates are extended to the most vulnerable patients, like the uninsured.

Second, we should promote value-based arrangements that give innovative companies, physicians, and hospitals equal skin in the game to match patients to treatments that work. Regulators can help accelerate the transition to these contracts by removing regulatory barriers that discourage companies from testing the full potential of indication and outcomes-based contracts to improve patient outcomes and match the performance of medicines to their real world outcomes.

Finally, I would encourage Congress to consider a broader menu of reforms that would allow payers to take a longer term view of the value and costs of new medicines. Such reforms would include encouraging the uptake of value-based designs within high deductible health plans; new financing tools for State Medicaid programs that would allow them to purchase curative technologies like Hepatitis C drugs upfront, but spread the costs over longer periods of time; and multiyear private insurance contracts that may align payers' incentives with patients' long term health.

In conclusion, for the last 30 years, the United States has benefited from arrangements that have put us on the cusp of tremendous new medical achievements. The system is under strain today because the pace of the innovation is accelerating while our healthcare system is still divided into payment silos that create the appearance of a zero sum game between stakeholders.

I am confident that policymakers can work together on a bipartisan basis to update and improve America's virtual cycle of innovation and affordability for the next 30 years.

Thank you.

[The prepared statement of Dr. Howard follows:]

PREPARED STATEMENT OF PAUL HOWARD, PHD

Summary

An effective balance between strong upfront patent rights and rapid generic competition has helped make the United States the unquestioned global leader in medical innovation, while also assuring broad affordability, for the last several decades. However, there are real challenges facing the health care system today, specifically for patients with serious chronic illnesses who face high coinsurance or deductibles. The U.S. health care system is in dire need of competition to reduce wasteful and ineffective care. However, addressing drug prices directly, in a silo, is inadvisable because we want technology to substitute for labor, something that happens only through innovation.

The Centers for Medicare and Medicaid Services (CMS) expects that medicine's share of total health care costs will closely track overall health care spending growth over the next decade. However, costs attributable to expensive specialty medicines are rising significantly faster than for traditional drugs, with the result that a small fraction of all prescriptions account for a disproportionate share of all out-of-pocket spending on prescription medicines.

Fortunately, there are promising signs that payers and manufacturers are edging toward agreement that patients with serious diseases facing coinsurance should have access to PBM-negotiated discounts. There is also growing agreement that contracts for high-cost, high-value medicines should reflect evidence of their real-world performance.

Congress, CMS, and FDA have important roles to play in encouraging the market to shift to new arrangements that lower barriers to patient access.

First, Congress should reform the 340B program and return it to its original intent to assist hospitals serving largely indigent and uninsured populations. The current system instead encourages profit skimming and hospital consolidation.

Second, HHS and FDA should coordinate on creating safe harbors from Federal regulations that would allow stakeholders to experiment with new contractual arrangements. This allows manufacturers to bear financial risk for new medicines, without discouraging innovation.

Finally, Congress should consider opportunities to encourage using value-based insurance designs, new financing tools for State Medicaid programs, and longer-term insurance contracts that better align payers' incentives with patients' long-term health.

DRUG DEVELOPMENT AND DELIVERY FOR THE NEXT 30 YEARS: AFFORDABILITY IN AN ERA OF PRECISION MEDICINE

By Paul Howard, PhD
Director and Senior Fellow, Health Policy Manhattan Institute

Chairman Alexander, Ranking Member Murray, members of the Committee, I'd like to thank you for the opportunity to testify today about "The Cost of Prescription Drugs: How the Delivery System Affects What Patients Pay." I'm truly honored to be speaking to you today.

Bipartisan support for medical innovation, including strong support for FDA user fee agreements, an encouraging environment for translating basic medical research into promising new treatments, and an effective balance between strong upfront patent rights and rapid generic competition once those patents expire has made the U.S. the unquestioned global leader in medical innovation for the last several decades.[55]

Broadly speaking, robust generic competition, along with the advent of large and sophisticated payers, has kept the relative share of health care costs attributable to medicines broadly stable, even as new medicines have become a cornerstone of treatment for acute and chronic illness.[56]

---

[55] For a fuller discussion, see Biopharmaceutical Policy for American Leadership 52 in the 21st Century, Peter Huber & Paul Howard. https://nationalaffairs.com/storage/app/uploads/public/doclib/20161209_Unleashing OpportunityInnovationPolic yBooklet.pdf.

[56] Total U.S. health care spending in 2015 was $3.2 trillion dollars. Approximately two-thirds of those costs are attributable to hospital care (roughly 30%) and physician services (around 25%). Outpatient prescription drug spending has held steady at around 10% of total expenditures for decades. Adding in hospital administered

However, there are real challenges facing the health care system today, specifically for patients with serious chronic illnesses who are facing high coinsurance or deductibles largely for what are called "specialty" medicines, and that challenge needs to be addressed.

Ironically, part of that challenge is due to the advent of highly effective new treatments for hepatitis C, cystic fibrosis, some cancers, and rheumatoid arthritis.

A wave of even more powerful treatments, including gene therapies, new immuneoncology therapies, and regenerative medicine approaches are already on the horizon and likely to be approved by the FDA over the next 5 to 10 years. The outlook for innovation has never been brighter, even as the industry has become a lightning rod for product pricing controversies.[57]

But I would remind critics that having too many effective therapies is an enviable problem to have, and can largely be addressed by enhancing market competition and creating new financing and reimbursement tools that allow payments for treatments to be pegged to their real-world outcomes—like lowering costs elsewhere in the health care system, improving patient survival or quality of life, or simply delivering a comparable outcome to existing technologies less expensively.[58]

The U.S. health care system is in dire need of competition to reduce wasteful and ineffective care, and new technological platforms can allow the rapid analysis of large volumes of patient data – enabling competition not only between medicines, but among providers and different payment platforms. In short, Congress should create incentives that reward providers who use medicines (both generic and branded) and technology to deliver care as efficiently as possible, while also empowering patients with the information they need to identify high quality providers.[59]

Fixing drug prices in a silo is inadvisable because we want technology to substitute for labor, including unnecessary hospitalizations, doctor's visits, or debilitating stays in a nursing home.[60] Bending the curve of health care cost growth and delivering state-of-the-

---

drugs raises that share to 14-15%. Fein, Adam J., *The 2017 Economic Report on U.S. Pharmacies and Pharmacy Benefit Managers*, Drug Channels Institute, 2017.

[57] Many critics point to European drug price controls as the solution – ignoring the outsized role that the U.S. market plays in global innovation generally. See To Lower Drug Prices, Innovate, Don't Regulate. https://www.nytimes.com/roomfordebate/2015/09/23/should-the-government-impose-drug-price-controls/to-lower-drug-prices-innovate-dont-regulate.

[58] For a fuller discussion of the role of analytics, diagnostics, and outcomes based payments see Precision Medicine in the Era of Health Care Reform. https://www.manhattan-institute.org/sites/default/files/ R-PH-0416.pdf.

[59] As researchers in a Health Affairs blog wrote in 2015:

> Adherence to treatment guidelines and quality remain highly variable across providers in a wide variety of oncology domains, including end-of-life care, prostate cancer, ovarian cancer, and colorectal cancer screening. Problems range from underuse of highly effective therapies and procedures to overuse of ineffective ones. Thus, while today's typical cancer patient is likely better off than her counterpart from earlier years, not all patients are receiving the most effective care.... Rewarding physicians for patient health improvement moves physician incentives closer to the values and needs of patients.

[60] See Michael Mandel, Rising Labor Costs Accounted for 47 percent of Increased Personal Health Care Spending in 2015. http://www.progressivepolicy.org/blog/rising-labor-costs-accounted-47-percent-increased-personal-health-care-spending-2015/.

art care can, and must, go hand in hand if we are to meet America's most pressing health care challenges.

There is no accounting or discount scheme that will enable us to grapple with the scourge of Alzheimer's short of medicines that delay, or perhaps even prevent it entirely. Innovation is our best hope for lowering costs *and* improving outcomes.

With that in mind, I'd like to frame my remarks with some observations that I hope will guide our discussion today.

We stand at the precipice of a Golden Age of medicine, with new treatments that allow us to treat diseases at their molecular and genetic roots, where we can begin to speak of lasting remissions, sharply reduced disability, and even true cures—as from gene therapy.

Nonetheless, broadly speaking, the vast majority of prescriptions in the U.S. today are highly affordable, with roughly 30% having a zero-dollar copay. Most Americans who take prescription drugs regularly say they are affordable. In fact, close to 90% of all retail prescriptions in the U.S. today are for generics[61], which have saved payers hundreds of billions of dollars over the last decade.

Apart from a sharp surge in drug spending in 2014, when a new class of highly effective medicines for hepatitis C were introduced, drug price growth has been moderate, especially when we disaggregate price increases from increased utilization. A growing number of Americans are taking medicines, which is unsurprising given that age is one of the leading risk factors for developing a chronic illness. Payers, however, have been able to leverage large purchasing networks to increase manufacturer rebates as a share of gross revenues.

As a result, the Centers for Medicare and Medicaid Services (CMS) expects that medicine's cost growth will closely track overall health care spending growth over the next decade.[62]

When we drill down into the market, however, costs attributable to so-called specialty medicines are rising significantly faster than for traditional drugs, and today constitute close to 30% of all drug revenues. Prices for these medicines are rising significantly faster than other costs, although they also treat especially serious chronic diseases. They also face less generic competition, including, at least for now, from biosimilars.

That overall drug spending has not risen faster is a testament to the success of insurers and pharmaceutical benefit managers (PBMs) cost containment strategies. They have employed utilization management tools like prior authorization, drug tiering and coinsurance, and larger deductibles for non-preferred medicines manage the uptake of specialty drugs.

---

[61] Fein, Exhibit 2: Unbranded and Branded Generics, Share of U.S. Prescriptions, 2005-2021.

[62] Howard and Feyman, Drug Price Controls Hurt Patients Most. https://www.manhattan-institute.org/html/issues-2016-drug-price-controls-hurt-patients-most-7949.html.

To retain formulary access for specialty medicines, companies often offer quite substantial rebates. One PBM, Express Scripts, noted in the last year that it held contain price increases for its members to under 3%.

How is it possible, then, that payers can complain about a drug pricing crisis, while pharmaceutical firms note that drug spending, and especially net pricing after accounting for rebates and utilization increases, are fairly stable?

The he-said, she-said debate can be resolved by simply noting that there are an increasing number of patients with high deductible plans, where medicines are part of a single combined medical and pharmacy deductible, and of patients with traditional insurance who are prescribed medicines where they pay coinsurance based on the list prices of these medicines, and thus do not benefit from PBM-negotiated discounts.

For patients who may need a medicine that is excluded from the PBMs formulary entirely, short of manufacturers' patient assistance programs, they may have to bear the full costs of these medicines themselves. (PBMs respond that they pass along these rebates to employers and other payers, helping to keep overall health insurance increases lower than they would otherwise be.)

To summarize: Patients with serious chronic illnesses may find themselves caught between the hammer of rising cost control efforts at a time of rapid therapeutic innovation.

There are some promising signs that payers and manufacturers recognize that the status quo is unsustainable, and are edging toward agreement that patients with serious diseases should have access, at the point of purchase, to PBM-negotiated discounts.

There is also growing agreement that reimbursement contracts for high cost, high value medicines should reflect evidence of their real-world performance, which may be very different than outcomes generated in clinical trials used for FDA approval—or for an entirely new indication, where evidence may be lacking at the time of approval.

Congress, HHS, and FDA have critical roles to play in encouraging the market to shift to new arrangements that lower barriers to patient access and encourage greater collaboration in getting the right medicine to the right patient at the right time – and at a price that is sustainable for patients, payers, and innovators.

I have three recommendations for Congress today.

First, fix the 340B drug discount program. 340B was originally designed to assist hospitals serving indigent patients, but has expanded to cover approximately 50% of the market for infused oncology medicines.

While hospitals acquire these drugs at large mandatory discounts, several studies suggest that they are billing commercial insurers a percentage of allowable charges, which is significantly higher than their acquisition price. As a result, such sales have become a major source of hospital revenues and an inducement for vertical hospital consolidation—i.e., for hospitals to acquire oncology practices and then charge far higher prices than standalone oncology practices (who charge Medicare ASP+6%).

Commercially insured patients and Medicare Part B patients thus may find themselves paying coinsurance on these highly inflated prices. Congress should reform 340B, returning it to its original intent to assist hospitals that largely serve indigent and uninsured populations, and ensure its rebates are extended to vulnerable patients (like the uninsured), and commercially insured and Medicare Part B patients who may be treated at these hospitals and find themselves paying coinsurance. Reducing the financial arbitrage available to hospitals would also reduce the incentive for hospitals to acquire oncology practices, reduce pricing pressures on oncology payers and patients, and reduce pricing distortions in other parts of the market.

Second, stakeholders also seem to be in broad agreement that novel reimbursement contracts should reflect medicines' value, both through indication-or outcomes-based designs. Regulators should help accelerate the transition to these contracts by removing regulatory barriers that discourage companies from testing the waters.

Specifically, HHS and FDA should coordinate on creating safe harbors from federal regulations that would allow stakeholders to experiment with innovative new contractual arrangements. These might allow for reimbursement to track a medicine's real-world performance, or for pricing to evolve as the weight of evidence evolves.

For instance, recently Eli Lilly and Anthem petitioned HHS and the FDA to grant them safe harbor from regulations, like Medicaid Best Price and Stark anti-kickback rules, which prohibit them from experimenting with these types of contracts.

With the FDA at the table, regulators could also create standards for the collection of real-world evidence that would allow the agency to update a drug's label to reflect new information on safety and efficacy, expand to new label indications, and generally support the development of a "health care learning system." This system uses information on patient outcomes, medication regimens, and even delivery system reforms to create a rapid feedback loop that helps ensure that the right medicine reaches the right patient at the right time—and all in a framework pushing every dollar spent on patient care to be used as efficiently as possible.

Finally, I would encourage Congress to consider a broader menu of reforms that would allow payers to take a longer perspective on the value and costs of new medicines. Such reforms would include encouraging the uptake of value-based insurance designs; new financing tools for state Medicaid programs to purchase curative technologies rapidly, but spread the costs over longer periods of time; and multi-year private insurance contracts that may align payers' incentives with patients' long-term health. Congress should also continue to empower patients with more information about both provider pricing and outcomes for specific indications – helping the market to reset on a competitive basis.

In conclusion, once we start asking questions about how to deliver better value to patients, to society, and to future generations, we are apt to look far past our current drug pricing debates – and towards the future of precision medicine.

For the last 30 years, the U.S. has benefitted from arrangements that have put us on the cusp of tremendous new medical achievements. The system is under strain because the pace of innovation is accelerating, while our health care system is still divided into payment silos, with a short-term framework that undervalues the long term impact medicines can play in resolving our most pressing health care challenges – including cancer, major depression, diabetes, and Alzheimer's.

Rather than pointing fingers, I hope that Congress can construct arrangements that will serve patients better for the next 30 years, unleashing the full potential of precision medicine to improve and lengthen patients' lives, here and around the globe.

Thank you, and I'd be happy to answer any questions you may have.

The CHAIRMAN. Thank you, Dr. Howard. Dr. Anderson, welcome.

STATEMENT OF GERARD ANDERSON, PHD, PROFESSOR OF MEDICINE, JOHNS HOPKINS UNIVERSITY SCHOOL OF MEDICINE, BALTIMORE, MD

Mr. ANDERSON. Thank you, Chairman Alexander, Senator Murray, and members of the HELP committee today.

This summer, I will have the opportunity to teach 250 of our new MPH students and I am fortunate enough to have Barbara Mikulski as one of my professors in the class.

I do not receive any financial support from pharmaceutical companies, entities involved in the pharmaceutical supply chain, or health insurers.

My main concern today is that healthcare prices are limiting access to essential drugs. Innovation is absolutely wonderful, but all Americans need to be able to afford these innovative drugs.

In my written testimony, I focus on four categories of people with the most problems accessing drugs. Almost one-quarter of all Americans have a chronic condition and one-quarter of them have two or more chronic conditions. In my testimony, I talk about a woman with multiple chronic conditions with insurance who has monthly bills of $1,700.

The second category of patients are those who are prescribed very expensive prescriptions drugs. One of my physician colleagues at Johns Hopkins came to me very upset last year. He treats babies with neuromuscular defects and was thrilled to learn that the FDA has approved a new drug to help these babies. A month later, he learned that the drug company had set the price at $750,000 for the first year of treatment and $375,000 in subsequent years.

Who wants to hear that your new baby has a genetic defect that will make them incompetent of doing most anything, and then to learn the drug that treats them costs $750,000? In Baltimore, you can buy a mansion for $750,000.

A third category is people taking off-patent drugs where the price has increased dramatically because there are no competitors. This is what Martin Shkreli did. The Senate Aging Committee, led by Senator Collins, did a wonderful report on this topic recently.

The fourth category is public programs that cannot afford to pay for drugs. We are working with Louisiana to help them find ways to fund Hepatitis C drugs for the 35,000 Louisianans with Hepatitis C. Hepatitis C is the infectious disease that kills more people than any other infectious disease including AIDS.

The drug costs over $20,000 even with several competitors and Louisiana simply does not have the $764 million at current prices to treat everyone with Hepatitis C.

The next part of my drug testimony discusses drug pricing. Drug pricing is exceedingly complex. I wore my tie with the writing of Leonardo da Vinci as a reminder of how complicated drug pricing systems have become. I am not even sure Leonardo da Vinci could understand drug pricing today.

It begins, though, with a drug company setting a list price for their drug. It is important to recognize that the Government gives that branded drug company patent and market exclusivity periods. These are government-given monopolies that protect the intellectual capital of the drug company and make it profitable for the drug company to engage in research and development.

However, as any economist can tell you, when a company has a monopoly, it sets the price that maximizes its profits. The monopoly price is not the price that allows everyone to get access to the drug.

The Senate Finance Committee did a very nice report on how Gilead had set the price for their Hepatitis C drug assuming that most people would not get access to the drug.

Few people have argued that the list price is irrelevant because few people actually pay the list price. However, the list price is used to determine the amount of cost sharing that many patients pay. Thus, patients are harmed when the list price increases.

Other experts in this panel have discussed the relationships between the drug companies, the PBM's, the wholesalers, and the pharmacies. It is important to recognize, however, that the process begins with the drug company setting the price.

The last portion of my testimony discusses several options for the committee to discuss, and I only have time for two of them right now.

One is a policy that would keep people like Martin Shkreli from putting a drug into something called limited distribution chain. Limited distribution chains prevent competitors from getting access to the drug, establishing bioequivalence, submitting an ANDA to the FDA, and then competing. So it is very anti-competitive.

Most drugs are paid on a fee for service basis. Putting drugs, as some of the others have talked about, into value-based purchasing—like bundled payments and accountable care organizations—would allow the physicians to decide which drugs are necessary for the patient taking into account the cost of the drug and alternative approaches. This would fundamentally change the drug purchasing system by putting physicians, not PBM's and health insurers, in charge of the process.

I am happy to answer any questions.

[The prepared statement of Dr. Anderson follows:]

PREPARED STATEMENT OF GERARD ANDERSON, PHD

Summary

High drug prices are causing access problems. Patients in four categories are having the greatest difficulty accessing drugs:

1) Patients with chronic diseases who cannot afford all of their medicines.
2) Patients prescribed very expensive specialty drugs.
3) Patients prescribed off-patent drugs whose prices have recently skyrocketed due to a lack of competition.
4) Patients on public programs where the public program cannot afford to purchase the drug.

In my written testimony, I provide examples of people in each of these situations.

How Drug Prices Are Set and Why This Matters to Patients

1) It begins with a drug company setting a list price for the drug. No regulatory or market forces constrain the list price.
2) Branded drug companies have government-issued monopolies (patents and market exclusivity periods).
3) The list price matters because it is often used to determine the amount of cost sharing that patients pay.
4) Pharmaceutical benefit managers (PBMs) earn their profits primarily by negotiating discounts off of the list price. The greater the list price, the greater the spread between the list price and the actual transaction price and the greater the profit the PBM earns. As a result, there is a financial incentive for the PBMs to try to get the drug company to increase the list price. This in turn increases the amount of cost-sharing the patient pays.
5) Wholesalers bring the drug from the manufacturer to the pharmacy or hospital and earn a small profit doing so.

6) Pharmacies and hospitals sell the drug to the patient after they negotiate a price with the drug manufacturer and add a dispensing fee.
7) Most patients pay something out-of-pocket for the drug that is based on their insurance.
8) All of this information is confidential and the patient cannot understand how the cost-sharing amounts are set.
9) Sometimes the patient would pay less if they ignored their insurance coverage and paid cash.

Policy Recommendations

Finally, I briefly present a series of recommendations about how to increase the level of competition in the supply chain for pharmaceuticals and lower pharmaceutical prices while still providing incentives for innovation.

Two policy recommendations warrant special considerations:

1) Preventing companies from putting drugs into limited distribution chains that keep generic companies from accessing the drug, testing for bioequivalence, and submitting applications to the FDA.
2) Placing drugs into value-based purchasing arrangements like bundled payments and ACOs. This is a disruptive system putting doctors in charge.

Johns Hopkins
The Center for Hospital Finance and Management
624 North Broadway, Room 304
Baltimore MD 21205
June 12, 2017

Chairman Alexander, Ranking Member Murray and members of the HELP Committee, my name is Gerard Anderson. I am a professor at Johns Hopkins Schools of Public Health and Medicine and Director of the Johns Hopkins Center for Hospital Finance and Management.

This summer, I will have the opportunity to teach our 250 entering MPH students a course on public health policy, and Senator Barbara Mikulski will be giving them a lecture based on her years of experience on the HELP committee.

I do not receive any financial support from pharmaceutical companies; entities involved in the pharmaceutical supply chain, or health insurers. I am also not testifying on behalf of Johns Hopkins University, but in my role as a professor at Johns Hopkins University.

Today, I will cover three topics.

First, my main concern about high drug prices is that they are limiting access to essential drugs. Innovation is wonderful, but people need to be able to afford the innovative drugs. I begin by showing how high drug prices are affecting access to care. I will focus on four areas where people are having the greatest difficulty accessing drugs.

1) Patients with chronic diseases who cannot afford all of their medicines.
2) Patients prescribed very expensive specialty drugs.
3) Patients prescribed off patent drugs whose prices have recently skyrocketed due to a lack of competition.
4) Patients on public programs where the public program cannot afford to purchase the drug.

Second, I will attempt to summarize how drug prices are set and how this process can affect patients' access to these medications.

Third, I briefly present a series of recommendations for increasing the level of price competition, revising regulations and legislation, lowering pharmaceutical prices, and improving patients' access to essential drugs, while still providing healthy returns and incentives for innovation.

How High Drug Prices Affects Access to Care

While many patients have some level of difficulty paying for their drugs, patients taking a large number of drugs or very expensive drugs face an even greater health challenge.

Almost Half of All Americans Have One or More Chronic Conditions

Perhaps less well known is that one-quarter of all Americans have multiple chronic conditions, and there are about five million Medicare beneficiaries with five or more chronic conditions. Many of these chronic conditions require people to take multiple drugs, and having access to the drugs to treat these conditions is critical for patients to remain healthy.

The problem is that many people taking these drugs cannot afford to fill their prescriptions. As a result, they are forced to make choices between paying the rent, purchasing food, caring for their children and being able to afford the drugs that will keep their chronic illnesses from becoming even worse. A December 2016 Kaiser Family Foundation poll found that one in five Americans did not fill a prescription last year because of cost and one in six Americans cut pills in half or skip doses in the prior year. This is rationing based on price.

I am working with an organization called Patients for Affordable Drugs, an organization that has been collecting stories from over 7000 people who are having difficulty paying their prescription drug bills. Its founder, David Mitchell, told me that the most challenging stories that he gets every day are from people with chronic conditions that cannot afford to purchase their drugs or need to split pills or skip doses in order to have the prescription last longer. High drug prices are impeding their access to essential medicines that directly affects their health.

A woman from Schenectady, NY wrote him:

> "I am a 53 year old diabetes patient who was diagnosed with bipolar disorder. I have also suffered 8 strokes in the last 20 years. As I've gotten older, controlling my blood sugar has become harder and harder. I had never had a problem paying for my daily medications until a year and a half ago. The diabetes supply that I need are [she lists five drugs] and other supplies such as a blood meter, needles, test strips, etc. Combine that with the costs of the other 10 drugs I take to control my other medical issues, co-payments, [and] hospital tests needed; I am unable to afford these increasing monthly costs. Under my Part D coverage with Medicare and Humana, my monthly supply of these drugs will cost me approximately $1,700 monthly."

She is one of the millions of patients who are unable to afford drugs to treat chronic conditions in spite of having health insurance coverage.

Other Patients Struggle to Afford Their Treatment because They Have Been Prescribed an Extremely Expensive Specialty Drug

Recently, a number of very effective new drugs have entered the market offering complete cures or ways to maintain a high level of functioning. These are the kinds of innovations that will improve health status and increase life expectancy. The problem is that many of these drugs are so expensive that most people cannot afford them.

One of my colleagues at Johns Hopkins who treats babies with genetic neuromuscular defects was thrilled when he learned that the FDA had approved the first drug to help these babies. The drug, a new molecular entity, essentially repairs the genetic defect and will allow the baby to live a normal life. The treatment is only truly effective if it is given immediately following birth before the generic defect leads to muscular deterioration. A month later, the doctor was mortified to learn that the drug company set the price at $750,000 for the first year of treatment, and $375,000 per year after that for the rest of the child's life. Who wants to hear that your newborn has a genetic defect and then learn that your young family will need to raise $750,000 in the next two weeks in order for your infant to progress normally? If the insurance company initially denies the payment, then the appeal will almost always require more than two weeks. It is hard to imagine the stress that young families feel when faced with this situation.

The Senate Finance Committee conducted a study of the pricing of one of these specialty drugs. Gilead was the first drug company to develop a cure for hepatitis C. This was a major clinical innovation offering a cure for an infectious disease. Hepatitis C is the infectious disease responsible for the greatest number of deaths in the United States every year – even more than HIV/AIDS. However, the drug company set a price that few could afford, and Gilead did this knowing that not everyone with hepatitis C would be able to afford the drug. Let me simply quote one line from the executive summary of the Senate Finance Committee's report:

> "Gilead's own documents and correspondence show its pricing strategy was focused on maximizing revenue — even as the company's analysis showed a lower price would allow more patients to be treated."

While we do not have exact numbers of the percent of people with hepatitis C that have been treated, the best estimate is that less than 20% of people with hepatitis C have been treated for a potentially fatal, but curable infectious disease. Even after the drug has been on the market for three years and two additional competitors have entered the market, still less than 20% of hepatitis C patients have received treatment.

Apparently, simply having competition for branded drugs is not sufficient to bring the price down to a level that most people can afford. The United States should have prices that allow everyone to have access to these life saving drugs. While we need innovation, we also need access and high drug prices set by the drug companies should not ration access.

The Kaiser Family Foundation conducted a study of Medicare beneficiary cost sharing for specialty drugs. For Medicare beneficiaries with Part D coverage, out-of-pocket costs averaged $7000 for drugs to treat hepatitis C, $6000 for drugs to treat multiple sclerosis, $4000 for drugs to treat rheumatoid arthritis and $8000 for drugs to treat certain types of cancer. For a social security recipient earning $26,000 per year, these out-of-pocket costs represent 16% to 32% of the person's total income for the year and clearly are prohibitively expensive. At these prices, it is not surprising that many Medicare beneficiaries with Part D insurance cannot afford these drugs.

Even for off Patent Drugs, High Prices Can Still Create Access Problems

Much of the recent attention has focused on the rapid increases in prices of off patent drugs that do not have any competitors. The generic drug industry works reasonably well when there are three or more competitors selling the same drug. Since the drugs are interchangeable, competition works to keep prices affordable.

However, problems occur when there are no competitors (or even just one or two). When there is little competition for off patent drugs, companies can raise the prices without fear that consumers will choose a lower priced competitor. This is exactly what

Martin Shkreli did with his drug. He took an off patent drug that had been on the market for many years, raised the price by 3500%, and created mechanisms to prevent other competitors from entering the market.

Analysis by Senator Susan Collins and the Senate Aging Committee staff showed how Martin Shkreli and others have been able to keep competitors from entering the market. First, the company acquired a "sole-source drug, for which there was only one manufacturer, and therefore faces no immediate competition, maintaining monopoly power over its pricing." Second, "the company ensured the drug was considered the gold standard—the best drug available for the condition it treats, ensuring that physicians would continue to prescribe the drug, even if the price increased." Third, "The company selected a drug that served a small market, which were not attractive to competitors and which had dependent patient populations that were too small to organize effective opposition, giving the companies more latitude on pricing."

Fourth, the company created a closed distribution system to stifle competition. As the report notes, "The company controlled access to the drug through a closed distribution system or specialty pharmacy where a drug could not be obtained through normal channels, or the company used another means to make it difficult for competitors to enter the market." Without access to the drug, a competitor cannot conduct bioequivalence studies in order to submit a drug application to the FDA. Increasingly, drug companies are using these closed distribution systems to stifle competition. This is an area that Congress could address, as I will discuss later.

The Senate Aging Committee concluded by stating, "Lastly, the company engaged in price gouging, maximizing profits by jacking up prices as high as possible. All of the drugs investigated had been off patent for decades, and none of the four companies had invested a penny in research and development to create or to significantly improve the drugs. Further, the Committee found that the companies faced no meaningful increases in production or distribution costs."

There have been hundreds of stories written about the problems created by these rapid price increases in off patent drugs without competition. Let me quote from another email that Patients for Affordable Drugs received: My wife "has seen [her drug's] price increase by over 3600% since 2014." Again, this is for an off patent drug. "Today her medications cost $283,000 per year or about $200 per dosage - from the 1980-'s to 2006 [drug name eliminated for confidentiality reasons] was $1.00 per dose/$1500 per year." People simply do not have the resources to afford these drugs and often the cost sharing is prohibitively expensive.

Finally, Public Programs Cannot Afford These Expensive Drugs

States and the federal government have budget constraints and high prices are forcing public programs to make very difficult life or death decisions.

For example, the state of Louisiana wants to expand treatment for hepatitis C, but cannot afford to offer the care to everyone at current prices. According to the Secretary of Health in Louisiana, it would cost $764 million dollars at current prices to cover the 35,000 uninsured and Medicaid recipients with hepatitis C in the state. Louisiana simply does not have these resources, without dramatically reducing spending for things like education or public safety.

We, at Johns Hopkins, are working with the Secretary of Health in Louisiana to help her develop ways so that Louisiana can afford to purchase the drugs and prevent the spread of an infectious disease. Similar concerns about the affordability of certain drugs have been expressed by other states and by federal agencies such as the Veterans Administration and the Indian Health Service.

A woman from Alabama writes to Patients for Affordable Drugs: "My husband and I are currently doing without needed medication because of the cost. We recently lost our health coverage. With the high cost of medication, we simply cannot afford to fill our prescriptions. My daughter is in the same position, however she is on Medicaid. She has numerous health conditions and without her needed prescriptions, which Medicaid won't cover due to the cost, she ends up being forcibly hospitalized for treatment." States must make difficulty choices. And simply telling them to cover everyone that needs a drug ignores the fiscal realities.

How Drug Prices Are Set and Why This Matters to Patients

The establishment of the initial drug price, how this then gets translated into the price that the pharmacy or hospital pays to acquire the drug, and how it ultimately impacts the price that the patient pays to obtain the drug is extremely complicated. Much of the process is not transparent. My summary by necessity is an oversimplification of the process. A full description would consume a book.

It begins with a drug company setting a list price for the drug. There are no regulatory or market forces that determine the list price that the brand name drug company can set, and the drug company has full discretion and market power to set whatever list price it chooses when the drug is launched or to change the list price at any point of the life cycle of the drug.

It is important to recognize that the branded drug company has patent and market exclusivity periods that prevent other drug companies from manufacturing the drug. These are government given monopolies that protect the intellectual capital of the drug company and make it profitable for the branded drug company to engage in research and development.

However, any economist can tell you the dangers when a company has a monopoly; the drug companies are able to set the price that maximizes their profit. The monopoly price is not the price that allows everyone to get access to the drug. They set a price that is much higher than they would set in a competitive environment.

There are a number of factors that go into the drug company setting the list price. One factor is the cost of research and development. However, the list price is typically not based on the research and development that went into developing that specific drug; instead, the company looks at their entire portfolio of drugs to determine the profits they will require to create the next generation of drugs. Even using the pharmaceutical industry's own data, it is clear that branded drug companies typically spend less than 25% of their revenues on research and development, and far more on advertising and marketing.

Many people have argued that the list price is irrelevant because few entities actually pay the list price. However, the list price is often used to determine the amount of cost sharing that many patients will pay. Since the list price is the only price that is publicly announced, it becomes the basis for many cost-sharing agreements. Thus, patients are harmed when the list price goes up.

Most people with health insurance have their drug benefits determined by pharmaceutical benefit managers (PBMs), who negotiate prices with drug companies on behalf of health insurers or large employers. Only three PBMs control 80% of the market, which is troubling from a competitive vantage point.

Increasingly, it is being reported that PBMs are responsible for some or even most of the price increases. While they do have a role in the price increases, PBMs also serve to negotiate lower prices because of their tremendous buying power.

PBMs earn the majority of their profits by negotiating rebates off of the list price. The greater the list price, the greater the difference between the list price and the actual transaction price, and the greater the profit the PBM can earn. As a result, there is a financial incentive for the PBMs to try to get the drug company to increase the list price to show the insurance company or the large employer that they are getting a larger discount. However, this also serves to maximize the PBM's own rebates. For example, if the list price is $100 instead of $50, and if the actual transaction price is $30, then the discount appears much greater when the list price is $100. Also the PBM's rebate might be greater. Neither the size of the rebate nor the actual transaction price is transparent. Congress might want to use its subpoena power to investigate.

The fact that a higher list price can result in greater sales for the drug company is contrary to all economics principles. In nearly all markets sales decline when prices increase. However, for drug pricing, higher list prices and the greater rebates can help drugs get better placement on the formulary and hence more sales. The challenge is to change the rebate structure for PBMs a topic that I discuss later in the testimony.

Wholesalers bring the drug from the manufacturer to the pharmacy or hospital. The profit margins of the large wholesalers add only 1-2% to the price of the drug.

Pharmacies and hospitals sell the drug to the patient after they negotiate a price with the drug manufacturer and add a dispensing fee. Doctors, pharmacies and hospitals can get rebates from drug companies for using their drug as well. These rebate arrangements are almost never disclosed to patients.

Most patients pay something out-of-pocket for the drug. The exact amount is based on their insurance coverage. Insurance companies and PBMs determine the price that the patient will pay out of pocket by placing drugs on different tiers with different levels of cost sharing. PBMs and the branded drug companies negotiate aggressively on tier placement and this also helps determine the amount of the rebate. Again, all of these negotiations are confidential and the patient cannot understand how the cost sharing amounts are set. As a result, there have been calls for greater transparency in the pharmaceutical supply chain.

What we have recently learned is that some PBMs have instituted gag clauses with the pharmacy that prevent the pharmacy from telling their patient that if the patient paid cash instead of using their insurance card the price would be lower. Placement of the drug on a cost-sharing tier where the drug has a very high list price and low transaction price could mean that paying the cost sharing based on the list price is greater than the cash price. Pharmacies have reported this occurs quite often.

However, it is important to note that it all starts with the drug company setting the list price. Brand name drug companies have complete discretion on the price that they set and can raise it at any time. The government does not determine or limit the price. In fact, the government gives the branded drug company a government issued monopoly to set the price. Off patent drugs face market competition if there are multiple competitors. The problem in the off patent market occurs when there is only one or two off patent drug companies making a drug.

Policy Options to Increase Competition, Decrease Drug Spending, and Improve Patient Access While Encouraging Innovation

We are examining policy options for the HELP committee to consider. We have divided them into two categories

1) Policies that increase the level of competition
2) Policies designed to increase access to pharmaceuticals

Initiatives to Increase the Level of Competition

Curb Use of Limited Distribution Networks that Restrict Ability of Generic Companies to Copy Drugs and Submit ANDAs to FDA

Generic drug companies need access to brand and off patent drugs in order to demonstrate bioequivalence to the FDA for abbreviated new drug applications (ANDAs). However, some brand and off patent drug companies are putting their drugs in limited distribution networks, making it virtually impossible for a generic drug company to access the drug.

Hearings at the Senate Aging Committee and House Government Oversight Committee have shown how Martin Shkreli and others have used this tactic to stifle competition for old and off-patent drugs. Requiring drug companies to make their drugs easily available to generic firms would accelerate the introduction of generic drugs in the market and could save $2.8 billion, according to the Congressional Budget Office.

Include Drugs in Bundled Payments and ACOs

This is a potential game changer. Most drugs are still paid under a fee-for-service model. Payment reform is moving towards value based purchasing; however, drugs are typically not included in these approaches. Including drugs in reforms like bundled payments and Accountable Care Organizations (ACOs) would allow the physicians and other providers to make allocation decisions that include tradeoffs between a drug and other treatment modalities. Including drugs in bundled payments and ACOs would fundamentally disrupt the drug purchasing process and lead to more transparent pricing and put doctors in charge of deciding which drugs the person receives instead of the PBM or insurer. The doctor would have the financial incentive to make the decision that is in the best interest of the patient. Drugs are already included in the Medicare DRG payment that hospitals receive; this would simply expand the scope to value based purchasing arrangements.

Eliminate Rebates in PBMs and PDPs

PBMs earn most of their profit by getting rebates from the drug companies. The rebate is based on the difference between the list price and the transaction price. Increasing the list price therefore results in greater rebates, which totally distorts the pricing system. The higher list price also means greater cost sharing for patients because cost sharing is typically based on the list price. Forcing the PBMs and indirectly the prescription drug plans (PDPs) to pass on all of the rebates to the government, health plan or self-insured company would eliminate the market distortions, reduce prices, and should be used to reduce premiums or patient cost sharing. The PBMs would earn a fee for their services instead of a portion of the rebate. Giving the rebate to the patient--although it sounds good in principle--serves to distort the market since the patient would no longer be affected by the price and the drug company could increase the price even further. Some "skin in the game" for patients is needed to keep prices down, as long as it does not prevent access.

Restrict Pay for Delay Behavior

Branded drug companies have used a variety of mechanisms to prevent generic drug companies from entering the market, including paying them to delay the introduction of a competitor generic drug. While the courts have continually said this is illegal, some abuses continue. Litigation is time consuming and allows the branded drug company to continue to earn substantial profits while the case is still being litigated. An alternative is to penalize the generic company that applies to be the first entrant into the market after the patent expires, but then does not actually manufacture the drug. Congress could, for example, give the FDA the authority to keep the generic manufacturer from making an ANDA application for a second drug until it has actual sales on its first application. Generic drug companies would be motivated to get the drug to market as soon as possible and pay for delay would be eliminated.

Restrict Use of Patient Assistance Programs

While public programs like Medicare and Medicaid do not permit drug coupons, they do permit patient assistance programs that provide billions of dollars in financial support to Medicare and Medicaid beneficiaries. Some of the largest foundations in the US are now patient assistance programs sponsored by drug companies, with several of them giving out almost a billion dollars a year. The problem with patient assistance programs is that they allow drug companies to raise prices while keeping patients immune from all cost sharing. A recent Wall Street Journal analysis suggests for every $1 million funneled to patient assistance programs by drug companies resulted in $21 million in increased drug sales.

This is problematic considering the IRS considers patient assistance program donations to be charitable deductions. Again, some "skin in the game" for patients is necessary, as long as it does not harm access.

Reduce Abuse of Orphan Drug Designations

Some branded drugs have multiple orphan drug approvals that extend their period of market exclusivity and give them significant tax advantages. While the Orphan Drug Act had good intentions, the legislation needs revision to prevent companies from applying for multiple orphan drug designations and receiving multiple approvals and therefore market exclusivity extensions for the same drug. Revision of the law would lower prices by moving branded drugs to the generic market sooner.

Restrict Mergers of Generic Drug Companies

The Hatch Waxman Act effectively controls drug prices for generic drugs when there are three or more generic competitors manufacturing the drug. However, the generic industry has undergone a series of mergers that have reduced the number of competitors and lessened price competition. Recently, the largest and the third largest generic manufacturers merged. Because generic drugs are responsible for almost 90% of drug sales in the US, Congress and the FTC need to take a careful look at the level of competition in the generic market to make sure there are more than three competitors for all generic drugs. The recent mergers have lessened the level of competition in the generic market.

Additional Initiatives to Improve Access to Pharmaceuticals

Revise Medicare Catastrophic Drug Spending Rules

The main reason for the rapid increase in Medicare Part D spending is the advent of the high priced specialty drugs costing more than $7000, for which the Medicare program pays 80% of the cost. In spite of paying 80% of the cost, Medicare is prohibited from negotiating these drug prices. MedPAC has proposed shifting 80% of the cost to the PDPs and dropping the Medicare proportion to 20% so that the PDPs have a greater incentive to negotiate lower drug prices for these specialty drugs. However, this could cause the PDPs to discriminate against people with multiple chronic conditions (who take lots of drugs).

Instead, Medicare should be able to negotiate prices directly for these high priced specialty drugs. If negotiation fails, Medicare could use reference pricing, binding arbitration or value based pricing to set prices.

Enact Price Gouging Legislation

This year, the State of Maryland enacted bipartisan legislation to empower the Attorney General to take legal actions against drug companies enacting "unconscionable" price increases for off patent drugs with fewer than three competitors. It is designed to keep people like Martin Shkreli from raising prices on an off patent drug for which there is the only one manufacturer. It is the first legislation to address the problem of rapid price increases for off patent drugs. Congress could consider similar legislation to stop actions by people like Martin Shkreli.

Allow One Single Federal Agency to Negotiate Drug Prices

Currently many different government agencies negotiate drug prices, with each federal agency paying very different rates with different or no formularies. Looking at those 30 drugs for which we can directly compare prices, the Medicare program pays

30% higher prices than the DOD. Considering the similarities in the drugs needed by these agencies, the federal government would have a better procurement process if there was only one federal agency purchasing drugs. Because the prices are highest in the Medicare program and Medicare beneficiaries pay the highest cost sharing, Medicare beneficiaries are the biggest losers when government agencies pay different prices. While some federal agencies might pay more in one price arrangement, the entire federal government could pay less. Savings would be dependent on where the single federal entity set the price – at the highest level (Medicare), the lowest (DOD), or at the weighted average.

Use 1498 Authority to Negotiate Drug Prices

The federal government has the existing authority (28 U.S.C. § 1498) to take away the patent of a company, such as a pharmaceutical company; provide reasonable compensation to the drug company for the use of the patent, and allow a generic manufacturer to manufacture the drug. The Department of Defense, the National Gallery of Art and many other federal agencies have used this authority to purchase patented materials at reasonable prices. Health and Human Services Secretary Tommy Thompson threatened to use 1498 authority to purchase Cipro following 9/11 and Bayer lowered its price in response. The state of Louisiana is currently considering asking Secretary Price to use his authority under 1498 so that Louisiana can purchase hepatitis C drugs for the uninsured and Medicaid populations.

The CHAIRMAN. Thank you, Dr. Anderson. Thanks to all of you; very interesting testimony.

We will now begin a round of 5-minute questions. At about 11:20, I am going to ask Senator Cassidy to come over and chair the committee so that I can attend another hearing for a few minutes.

One purpose of this hearing is to see if we can establish some base facts. Let me ask this question and if you can answer it as close to yes or no as possible, I would appreciate it.

I have heard drug spending accounts for roughly 15 percent of health spending. Of that 15 percent, 10 to 11 percent is on drugs purchased at the pharmacy or ordered online, and 4 or 5 percent is spent on drugs given in the hospital and the doctor's office.

Is that correct? Does anyone disagree with that? [Panel nods in assent.]

Thank you.

Dr. Howard, you said, I believe, that 30 percent of branded generic prescriptions had a zero out-of-pocket cost for the patient in 2016. In other words, that when the patient picked up the prescription at the drugstore, 30 percent of the prescriptions cost zero. Dr. Adam Fein has said that as well in a meeting that we had here.

Is that an accurate reflection of what you said?

Mr. HOWARD. Yes, it is.

The CHAIRMAN. Does anyone disagree with that of the panel?

[No audible response.]

Thirty percent of the prescriptions, brand and generic, picked up at the pharmacy or online costs the patient zero.

Mr. Mendelson, you observed, if I heard your testimony correctly, that patients are bearing more of the cost of prescription drugs out-of-pocket in an effort to keep monthly premiums low.

Is it accurate to say, and I would ask this of other panel members as well, that in some situations or many situations consumers are paying more for drugs while insurance companies and employers are paying less for drugs.

Did I say that right or how would you characterize it?

Mr. MENDELSON. I would characterize it as saying that changes in benefit design are resulting in consumers paying more.

The CHAIRMAN. Changes in benefit design. Now, what does that mean to the untutored of us?

Mr. MENDELSON. As the cost sharing associated with a drug goes up, you are paying more of the portion of that price.

The CHAIRMAN. Then who is paying less if the patient is paying more?

Mr. MENDELSON. It depends on whether the cost—I know you do not like the word "depends," no Senator ever does—but it depends on whether the cost is going up as a result of a rise in the price of the drug or just the change in the benefit design.

What is happening is that patients are being asked to pay a larger and larger percentage of the cost of the drugs that they take.

The CHAIRMAN. That would mean someone is paying less. Is that right?

Mr. MENDELSON. That is right. It could be reducing the premium.

The CHAIRMAN. It would be the employer or the insurance company. Right?

Mr. MENDELSON. Or it could be reducing the premiums to the consumer.

That is the other thing that is important, which is that if a health plan can reduce premiums to the consumer, they want to do that, and part of the way they are doing that is by putting higher prices for drugs to consumers at the same time.

The CHAIRMAN. To lower the price of the premium. Any other comment on that? Dr. Anderson.

Mr. ANDERSON. Essentially what we are seeing in the private insurance market and the PBM's, is about a 3 percent growth rate in drug expenditures. What we have is if the price——

The CHAIRMAN. A 3-percent growth rate.

Mr. ANDERSON. The expenditures by the health insurers, by the employers, by people. It is not that the prices are going down for the employer; they are just not going up as fast.

What we have is a balloon here. What happens when the price increases are people, the insurance companies, squeeze the balloon a little bit to keep their price increase by only going up by 3 percent. Somebody else has to pay part of that increase and that is the consumer.

When the employers squeeze the balloon, the consumer pays.

The CHAIRMAN. Who else had a comment? Dr. Howard.

Mr. HOWARD. Yes, I am sorry. I just wanted to comment.

What happens when the person goes to the pharmacy to pick up their prescription, the pharmacy does not know the rebate. They are reimbursed based on what is called, I think, the average wholesale cost.

The coinsurance that a patient is paying is based on the price that the pharmacy has. That rebate is given to the PBM. I think Dan commented that that rebate is then, at least some portion of it, passed along to the employer. The patient is experiencing a co-insurance based on a list price and that is a problem. That is what we are honing in on now.

As Express Scripts said last year, it held cost growth for its commercial clients to under 3 percent, but more of that cost is being shifted to patients buying these specialty medicines.

The CHAIRMAN. I am afraid I am out of time, but I am going to submit to each of you two or three questions, if I may in writing. One of them is going to be if we should not focus on the list price, then what should we focus on instead in trying to understand pricing?

Senator Murray.

Senator MURRAY. Thank you very much, Mr. Chairman.

Before I ask the witnesses any questions, I wanted, since you are going to be leaving, to ask you a question. I really do appreciate you having this hearing, prescription drug prices is extremely important. I appreciate this and it is an important topic. I will have questions.

You have not yet scheduled a hearing on the Republican Trumpcare bill. I know you are a part of the discussion. You know what is in it. We have no idea. We have not seen it. The people we represent do not have any idea. Senator McCaskill raised this at a hearing, powerfully, last week and I want to raise it here too.

Do you intend to have any hearings before the bill comes to the floor?

The CHAIRMAN. I have none planned, Senator Murray, but let me respond to that in two ways.

No. 1 is that bill, if you are referring to the House bill, would be referred to the Finance Committee, not this committee. So you might take it up with Chairman Hatch.

No. 2, I had a hearing in late January, early February. We had terrific witnesses. My hope was to focus on the individual market and changes that we might agree on in a bipartisan way. Most Senators came to the meeting and made their Obamacare speeches that they have been making for the last 7 years.

I would summarize it by saying that the witnesses did very well at the hearing. The Senators did very poorly.

If we are not able to focus in a bipartisan way when we have a bipartisan hearing, I do not think there is much promise for a bipartisan result.

Which leads me to my third point, which is that this is a hearing that you asked for—

Senator MURRAY. Right.

The CHAIRMAN [continuing]. That other Democrats asked for, and that Senator Cassidy and Republicans asked for. We agreed on who the witnesses should be. We have exceptional witnesses today. It is a chance to address drug pricing, which is important to every American family.

I would think that this committee is a group of grown-up adults who are able to do more than one thing at a time.

We could discuss Obamacare, if you would like, but today we are trying to discuss drug pricing which is up to 15 percent. You brought up the issue.

Senator MURRAY. I just asked you a question.

The CHAIRMAN. You asked me the question about Obamacare, which is not the subject of today's hearing.

Senator MURRAY. I agree.

The CHAIRMAN. If that is the way you want to spend your time, fine. I do not know why I should call hearings requested by the Democrats with bipartisan hearings when you will not focus on the hearing.

Senator MURRAY. Mr. Chairman, I appreciate that you are having this hearing. I also would very much appreciate that we have a hearing on a bill that we are going to see that our folks have not seen, people across the country have not seen.

When we passed the ACA, we had 57 bipartisan HELP committee hearings, and meetings, and roundtables. I will just say that that is disconcerting.

The CHAIRMAN. You passed the ACA in the middle of a snow-storm with 60 votes and crammed it down the throats of Republicans.

Senator MURRAY. Well.

The CHAIRMAN. If you want to talk about that, we can. Today we are talking about drug pricing.

Senator MURRAY. We are talking about drug pricing. It is an important part of the healthcare program, but I think people in the country are deeply worried about what is happening to the healthcare system.

Mr. Coukell, let me go to you first.

Our hearing today is about the supply chain impacts and costs, and we have heard that the interactions between drug companies, pharmacies, and payers is a complicated one, but let me ask you a simple question.

We all know prescription drug prices are harder and harder for our families to bear. Some Republicans have been blaming this on the skimpier insurance coverage that forces patients to pay more out-of-pocket.

If that were the case, the total spending on drugs should stay constant as just the patient share of the costs would be increasing.

Based on your testimony, my understanding is that total spending on drugs is not only increasing, it is increasing faster than spending on other types of healthcare services.

Is that correct?

Mr. COUKELL. That is correct, Senator, and it is projected to continue increasing at about the current rate through 2021.

Senator MURRAY. Why is that?

Mr. COUKELL. That is based on a combination of high launch prices of new drugs, and year-on-year increases in the prices of brand drugs that are on the market. Drug spending is also being increased, by the increased volume growth as the population ages and we use more drugs. Those are the three major drivers of drug spending.

Senator MURRAY. Dr. Anderson, about 10 to 15 percent of U.S. healthcare spending goes to pay for prescription drugs. We established that. That is a cost patients feel every day.

I wanted to ask you in my short amount of time left, how can we tell if a high-priced new drug—you mentioned some of the bipartisan report were produced—how can we tell if a high-priced new drug is actually saving money down the road?

Mr. ANDERSON. We really cannot in most cases. We have some methodologies out there that are trying to do that, but it is exceedingly complicated.

That is why I would rather have the doctor make the decision as to which drug you get by giving that doctor the financial incentives to make the choice given the fact that they have a certain amount of money to spend.

Senator MURRAY. Thank you very much.

The CHAIRMAN. Thank you, Senator Murray.

Senator Cassidy.

STATEMENT OF SENATOR CASSIDY, MD

Senator CASSIDY. Thank you all.

A couple of things. Let me just make a comment at the beginning. I am a little bit betwixt and between the two sides.

I will say as a physician, when I was a medical student, one of the most common surgeries was gastric resection, taking out a part of the stomach for peptic ulcer disease. Along comes Cimetidine, which is now an over the counter drug, and we just stopped doing the surgery.

Then when I was a resident and fellow, Crohn's disease surgery was so common. No one does Crohn's disease surgery anymore because now we have these new drugs that just eliminate it.

Yet, on the other hand, I will agree. Dr. Anderson, you made the point and it was made by others, that there are some drugs that are so priced that some people do not achieve the benefit.

I always said we have a social contract with pharmaceutical companies in which we reward them for the risk and the social benefit they bring. I was on a call the other day and somebody said, "Well, our first loyalty is to our stockholder, our shareholder. We should charge whatever we can."

It seems like our social contract has now fallen apart. I just say that as a physician that understands there are lifesaving medicines which some people cannot access.

Dr. Anderson, you mentioned the Louisiana Hepatitis C. I am actually working on that. I am a hepatologist. I did a spreadsheet and saw that we could actually save money on long-term care—cirrhosis, a better share of the cancer, et cetera—if we upfront the treatment. The question is how do you pay for it? I do think that is something that we have to address.

Let me toss out something which is kind of radical.

When I look at the rebates, I am not sure that on net the rebates are actually bringing benefit to our society. As a physician, I look at the person paying cash and she is not benefiting from that rebate unless that is one of the rare companies, like CVS, I think you mentioned Dr. Howard, that does a point of sale rebate.

One of you mentioned in your testimony that we are pushing people more rapidly into the catastrophic portion of their Medicare Part D by a higher price. Sure, it is rebated, but the person is paying out-of-pocket. So their true out-of-pocket cost is inflated. They are moving more rapidly into the Medicare Part D.

Both for that cash person and their deductible, or with their health savings account, and the Federal taxpayer who is pushed more rapidly into the catastrophic portion. It seems like the rebate is kind of not working as well.

Mr. Mendelson.

Mr. MENDELSON. Yes. I would respectfully challenge that. I think that rebates are benefiting American consumers. They are benefiting American consumers because they leverage effective price competition and they ultimately reduce——

Senator CASSIDY. Let me interrupt. Why not just have a price based? When my wife buys jeans, she does not get a rebate from Levi's or Lee. She actually just gets a net price.

Tell me why that does not just translate into a net price?

Mr. MENDELSON. Rebates are a way that pharmaceutical companies give price concessions.

Senator CASSIDY. I accept that. I guess what I am just stumbling on, why not have a little upfront price which would be the ultimate concession?

Mr. MENDELSON. Because when drugs are first launched, there is a launch price and then competition comes in. The Hepatitis C market is a great example of this.

Senator CASSIDY. Somehow I think we are talking past each other.

Mr. COUKELL. Senator, may I? Senator CASSIDY. Yes.

Mr. COUKELL. If your wife were buying tens of thousands of pairs of jeans, she would go to the manufacturer of the jeans and say, "I do not want to pay list price. I am going to buy a lot of jeans and let us have a negotiation about what I should pay."

Senator CASSIDY. I get that, but when you look——

Mr. COUKELL. If we do not have that mechanism, then the question is how do we set a price for drugs? Some other countries, the Government sets that price.

Senator CASSIDY. Mr. Coukell, let me just say, though you can either do that with a rebate or you can say, "Give me a better price upfront." If I am buying a fleet of automobiles from Ford, I say, "Just knock $1,000 off," or I could say, "Give me $1,000 later."

The reason I say that is because that manufacturer's price is factoring in to what the person paying cash is paying and therefore that inflates their true out-of-pocket costs, moving them more rapidly into the Medicare Part D.

Mr. Howard.

Mr. HOWARD. Senator Cassidy, I think you make a very interesting point, which is companies could shift to a flat discount, as per CVS has done, make it available at the point of purchase.

They could also turn to providers and say—the reason they give the discount is to get on the formulary—but they could go to providers under some systems and say,

> "Here is your mix of patients. These are the medicines they need. Here is the price we will charge you and because you are operating in a value-based contract or a capitation contract as an HMO, you can save money. We will demonstrate and share our savings with you."

There is a different way of thinking about this that utilizes health technologies and informatics we have at our disposal and that are coming online to try and make the value proposition clearer to the provider and the patient.

Senator CASSIDY. I get that. It seems like there is a complexity there which is so incredible, that it is hard for one side of that to actually fully understand if they are getting the value that they are promised.

Mr. ANDERSON. It is absolutely true that it is totally confidential. What you have got to recognize is the consumers, if you go to the pharmacy with your insurance card, you might be paying more because you have insurance than if you did not have that insurance card. That is because of the rebates and those activities.

Senator CASSIDY. I will say that Louisiana is one of the few States that has said that pharmacists cannot be gagged. Meaning that they can inform a patient that she would pay less if she paid cash as opposed to paying her deductible, and that may be something we wish to look at.

The CHAIRMAN. OK.

Senator CASSIDY. Which is a very pro-consumer, pro-patient perspective.

The CHAIRMAN. Thank you, Senator Cassidy.

It is hard within 5 minutes to really dwell into this for each Senator. We might explore, as time goes on, whether we want to have a different forum, a roundtable, for example, where we can have more of a conversation and discussion between, perhaps, the four of you and Senators who are especially interested in this issue.

I am open to any kind of discussion that will help us understand what we are talking about. We talk about list prices, rebates, et cetera.

Senator Casey.

STATEMENT OF SENATOR CASEY

Senator CASEY. Mr. Chairman, thank you.

I want to thank you and Ranking Member Murray for having this hearing, and for those that made it possible. It is a critically important issue and I know we are going to have more than one.

I have to say, that stands in contrast to what is not happening on an even larger issue. This is a big issue, drug prices and affordability.

The even larger issue of what is going to happen to our healthcare system because of what the Senate Republican members are doing right now. I would hope that we would have hearings on the healthcare proposal just like we are having hearings on this issue.

In my judgment, there are lots of ways to argue against what happened in the House and what likely will happen in the Senate because there is reporting, just last week, that the Senate bill will be 80 percent of the House bill. So it is substantially similar.

In that case, just in terms of the Medicaid proposals, which I do not think will change all that much House to Senate, it is not repeal and replace. In my judgment it is repeal and decimate when it comes to children who get their good healthcare through Medicaid. People with disabilities in my State over 720,000 people have a disability and receive Medicaid, and about a quarter of a million seniors cannot get into a nursing home absent Medicaid.

If we enact what is being proposed in the House bill, if we enact what is being, credibly assessed as to where the Senate bill is, a lot of those Pennsylvanians will be hurt. I hope we have a hearing on that bill as well.

This issue for people in my State is of paramount concern. Other than questions about national security on the domestic side of what people are concerned about, and I would say other than maybe healthcare itself more broadly, I am asked about no issue more than drug prices.

It is of great concern to people. It is making it very difficult for people to get the medications they need. Millions of Americans do not get the medication they need because of prices.

Dr. Anderson, I will start with you. You heard what I said about Medicaid and what would happen in the event that a bill is enacted substantially similar to what has been talked about and what has been legislated.

Can you discuss high drug prices, especially around curative treatments like Sovaldi, which can cure someone with Hepatitis C, but will impact State Medicaid programs under capped funding?

Mr. ANDERSON. I would be glad to.

If you have a drug like Hepatitis C, and people have it at the age of 40 or 50, it makes it difficult for them to work. Some of them are in prisons, many have been on Medicaid.

However the benefit, in terms of financial benefit, of them getting ill typically does not accrue to the Medicaid program. They get ill when they are eligible for Medicare, and so the State is putting out all of this money, and the Medicare program is the one that is benefiting.

Figuring out a way for the State to have an incentive to invest in a curative disease, an infectious curative disease is absolutely important.

Senator CASEY. One of my basic concerns is that one of the changes that will take place at the State level is to a large extent, maybe not completely, but to a large extent if the Medicaid changes that are being proposed were enacted, the Federal officials would wash their hands of it. State officials, who have to balance their budgets, would have to take up and deal with the consequences, I should say, of no more guaranteed funding for Medicaid.

Mr. ANDERSON. That is exactly why we are working with Senator Cassidy in Louisiana to try to do that. We would be happy to work with Pennsylvania or any State as well.

Senator CASEY. I am grateful.

In the remaining time I have, Mr. Mendelson, on Page 5 of your written testimony, you cite the higher out-of-pocket costs as a key factor in patients' adherence to prescribed medications. For Americans with chronic diseases, adherence to a prescribed medication regimen can reduce unnecessary health spending such as hospital stays, doctor visits, et cetera.

Can you talk about that part of your testimony?

Mr. MENDELSON. Absolutely. Adherence is a key aspect and especially when a patient is using a medication that is of critical benefit to them or, frankly, reducing health system costs like the cardiovascular generics that we discussed before.

There is tremendous potential in fielding digital compliance programs where patients are tracked and the plan, or the Pharmacy Benefit Management company, is able to remind the patient, make sure that they are adhering to the therapy. Those are programs that could very well be supported by this committee.

Senator CASEY. My final point and I know I am done. I do not know how you—even if the result of these hearings over time ended with lower drug prices—I do not know how that is benefiting many people when you rip away healthcare to 23 million people, which is the CBO number based upon the House bill. If you do the math on the Senate bill——

The CHAIRMAN. Time is up, Senator Casey.

Senator CASEY [continuing]. You have millions of people without Medicaid coverage.

The CHAIRMAN. Senator Young.

STATEMENT OF SENATOR YOUNG

Senator YOUNG. I thank all of our panelists for being here today. Each of you indicated in your written testimony that you alluded to the piloting of innovative outcomes-based contracts by insurers and by biopharma companies. I would like to explore this idea of outcomes-based contracts with each of you.

Can you first explain how these contracts work and perhaps what their potential might be to lower drug costs for patients? Any of you can respond.

Mr. COUKELL. There is a vast range of potential ways these contracts could work.

Some could be purely financial instruments around a volume of sales and so on. Some could tie reimbursement payment for the drug to achieving specific outcomes, preventing hospitalization, or lowering cholesterol to a certain level. There are a lot of ways they can be structured.

This is still very new territory. There are not that many of these arrangements in place. Avalere just did an analysis that Mr. Mendelson could talk about.

There is relatively little in the public domain about how they are structured. They are complex to negotiate. They require a lot of data to monitor and followup on, and it is as yet unclear whether they will reduce spending.

Senator YOUNG. Yes.

Mr. MENDELSON. Yes, I am sorry, if I could?

Our analysis actually showed that 70 percent of health plans were very enthusiastic about initiating these contracts, and that 40 percent had actually initiated these contracts and felt they were successful.

I completely agree with Allan's characterization of the programs, but these are critical programs that are in place today, and I think really could be facilitated by making a few small changes to enable better contracts between health plans and pharmaceutical companies.

Senator YOUNG. To followup on that, are there policy barriers to implementation of these contracts?

Mr. MENDELSON. Yes.

Senator YOUNG. If so, what are they?

Mr. MENDELSON. I would point to three.

The first is that certain aspects of the Stark Regulations prevent the engagement with patients to make sure that some of the compliance programs—for example, that Senator Casey mentioned— could actually be adopted.

The second, ironically, is Medicaid best price where sometimes a pharmaceutical company does not want to enter into an agreement with a health plan if they think that the price that they will ultimately grant will go below what they granted to Medicaid.

It is ironic in the sense that it is really preventing the healthcare system from moving forward on the basis of the price floor that was set under Medicaid. So those are two.

Then I think there is a third set of policies around enabling more digital engagement by plans into the pharmaceutical area, and I would be happy to followup with more detail on that for the record.

Senator YOUNG. I will look forward to that.

Can others identify policy barriers to implementation of these contracts? Or, if you have strong opinions about their viability and effectiveness as we transition from a fee-for-service model, I would like to hear your thoughts as well. Yes, Doctor.

Mr. HOWARD. Dan is absolutely right.

I just had one thing. From the perspective of the FDA—and the engagement of companies, providers, and payers—there can be limitations on what companies can provide in terms of what is called off-label information on a product's effectiveness or safety profile that is not contained on the label. It is gathered through other sources, other clinical sources, electronic medical records, other studies.

Being able to transmit that information and incorporate it into these contract designs, testing new value and pricing arrangements, would be very helpful. The FDA's concern is that manufacturers would not have an incentive to go back and get new label indications, or expanded label indications.

The FDA could create safe harbors for these and then develop the use cases where they could capture that information and more rapidly expand the label and update the label more quickly than they do today. That would also allow for drug repurposing, drugs competing head to head based on their real world performance, which is another way to drive competition.

Mr. ANDERSON. What I would be concerned about in this formula approach is determining the value of a human life.

You really need to do that in most of these formulas and I do not know how you are going to do that. If you want to try to do that, go ahead. Also, every single patient——

Senator YOUNG. Would we, perhaps, look to some other areas, through regulation? We have seen that regulators here at the Federal level on a daily basis do determine cost value. Whether it is through auto safety rules, or other decisions over at the FDA, they do, in fact, determine a cost value, as uncomfortable as that notion is to all of us, a cost value——

Mr. ANDERSON. Right.

Senator YOUNG [continuing]. Per life.

Mr. ANDERSON. So the first thing you would have to do is that.

Senator YOUNG. Yes.

Mr. ANDERSON. The second thing is each patient is unique. Talking about a value for a drug for you is different than for Senator Collins.

Senator YOUNG. Dr. Howard and Mr. Mendelson, this cost value, they see that as a red herring based on their facial expressions.

Mr. ANDERSON. Right.

Senator YOUNG. I want to get that on the record.

The CHAIRMAN. Thank you, Senator Young.

Senator Franken.

STATEMENT OF SENATOR FRANKEN

Senator FRANKEN. Thank you, Chairman Alexander and Ranking Member Murray for holding today's hearing on prescription drug costs.

I also want to thank Senator Cassidy and the eight other Members from both sides of the aisle who joined me in requesting this hearing. I hope that we can continue this work together to tackle prescription drug costs and that is why we are here.

I am also glad that we will have additional hearings on prescription drugs. The roundtable is a great idea, Mr. Chairman.

I do agree with the Ranking Member and with Senator Casey that we do need to have hearings on the current effort in the Senate to repeal the ACA. I think the fact that we are not, should show the people of Tennessee, once again, that the Chairman is a rabid right-wing partisan.

Is that helpful for you? [Laughter].

The CHAIRMAN. Actually, that might get me through the next election.

Senator FRANKEN. OK.

The CHAIRMAN. Thank you for that.

[Laughter].

Senator FRANKEN. Our No. 1 focus today and always needs to be on patients.

Consider Carol from St. Paul, who has M.S. and has been denied coverage for her drugs that charge nearly $3,000 for her co-payments.

Or take Clare, who lives in Stillwater, MN. Clare used to pay $60 for her Remicade treatment for her rheumatoid arthritis. My mother had rheumatoid arthritis. But the price shot up to $1,400 for her prescription. Clare had to choose. Take her medicine or keep her home. It has been 2 years since her last treatment, and now she is having trouble holding a knife and fork.

No one should have to choose between affording their medications or their home.

Clare is angry. Her condition now interferes with her ability to do basic tasks and she feels like she is being robbed of her ability to age gracefully.

Frankly, I am angry too. It is our job, all of us here, to help people like Clare.

These stories are not unique to Minnesota. I have given all of you these stories from your constituents and your States. I hope that you will read them, everyone here, and internalize them, and make these stories your test of whether what we are doing here is good enough.

Senator Cassidy has been talking about the "Jimmy Kimmel Test," and I am glad he has been. For drug prices, let us use the "Clare Test." Will the proposals we support help Clare keep her home and get the medicine she needs to hold her knife and fork.

That is why I worked with 15 of my colleagues, many of them here today, to introduce comprehensive legislation to bring down prescription drug prices. This bill includes more than a dozen policies to increase transparency, improve affordability, reward high value innovation—I thank the Senator from Louisiana for bringing that up—and accelerate competition.

I do not expect every member on this committee to endorse all the provisions in my bill, but I hope we can work across party lines to build on them.

I would like to turn to my questions.

Skyrocketing drug prices obviously affect Clare, but they actually affect all of us.

Mr. Coukell, can you describe for Americans who are listening today who do not take expensive prescription drugs all the different ways that high drug prices affect them as well?

Mr. COUKELL. Thank you, Senator.

We all pay the cost of prescription drugs. We pay it through insurance premiums that we pay. We pay it indirectly through insurance premiums that businesses pay. We pay it through taxpayer programs that support Medicare, and Medicaid, and the V.A., and DoD, and all of those programs.

Every prescription that is covered by insurance ultimately is covered by the American public.

Senator FRANKEN. All of you would agree, right?

[Panel nods in assent.]

I only have 30 seconds left, Mr. Acting Chairman, can I go to my next question?

SENATOR CASSIDY [presiding]. Yes.

Senator FRANKEN. Thank you.

Reuters recently conducted an investigation on price increases for the top 10 drugs sold in the United States. Between 2011 and 2014, all of these 10 drugs had price increases of at least 50 percent.

Clare's arthritis drug, Remicade, went up 63 percent. Humira, another arthritis drug, had 126 percent price increase. M.S. drugs, too, have increased from about $8,000 a year to upwards of $60,000 a year annually, even though many have been in the market for years.

Mr. Coukell, or anyone who wants to answer this. How do drug companies justify these year over year price increases? For example, are their products improving in any way from year to year to justify the price? Or, are companies conducting valuable new research and development on these existing drugs? If neither of these, what do you think drives these increases? Again, for anyone, but I will go first to Mr. Coukell.

Mr. COUKELL. Thank you, Senator.

It is always important in this space to recognize when we are talking about list prices or net prices. Both are important.

Net prices are projected to rise 2 to 5 percent a year over the next 5 years. So compounded, that is 10 to 30 percent.

List prices are rising much faster and rebates are rising with them. For the patient who is paying an out-of-pocket share based on a list price, or something like a list price, that has huge implications at the pharmacy.

Obviously, once the products are on the market, there are some ongoing costs for the companies, but if the drug comes to market at a price that reflects its value, it is unclear why it would increase faster than medical CPI.

Senator FRANKEN. I am sorry. I will be here for a second round. Thank you for your indulgence.

SENATOR CASSIDY. Senator Collins.

STATEMENT OF SENATOR COLLINS

Senator COLLINS. Thank you.

Dr. Anderson, let me start by saying it is great to see you here again. You were extremely helpful last year when the Senate Aging Committee conducted a year-long investigation into the four drug companies that had acquired decades-old, off-patent drugs, and then dramatically increased the prices, in one case by literally 5,000 percent overnight.

What we found in that investigation is that companies were able to ward off competition by putting their drugs in closed distribution systems, or specialty pharmacies that made it very difficult for generic companies to get sufficient quantities of the drugs to do the bio-equivalency studies that are required by the FDA.

We particularly found that there were problems with abuses of the Risk Evaluation and Mitigation Strategies program. That is what is known as REMS. It is used for drugs with increased risk factors. Instead, it was being misused to prevent potential competitors from getting the drugs that they needed for the bio-equivalency studies. Indeed, Janet Woodcock, from the FDA, testified that this was a real problem.

Could you elaborate on that issue and what we could do to ensure that companies do not block access to the quantities of drugs that are needed for the bio-equivalency studies?

Second, since this is going to be the only question I am going to get, another idea would be to amend the Medicare Part D contracts that outline the participation in the formularies that are covered by Medicare Part D to require companies participating in Part D to make available sufficient quantities of their medications for these bio-equivalency exams conducted by potential competitors.

Could you comment on those two issues?

Mr. ANDERSON. I will do my best.

Senator COLLINS. Thank you.

Mr. ANDERSON. Thank you for those kind words.

It has been great to work with you and your staff over the last year and a half helping to put together your report, and then the legislation I know that you have been able to get through this committee. It has been a great effort, and I appreciate my little part in that activity.

What is happening right now is you have this REMS program which is established by the Congress and it is to make sure that the drugs are safe.

However, what is happening is that companies are using this idea to block other companies from actually getting access to the drug. People like Martin Shkreli, which your report showed, essentially created this entity called a limited distribution chain to keep everyone from getting access to his drug who was a competitor to him, so no one could actually get access to the drug.

There are a number of ways that you and others could deal with this problem. One of which is to essentially say to every drug company, "You have to make that drug available to anybody who wants to manufacture it."

I was on a panel with Janet Woodcock over in Government Oversight a little while ago, and she said,

> "I cannot do anything about it. I can say that you can make it available if it is on REMS, but I cannot force you to make it available."

I think only the Congress can essentially say that.

There is about a $3 billion savings that the Congressional Budget Office has estimated could happen if essentially Congress were simply to say to the company, "You have to make that available."

There are a number of bills, and you have one of them, that are about that particular area.

You could amend the Part D activities. You could do a whole variety of different activities, but essentially the idea here is to make sure that there is, in fact, competition in the marketplace.

Senator COLLINS. Thank you so much. Those are clearly areas that we need to pursue.

Thank you, Mr. Chairman. Senator CASSIDY. Senator Bennet.

STATEMENT OF SENATOR BENNET

Senator BENNET. Thank you, Mr. Chairman.

I would like to thank the Chairman and the Ranking Member for holding this hearing on drug pricing.

It is a critical issue for people all across Colorado. I hear about it regularly and I have heard about it over the last several weeks as I have held town halls all over my State in republican and democratic parts of Colorado where people are expressing their deep concern—I should say to my colleagues on the other side of the aisle—over the House-passed healthcare bill.

Based on what we know, 23 million people may stand to lose health insurance, and those who are older and sicker may be charged more. The effect of this is going to be felt more in rural areas than in urban areas.

In Otero County, where I held one of these town halls, the republican part of my State, 43 percent of the people who live there depend on Medicaid. I think they have a right to know what is in the bill, what is in the Senate plan. A right to know what is being currently drafted behind closed doors. Their health, the well-being of their families is at stake.

In 2009, while amending the process the Democrats used to pass the Affordable Care Act, Speaker Ryan said, "I do not think we should pass bills that we have not read, that we do not know what they cost."

He said,

"Congress is moving fast to rush through a healthcare overhaul that lacks a key ingredient, the full participation of you, the American people."

Speaker Ryan said,

"Congress and the White House have focused their public efforts on platitudes and press conferences, while the substance and the details have remained behind closed doors."

In 2010, Leader McConnell said,

"When it comes to solving problems, Americans want us to listen first and then if necessary, offer targeted step-by-step solutions. Above all, they are tired of a process that shuts them out. They are tired of giant bills negotiated in secret then jammed through on a party line vote in the middle of the night.

"It should be clear now, Americans are tired of grand schemes imposed from above."

They said this about a process that took years, literally years, and provided numerous opportunities to members of both parties to provide input. Almost countless bipartisan hearings were held, countless bipartisan roundtables were held. Hundreds of amendments were considered. Republican amendments were adopted in the process.

When the bill came to the floor, the Senate spent 25 days in broad daylight in front of the American people debating the health reform bill. We have not had a single hearing about this product, which may be on the floor and voted on next week. Not a single hearing. What an abusive process. At the very least, we should meet the standards that Speaker Ryan and Leader McConnell set for the Affordable Care Act.

I say to my colleagues on both sides of the aisle based on the hearings that I held, the town hall meetings that I have held in Colorado. There is going to be a lot of grief that is going to come to this body if we do not slow down and have the kind of public discourse we should be having about 16 percent of our economy and something that affects so materially every single family in our States.

I am glad we are having a hearing today on drug pricing because it is one of the things I hear about at every single one of my town hall meetings. As I mentioned, I think people do not understand why people in America seem to pay such a higher price than people around the world do.

I wanted to ask with my remaining time a question of the panel. It seems to me, based on your testimony and other work that I have seen, that we really need different solutions to address different categories of the drugs.

I would like to ask first whether you think my categories are off-base or on-base. Second, what would you say are the ways we could most materially affect the price of drugs.

The categories, I would suggest, are specialty drugs which are innovative treatments and cures that do not have a competitor, branded drugs that may not have a generic version, but may face competition with drugs that treat the same disease, and generic drugs.

I would ask the panel, do you agree? I have 2 minutes left, so I am just going to go down the row starting with Mr. Mendelson.

Do you agree with this break down and the need for different solutions to address the rising costs of each of these categories? What policy would make the biggest difference, Mr. Mendelson?

Mr. MENDELSON. I agree that different approaches are necessary for products that have limited competition versus those that have robust competition.

My view is that the best opportunity is really in fashioning policies that enhance the competition across all of these different categories, but it has to be selectively done in ways that make sense.

I do want to kind of point out one thing from the prior aspect which is that, as Allan mentioned, drug prices are going up between 2 and 5 percent in the past period. Overall, healthcare prices are going up by about 6 percent.

If these different categories are associated with different levels of price increase and, in fact, for drugs with generic competition, you see substantial reductions in cost.

I just wanted to kind of address that in the premise of the question.

Mr. HOWARD. Just the recognition, to followup on Dan's point, this is a problem we are going to have about every 10 or 11 years because that is when patents expire.

For the first part of this century through about 2012, in 2012 real drug spending actually fell because about a trillion dollars worth of branded medicines went generic.

Then we just need to focus on keeping the drugs in the picture of this is 15 percent of the cost. There is 85 percent of the rest of the costs that is a more appropriate use of medicines and a more appropriate reimbursement for outcomes that includes all of the other pieces of the system can help us to bend the curve.

I would just caution that. Keep them in sight of all the other things they do in the system and the ability to promote competition among other providers.

Mr. ANDERSON. I would just amend your three categories and make it four.

Within the generic space, for most generic drugs where there are three or more competitors, the system works incredibly well. When there are one or two competitors, the system is broken and that is when you get the Martin Shkreli's of the world and that is what Senator Collins and I were talking about.

I would just make that slight modification to your groupings.

Mr. COUKELL. May I quickly?

Senator CASSIDY. Very quickly.

Mr. COUKELL. I agree with that taxonomy. I just want to followup on one point that Dr. Howard made which is this is a 10-year cycle.

The concern here is your first category, which are specialty drugs. We know now that 1 percent of prescriptions are 30 percent of spending. If biomedical innovation continues the way it is going, and let us hope that it does, more and more diseases will fall into that 1 percent and that is the trend that looks unsustainable.

Senator BENNET. Thank you.

Senator CASSIDY. Senator Murkowski.

STATEMENT OF SENATOR MURKOWSKI

Senator MURKOWSKI. Thank you, Mr. Chairman. Thank you to the panel.

Many of my constituents back in Alaska live in communities where there is not a pharmacy in town, or if there is a pharmacy, it is a very small pharmacy and they likely do not stock a lot of specialty drugs. Much of what Alaskans receive by way of pharmaceuticals comes to them through the mail.

A pretty basic question here, then, is if it is going to come through the mail, why not work to expand that available market? For many, they look at our closest neighbor, which is Canada and say, "Well, why can we not just get our pharmaceuticals through the mail and through licensed providers in Canada?"

Obviously, that has been a subject of discussion here in this committee room.

What is the answer to a situation like Alaska, or many parts in rural America where you receive your drugs by mail? How do we work to ensure, not only the safety and the quality—which of course, we want to do and make sure that the FDA is regulating appropriately—but really to allow for a level of access to people in rural America?

I will throw it out to any of you. Dr. Anderson.

Mr. ANDERSON. We are working and getting a lot of mail order activities in the drug system. In most of the places in Alaska, if Federal Express gets there, your pharmaceuticals do.

Senator MURKOWSKI. No Federal Express in a village.

Mr. ANDERSON. No, I understand that.

Senator MURKOWSKI. Yes.

Mr. ANDERSON. But in many places.

Senator MURKOWSKI. They would like it.

Mr. ANDERSON. Exactly. But in many places it is, in fact, available and they are.

The delivery system is working very well in the system. Maybe not in the villages in Alaska, but in most parts of the United States, the distribution system is working as long as if it is not a very limited distribution system, as Senator Collins and I were talking about earlier. I think that is it.

The cost increases that are occurring are not occurring in the distribution system. It is really in the cost of the BPM's.

Senator MURKOWSKI. Right.

Mr. ANDERSON. It is the cost of the basic pharmaceutical company. That is where the cost is. I do not think we are going to be talking a lot about distribution systems here.

Senator MURKOWSKI. Mr. Mendelson.

Mr. MENDELSON. I agree with the comments about home delivery that it is a vital aspect, and I do not think that is going to change, but we will see more and more of that as more benefit managers encourage those programs.

With respect to the importation issues and this dates back to when I was running OBM Health under the Clinton administration and that was also being proposed around that time. And talking about things that are cyclical, every 3, 4, or 5 years there is an example of a drug that comes in from outside our borders and really hurts somebody.

As a result, I know that Congress had essentially put a certification in front of the FDA Commissioner and said, "We need the Commissioner to certify." And it had Democrats and Republicans in those positions and to date, no one has been willing to certify to the safety of the importation program.

That does give me some level of pause in terms of essentially abandoning the protections that we have in this country that are tightly regulated, not only by the Federal Government, but also by States and essentially kind of adopting an external regulatory regimen.

Senator MURKOWSKI. Let me ask about the PBM's because you have raised that and it just seems that we have kind of a self-rein-forcing spiral when it comes to certain drug costs.

First, you have new drugs and they cost more money, and that drives up the cost of insurance. Then in an effort to reduce the monthly insurance premiums, insurers offer this array of plans that expose patients to more out-of-pocket costs. Then PBM's can negotiate some sort of a discount from the manufacturer in exchange for certain concessions, but those savings, then, are not passed on to the patient buying the drug. Instead, those savings are already built in to the cost of the patient's insurance premium.

Somebody who has bought only the insurance that they can afford, cannot afford the steep price of the drug because the insurance has a co-pay or a high deductible. The higher the list price of the drug, the more of a discount, then, that the PBM can negotiate and the more money then that PBM earns.

It seems that you are incentivizing the pharmaceutical companies to set a list price that is nowhere close to the actual cost of the drug, even when the R and D factored in and the cycle starts over again.

What do we do? I understand that Dr. Anderson would either eliminate the rebates to PBM's and PDP's, or mandate transparency. How do we get out of this cycle that it clearly appears that we are in?

Mr. ANDERSON. What you want to do is pay the PBM a fee for their services. They are performing a very valuable service. What you do not want to do is pay them, give them a portion of that rebate because that gives them the incentive to raise the price.

Senator MURKOWSKI. Just a flat fee or——

Mr. ANDERSON. A flat fee or some kind of incentive payment, but not based upon the price of the drug. You take away that rebate incentive to do it. If they can negotiate a better price, they can get a bigger fee, but they do not get a rebate.

Senator MURKOWSKI. Got it.

Dr. Howard.

Mr. HOWARD. Some employers do just that. I forget what the exact numbers are off the top of my head. About half of large employers ask for 100 percent of the rebate to be passed through to them, so they capture the full value of that, and then the PBM can be paid on a per member, flat fee basis. You can ask the other 50 percent of the employers who do not do that, why they do not do that.

I just wanted to draw attention to some innovative approaches on the payment end.

There was a study that United Health is trying to replicate where they tried to bundle physician payment services for cancer medicines, and for cancer care that physician delivered in the hospital.

In a nutshell, they found that drug costs went up by, I think, 136, 139 percent. But total healthcare costs for treating those cancers fell by 36 percent because the physician had an incentive to use a regimen at their own discretion that they felt would prevent other complications, prevent hospitalizations. They are trying to duplicate that experiment.

That is one way of putting the medicine at the center of a better outcome that can lower total cost and still force the manufacturers to demonstrate how they are impacting that outcome.

Senator MURKOWSKI. Thank you, Mr. Chairman.

Senator CASSIDY. Dr. Howard said they put the patient at the center of that, not the drug.

Mr. HOWARD. Correct.

Senator CASSIDY. Yes.

Senator Baldwin.

STATEMENT OF SENATOR BALDWIN

Senator BALDWIN. Thank you.

Mr. Chairman, Ranking Member, it is absolutely clear that we have a problem with drug prices when price increases accounted for 100 percent of the pharmaceutical industry's $8.7 billion bump in earnings last year.

I fear that it is about to get even worse with the very partisan healthcare bill that is about to be brought to the Senate floor, which I believe will make many, many, many Americans pay a lot more for less care.

I am glad this is a bipartisan hearing. We should be working on bipartisan solutions to improve costs instead of pulling the rug out from under so many of our constituents, like my Wisconsin constituents, who are already struggling to pay for lifesaving medications.

Wisconsinites like Diane. Diane is from Webster, WI. She recently had to stop taking her Multiple Sclerosis medication that costs more $90,000 annually today. She has seen the price increase over the last 23 years and she has seen her savings be just completely drained.

It is why I had the opportunity to introduce the Fair Drug Pricing Act with my colleague, Senator John McCain, to require basic transparency and accountability—like Research and Development costs, like marketing and advertising spending—for drug companies that choose to increase the price of certain drugs by more than 10 percent a year.

Holding drug companies accountable is a first step to addressing these dramatic price hikes that are making healthcare more and more unaffordable for too many families in Wisconsin.

I believe that the market is broken when people like Diane have to make that sort of decision and we continue to see these yearly price increases.

Pfizer has already raised the price of 90 of its existing drugs by about 20 percent this year. While drug companies often argue that their price hikes are due to product improvements, and new R and D, we have absolutely no way to verify this.

What could we do to limit these price increases for existing drugs? Do we need more information surrounding drug company pricing decisions to help improve access?

I want to start in answering that question with you, Mr. Coukell.

Mr. COUKELL. Thank you, Senator.

You started with Multiple Sclerosis, and it is an interesting area where there are a dozen drugs or so, and every time a new one comes along, the price of all the old ones go up. So that shows us that the market is not working the way markets are supposed to be working.

It is absolutely a difficult area to make policy in because there is such a lack of transparency about who is paying what. It is very, very complex.

I think the question of whether R and D costs have a direct relationship to price is an important one and clearly it is an expensive undertaking to develop a drug. But if two virtually identical drugs came to market with really different R and D costs, we would not expect them to have a different price.

Really as the consumer, what I want to buy is a clinical outcome, and it does not matter to me that much what the R and D cost is.

Senator BALDWIN. Thank you.

Mr. ANDERSON. Senator Baldwin.

Senator BALDWIN. I have a separate question for you, Dr. Anderson.

Since 2002, three major drug companies have increased the price of insulin by more than 200 percent. I heard from a constituent— his name is Greg from Stoddard, WI— who has two sons and is struggling to afford the costs of their diabetes and insulin treatment that costs more than $1,000 a month.

I want to know if the drug maker that increases their price every year considers Greg's sons or any of the other families who depend on their drugs to function?

Dr. Anderson, can you discuss why companies who make life-saving drugs are incentivized to regularly increase their price or launch new drugs at radically high prices? How much does the impact of these high prices on real patients factor into any of their decisions?

Mr. ANDERSON. I had the opportunity to go to meet with the investment bankers and the drug companies, and ask pretty much that same question.

The simple answer is because they can.

Essentially, there is no regulation and because they have a monopoly, they can set the price at whatever they want to set it. So they essentially have that ability.

What they have seen from people like Martin Shkreli, who have done it and gotten away with it, that they should be able to do it. The investment bankers are often telling them, "You should do the same thing as Martin Shkreli did."

Senator CASSIDY. Senator Warren.

STATEMENT OF SENATOR WARREN

Senator WARREN. Thank you, Mr. Chairman.

I am glad we are having a hearing to talk about the skyrocketing price of prescription drugs. It is obviously a massive problem and there are a lot of different things we could do to help.

Senator Franken and I have a bill with a whole group of Senators that has a whole menu of options in it.

Senator Sanders and I have a bill with a group of Senators to allow medicines to be imported, cheaper medicines to be imported from Canada. Those are things we should be talking about.

Let us be blunt. It is insane to pretend to have a bipartisan hearing on lowering drug prices when right now, today, 13 Republicans are writing a secret bill to kick 23 million people off health insurance and their prescription drug benefits, and we cannot even get a look at it.

Let us start there. Dr. Anderson, you are an expert in health policy. Before the Affordable Care Act, if you bought a plan on an individual market, did it have to cover prescription drugs?

Mr. ANDERSON. It did not.

Senator WARREN. It did not. And now the ACA requires that plans sold on exchanges cover prescription drugs as essential health benefits. Is that right?

Mr. ANDERSON. Yes, they are essential health benefits written into the law.

Senator WARREN. Yes. All right. Let us talk about a second part.

Before the ACA, insurance plans could also impose annual and lifetime limits, meaning that once patients had run up prescription drug costs to a certain point, the patient, not the insurer, would be on the hook for all the prescription costs after that. Is that right?

Mr. ANDERSON. Absolutely. People were being thrown into bankruptcy court as a result.

Senator WARREN. Let us talk about potentially who gets especially hurt.

How did those out-of-pocket costs hurt someone with a disability or a chronic illness?

Mr. ANDERSON. Well, they are the people that are taking the most drugs. If you have five or more chronic conditions, which is about 5 million Medicare beneficiaries, you are filling a prescription every week and that is just exceedingly expensive.

Senator WARREN. Before we had the ACA, we lived in a world where insurance stopped for those who needed it most and stopped whenever anyone needed it most.

I know the ACA's coverage of prescription drugs is not perfect, but if the secret Republican plan is anything close to the House bill, then millions of Americans will lose their access to prescriptions. The Republican plan will also gut Medicaid, which means millions more will not get access to their medicine.

In fact, I want to ask about Medicaid for a just a second.

While the Federal Government pays for prescriptions through a lot of different Federal programs, the best deal is Medicaid. A 2014 GAO study found that TRICARE paid 34 percent more than Medicaid for brand name drugs. Medicare Part D paid 69 percent more.

There are a lot of ways that we could lower drug prices. We could negotiate with Medicare, let Medicare negotiate. We could import cheaper medicines. And instead, the Republicans are talking about slashing the one Government program that does a good job of keeping prescription drug costs low.

My question goes in the other direction. Mr. Chairman, I assume that you have seen the bill, and I am not asking for details on this. Can we get some general outlines of the Republican plan? Will the secret Republican bill let insurance companies go ahead and drop prescription drug coverage or kick people off Medicare?

Senator CASSIDY. Senator Warren, I cannot answer that.

Senator WARREN. I appreciate that and you have been someone who has really tried to work in a bipartisan way on this issue.

This is just enormously frustrating. We are in here to talk about the importance of access to prescription drugs and the need to bring down the costs, at the same time that 13 people are negotiating in secret to take away prescription drug coverage from millions of Americans.

There are people who want to be able to work in a bipartisan way. We have had our differences on this committee with Chairman Alexander and with others, but we try to sit down and work in a bipartisan way.

We cannot work in a bipartisan way if we cannot see the bill.

What is happening right now to deny Democrats and the rest of the Republicans access to this bill so that we can see the details, so that we can debate them out in public, so that we can have experts review them, so the American people can see them.

To deny the opportunity to see any of that is just flat wrong. In fact, it is shameful.

That is it for me, Mr. Chairman.

Senator CASSIDY. Briefly, Senator Baldwin.

Senator BALDWIN. Mr. Chairman, I want to request that testimony from the Campaign for Sustainable Prescription Drug Pricing be submitted for the record.

Senator CASSIDY. Without objection.

[The information referred to may be found in Additional Material.]

Senator CASSIDY. Senator Hassan.

STATEMENT OF SENATOR HASSAN

Senator HASSAN. Thank you, Mr. Chair and Ranking Member Murray.

As is true for all of my colleagues, I think the topic of today's hearing is incredibly important, and I appreciate the chance to discuss it.

I would venture to guess that just about every Member of Congress has heard from their constituents about the rising cost of prescription drugs. I hear about it from Granite Staters all the time.

I also right now, am hearing from Granite Staters all the time about Trumpcare and what the Senate is doing with Trumpcare.

Mr. Chair, I come from a State with a large citizen legislature, 424 volunteer legislators, where every single bill is required to get a hearing. You cannot pass legislation in New Hampshire if the bill has not had a hearing.

I am new to DC, but I continue to be amazed that we would not talk about a bill that impacts so many people and one-sixth of our economy. We hear references to it in the press. We know it is being worked on in secret, but we do not have even an outline of that bill for us to be able to examine ourselves or to get feedback from our constituents about which is what the other purpose of having hearings is about, so people can see it and they talk to us about it.

I appreciate this expert panel so much. But we have been talking today about the nuances of benefit plan design when, in fact, if Trumpcare passes, a whole lot of our constituents may not have a plan to begin with.

I join with my colleagues in being so frustrated that we are needing to spend time today when we want to be talking about the very important issue of access to lifesaving prescription medications for our constituents. But we need to be talking about Trumpcare because if Trumpcare passes in anything near the form that the House bill is in, and we are told that the Senate plan is similar to the House bill, this will be kind of an academic discussion for a whole lot of our constituents.

I will join with my colleagues in asking the majority party to please share their plan with us, and to please include us, and to have a hearing so that our country can collaborate, and come together, and find a way forward.

One of the things that I am also very concerned about is that we are hearing that the Trumpcare plan will cut Medicaid. I think a lot about the people who are covered by Medicaid in my State with long term disabilities, who do not have the physical capacity to actually take the medicine themselves. We need nurses, and licensed nursing assistants, and homecare workers who can actually help. If Medicaid is slashed again, access to prescription drug medicine for a lot of our constituents is an academic issue if there is not somebody who can help them take it.

That is what I think we should be talking about in a companion hearing to this one—the overall Trumpcare bill.

I do have a couple of questions about some fundamental issues that affect drug pricing because, again, I appreciate the discussion about benefit plan design, but we are still talking about underlying costs that keep rising very quickly.

As you know, and Dr. Anderson, we began to talk about this in one line of questioning. Drug manufacturers often point to high research and development costs to justify high drug prices.

In December, Health and Human Services released a report that concluded drug manufacturers set prices to maximize profits. This finding is obvious, especially for those who struggle every day to afford their medications. But I want to point out something from this report that I find interesting and would ask for you to comment on it.

The HHS report said that the relationship between research and development costs and drug prices is subject to a number of misconceptions. In reality, the prices charged for drugs are unrelated to the development cost. Drug manufacturers set prices to maximize profits. At the time of marketing, R and D costs have already occurred and do not affect the calculation of a profit-maximizing price.

Dr. Anderson, your testimony echoes this finding. I really am curious to find out from you, as an expert in this field, do companies spend more on research and development or on marketing, advertising, and then add to it in the profits they take?

Mr. ANDERSON. Thank you for that question.

They spend less on research, and more on marketing and sales than most of the companies. Essentially, you are correct that there is no typical relationship between the amount invested in a particular drug and the price of that drug.

Overall, the companies need the money for R and D, but they do not actually price on the basis of how much R and D they put in to a particular drug.

Senator HASSAN. Thank you very much for your answer.

Thank you, Mr. Chair.

Senator CASSIDY. Senator Murphy.

STATEMENT OF SENATOR MURPHY

Senator MURPHY. Thank you very much, Mr. Chairman.

My apologies to the panel; I am not going to ask them any questions. I am not. I think this is a really interesting discussion, but I think it is totally irrelevant to the most important discussion that is happening right now, which is not in this committee. It is not anywhere that the American public can see.

It is behind closed doors where there are a certain number of Republican Senators that are perpetuating a fraud on the American public and they are not here. I mean, Democrats have been here at this hearing pretty consistently throughout the morning. Republicans have been in and out.

If you want to believe the Republicans are behind closed doors writing a healthcare bill that is going to steal insurance from 23 million American in order to pass along a tax cut to the richest amongst us. Then this visual is evidence, potentially, of what is going on right now.

Senator Hassan has it perfect. We can talk all we want about benefit design, but if 23 million Americans lose their access to health insurance, then they cannot afford prescription drugs. So it does not really matter what we do with respect to adjusting the intellectual property laws, or trying to differently regulate PBM's.

If there is a massive fall off of the number of people who have insurance, then nobody can afford the drugs that we are talking about here today. With all due respect to the chairman, not the chairman who is sitting there today, but the Chairman who made opening remarks, what does it matter that the bill was passed in 2009 in the middle of a snowstorm? What does it matter what the weather was outside?

There were 25 days of debate in the U.S. Senate before that bill came up for a vote. The American people had a month to watch the Senate debate that piece of legislation and offer amendments. And as the Ranking Member said that was on top of exhaustive committee processes.

It is just not true that that bill was rammed through. That is not true. The House and the Senate debated that bill for a year and a half. It was there for the American public to see.

The reason that we are watching this process play out in secret, the reason why no one in this country will see this piece of legislation until it is already passed is because Republicans learned a lesson from 2009 and 2010. That it did not accrue to Democrats' benefit to have that process play out over such a long period of time, so that is why they are going to keep this secret.

They are going to keep it secret because inside that bill are massive giveaways for their friends. $145 billion of tax breaks for health insurers. $28 billion of tax breaks for pharmaceutical companies. $663 billion of tax cuts, almost none of which is going to anyone in this country who makes under $200,000 a year.

There is good reason why there are no Republican Senators here except for Senator Cassidy. There is good reason why they are doing this behind closed doors because it is a fraud.

It is a fraud to take insurance from middle class folks, folks who might be struggling in this country so that you can muster up enough money to hand another big tax break to people that do not need it.

I hope eventually we can sit down and have a conversation about drug pricing that is meaningful and relevant, but this is not. This is just a distraction from what the real story is, which is this committee becoming irrelevant as a secret process unfolds to radically change one-sixth of the American economy.

Senator CASSIDY. Senator Sanders.

STATEMENT OF SENATOR SANDERS

Senator SANDERS. Thank you very much, Mr. Chairman.

I want to talk about prescription drugs, but I want to concur with Senator Murphy, and Senator Murray, and I suspect others. We are talking about one-sixth of the American economy and there will be no public discussion. No committee hearings. No witnesses coming forward. This is really outrageous.

I want to focus on an issue which is also outrageous and that is I am hearing from my constituents in Vermont—that I suspect every other Senator here is hearing from his or her constituents back home—that they are sick and tired of being ripped off by the pharmaceutical industry, and they are very tired of paying by far the highest prices in the world for prescription drugs.

At a time when drug prices are soaring, millions of Americans are unable to afford the medicine they need. This is the United States of America, approximately one out of five Americans under the age of 64 who gets a prescription from a doctor cannot afford to fill that prescription.

How many of those people die? We do not know.

How many of those people suffer, become much sicker than they should have been? We do not know.

How much cost occurs when people end up in the hospital because they did not take medicine when they should have? We do not know, but clearly it is many billions of dollars.

Mr. Chairman, there is no rational reason why in the United States, Gleevec, which is used to treat leukemia, costs over $10,000 in our country, but $2,100 in Norway.

Why does a drug called Lantus, a diabetes drug, cost $186 in America, but $47 in France?

Why does Crestor, a popular drug for high cholesterol, cost $86 in the United States, and $29 in Japan?

Why does Advair, used to treat asthma, cost $155 in the United States, $38 in Germany? On and on and on it goes. We are not just picking these drugs out. That is all across the board. Some cases the discrepancy is more, some it is less.

Without exception, we pay the highest prices in the world for prescription drugs. Why is that? That really should be the simple question that is debated today, and I apologize. I have been to other hearings and I hope it has been discussed, but that is the question.

Why in this country do we pay the highest prices in the world compared to every other country on earth? The answer is simple. Follow the money.

Since 1998, the pharmaceutical industry has spent more than $3 billion in lobbying. This is not some kind of high technical, medical issue. Three billion dollars in lobbying and they have spent hundreds of millions of dollars on campaign contributions.

We have a corrupt campaign finance system. We have a corrupt lobbying system. The reason we pay the highest prices in the world is an example of that for prescription drugs.

An incredible example, last year—I was involved in this—people of California wanted lower prescription drug costs. The drug companies spent $131 million in one State to prevent the people of California from lowering drug prices in their own State.

Meanwhile, while Americans are dying because they cannot afford the medications they need, the five largest drug companies in the country made over $50 billion in profits in 2015, while the top 10 pharmaceutical industry CEO's made $327 million in total compensation.

This is not a complicated issue. The drug companies are enormously powerful. They own much of the U.S. Congress. They make outrageous profits. Their CEO's earn outrageous levels of compensation, and yet back in Vermont, we have elderly seniors cutting their pills in half because they cannot afford the price.

There are a number of solutions to this problem. They are fairly obvious. They have been discussed here for a long, long time. The real issue is whether the Congress has the guts to take on the very powerful pharmaceutical industry. I must say, there is not any particular evidence to believe that that will occur.

What we need right now in this country are people from coast to coast standing up and fighting back for their own health, for the health of their children, for the health of their parents. Demand support for legislation like drug re-importation.

My colleague, Senator Franken, has issued a very good, comprehensive piece of legislation and other people have demanded that Medicare, for example, start negotiating prices with the pharmaceutical industry.

There are a lot of things that we can do. We know what the answers are. The question is, will the Congress have the guts to stand up to one of the most powerful political forces in the United States of America? That is the pharmaceutical industry.

Thank you.

Senator CASSIDY. Senator Whitehouse.

Statement of Senator Whitehouse

Senator WHITEHOUSE. Thank you, Chairman.

I can remember once when our Republican colleagues were so sensitive to regular order in the Senate that they were accusing the Affordable Care Act of being a cooked up, closed door deal even when that was not even true.

We had in this committee, in this very committee, 47 bipartisan hearings, meetings, roundtables, and/or sessions. We considered 300 amendments. There were 160 Republican amendments adopted. We sat in that big conference room day, after day, after day going through huge stacks of amendments.

It looks like what is going to happen here is that the majority leader is going to call up the wretched House bill on the floor. If there is an amendment process, it will be a sham because all amendments will be stripped out because he will offer a complete replacement, which will be the secret Senate bill, the first chance anybody will have to see it.

No amendments will then be in order and they will cram it through on a fixed vote with only then the secret CBO score being provided. Then they will go off to conference with the House, which did the original wretched bill. It will obviously get even worse in conference with the House.

That may be the most disgraceful Senate process in the history of this body and it is certainly a closed door deal that bears no comparison to the open, robust process by which we got to the Affordable Care Act. Let me just make that point.

Let me ask the panel, where there is, in fact, competition among pharmaceuticals, how does the market tend to work?

Mr. ANDERSON. There are two answers to your question. Senator WHITEHOUSE. Make it quick.

Mr. ANDERSON. When there is generic competition with a lot of competitors, it works incredibly well.

Senator WHITEHOUSE. OK. Next. Howard.

Mr. HOWARD. When there are close therapeutic substitutes, the drugs are very similar, rebates are very large and the competition is fierce.

Senator WHITEHOUSE. Mr. Coukell.

Mr. COUKELL. I agree.

Mr. MENDELSON. Agree.

Senator WHITEHOUSE. OK. When there is real competition, it tends to work.

Next question, how hard is it to determine when a drug pricing monopoly exists for people who have some familiarity with this market? Is this, like, a really impossible thing to figure out?

On a scale of 0 to 10, how hard is it to figure out that a drug enjoys an effective pricing monopoly?

Mr. COUKELL. All brand drugs enjoy a pricing monopoly. Some have competition from other products. It is a little harder to tell when a generic has a monopoly, when it is the only product in the market, but not impossible.

Senator WHITEHOUSE. You can tell. There are some drugs that clearly do have a monopoly where monopoly rents can be extracted. Correct?

Mr. COUKELL. Yes.

Senator WHITEHOUSE. And that is visible. People can see that.

Mr. COUKELL. Yes.

Senator WHITEHOUSE. Yes? Economists can look at it and say yes, that is monopolistic behavior. Correct?

Mr. COUKELL. Correct.

Senator WHITEHOUSE. Correct. OK.

What do we do as a country when we see that monopolistic behavior? Who steps in at that point and says, "But wait a minute. That is actually an effective monopoly. We are going to have to do something about this pricing."

Long pause because nobody does.

That takes me to Senator Sanders' point. As Senator Baldwin mentioned, the Credit Suisse just found that price increases have added $8.7 billion in net income to the companies that they analyzed; $8.7 billion in added net income.

Also, we have this wretched decision called Citizens United, which allows industries to come in and spend unlimited amounts of money on influence in Congress.

If you are making an extra $8.7 billion, how much money might it make sense to spend to try to exert influence in Congress? The answer is probably around $8.7 billion. Of course, they do not need to spend that much because we tend to come cheaper than that.

It is impossible to imagine that we could not solve, in good faith, the pharmaceutical pricing problem, or at least take a good whack at it in this country, in a week if it were not for the special influence operations that control the Senate and control the House.

It is not just the unlimited money that we see spent. Once Citizens United let the pharmaceutical industry, and the fossil fuel industry, and the other big players here spend unlimited amounts of money. That also allowed them to go to the dark money channels and blow them out so that they could spend unlimited dark money so that you do not even see their hands in operation.

I associate myself with the comments of Senator Murphy, Senator Baldwin, Senator Sanders, and Senator Murray. This is a solvable problem except for the fact that we are too in tow to big special interests.

Look out for the special interest prizes buried in the secret Senate Republican healthcare bill.

Senator CASSIDY. Senator Franken, second set of questions. Senator FRANKEN. Thank you, Mr. Chairman.

Let me speak to what my colleagues have been speaking to, which is this Republican process that is going on behind closed doors.

There is a hope here, which is that they need 50 votes. And there is the hope that enough of my Republican colleagues do not vote for a bill that will hurt the American people. These are colleagues. They are colleagues on the other side of the aisle, the acting chairman among them, who cares about patients, who has run a clinic for patients who are in need.

There is hope that there are enough colleagues on the other side of the aisle that will not allow something to get passed that will hurt the American people and that will make this discussion completely moot.

I am here because I go around the State of Minnesota, and everyone knows that the prices of pharmaceuticals have shot up in the last 3 years, and they are feeling it.

We have you four here, and I want to use your expertise to talk about that, and put aside this process that none of us, on this side, anyway, like—and I suspect that many on the other side do not like—and use the fact that you are here.

I hope we do have a roundtable with you and I hope we can do it under maybe different circumstances where we are not talking just at the margins. We are talking about something that is very key to the American people and not just on the margins considering something very bad getting passed.

I want to ask you about this idea of the R and D costs. I have heard some testimony from both Mr. Coukell and Dr. Anderson about the R and D. Very often it is said, "Well, you have got to let them charge this much because otherwise they would not be able to develop drugs."

This is what an article recently published in the *Journal of American Medical Association* said,

> "Although prices are often justified by the high costs of drug development, there is no evidence of an association between research and development costs, and prices. Rather, prescription drugs are priced in the United State primarily on the basis of what the market will bear."

Do you think JAMA is correct?

Mr. COUKELL. Senator, one of the areas we work on is antibiotics. It is really hard to make money on antibiotics because when a new one comes to market, it is competing with old ones that are really cheap. And so that goes to show you that it is not related directly to the R and D costs. It is related to what the market is willing to pay based on the outcomes you get.

Mr. HOWARD. To put that in a slightly different way, so that returns on investment are very sensitive to the prices that drugs command. So that when there is an attractive environment for investment, more money goes into R and D.

There has been a great deal of econometric work from RAND and other places that shows when those returns decline, money going into R and D can decline as well.

The problem is that investors have alternatives. If they can look at getting the next Snapchat or pick your favorite Web application that they can make a billion dollars on in a few years and not face regulatory approval compared to a product that performs at term.

Senator FRANKEN. Let me ask to that end. What are the profit margins of pharmaceutical companies versus, say, other sectors in the economy, say steel?

Mr. HOWARD. The CBO has found that returns on investment for the industry are comparable to other high tech industries.

Senator FRANKEN. Other high tech. OK. I said steel. You did not answer my question.

Mr. HOWARD. Should we compare them to donuts? We should compare them to other high R and D industries.

Senator FRANKEN. You should answer my question first.

Mr. HOWARD. Right. There are lower returns for commodity-based industries like steel than there are to other returns like software where there are important I.P. protections and higher returns as well.

Senator FRANKEN. At least that was an answer. Thank you. I appreciate that.

I am out of time, but there are so many—can I make a couple of points?

Senator CASSIDY. If you can make them quickly, because I have to head out.

Senator FRANKEN. We should be able to import from Canada. We should be able to have a safe path and I think we also pay with NIH funding; I do not think that is talked about enough. We should negotiate within Medicare Part D.

I would like to get that roundtable, so we can discuss all that again.

Dr. Howard, thank you again for your answer. Thank you.

Senator CASSIDY. Senator Murray.

Senator MURRAY. Thanks very much, Mr. Chairman.

I want to thank all of our witnesses. This is an important hearing. It is a hearing about a cost to American families that is dramatically growing that they are deeply concerned about. We do need to figure out a way to proceed forward in a bipartisan way.

Mr. Chairman, thank you for your forbearance and patience. I know you want to go crash the secret meeting, so I do not want to hold you up too much longer.

Senator MURRAY. Can I come with you and crash that meeting? Because I will tell you, people across the country want to know what is in it because the cost of healthcare is critical to every family, every business, every community, everyone.

The fact that a Republican Trumpcare bill is going to be jammed through here in a few weeks without any look at it by this committee, to me, is really appalling.

We have a responsibility to our constituents to ask questions, to offer amendments, to be a part of that process particularly when millions of Americans are going to lose their coverage, pay higher costs, and feel the impact of that.

I know you want to get to the meeting. I appreciate that. I will just say we are really appalled that this is being done in secret, and I hope you pass that onto your colleagues.

Thank you very much.

Senator CASSIDY. I will also thank you and what I kind of draw from our meeting today is that there is a tension between how do we drive innovative for that antibiotic, for example, and how do we keep drugs affordable?

Dr. Howard, your point at the end—about drug company profits are comparable to other high tech R and D—is appropriate. We cannot ignore the fact that some people cannot access drugs.

Also my own concern, but I think I heard it here, is that we are driving some patients into the catastrophic portion of Medicare Part D which is really increasing the bill for the Federal taxpayer as well as for that person who is not getting that point of sale rebate.

Two more things we heard. We need to leverage outcomes data to identify and reward value. Last, the whole process is opaque, so pity the poor patient who is trying to make a sense of it. So if we can get transparency, That could help.

Let me finish by saying the hearing record will remain open for 10 days. Members may submit additional information for the record within that time should they wish.

Thanks again for being here.

The committee stands adjourned.
[Additional Material follow.]

Testimony Submitted for the Record, U.S. Senate Committee on Health, Education, Labor and Pensions, Full Committee Hearing on "the Cost of Prescription Drugs: How the Drug Delivery System Affects What Patients Pay," John Rother, Executive Director, the Campaign for Sustainable Rx Pricing (CSRxP), June 13, 2017

Chairman Alexander, Ranking Member Murray, and members of the Senate HELP Committee, the Campaign for Sustainable Rx Pricing (CSRxP) thanks you for the opportunity to submit testimony for the record on the critically important issue of unsustainable growth in prescription drug prices.

CSRxP is a project of the National Coalition on Health Care Action Fund. We are nonpartisan coalition of organizations committed to fostering an informed discussion on sustainable drug pricing and to developing bipartisan, market-based solutions that improve affordability while maintaining access to prescription drugs for American patients and their families. Our members represent organizations including consumers, hospitals, physicians, nurses, pharmacists, employers, pharmacy benefit managers and health plans.

We look forward to continuing our work with the Committee to address the unsustainable growth in prescription drug prices, which can threaten the financial security, health and wellbeing of American patients and their families. Below we describe how the current marketplace enables the brand pharmaceutical industry to engage in anti-competitive practices that drive up prescription drug prices for consumers and present market-based, bipartisan solutions that would allow U.S. patients to continue to access the medicines they need at prices more affordable than currently available to them.

Spending Growth on Prescription Drugs Far Exceeds Spending Growth in the U.S. Healthcare Sector More Broadly

U.S. spending on prescription drugs is unsustainable and growing at a rate faster than the rest of the healthcare sector. In 2015, for example, while overall growth in U.S. healthcare spending increased by 5.8 percent, growth in spending on prescription drugs increased by 9 percent and outpaced spending on all other medical services.[63] Medicare has followed a similar trend in recent years, as spending growth on drugs has exceeded spending growth in other parts of the program. The Medicare Trustees stated in their 2016 report, for example, that per capita drug spending in Part D grew faster than historical rates in 2015, driven in large part by continued growth in prescription drug prices and a "surge" in spending on expensive specialty medicines, and they project such accelerated growth will continue in the future for similar reasons.[64] Likewise, Medicare Part B spending on prescription drugs increased at a rapid average annual rate of 7.7 percent from 2005 to 2014; during that period, specialty biologic medicines grew at a particularly fast rate, increasing from 39 percent to 62 percent of total spending, with a significant share of the growth due to price increases rather than number of patients using the medications.[65]

The Brand Pharmaceutical Industry Is Driving Excessive Drug Cost Growth by Setting Needlessly High List Prices for Its Products and Increasing Those Prices by Amounts That Substantially Exceed Inflation after They Enter the Market

Despite efforts from the brand name drug industry to suggest otherwise, the pharmaceutical industry is the primary driver of the unsustainable and needless growth in prescription drug costs that American patients and their families face today. The industry sets high initial prices for its products and consistently increases those prices at rates that typically exceed inflation.

The brand pharmaceutical industry acknowledges that the list prices it sets represent the majority of the cost that U.S. patients pay out-of-pocket for their prescription drugs. "More than half of what commercially-insured patients pay out-of-pocket for brand medicines is based on the list price," the Pharmaceutical Research & Manufacturers of America states.[66] In other words, the industry alone sets the lists price that comprises a majority of the patient's out-of-pocket spending, meaning that the brand drug industry has significant control over the excessive and unsustainable costs that U.S. patients and their families bear in purchasing prescription drugs.

---

[63] Centers for Medicare and Medicaid Services. "NHE Fact Sheet." See link: https://www.cms.gov/Research-Statistics-Data-and-Systems/Statistics-Trends-and-Reports/NationalHealthExpendData/NHE-Fact-Sheet.html.

[64] 2016 Annual Report of the Boards of Trustees of the Federal Hospital Insurance and Federal Supplementary Medical Insurance Trust Funds, page 108. See link: https://www.cms.gov/research-statistics-data-and-systems/statistics-trends-and-reports/reportstrustfunds/downloads/tr2016.pdf.

[65] HHS Assistant Secretary for Planning and Evaluation. "Medicare Part B Drugs: Pricing and Incentives," page 6. March 8, 2016. See link: https://aspe.hhs.gov/system/files/pdf/187581/PartBDrug.pdf.

[66] Pharmaceutical Research & Manufacturers of America. "More Than Half of Patients' Out-of-Pocket Spending for Brand Medicines Is Based on List Price." March 27, 2017. See link: http://www.phrma.org/graphic/more-than-half-of-patients-out-of-pocket-spending-for-brand-medicines-is-based-on-list-price.

Indeed, the brand industry today is using its ability to set high list prices for its products – and add to the already unwarranted costs consumers pay out-of-pocket for the prescription medications they need. One recent analysis found, for example, that list prices for prescription drugs grew 9.8 percent in 2016 after a 10.8 percent increase in 2015.[67] By way of comparison, the CPI increased by 2.1 percent and 0.7 percent, respectively, in 2016 and 2015.[68]

The industry also acknowledges the important role that pharmacy benefit managers, wholesalers, pharmacies and other intermediaries play in reducing the list price by negotiating discounts and rebates off that list price, thereby lowering overall cost of medicines for U.S. consumers. However, brand drug makers find ways to keep costs unsustainably high even after these discounts and rebates are negotiated for consumers by implementing excessive price increases that typically exceed inflation after a product enters the market.

AARP found, for instance, that retail prices increased in 2015 for 97 percent of the widely-used brand name prescription drugs and all of these increases exceeded the rate of general inflation that year.[69] Another study showed that prices for four of the 10 top-selling drugs in the U.S. increased by more than 100 percent between 2011 and 2014 and for six of the 10 top-selling drugs in the U.S. grew by more than 50 percent during that same period.[70] The trend appears to be continuing in 2017, as another analysis determined that there were 40 drug price increases in the first quarter of 2017 – up from 33 in 2016.[71]

Manufacturers of expensive specialty medications in particular significantly contribute to this critical problem of unsustainably high list prices and price increases in excess of inflation. AARP determined, for example, that the average cost of a specialty medication in the U.S. was $53,000 in 2013.[72] In that year, that amount was more than: (1) the average annual U.S. household income - $52,250; (2) two times the median income of a Medicare beneficiary - $23,500; and (3) three times the average Social Security retirement benefit - $15,526.[73]

---

[67] Saganowsky, Eric. "Report: Price Hikes Are Still Driving Pharma's Earnings Growth. Who's Most At Risk?" *Fierce Pharma.* April 19, 2017. See link: http://www.fiercepharma.com/pharma/despite-scrutiny-price-hikes-still-driving-pharma-s-eps-growth-report.

[68] Bureau of Labor Statistics. "CPI Detailed Report. Data for December 2016," page 2. See link: https://www.bls.gov/cpi/cpid1612.pdf.

[69] AARP Public Policy Institute. "Rx Price Watch Report: Trends in Retail Prices of Brand Name Prescription Drugs Widely Used by Older Americans, 2006 to 2015," page 10. December 2016. See link: http://www.aarp.org/content/dam/aarp/ppi/2016-12/trends-in-retail-prices-dec-2016.pdf.

[70] Humer, Caroline. "Exclusive: Makers Took Big Price Increases on Widely Used U.S. Drugs." Reuters Health News. April 5, 2016. See link: http://www.reuters.com/article/us-usa-healthcare-drugpricing-idUSKCN0X10TH.

[71] Tirrell, Meg. "The Drug Industry Is Addicted to Price Increases, Report Shows." *CNBC*. April 20, 2017. See link: http://www.cnbc.com/2017/04/20/the-drug-industry-is-addicted-to-price-increases-report-shows.html.

[72] AARP Public Policy Institute. "Trends in Retail Prices of Specialty Prescription Drugs Widely Used by Older Americans, 2006 to 2013," page 8. November 2015. See link: http://www.aarp.org/content/dam/aarp/ppi/2016-12/trends-in-retail-prices-dec-2016.pdf.

[73] AARP Public Policy Institute. "Rx Price Watch Report: Trends in Retail Prices of Prescription Drugs Widely Used by Older Americans, 2006 to 201," page 1. February 2016. See link: http://www.aarp.

Within specialty medicines, one area of particularly significant concern is the treatment of patients with cancer. In the U.S., a novel anti-cancer drug routinely costs more than $100,000 per year or course of treatment and the median launch price of a new oncology drug has increased in each decade from the 1960s to today from $100 to $10,000 per month of treatment.[74] Similarly, a separate analysis demonstrated that the inflation-adjusted price of an anti-cancer medicine often increases after launch, by as much as 44 percent over the course of the decade.[75] These rapidly growing and excessive oncology drug costs represent potentially significant barriers for patients in accessing lifesaving and life-sustaining treatments who simply may not be able to afford them.

In analyzing this extreme and rapid growth in cancer drug costs, researchers emphasized how these costs both hurts patients, who in many cases may not be able to afford these expensive medications, and society at large, which simply will not be able to financially bear the unsustainable burden of excess drug cost growth over the long-term:

> "Not only are launch prices high and rising, but individual drug prices are often escalated during exclusivity periods. High drug prices harm patients – often directly through increased out-of-pocket expenses, which reduce levels of patient compliance and lead to unfavorable outcomes – and harms society – by imposing cumulative price burdens that are unsustainable."[76]

Drug Manufacturers Suggest That Research and Development Justifies High Drug Prices – but Data Show That the Excessive Amounts Charged to *U.S.* Patients in Aggregate Exceed the Industry's *Global* R&D Budget

A recent analysis concluded that the drug prices paid by *U.S.* consumers create significantly more revenue for the brand pharmaceutical industry than the amount the industry expends *globally* on research and development. Specifically, the analysis found that 15 drug companies that manufactured the 20 best-selling drugs worldwide in 2015 made $116 billion in excess revenue from U.S. drug prices.[77,78] Meanwhile, brand drug makers only spent $76 billion – or $40 billion less – on global research and development

---

org/content/dam/aarp/ppi/2016-02/RX-Price-Watch-Trends-in-Retail-Prices-Prescription-Drugs-Widely-Used-by-Older-Americans.pdf.

74 Prasad et al. "The High Price of Anticancer Drugs: Origins, Implications, Barriers and Solutions." *Nature Reviews Clinical Oncology*. 2017. Advanced Online Publication, page 1.

75 *Ibid.*

76 *Ibid.*

77 Note that this study looked at net prices – not list prices – that U.S. consumers paid for prescription drugs. Net prices reflect discounts and rebates that pharmacy benefit managers, wholesalers, pharmacies, and other members of the supply chain negotiate with drug manufacturers to lower the list price initially set.

78 Yu, Nancy et al. "R&D Costs for Pharmaceutical Companies Do Not Explain Elevated US Drug Prices." *Health Affairs Blog*. March 7, 2017. See link: http://healthaffairs.org/blog/2017/03/07/rd-costs-for-pharmaceutical-companies-do-not-explain-elevated-us-drug-prices/.

that same year.[79] As one author of the analysis Dr. Peter Bach, Director of Memorial Sloan Kettering Cancer Center's Center for Health Policy and Outcomes, clearly said: "the math doesn't work out."[80]

Moreover, brand drugs with the highest prices sometimes are the ones that are the least costly to develop, indicating that a drug maker's R&D budget does not necessarily justify the setting of high drug prices or excessive price increases. In other words, as one recent study found, high prices do not necessarily correlate with the innovative R&D that the pharmaceutical industry maintains it is supporting in part through excessive drug cost growth.[81] Specifically, the study explains that the

> "costliest drugs to develop are those which require large phase III clinical trials involving tens of thousands of patients, such as drugs for diabetes, high blood pressure, and heart disease....But, in fact, new drugs in these areas have little pricing power, because doctors have the ability to prescribe effective and inexpensive generics for these conditions."[82]

By contrast, the

> "cheapest drugs to develop are those which require small clinical trials involving dozens of patients, such as drugs for ultra-rare, or 'ultra-orphan' conditions....Phase III trials for these conditions, which only affect several thousand people in the United States, run in the tens of millions. But manufacturers have generated billions in revenues from them."[83]

Excessive Drug Prices Paid by American Patients and Families Enable the Drug Industry to Pay for Needless Advertising and Marketing – and Contribute to Drug Makers' Bottom Lines

If the drug industry does not spend all of the money it receives from U.S. consumers on its products on R&D as shown above, the question arises as to where the industry actually spends those excessive revenues. It turns out that brand manufacturers are using a significant portion those funds for marketing and advertising – and to increase their bottom lines.

---

[79] *Ibid.*

[80] Sagonowsky, Eric. "High U.S. Drug Prices Cover Pharma's Global R&D – And a Whole Lot More, Study Finds." *Fierce Pharma*. March 10, 2017. See link: http://www.fiercepharma.com/pharma/high-u-s-drug-costs-pay-for-pharma-s-global-r-d-plus-more-study-finds.

[81] Roy, Avik. "The Competition Prescription: A Market-Based Plan for Making Innovative Medicines Affordable," page 7. See link: http://www.csrxp.org/wp-content/uploads/2017/05/The-Competition-Prescription1.pdf.

[82] *Ibid.*, page 7.

[83] *Ibid*, page 8.

First, many members of the brand drug industry spend more on advertising and marketing than R&D; one analysis determined that nine of the 10 largest drug companies spent more on marketing than they did on research in 2013.[84] A separate analysis found that drug makers specifically are increasing their spending on television advertising in the U.S., spending $6.4 billion on TV consumer advertising in 2016 – an increase of 5 percent over 2015 and of 62 percent since 2012.[85] Along those same lines, in 2016, drug advertising represented the sixth largest category of TV advertising, accounting for eight percent of total TV advertising revenue and increasing six places from twelfth place in the category in 2012.[86]

Importantly, while drug makers suggest marketing and advertising help inform patients and their providers of treatment options, these industry tactics also drive up health care costs for all consumers – not just those that take prescription drugs. Television advertisements often induce unnecessary demand, encouraging patients and their families to ask physicians for drugs they may not need.[87] Similarly, drug makers' direct marketing to physicians informs prescribers about the availability of specific treatment options – and not necessarily those that treatments that are the most effective and least costly for the patient. Both cases needlessly and unfairly increase healthcare costs for all Americans – not just those using prescription medicines – by unnecessarily increasing spending on prescription drugs overall, thereby driving up overall insurance premiums for all U.S. consumers.

Second, and very importantly, brand drug manufacturers depend on these unsustainable high drug prices to help support their bottom line growth; price increases now are replacing a decline in prescription volume that the industry is facing for at least certain types of medications. To this point, one recent analysis found that between 2011 and 2014, *sales* from the top 10 drugs increased 44 percent even though *prescriptions* for the medications decreased by 22 percent.[88] Likewise, another analysis determined that drug price increases contributed $8.7 billion to net income for 28 companies analyzed, representing 100 percent of earnings growth for those companies in 2016.[89] Hence, it seems very unlikely that many brand drug makers have much incentive to curb the unsustainable and excessive drug price growth absent bipartisan action to change these unfair pricing practices that hurt American patients and their families.

---

[84] Swanson, Ana. "Big Pharmaceutical Companies Are Spending Far More on Marketing than Research." *The Washington Post*. February 11, 2015. See link: https://www.washingtonpost.com/news/wonk/wp/2015/02/11/big-pharmaceutical-companies-are-spending-far-more-on-marketing-than-research/?utm_term=.916fc28032c9.

[85] Appleby, Anne and Horovitz, Bruce. "Prescription Drug Costs Are Up; So Are TV Ads Promoting Them." *The USA Today*. March 16, 2017. See link: https://www.usatoday.com/story/money/2017/03/16/prescription-drug-costs- up-tv-ads/99203878/.

[86] *Ibid*.

[87] *Ibid*.

[88] Humer, Caroline. "Analysis: Drugmakers Take Big Price Increases on Popular Meds in U.S." *Scientific American*. See link: https://www.scientificamerican.com/article/analysis-drugmakers-take-big-price-increases-on-popular- meds-in-u-s/.

[89] Tirrell, Meg. "The Drug Industry Is Addicted to Price Increases, Report Shows." *CNBC*. April 20, 2017.

Rules Embedded in the U.S. Regulatory System Permit the Brand Drug Industry to Engage in Anti- Competitive Practices That Block Affordable Generic Competition and Keep Drug Prices High, Driving up Prescription Drug Costs for Patients and Families and All U.S. Consumers

The brand drug industry often manipulates the current U.S. regulatory system in an anti-competitive manner to limit and restrict patient access to the affordable medications they need.

First, the Orphan Drug Act introduced a range of incentives – most importantly seven years of market exclusivity with no competition – to encourage the development of medications to treat rare diseases, or those diseases that affect fewer than 200,000 patients. Since passage of the Orphan Drug Act, hundreds of orphan drugs have been approved. Many of these medications are helping patients who previously had no treatment options.

However, an increasing number of orphan drugs have achieved blockbuster status, with billions of dollars in sales annually. Oftentimes in these cases, drug manufacturers have secured a single "orphan" indication for a drug's use and then, after FDA approval, patients use the drugs off-label far more broadly beyond that single indication use. In effect, manufacturers benefit from having the special orphan exclusivity period that restricts competition but allows their products to be used off-label for treatments of other types of disease – and oftentimes at very high prices for patients. To this point, a recent analysis found that seven of the top 10 best-selling drugs in the U.S. in 2014 came on the market with an "orphan" designation.[90]

Second, brand name drug companies are using FDA regulations to engage in anti-competitive behavior that blocks competition of certain drugs that require additional safety protections. For specific drugs with specific safety risks, FDA requires manufacturers to develop detailed Risk Evaluation and Mitigation Strategies (REMS) prior to entering the market. While this type of information creates additional safety information for patients and offers safeguards for providers, brand drug manufacturers have manipulated REMS to block generic manufacturers from obtaining samples of brand drugs under the guise of addressing patient safety concerns. This practice restricts competition in the market and often leaves patients with fewer choices for their medications. As a result, patients may be at the mercy of a single drug company for the medication they need to stay healthy, and that company is free to set the price for that medication indiscriminately. This practice stifles the introduction of generic competition, thus preventing lower-priced options from being available to patients and increasing costs for everyone. Bipartisan legislation has been introduced in both the Senate and the House

---

[90] "'Orphan Drug' Loophole Needs Closing, Johns Hopkins Researchers Say." November 19, 2015. See link: http://www.hopkinsmedicine.org/news/media/releases/orphan_drug_ loophole_needs_closing_johns_hopkins_re searchers_say.

– the CREATES Act and the FAST Generics Act – that would stop this anticompetitive practice. We therefore encourage the Committee to consider bipartisan legislation that addresses these abuses by prohibiting companies from restricting access to samples.

Market-Based Solutions Can Help Rein in Excessive Drug Cost Growth for U.S. Patients and Families

CSRxP supports adoption of bipartisan, market-based solutions to help curb the excessive and unsustainable growth in prescription drug spending for U.S. patients and their families. To that end, CSRxP strongly urges the Committee to support and adopt the following policies that promote transparency, foster competition, and incentivize value in the marketplace, making drugs more affordable and accessible for the patients who need them.

Promote Transparency

- Drug manufacturers should release details of a drug's unit price, cost of treatment, and projection on federal spending before FDA approval. Given the significant impact pharmaceuticals have on overall health care spending, manufacturers should be required to disclose information on the estimated unit price for the product, the cost of a course of treatment, and a projection of federal spending on the product.
- Drug makers should annually report increases in a drug's list price. Similar to requirements already in place for other entities like health plan issuers, hospitals and nursing facilities, pharmaceutical companies should report increases in drug's list price. Furthermore, HHS should provide an annual report to the public that includes the top 50 price increases per year by branded or generic drugs; the top 50 drugs by annual spending and how much the government pays in total for these drugs; and historical price increases for common drugs, including those covered by Medicare Part B.
- Manufacturers should disclose drug R&D costs. Drug makers should be required to disclose how much drug research was funded by public entities like the National Institute of Health (NIH) or other academic entities or by other private companies, so that regulators and taxpayers can properly weigh return on investment.

We encourage the Committee to consider bipartisan legislation, the FAIR Pricing Act, sponsored by Senators Baldwin and McCain that would bring great transparency to the pharmaceutical industry.

Foster Competition

- Speed FDA approval of generic drug applications – especially for lifesaving drugs and for drugs with no or limited generic competition. The FDA faces a backlog of nearly 4,000 generic drug applications, yet approval times can be three or more years. The FDA should receive the resources necessary to clear this backlog and prioritize generic drug approval applications, especially for lifesaving drugs and drugs with no or limited generic competition.
- Reduce drug monopolies by incentivizing competition for additional market entrants. Several FDA programs are intended to expedite review of new drugs that address unmet medical needs for serious or life-threatening conditions. Incentives should drive competition for expensive treatments where no competitors exist and encourage a second or third market entrant.
- Strengthen post-market clinical trials and surveillance. Currently, expedited drug approvals often involve small clinical trials with a narrow patient population and trials are not regularly reported publicly. Once a drug enters the market, research into the long-term efficacy and side effects should continue within specific timeframes and reporting requirements. Even if a product is not approved, manufacturers should be required to report data for all trials that summarizes non-identifiable demographics and participant characteristics, primary and secondary outcomes results, and adverse event information.
- Target exclusivity protections to the most innovative products. Currently, pharmaceutical manufacturers can extend market exclusivity protections by seeking approval for a "new" product that is essentially the same as the original. Prohibiting such tactics will bring consumers more options and lower prices more quickly. Anti-competitive pricing schemes should be closely monitored by federal agencies and prosecuted if violations of antitrust law are found.
- Curb misuse of REMS. As we noted above, the FDA uses REMS to allow products with potential safety issues to enter the market. Drug manufacturers often manipulate REMS to block generic drugs from obtaining samples of brand drugs under the guise of addressing patient safety concerns, effectively preventing them from pursuing the research needed to bring generic drugs to market. Bipartisan legislation has been introduced in both the Senate and the House – the CREATES Act and the FAST Generics Act – that would stop this anticompetitive practice. CSRxP encourages the Committee to consider this bipartisan legislation that addresses these abuses by prohibiting companies from restricting sample access.
- Promote a robust biosimilars market. Regulatory policies should encourage market entry and uptake of biosimilars, as they have significant potential to expand treatment options and reduce costs by increasing competition in the

marketplace. For example, one study found that 11 biosimilars already approved for sale in Europe and elsewhere could generate approximately $250 billion in savings over 10 years if they were available in the U.S.[91] We urge the Committee to consider provisions – such as reducing the market exclusivity period for brand name biologics – that would help support the development of a robust biosimilar market and help ensure that patients have access to lower cost alternatives to existing, expensive biologics.

Incentivize Value

- Increase funding for private and public research efforts like the non-profit Institute for Clinical and Economic Review (ICER) to test the value of medical tests and treatments. Investment in objective information is critical for physicians, patients and payers as more and more high-price drugs enter the healthcare system.
- Require drug makers to conduct comparative effectiveness research (CER) studies of new versus existing drug products. Through CER studies, manufacturers should have to demonstrate that their product is better than others, so that physicians and patients can make smart decisions about the value of different treatments, particularly those with very high costs. Many other countries currently require drug manufacturers to provide CER studies; they should be expanded in the U.S. to reduce spending on unnecessary or ineffective treatments.
- Expand value-based pricing in public health programs like Medicare and Medicaid. Currently Medicare and Medicaid purchase prescription drugs for their beneficiaries, but not generally in a manner to accommodate value-based payment models. Steps should be taken to ensure these program can best take advantage of recent developments in value-based purchasing to ensure all parts of the U.S. healthcare system benefit from market-based negotiating efforts to lower drug prices.

Conclusion

In conclusion, CSRxP appreciates the leadership from the Committee and again thanks the Committee for the opportunity to submit testimony for the record to address the unsustainable and excessive growth in prescription drug costs in the U.S. The

---

91 Express Scripts. "The $250 Billion Potential of Biosimilars." April 23, 2013. See link: http://lab.express-scripts.com/lab/insights/industry-updates/the-$250-billion-potential-of-biosimilars.

Campaign looks forward to continued work with the Committee in the future in developing market-based policies that promote competition, transparency, and value to make prescription drugs more affordable for all American patients and their families while at the same time maintaining access to the treatments that can improve health outcomes and save lives.

LOBBYING REGISTRATION FORM SUBMITTED BY SENATOR FRANKEN

Clerk of the House of Representatives	Secretary of the Senate
Legislative Resource Center	Office of Public Records
B-106 Cannon Building	232 Hart Building
Washington, DC 20515	Washington, DC 20510

SECRETARY OF THE SENATE
00 SEP -5 PM 4:44

LOBBYING REGISTRATION

Lobbying Disclosure Act of 1995 (Section 4)

Check if this is an Amended Registration ☐ 1. Effective Date of Registration 08/01/2000

2. House Identification Number ________ Senate Identification Number ________

REGISTRANT

3. Registrant Name PRESTON GATES ELLIS & ROUVELAS MEEDS LLP

Address 1735 NEW YORK AVE, NW SUITE 500

City WASHINGTON State DC Zip 20006

4. Principal place of business (if different from line 3)

City State/Zip (or Country)

5. Telephone number and contact name Contact E-Mail (optional)

202-628-1700 ROSANNE PHILLIPS

6. General description of registrant's business or activities

Law Firm

CLIENT *A lobbying firm is required to file a separate registration for each client. Organizations employing in-house lobbyists should check the box labeled "Self" and proceed to line 10.* ☐ Self

7. Client Name Commonwealth of the Northern Mariana Islands

Address Office of the Governor Caller Box 10007

City Saipan State MP Zip 96950

8. Principal place of business (if different from line 7)

City State/Zip (or Country)

9. General description of client's business or activities

United States Territory.

LOBBYISTS

10. Name of each individual who has acted or is expected to act as a lobbyist for the client identified on line 7. If any person listed in this section has served as a "covered executive branch official" or "covered legislative branch official" within two years of first acting as a lobbyist for this client, state the executive and/or legislative position(s) in which the person served.

Name	Covered Official Position (if applicable)
JACK ABRAMOFF	
TODD BOULANGER	Legis. Aide - Sen. Bob Smith
WERNER BRANDT	
DARRELL CONNER	

Form LD-1 (Rev. 06/98) Page 1

Registrant Name: PRESTON GATES ELLIS & ROUVELAS MEEDS LLP

Client Name: Commonwealth of the Northern Mariana Islands

Item	Description	Data
10a	Lobbyist Name	DAVID FUNDERBURK
10b	Covered Official Position	CONGRESSMAN
10a	Lobbyist Name	BRUCE HEIMAN
10b	Covered Official Position	
10a	Lobbyist Name	WILLIAM JARRELL
10b	Covered Official Position	
10a	Lobbyist Name	LLOYD MEEDS
10b	Covered Official Position	
10a	Lobbyist Name	SOL MOSHER
10b	Covered Official Position	
10a	Lobbyist Name	RALPH NURNBERGER
10b	Covered Official Position	
10a	Lobbyist Name	MICHAEL O'NEIL
10b	Covered Official Position	
10a	Lobbyist Name	TIM PECKINPAUGH
10b	Covered Official Position	
10a	Lobbyist Name	PATRICK PIZZELLA
10b	Covered Official Position	
10a	Lobbyist Name	KEVIN RING
10b	Covered Official Position	Ex. Dir. Hs Cons. Act Team;Counsel US Sen. Jud.Com
10a	Lobbyist Name	EMANUEL ROUVELAS
10b	Covered Official Position	
10a	Lobbyist Name	ALAN SLOMOWITZ
10b	Covered Official Position	
10a	Lobbyist Name	DENNIS STEPHENS
10b	Covered Official Position	
10a	Lobbyist Name	STEVEN VALENTINE
10b	Covered Official Position	Leg. Dir & Gen. Counsel Sen. Bob Smith
10a	Lobbyist Name	SHAWN VASELL
10b	Covered Official Position	
10a	Lobbyist Name	PADGET WILSON
10b	Covered Official Position	Legis. Corres. Sen. Paul Coverdell

Registrant Name: PRESTON GATES ELLIS & ROUVELAS MEEDS LLP

Client Name: Commonwealth of the Northern Mariana Islands

LOBBYING ISSUES

11. General lobbying issue areas. Select all applicable codes listed in instructions and on the reverse side of Form LD-1, page 1.

IMM, LBR, TAX

12. Specific lobbying issues (current and anticipated)

AFFILIATED ORGANIZATIONS

13. Is there an entity other than the client that contributes more than $10,000 to the lobbying activities of the registrant in a semiannual period and in whole or major part plans, supervises, or controls the registrant's lobbying activities?

☐ No. Go to line 14. ☒ Yes. Complete the rest of this section for each entity matching the criteria above, then proceed to line 14.

Name	Address	Principal Place of Business (city and state or country)
Western Pacific Economic Council	P.O. Box 144 Saipan, MP 96950	

FOREIGN ENTITIES

14. Is there any foreign entity that:

a) holds at least 20% equitable ownership in the client or any organization identified on line 13; or
b) directly or indirectly, in whole or in major part, plans, supervises, controls, directs, finances, or subsidizes activities of the client or any organization identified on line 13; or
c) is an affiliate of the client or any organization identified on line 13 and has a direct interest in the outcome of the lobbying activity?

☒ No. Sign and date the registration. ☐ Yes. Complete the rest of this section for each entity matching the criteria above, the sign and date the registration.

Name	Address	Principal Place of Business (city and state or country)	Amount of contribution for lobbying activities	Ownership percentage in client

Signature [signature] Date 09/05/2000

Printed Name and Title MICHAEL O'NEIL - ATTORNEY

Form LD-1 (Rev. 06/98)

Registrant Name: PRESTON GATES ELLIS & ROUVELAS MEEDS LLP

Client Name: Commonwealth of the Northern Mariana Islands

Item	Description	Data
12	Specific Lobbying Issues	H.R.730; United States Commonwealth of the Northern Mariana Islands Human Dignity Act; S.1052; Northern Mariana Islands Covenant Implementation Act. H.R. 325; Fair Minimum Wage Act of 1999. S.192; Fair Minimum Wage Act of 1999. S.922; Made in the USA Label Defense Act of 1999; H.R.1671; Made in the USA Label Defense Act of 1999; Legislation affecting the tax status of goods produced in the Commonwealth of the Northern Mariana Islands. Legislation affecting the minimum wage in the Commonwealth of the Northern Mariana Islands.

RESPONSE BY DAN MENDELSON TO QUESTIONS OF SENATOR ALEXANDER

Question 1. To confirm feedback received at the hearing, I have heard that drug spending accounts for roughly 15 percent of health spending. Of that 15 percent, 10 to 11 percent is on drugs purchased at the pharmacy or ordered online, and 4 to 5 percent is spent on drugs given in a hospital or at the doctor's office.

Do you agree, that is how much is spent on drugs in the United States?

Answer 1. Those statistics are generally accurate, though estimates vary based on source and spending categories analyzed. According to the Centers for Medicare and Medicaid Services, National Health Expenditure Data, drugs dispensed in the pharmacy and medical benefit account for approximately 13 percent of total U.S. healthcare costs. This frequently cited figure uses total national health expenditures as a basis for calculating the percentage. Other experts sometimes use a subset of national health expenditures or total medical claims as the denominator, which accounts for the range of percentages often cited in this context.

Question 2. In 2015, 89 percent of all prescriptions picked up at pharmacy or online were low-cost generic drugs. According to Adam Fein, an expert on drug spending and the delivery system, nearly 30 percent of brand and generic prescriptions had a $0 out-of-pocket cost for the patient in 2016, up from 11 percent in 2011. So there appears to be a growing number of prescriptions available at no cost to a patient when you pick up your prescription at the drug store. Do you agree with that statement?

Answer 2. I agree that the majority prescriptions filled at the pharmacy or online are generic drugs and that generic drugs typically have lower associated cost sharing for patients.

Question 3. Would it be accurate to say a drug list price does not accurately reflect costs to patients? What should we as Congress be focusing on, instead of list prices?

Answer 3. Generally, a drug's list price and actual patient costs differ based on a series of negotiations and decisions. Specifically, as multiple products for a given indication come to market, plans and PBMs may negotiate rebates and other price concessions from manufacturers in exchange for preferred formulary placement and improved access. Typically, payers use these price concessions to reduce overall premiums, but the rebates are not shared directly with patients at the point of sale. As a result, most patients who fill a prescription are paying cost-sharing based on a price that is generally not reflective of rebates negotiated by a health plan or PBM.

Question 4. Can you comment on whether the costs for drugs have gone up, down, or remained steady in the last 5 to 10 years?

Answer 4. Like spending for all medical services, spending on prescription drugs has increased over time as innovation has enhanced capabilities. In recent years, new innovations have increased spending on specialty medications, which now account for $384 of the $895 per person per year spent on drugs. However, list prices (11.5 percent) have increased more slowly than net prices (6.1 percent) over the past 5 years.

Question 5. We hear quite a bit about a need to have more transparency around drug prices and within the drug delivery system. Do you think transparency would help, and if so, where?

Answer 5. The impact of transparency proposals depends on how they are constructed. In some areas, price transparency causes consumers to make better competitive decisions, which could potentially result in lower costs. On the other hand, certain types of transparency requirements can present challenges, and have the potential to inhibit competition and create market distortions. For example, the Congressional Budget Office (CBO) estimates that disclosure of drug rebate information "would facilitate tacit collusion among those manufacturers, which would tend to raise drug prices."

Question 6. We hear a lot about passing on rebates directly to consumers. What is your perspective on this proposal and what would be the impact on costs (for drugs or their premium) to patients?

Answer 6. Rebates have been growing in recent years, and generally are not passed on to consumers in the form of lower copays, but rather used to reduce premiums in the context of competitive markets. There is good potential to find ways to use rebates to reduce patient-cost sharing. While this type of proposal may lead to a small increase in premiums, the impact of the proposal on patient-cost sharing will depend on the structure of the policy and the healthcare needs of a particular patient. Undoubtedly, patients with chronic illnesses would benefit from this type of change, and point-of-sale adjudication/estimation of rebates is technically feasible.

Question 7. Can you comment on what tools are available within the delivery system to directly reduce patient costs?

Answer 7. Increased competition in the pharmaceutical markets holds promise for reducing costs. Speeding the approval of the second- and third-branded drugs in a therapeutic class would expedite competition and lead to more rapid price concessions.

Ensuring a continued robust market for generic pharmaceutics is vital for effective cost management and improvement of population health outcomes.

In addition, outcomes-based contracts also represent a significant opportunity to shift away from prescription drug list prices toward value-based reimbursement models. Effective outcomes-based contracts require next-generation data analysis and interventions that enable payers and manufacturers to identify patients eligible for treatment, target outreach to ensure appropriate adherence and quality improvement, and measure product performance against pre-agreed-upon outcomes on an ongoing basis. Consumer benefit can be substantially enhanced through data-based engagement around pharmaceuticals.

Question 8. What do you think of the suggestion that concerns related to drug costs have grown as patients have been forced personally to take on more and more of the drug costs?

Answer 8. Insurance benefit designs increasingly expose consumers to the full cost of their medicines through deductibles or percentage coinsurance for drugs, as payers have been under pressure to meet consumer demand for constrained premium growth. Of course, other factors also contribute to increased consumer payments, such as the cost of newly launched products and the increases in list prices over time.

RESPONSE BY ALLAN COUKELL TO QUESTIONS OF SENATOR ALEXANDER

Question 1. To confirm feedback received at the hearing, I have heard that drug spending accounts for roughly 15 percent of health spending. Of that 15 percent, 10 to 11 percent is on drugs purchased at the pharmacy or ordered online, and 4 to 5 percent is spent on drugs given in a hospital or at the doctor's office. Do you agree, that is how much is spent on drugs in the United States?

Answer 1. The Office of the Assistant Secretary for Planning and Evaluation (ASPE) estimates that pharmaceuticals accounted for almost 17 percent of U.S. personal health care services, or $457 billion, in 2015—retail and mail order prescription drugs accounted for 12 percent of personal health care services, while nearly 5 percent was for pharmaceuticals given in the hospital, physician's office and other non-retail settings.[92] The Altarum Institute, a nonprofit health organization, estimates that retail and non-retail prescription drug spending totaled $450 billion in 2016, or 14 percent of health

[92] Health and Human Services Assistant Secretary for Planning and Evaluation, "Observations on Trends in Prescription Drug Spending," March 2016, Available at: https://aspe.hhs.gov/sys- tem/files/pdf/187586/Drugspending.pdf.

expenditures.[93] Of total health expenditure, 10.1 percent was for retail spending on pharmaceuticals, and 4.3 percent was for non-retail spending.[94,95]

Question 2. In 2015, 89 percent of all prescriptions picked up at pharmacy or online were low-cost generic drugs. According to Adam Fein, an expert on drug spending and the delivery system, nearly 30 percent of brand and generic prescriptions had a $0 out-of-pocket cost for the patient in 2016, up from 11 percent in 2011. So there appears to be a growing number of prescriptions available at no cost to a patient when you pick up your prescription at the drug store. Do you agree with that statement?

Answer 2. The growth in the share of prescriptions with no out-of-pocket costs for patients is driven by generics. An IMSQuintiles analysis found that last year 26 percent of prescriptions dispensed were for generic drugs with no out-of-pocket costs.[96]

An additional 3.9 percent of prescriptions were for brand drugs with no out-of-pocket costs. Insurance plan design determines out-of-pocket costs for any individual patient, but other policies also contribute. For example, most Medicaid patients have zero dollar or low out-of-pocket costs and the Affordable Care Act (ACA) requires generic contraceptives to be dispensed with no out-of-pocket costs. In addition, the ACA limits annual patient out-of-pocket spending for covered services in a health plan, including that of prescription drugs. Prescriptions dispensed for patients who have surpassed their annual maximum have no out-of-pocket costs.

However, some patients have seen their out-of-pocket costs increase significantly in recent years. The number of Medicare Part D enrollees reaching the catastrophic coverage phase reached 3.6 million in 2015, a 53 percent increase since 2010.[97] Enrollees not eligible for a low-income subsidy must pay 5 percent of the cost of their prescriptions in the catastrophic coverage phase, with no limit on annual out-of-pocket spending. In 2015 patients reaching the catastrophic coverage phase paid an average of $257 per month for each high cost prescription drug—defined as medications with an average price of more than $1,000 per month.

Question 3. Would it be accurate to say a drug list price does not accurately reflect costs to patients? What should we as Congress be focusing on, instead of list prices?

---

93 C. Roehrig, "Center for Sustainable Health Spending Data Brief: A Ten Year Projection of the Prescription Drug Share of National Health Expenditures Including Non-Retail," Altarum (Updated May 2017), *http://altarum.org/publications/a-10-year-projection-of-the-prescription-drug-share-of-national-health-expenditures-including.*

94 Ibid.

95 While Altarum and ASPE use similar methodologies, Altarum utilizes total health expendi- ture as a denominator, and ASPE uses personal health care expenditure. Personal health ex- penditure represents spending on medical care and excludes government spending on adminis- tration, public health, and investment into medical research. Personal health expenditure in 2015 was $2.72 trillion.

96 QuintilesIMS Institute, "Medicines Use and Spending in the U.S.: Review of 2016 and Out-look to 2021," May 2017, Available at: *http://www.imshealth.com/en/thought-leadership/quintilesims-institute/reports/medicines-use-and-spending-in-the-us-review-of–2016-outlook-to-2021.*

97 Department of Health and Human Services, Office of the Inspector General, "High-Price Drugs Are Increasing Federal Payments for Medicare Part D Catastrophic Coverage," January 2017, Available at: *https://oig.hhs.gov/oei/reports/oei-02-16-00270.pdf.*

Answer 3. List prices are a critical factor in determining out-of-pocket costs for many patients. This happens in at least three circumstances. (1) Patients without drug coverage are charged something close to list price at the pharmacy, even when the price paid by larger payers is far lower. (2) Patients enrolled in health plans with deductibles must pay the full cost of their medications until they meet an annual spending threshold. During this deductible phase, out-of-pocket payments are typically based on the drug's list price. (3) Patients in health plans with co-insurance,[98] which is usually applied to the most expensive prescriptions medications, typically pay a fixed percentage (e.g., 30 percent) of the drug's list price.

Among commercially insured patients in 2016, over half of patient out-of-pocket costs for brand prescriptions was based on list prices, and over 90 percent of patient out-of-pocket spending for specialty drugs was based on list prices.[99] While some payers are able to offer plans that pass on rebates and discounts off the drug list price to patients at the point of sale,[100] it is unknown to what extent plan sponsors are choosing these benefit designs.

Congress should focus primarily on overall drug spending, particularly in public programs. However, drug list prices are not an accurate measure of total U.S. spending on prescription drugs. Some organizations have published estimates for total drug spending, but each uses a different approach, some focusing on pharmaceutical manufacturer revenue, while others are based on pharmacy claims, which often do not take into account rebates and other discounts offered by manufacturers. One challenge in understanding drug spending is the range of entities involved in the prescription drug supply and payment chain, including wholesalers, pharmacy benefit managers, pharmacies, and insurers. Each of these entities retains a portion of total drug spending and flow of health care payer and consumer dollars throughout this complex system is little understood.

However, list prices are useful in establishing trend lines for prescription drug spending, as list and net prices tend to rise in tandem (though the average gap between list and net prices has increased slightly in recent years as rebates have increased).

Pew is pursuing additional research that will develop a national estimate of total spending on drugs, including contributions toward insurance premiums for drug coverage and a breakdown of what share of this total each supply chain entity retains.

Question 4. Can you comment on whether the costs for drugs have gone up, down, or remained steady in the last 5 to 10 years?

Answer 4. The costs for drugs have gone up in recent years. As discussed, methodologies vary widely, but there is widespread agreement that spending on drugs has

---

98 This differs from copays, under which patients pay a fixed dollar amount for a prescription.

99 QuintilesIMS Institute, "Medicines Use and Spending in the U.S.: Review of 2016 and Outlook to 2021," May 2017, Available at: *http://www.imshealth.com/en/thought-leadership/quintilesims-institute/reports/medicines-use-and-spending-in-the-us-review-of-2016-outlook-to-2021.*

100 CVSHealth, Consumer Transparency Helping Members with High-Cost Drugs at the Point of Sale, *https://payorsolutions.cvshealth.com/insights/consumer-transparency.*

increased significantly. A 2016 report by the Department of Health and Human Services Assistant Secretary for Planning and Evaluation found that "[e]xpenditures on prescription drugs are rising and are projected to continue to rise in the coming years as a share of total health care spending."

IMSQuintiles estimates that drug manufacturer revenue net of rebates and discounts has increased 42 percent since 2006, reaching $323 billion in 2016, with more than two-thirds of that growth occurring since 2013.[101] They have found that while both drug list prices and rebates and discounts to payers have increased substantially year over year, manufacturer net revenue has continued to rise, up 4.8 percent in 2016 alone.

New brand drugs have driven the majority of this spending growth each year since 2014. New drugs are increasingly specialty products, including biologics, and typically launch at high prices. Year-on-year increases in the prices of brand drugs that do not yet face generic competitors also contribute to rising spending. Conversely, spending on generic drugs decreased slightly in 2016. Generic drugs represent an ever-growing share of prescriptions dispensed, reaching over 89 percent in 2016. While there have been some individual generic products with extraordinary price increases in recent years, generic drugs as a class generate significant savings.

Question 5. Some have suggested that drug importation could lower drug prices. What are your views on that strategy?

Answer 5. Brand pharmaceuticals are generally more expensive in the United States than in other high-income countries, in part because some countries have implemented policies to limit prices, so allowing the purchase and importation of prescription drugs from other countries has the potential to give Americans access to some medicines at lower prices.[102] However, it is difficult to estimate the potential savings, which would have to be weighed against the costs to implement such a program, the potential safety risks of imported products, and the overall impact on the security of the U.S.-drug supply chain.

The importation of drugs from foreign sources would bypass current FDA review processes and could increase safety risks. Federal law currently provides the Secretary of Health and Human Services the authority to permit importation of prescription drugs from Canada, if the Secretary certifies to Congress that they would pose no additional risk to the public's health and safety, and would result in a significant reduction in the cost of the drugs to Americans. However, no certification has ever been made.

---

[101] QuintilesIMS Institute, "edicines Use and Spending in the U.S.: Review of 2016 and Outlook to 2021," May 2017, Available at: http://www.imshealth.com/en/thought-leadership/quintilesims-institute/reports/medicines-use-and-spending-in-the-us-review-of-2016-outlook-to-2021.

[102] The Pew Charitable Trusts, "Policy Proposal: Importation of Prescription Drugs," http://www.pewtrusts.org/en/research-and-analysis/fact-sheets/2017/04/policy-proposal-importation-of-prescription-drugs.

To address the potential risks associated with importing unapproved drugs, FDA would need significant additional resources and capacity. At a 2004 congressional hearing, FDA's then-commissioner speculated that a program to ensure the safety of imported drugs could cost hundreds of millions of dollars annually,[103] which could reduce the net savings from importation.

Furthermore, any importation system would need to conform to the requirements of the Drug Supply Chain Security Act (Title II of the Drug Quality and Security Act of 2013), which Congress passed to ensure that counterfeit and diverted drugs do not enter the pharmaceutical supply chain. This legislation requires pharmaceutical manufacturers and repackagers to put a unique product identifier on most prescription drug packages and outlines steps to build a system for electronically identifying and tracing each individual package of prescription drug as it is distributed in the United States. Manufacturers must put this unique code on products beginning November 2017, and by 2023, all participants in the pharmaceutical supply chain must participate. This will make it easier to detect when counterfeit or illegal product is introduced into the system, and will significantly enhance the speed and accuracy of implementing product recalls. However, if imported product could be sold into the U.S. system without the product identifiers necessary to comply with this drug security system, it would make it difficult for supply chain partners who encounter product that is not compliant to determine which products are counterfeit or otherwise illegal, and which are legally imported. As a consequence, the risk of importation is not only that FDA cannot ensure that the products being imported are legitimate, but that the introduction of products that are not a part of the supply chain security system (even if they are legitimate products) will compromise the ability of the system to identify counterfeit and diverted products from any source, thus significantly undermining the protections that Congress put into place in 2013.

The importation of drugs from abroad could also have unintended consequences in other countries. The U.S. population far exceeds that of most other OECD countries and therefore meeting even a portion of U.S. demand with foreign supplies could strain local markets. To mitigate decreased U.S. revenue, manufacturers could seek to increase their prices in foreign markets or restrict foreign entities from exporting medications to the United States. In addition, the U.S. market's large size could strain the supply of pharmaceuticals, resulting in drug shortages in other countries if importation were to be implemented on a large scale.

---

[103] Options for Safe and Effective Prescription Drug Importation: Hearing Before the Committee on Commerce, Science, and Transportation, U.S. Senate, 108th Cong. (2004) (statement of Mark McClellan, commissioner of the U.S. Food and Drug Administration), *https:// www.gpo.gov/fdsys/pkg/CHRG-108shrg76522/pdf/CHRG-108shrg76522.pdf.*

RESPONSE BY PAUL HOWARD TO QUESTIONS OF SENATOR ALEXANDER

Question 1. To confirm feedback received at the hearing, I have heard that drug spending accounts for roughly 15 percent of health spending. Of that 15 percent, 10 to 11 percent is on drugs purchased at the pharmacy or ordered online, and 4 to 5 percent is spent on drugs given in a hospital or at the doctor's office. Do you agree, that is how much is spent on drugs in the United States?

Answer 1. Yes, although the exact numbers vary by source. In 2015, *APSE estimated* that prescription drug spending in the United States was about $457 billion in 2015. That same year, *CMS found* that U.S. health care spending totaled $3.2 trillion, which would put total prescription drug (retail and physician-administered) spending at 14.28 percent for 2015. ASPE also notes that 70 percent of the increase in spending from 2010–14 was due to non-price-related factors (i.e., 10 percent population growth, 30 percent increase in the number of prescriptions per person, 30 percent overall, economy-wide inflation). By way of comparison, in 2016, the *Kaiser Family Foundation* found that retail pharmacy sales totaled $379 billion or 11.1 percent of the total health care spending ($3.4 trillion) in the United States for that year.[104,105]

Finally, totally net spending growth has *slowed considerably* since 2014, according to a May 2017 report from Quintiles/IMS (slide 1).

Question 2. In 2015, 89 percent of all prescriptions picked up at pharmacy or online were low-cost generic drugs. According to Adam Fein, an expert on drug spending and the delivery system, nearly 30 percent of brand and generic prescriptions had a $0 out-of-pocket cost for the patient in 2016, up from 11 percent in 2011. So there appears to be a growing number of prescriptions available at no cost to a patient when you pick up your prescription at the drug store. Do you agree with that statement?

Answer 2. I agree. The 2017 Quintiles/IMS report *shows this* (see slide 5). However, the Quintiles report shows that patient out-of-pocket spending is highly concentrated among patients with certain formulary or benefit designs. Quintiles notes that plans with drug "deductibles and coinsurance set patient out-of-pocket costs based on list prices and 19 percent of commercial brand prescriptions are paid in this way, accounting for 52 percent of out-of-pocket costs."

Specifically, "patients with a specialty prescription in the deductible accounted for 2 percent of prescriptions but 32 percent of out-of-pocket costs." It is the concentration of OOP spending in a relatively small subset of patients that I find worrisome:

---

[104] *http://www.drugchannels.net/2016/04/key-insights-on-drug-prices-and.html.*
[105] *http://www.drugchannels.net/2016/07/latest-cms-forecast-shows-big-drug.html.*

> "Abandonment rates for brands are 2.5 times higher when the patient is in the deductible phase of their plan and sees the full cost of the medicine they have been prescribed."

As I noted in my testimony, Congress' attention should be focused on addressing potentially excessive patient-cost sharing that impact patients' health outcomes.

Question 3. Would it be accurate to say a drug list price does not accurately reflect costs to patients? What should we as Congress be focusing on, instead of list prices?

Answer 3. That is correct. Data suggests that, net of rebates, drug price increases (on average) have been fairly modest. Congress should focus on insurance designs that increase patient-cost sharing without reflecting the rebates that manufacturers have negotiated with payers and PBMS.

Broadly speaking, we also need to ensure that insurers are not using formulary design (what drugs are covered, and what co-insurance they face) as a tool for *adverse selection*. Further, CMS and Congress should be carefully monitoring Part D plans, 340B, and exchange plans, to monitor insurance designs for potentially discriminatory impact.

However, this is a problem that will require a multi-stakeholder solution to further the bipartisan goal of expanding coverage, improving quality, and slowing cost growth across the health care system. I believe that Congress and the Administration should consider how to better encourage plans, manufacturers, and providers to take a longer term view of the role of medicines in keeping patients healthier, longer and reducing the use of other health care "inputs," including hospitalizations and emergency rooms visits.

Encouraging the uptake of value-based insurance designs, longer term (multi-year) insurance contracts, and safe harbors from Federal regulations like Medicaid Best Price and Stark anti-kickback can help the market evolve toward competition based on patient outcomes, rather than short-term price of a pill.

Experts on both sides of the aisle agree that there is hundreds of billions of dollars in excessive spending that could be cut from the U.S. health care system, while also improving patient outcomes. The incentives for collaboration and competition based on delivering best-in-class outcomes more efficiently for every dollar spent, however, remain weak.

Question 4. Can you comment on whether the costs for drugs have gone up, down, or remained steady in the last 5 to 10 years?

Answer 4. Average prescription drug spending steadily decreased from 2000–14. The 2014 spike in spending is almost entirely attributable to the entry of highly effective, yet expensive, treatments for hepatitis C into the marketplace.

Out-of-pocket prescription drug spending decreased from 2005–10, and remained stagnant through 2015. While out-of-pocket spending is expected to increase in the coming years, it is also expected to represent a continuously smaller share of total health care spending. Many new treatments that are expected to come online in the next several years, like C-ART for blood cancers, or gene therapies, are expected to be highly beneficial for patients—and thus highly valuable for society. Building a sustainable framework for rapid adoption of curative therapies is both a tremendous challenge, and a tremendous opportunity.

Question 5. We hear quite a bit about a need to have more transparency around drug prices and within the drug delivery system. Do you think transparency would help, and if so, where?

Transparency matters when it encourages patients and physicians to find the most effective therapy for that patient, given their medical needs and treatment preferences.

Transparency around list prices isn't helpful, since patient-cost sharing varies so widely based on plan design, or where the patient is within their annual deductible. It also doesn't help us understand the role medicines play in the wider health care system, where they are a vital tool for managing serious chronic illnesses that account for roughly 85 percent of U.S. health care costs.

Given the economics of the industry, we should also expect drug discounts to vary across payers—just as physician and hospital prices vary. There is no "one" right price for a medicine.

What we should be doing improving patients and physicians' ability to compare treatment strategies based on real world costs, benefits, and risks. Real world data on patient outcomes would give us much greater ability to drive competition across medicines, other treatment strategies, and providers. We should have a health care system that rewards the delivery of the best patient outcome, as efficiently as possible—whether that is through better diet, exercise, medical management, or a surgical intervention. Transparency in terms of being able to track and share data on patient outcomes and costs (with appropriate privacy protections) would save lives and help reduce the enormous waste and inefficiency we see today across the U.S. health care system.

Question 6. We hear a lot about passing on rebates directly to consumers. What is your perspective on this proposal and what would be the impact on costs (for drugs or their premium) to patients?

To my knowledge, CVS is the only PBM that has *embraced* this approach, but I believe it would be helpful to address current patient-cost sharing burdens. Depending on the rebate—say 20 percent or 30 percent—it could help patients substantially who otherwise find themselves paying based on the list price.

Ultimately, we need to shift to a different system of paying for medicines that does not depend on formularies based on the "bubble" between the list and net price. This is a step in that direction, but other approaches should be tried as well, including new insurance designs and tools for right-sizing patient-cost sharing based on outcomes (i.e., *value-based insurance designs*).

Question 7. Can you comment on what tools are available within the delivery system to directly reduce patient costs?

Manufacturers often offer co-pay/co-insurance assistance programs, and other means-tested programs that cap the out-of-pocket costs that patients pay for their medicines. Some PBMs, like Express Scripts, have begun to offer discounts for *uninsured patients* who would otherwise pay list price for their medicines. These programs are a relatively new phenomenon. Premera Blue Cross/Blue Shield in Washington State has offered a *value-based formulary* for employers where co-pays vary not based on price, but on how effective the medicine is—a very interesting approach that is, however, *data intensive*.

Encouraging providers, payers, and manufacturers to routinely generate and collect more real world data on patients could lower the cost of implementing these approaches. To do so, however, would require regulatory safe harbors from some FDA and CMS regulations.

Question 8. What do you think of the suggestion that concerns related to drug costs have grown as patients have been forced personally to take on more and more of the drug costs?

Answer 8. There have been dramatic shifts in insurance design over the last decade, including the rise of high deductible health plans, and the passage of the Affordable Care Act. Under the ACA, as insurers have been forced to cover more routine costs without any patient-cost sharing, and to standardize other benefits (no annual or lifetime cap on benefits, covering a broader collection of essential health benefits, greater scrutiny of annual premium increases), and the rise of maximum caps on annual spending that combine both medical and the pharmacy deductibles, more drug costs are being shifted onto patients for certain categories of high cost medicines, even though the long-term trends are toward lower overall OOP for health care in general.

RESPONSE BY GERARD ANDERSON TO QUESTIONS OF SENATOR ALEXANDER

Question 1. To confirm feedback received at the hearing, I have heard that drug spending accounts for roughly 15 percent of health spending. Of that 15 percent, 10 to 11 percent is on drugs purchased at the pharmacy or ordered online, and 4 to 5 percent is spent on drugs given in a hospital or at the doctor's office. Do you agree, that is how much is spent on drugs in the United States?

Answer 1. Yes, I agree with these numbers on drug spending. I would also add that, according to the Office of the Actuary in the Center for Medicare and Medicaid Services, prescription drug spending is expected to grow faster than overall health spending between 2016 and 2025 (an average of 6.3 percent per year compared to an average of 5.6 percent per year for overall health spending), which could affect these numbers moving forward.

As I highlighted in my testimony, these prescription drug costs are frequently passed onto patients, making it difficult for them to afford the medications that they need. For example, a Kaiser Family Foundation study found that for Medicare beneficiaries with Part D coverage, out-of-pocket costs averaged $7,000 for drugs to treat hepatitis C, $6,000 for drugs to treat multiple sclerosis, $4,000 for drugs to treat rheumatoid arthritis and $8,000 for drugs to treat certain types of cancer. For a social security recipient earning $26,000 per year, these out-of-pocket costs represent 16 percent to 32 percent of the person's total income for the year and clearly are prohibitively expensive.

RESPONSE BY DAN MENDELSON TO QUESTION OF SENATOR ISAKSON

Question. What would be the anticipated impact of allowing patients to appeal for lower cost sharing if the drug they need (as determined by their doctor and following any plan imposed utilization management procedures) happens to be on a Part D plan's "specialty tier?" Because the patient would be paying a total lower out-of-pocket cost, wouldn't this common-sense policy be good both for the patient (lowered OOP cost) and for Medicare (slower progression through the benefit and into catastrophic)?

Answer. There is growing interest in aligning insurance design to deliver value to patients. In particular, some patients have responses to medications or genetic makeups that require them to take a drug on the specialty tier, even if lower cost options are available. While this proposal represents an opportunity to align benefit design and the patient experience to such considerations, it could also potentially have implications for the market. Allowing patients to appeal for lower cost sharing for specialty tier drugs in Part D would lower patient out-of-pocket costs for some beneficiaries. This policy also has the potential to reduce costs to the Medicare program, as patients may take longer to reach the catastrophic phase of the benefit, where Medicare pays a greater share of costs. However, such policy would also alter the costs incurred by health plans, which could impact premiums.

RESPONSE BY DAN MENDELSON TO QUESTIONS OF SENATOR SANDERS

Question 1. Since online pharmacies were created about 15 years ago, there have been no reported examples of Americans dying by taking medication bought online from a *legitimate* and *regulated* pharmacy in Canada that requires valid prescriptions. And, this is after tens of millions of prescriptions have been filled online and internationally.

During the hearing, however, you raised safety concerns when the topic of drug importation was raised by Senator Murkowski. And, you stated that there have been cases of Americans being harmed by drugs they imported.

Can you provide specific instances you referenced generally during your testimony? Where (both in terms of country and type of distributor) did these drugs come from? Were they from legitimate, regulated online pharmacies? Did the patients have a prescription from a licensed health care provider?

Answer 1. The safety concerns I raised during my oral comments regarding the importation of medication from outside of the United States are based on statements from the Congressional Budget Office, the Food and Drug Administration, and the Federal Bureau of Investigation.

The Congressional Budget Office stated,

> "All products distributed in the United States must be produced in facilities registered with the FDA for production of those specific products. Much of existing worldwide sales volume does not satisfy that criterion, even drugs that otherwise meet safety and efficacy standards."[106]

For example in March 2017, 4 former Food and Drug Administration commissioners warned Congress that legalizing importation of drugs from other countries could endanger consumers by exposing them to fake, substandard, or contaminated drugs. The commissioners were concerned that there is no reliable way of knowing where imported drugs come from, particularly since the vast majority of online pharmacies are fake.[107]

Recently, the former director of the Federal Bureau of Investigation, released a report examining the degree to which current drug importation proposals, if implemented, would impact law enforcement's ability to protect the public health and ensure the safety of our drug supply. That report concluded that "importation proposals would force law enforcement agencies to make tough prioritization decisions that leave the safety of the U.S. prescription drug supply vulnerable to criminals seeking to harm patients."[108]

Question 2. In a January 2017 article published in "Chicago Business" you are credited with predicting that GOP legislators would follow President Trump's lead on drug pricing after the President commented that prescription drug companies were "getting away with murder." You also are credited with pointing out that pre-election poll data showed that Republican voters care more about high drug prices than they did about

---

[106] The Congressional Budget Office. Would Prescription Drug Importation Reduce U.S. Drug Spending? April 2004. https://www.cbo.gov/sites/default/files/108th-congress–2003-2004/re-ports/04-29-prescriptiondrugs.pdf.

[107] https://assets.documentcloud.org/documents/3519007/FDA-Commissioners-Drug-Reimporta tion.pdf.

[108] Freeh, Sporkin and Sullivan LLC, Freeh Group International Solutions LLC. Report on the Potential Impact of Drug Importation Proposals on U.S. Law Enforcement. March 2017 http:// freepdfhosting.com/ 84170a76e7.pdf.

repealing Obamacare. In fact, you are quoted as saying, "it's a populist issue" and one that "Trump is likely to move on."

My question is this: What is the best way for this issue to be addressed to ensure that drug companies do not continue "getting away with murder" and that the interests of the Republican voters you referenced in your article—lower high drug prices over repealing Obamacare—are front and center?

Answer 2. There are a range of opportunities to shift toward models that align drug prices to value, by promoting competition and pursuing other market-driven solutions. In particular, speeding the approval of the second-and third-branded drugs in a therapeutic class would expedite competition and lead to more rapid price concessions. Ensuring a continued robust market for generic pharmaceutics is vital for effective cost management and improvement of population health outcomes.

In addition, outcomes-based contracts also represent a significant opportunity to shift away from prescription drug list prices toward value-based reimbursement models. Effective outcomes-based contracts require next-generation data analysis and interventions that enable payers and manufacturers to identify patients eligible for treatment, target outreach to ensure appropriate adherence and quality improvement, and measure product performance against pre-agreed-upon outcomes on an ongoing basis. Consumer benefit can be substantially enhanced through data-based engagement around pharmaceuticals.

RESPONSE BY PAUL HOWARD TO QUESTIONS OF SENATOR SANDERS

Question 1. Dr. Howard, it is my understanding that the Manhattan Institute believes very strongly in the value of free trade. As you know, the United States safely imports lettuce, strawberries, tomatoes, fish and shrimp, and many other foods from Mexico, Singapore and other countries in Southeast Asia. For the most part, do you believe these fruits and vegetable and seafood are safe?

We do believe strongly in the value of free trade and free markets, and competition as a tool to drive value for consumers and patients.

However, with all due respect, the complexity of the drug supply chain—as demonstrated by recent scandals with fake or adulterated medicines originating in China or India—and the risks associated with patients receiving such fake or adulterated medicines for serious diseases *like cancer* are simply an order of magnitude higher than for foods. The economic incentive for sophisticated counterfeiters to find ways to slip fake medicines into higher cost markets like the United States are extraordinarily powerful, *and growing*. Opening the closed U.S. drug supply chain would increase these problems dramatically.

Issues with food safety are more easily detectible then in the case of chronically ill patients who may ingest fake or adulterated drug products imported from abroad, because they are already in compromised health. If a patient with high cholesterol or high blood pressure takes a fake medicine, the results may not be detected without regular testing—which might not occur for months, leaving the patient at increased risk of a serious adverse event. The progression of cancer might also go undetected for some time, and death could be attributed to the aggressiveness of the disease, rather than the use of counterfeit medicines.

Opening up the U.S. market to the wholesale importation of medicines from abroad has never been certified as safe by any FDA Commissioner from either a Republican or Democratic *administration*. Given the much smaller populations in Canada, or the UK, and the need for those populations to consume medicines for their own market, implies that extra quantities for the U.S. market would have to be generated by re-sellers from much farther abroad. This opens up opportunities for *fraud*, as has been the case in the EU.

Finally, I would note that attempting to link drug prices in wealthier countries to lower cost drug sales in poorer countries (again, as occurs in the EU, under parallel trade, where drugs for the UK and Germany are imported from poorer countries like Greece) provides an incentive for manufacturers to delay the launch of new medicines in poorer countries, or raises the prices lower income nations pay. Respectfully, I would suggest that this is the wrong way to address pricing challenges facing U.S. patients. Wealthier countries *should* pay higher prices for medicines than poorer countries, and attempting to arbitrage away the differences will only reduce the total supply of innovations available to future patients in both wealthy and poor countries alike. Instead, we should be finding ways to reduce unnecessary patient-cost sharing in the United States in ways that actually improve long-term patient health, as has been *suggested* by economists at RAND.

Question 2. If Americans can eat food from what some would call "developing nations," then shouldn't Americans be able to import safe and affordable prescription drugs, from regulated and legitimate pharmacies, from a "developed" nation like Canada? And, do you agree—yes or no—that Americans should have confidence in the safety of Canadian drugs much like they have confidence in the safety of shrimp from Singapore or lettuce and strawberries from Mexico? Please explain your answer.

Answer 2. Please see my answer to the previous question. I do not believe that the prices of poorer countries, like Mexico, should be linked to the sales of medicines in wealthier countries like the United States.

Differential pricing of medicines in wealthier and poorer countries is not only economically efficient, it raises the global supply medical innovations and thus global health.

To put this another way, wealthy countries subsidize drug development for poorer and middle income countries. Linking these markets is likely to raise prices for poorer countries beyond their ability *to pay*.

The economics and regulation of the pharmaceutical industry are simply very different than commodities like food. And the different size of the United States and Canadian markets makes it impossible for Canada to supply any significant part of U.S. market. As noted earlier, keeping a closed system would be virtually impossible.

Response by Gerald Anderson to Questions of Senator Sanders

Question 1. Dr. Anderson, you make it very clear in your testimony that a lack of transparency about drug pricing is a major part of the drug pricing crisis in the United States. Drug companies do not have to offer any transparency. In fact, they set a list price without being regulated or constrained. PBMs also are able to hide behind a zero transparency climate. In fact, despite what they claim to do, PBMs have a financial incentive to try to get drug companies to increase their list prices because they, then, make a greater profit. Wholesalers bring pharmaceutical drugs to hospitals and pharmacies, and they earn a profit in doing so without disclosing the amount. And, pharmacies and hospitals sell drugs to patients, and they make a profit in doing so, too. At the end of the day, the person who really pays is the patient and they often do so through higher cost sharing.

Dr. Anderson, as we work to expand transparency and to bring all of these varying amounts of money out into the open, do you think that we need to implement a drug importation system so that Americans can afford the medicines that they need today?

In regards to importation, my concern is that the pharmaceutical industry would likely adapt to any policy change in this area by rationing the number of drugs that they send to Canada or other countries. As a result, U.S. patients could still struggle to obtain needed medications, while creating access and affordability issues for patients in these other countries. Additionally, patients could face increased safety risks by consuming medications from manufacturers and countries outside of the current FDA-approval system.

However, I do think it is important to allow importation for off-patent drugs that have three or fewer competitors. I talked about this issue in my congressional testimony at the Senate Aging Committee and was a coauthor of a JAMA paper on this topic as well (Greene, Jeremy A., Gerard Anderson, and Joshua M. Sharfstein. "Role of the FDA in affordability of off-patent pharmaceuticals." *Jama* 315.5 (2016): 461–62.) It turns out that most of these drugs are being manufactured in other highly industrialized countries and it would be very easy to import these drugs from other countries without having the drug companies be able to penalize the other countries.

Instead, I would suggest looking at other policy changes that could quickly bring down drug prices and increase patients' access to the medications that they need, such as enacting price gouging legislation that empowers State Attorneys General to take legal actions against drug companies, restricting "pay for delay" behavior and other similar tactics that block generic drug companies from entering the marketplace, or using the Federal Government's current authority under 28 U.S.C. §1498 to provide reasonable compensation to a drug company for the use of its patent and allow a generic manufacturer to manufacture the drug.

[Whereupon, at 12:22 p.m., the hearing was adjourned.]

In: The Cost of Prescription Drugs
Editor: Alfred Bonsaint
ISBN: 978-1-53617-540-0
© 2020 Nova Science Publishers, Inc.

Chapter 2

The Cost of Prescription Drugs: How the Drug Delivery System Affects What Patients Pay, Part II*

Committee on Health, Education, Labor, and Pensions

The Committee met, pursuant to notice, at 10:03 a.m., in room SD–430, Dirksen Senate Office Building, Hon. Lamar Alexander, Chairman of the Committee, presiding.

Present: Senators Alexander [presiding], Collins, Cassidy, Young, Murkowski, Murray, Casey, Franken, Bennet, Whitehouse, Baldwin, Murphy, Warren, Kaine, and Hassan.

Opening Statement of Senator Alexander

The Chairman. The Senate Committee on Health, Education, Labor, and Pensions will please come to order.

Senator Murray and I will each have an opening statement, and then we'll introduce the witnesses. After the witnesses' testimony, Senators will each have 5 minutes of questions. There's a vote scheduled for 10:30. I think what we'll do is continue right on through until about 10:45, and then we'll alternate going back and forth to vote. I think we'll have time for all of us to hear the witnesses' testimony before we have to leave for the vote.

* This is an edited, reformatted and augmented version of Hearing Before the Committee on Health, Education, Labor, and Pensions United States Senate, One Hundred Fifteenth Congress, First Session, Serial No. 115–640, dated October 17, 2017.

Today, we're holding a hearing which is the second in a series on prescription drug costs in response to a bipartisan request led by Senator Cassidy, Senator Franken, along with Senators Collins, Baldwin, Murkowski, Whitehouse, Capito, Sanders, Enzi, and Warren, as well as other Senators who are interested in this subject. Not only was the request for these hearings bipartisan, but both this hearing and the first hearing on drug prices were bipartisan, which means Senator Murray and I agreed on the witnesses.

Despite this, our first hearing in June went so far off track that I delayed this hearing because Senators, instead of talking about drug prices, wanted to use the opportunity to talk about other issues, specifically, the Affordable Care Act. I acknowledge their deep feelings and differences of opinions on the ACA, but the Senate has been stuck in a partisan stalemate for 7 years over what is a relatively small part of healthcare, the individual health insurance market, where 6 percent of Americans purchase health insurance.

Senator Murray and I have been working for several weeks to see if we can find within the Senate a limited consensus bipartisan agreement to stabilize the individual market in the interim. But there are many other issues that have caused healthcare spending in this country to grow from consuming 9 percent of the gross domestic product in 1980 to nearly 18 percent in 2015 and a predicted 20 percent in 2025, according to the Center for Medicare and Medicaid Services.

We need to look at all aspects of healthcare spending—the 15 percent or so we spend on prescription drugs, including retail and prescription drugs administered in hospitals, and the other 85 percent of healthcare spending, which includes doctor visits, surgeries, and medical devices—and ways to get these costs under control. We're having a hearing on Thursday to discuss wellness and healthy lifestyle changes and how they could decrease serious illnesses and bring down healthcare costs.

While, of course, Senators are free to say and do whatever they wish to do, I would hope today that we could focus on the cost of prescription drugs while we have these excellent witnesses before us. Next month, the Committee will hold a third hearing to hear from Norm Augustine and consider a report he is leading from the National Academy of Sciences. This report is the result of a study called "Ensuring Patient Access to Affordable Drug Therapies."

We've set a good example of bipartisan success in the Food and Drug Administration user fee agreements. For 18 months, this Committee worked with our counterparts in the House to update and pass user fee agreements, including provisions from many Senators on both sides of the aisle, including measures that will provide additional staff and resources to the FDA to approve more biosimilars and generic drugs which provide more competition and lower drug costs. That bill became law this summer. Last year, the Committee worked together on 21st Century Cures to spur the development of new drugs and treatments.

My goal for these hearings is to continue these in a bipartisan way and learn the facts about what goes into the price patients pay when picking up their prescriptions and what, if any, steps we can agree on to lower those prices. We're in the middle of a remarkable time in science that is producing amazing discoveries for patients. We have drugs that can cure Hepatitis C, keep cancer at bay, and stop a stroke.

With this innovation comes new challenges. We need to make sure all patients can benefit. We've all heard from patients that the cost of new drugs is often too much for them to afford. We also need to make sure that any action we take doesn't jeopardize the innovation and the breakthroughs.

The prescription drug delivery system—how a drug gets from the manufacturer to the patient—is complicated. More than 4.4 billion prescriptions are written for drugs each year for Americans who then pick up these prescriptions at 60,000 drugstores or receive them from doctors or hospitals or online pharmacies, and those 4.4 billion prescriptions, estimated to cost $450 billion, are paid for in a similarly complicated way, which you're going to hear about today.

In addition to private insurance, many different government programs subsidize or pay for prescription drugs: Medicaid, 340B, Medicare Part B and Part D, Tricare, VA, and Indian Health Service. Patients often pay a set amount, called a copay, or a percentage, called coinsurance, when picking up their prescription as well, or sometimes patients have to cover the whole cost if they haven't met their deductible. What amount of the cost of the prescription drug they pay is determined by what health insurance they may have.

I hope our witnesses today will help us understand the drug delivery system and how their role in the system affects the price patients pay. Our witnesses represent the brand manufacturers, who take enormous risks; generic drug manufacturers, who over the last 30 years have grown to make up 89 percent of all prescriptions, lowering cost; drug wholesalers, who purchase drugs from manufacturers and deliver them all over the country daily; pharmacy benefit managers, who use their buying power to leverage lower prices on all drugs but also make difficult decisions about drugs to offer patients at what cost and with what copays or what insurance; and then, of course, pharmacists, who are on the front lines of helping patients that find out the cost of their medicine when picking it up at the drugstore and having to make that fit within their budgets.

As we look at it and hope to address the fundamental cost of healthcare, I hope we can continue to do this in a bipartisan way.

Senator Murray.

OPENING STATEMENT OF SENATOR MURRAY

Senator MURRAY. Well, thank you, Chairman Alexander, for your leadership in holding these hearings, and to all of our colleagues on both sides of the aisle for their commitment to address this critical challenge before us today, which is the increasing burden and soaring prices of prescription drugs. Much like our last hearing on the devastation being caused by the opioid crisis, this is truly an urgent discussion.

Like everyone here, I've heard from so many families who are forced to choose between some high-priced medication and paying their bills, between filling a prescription or putting food on the table, and between getting the care that they need or paying their mortgage or putting gas in the tank. So this is clearly a challenge we need to meet and meet it quickly.

Fortunately, we have taken some steps in the right direction. I'm very pleased this Committee worked to increase transparency and foster more competition in the generic drug market in the FDA Reauthorization Act. In these agreements, taking suggestions from both sides, we were able to accelerate the review of generics that can alleviate anti-competitive markets, improve the process for bringing a generic to market by increasing communication and transparency between the FDA and manufacturers, encourage new generics to compete with sole source products vulnerable to price hikes and shortages, and prevent gaming of the Orphan Drug Act which has brought hope to so many patients.

But as we know, generic competition alone will not address the high prices paid by so many patients and families in out-of-pocket costs and high premiums. We've got to make more progress to get at the root of the problem facing patients, which is the high prices set by drug manufacturers. That is why I'm glad that Democrats have put forward a number of ideas and legislation to demand more transparency from pharmaceutical companies about what's behind drug prices, allow Medicare to negotiate fair prices for prescription drugs, prevent manufacturers from engaging in price gouging, and crack down on the various anti-competitive practices that keep prices high. These measures would make a real difference when it comes to bringing down prices.

All this requires—and I've said it many times—this administration has to be our partner, not a hindrance to our efforts. As we all saw last week, President Trump continued to take unilateral steps to increase premiums and undermine protections for people with preexisting conditions and cause chaos in our healthcare system. That pattern of governing by sabotage is reckless and appalling and only makes it, I believe, more critical that Congress shows patients and families we can work together to undo the damage being caused and move on to actually doing some good when it comes to families' healthcare.

On drug prices, like so many other issues, President Trump talks a big game on Twitter but has not taken any actions to actually lower drug prices, and the little we have seen from this administration, a leaked Executive Order back in July, barely scratches the surface. Instead, many of the plans that have come out would do very little to actually target drug prices, and, in fact, some have actually targeted vital programs, like 340B, that support hospitals and clinics in serving the very communities who cannot afford the drugs they need to stay healthy.

I hope the administration chooses a different path, and I would just note, by the way, that President Trump could start by nominating a Secretary of Health and Human Services who will put families first when it comes to prescription drug prices and any issues, and I expect a thorough and rigorous nomination process when that comes before us. They have a very important role to play.

We have a lot to cover today, and I want to thank all of our witnesses for joining us. We are very much looking forward to your testimony.

I just want to again thank Chairman Alexander and all of our colleagues for their efforts to tackle this pressing challenge to make sure that prescription medication and lifesaving treatments are not just available, but accessible and affordable. I'm hopeful that our bipartisan work on insurance market stabilization and FDARA can lay the groundwork for serious action on drug prices, given that we all agree this is a priority. Actually, patients and families we serve can't wait much longer.

Thank you, everyone, and I turn it back over to you, Mr. Chairman.

The CHAIRMAN. Thank you, Senator Murray, and thank you for creating a bipartisan environment where we can work ahead, as you indicated, on trying to stabilize the individual health insurance market and begin to move away from health insurance to the larger issues affecting healthcare, such as drug prices.

We thank the witnesses for coming. I would ask you each to summarize your comments in about 5 minutes, and that will leave Senators more time to ask questions.

The first witness is Lori Reilly, the Executive Vice President of Policy, Research, and Membership at PhRMA. She leads the Policy and Research Department there, a trade association of brand drug manufacturers. Chip Davis is the President and Chief Executive of the trade association that represents generic drug manufacturers, distributors, and suppliers. Elizabeth Gallenagh is Senior Vice President for Government Affairs and General Counsel, representing prescription drug wholesalers. Welcome to you.

Mark Merritt is the President and Chief Executive Officer of the national group that represents America's pharmacy benefit managers, and Thomas Menighan is the Executive Director and Chief Executive of the largest association of pharmacists in the United States.

So, Ms. Reilly, let's begin with you, and then we'll hear from each witness.

STATEMENT OF LORI M. REILLY

Ms. REILLY. Thank you, Chairman Alexander, Ranking Member Murray, and Members of the Committee, for having me here today.

Over the past 20 years, the Food and Drug Administration has approved more than 500 new medicines to market, and those have resulted in significant progress against some of our Nation's most costly and challenging conditions. Through innovation, the HIV/AIDS death rate has dropped 86 percent in this country from the mid '1990's, and, more recently, progress that it's been making in the space of oncology has been heralded as game changers for many patients facing serious conditions such as cancer. Today, because of scientific advances, many other conditions are now manageable and sometimes even curable.

In the midst of the incredible scientific progress that we've seen, drug spending growth is actually declining from its peak in 2014. In fact, last year, prescription drug spending cost growth was 3 percent to 5 percent, according to public and private experts. That was in line with all other forms of spending growth. Spending on retail as well as physician-administered drugs continues to remain about 14 percent of what we spend in terms of total healthcare dollars in this country.

Oftentimes, when people talk about that 14 percent, there's a presumption that all of that comes back to the brand name manufacturer. In fact, less than half of that 14 percent—about 6.8 percent of what we spend on total healthcare in this country—comes back to the brand name industry. The rest goes to the generic industry and others in the supply chain.

One important part of the supply chain that isn't with us here today is the hospital sector. Just this morning, we released a paper that looked at 20 of the most commonly prescribed expensive medicines in hospital outpatient settings and found that, on average, hospitals increase and are reimbursed two and a half times the acquisition cost at which they purchase medicines in this country. They're an important part of the supply chain, and I hope we talk about that more later today.

Going forward over the next decade, medicines are projected to remain a stable share of healthcare spending at around 14 percent. To many, they question how can that possibly be the case? We know what's in the pipeline. We know that over the next 10 years, we're likely to have 40 to 45 new medicines approved every single year. But the reality is we have, for pharmaceuticals, some of the most stringent cost containment across the entire healthcare sector.

Pharmacy benefit managers use the fact that there's a great deal of competition within therapeutic areas to limit formularies, to place medicines on high cost-sharing tiers, and to use a host of utilization management techniques to keep costs under control. Over the next 5 years, over $100 billion worth of medicines will be coming off patents, and those medicines will become generics and cheaper for Americans to be able to afford, and, importantly, in the pharmaceutical benefit manager's space, about three pharmacy benefit managers today buy on behalf of 75 percent of all prescriptions in this country because of the leverage they can exert. In 2015, they were able to secure over $100 billion in rebates and discounts.

Unfortunately, what's happening today is those rebates and discounts often are not making their way back to patients at point of sale. Compounding this problem is, today, an increasing number of patients have high cost-sharing for their medicines, either because they have a deductible—today, 50 percent of commercially insured patients have a deductible for their medicine. When they have a deductible for their medicine, they're asked to pay a list price, in other words, a non-negotiated price for their medicine.

There are solutions that we think could be put forth to address some of the cost challenges we face. The first one is the fact that $100 billion of discounts and rebates should find its way back to patients at the retail pharmacy level. Those discounts should be passed back to patients to lower their healthcare costs. We also need to do more to reform government rules around how companies can contract today. There's a desire to move our healthcare system toward contracting toward value. But today, because of government rules and regulations, it makes it harder to have sensible contracting.

Third, we need to look at programs like the 340B program, which, yes, do provide a very important benefit to many, but, as I mentioned before, we know in the hospital sector, oftentimes hospitals are increasing the price of their medicine two and a half to three and a half times and are getting reimbursed oftentimes, again, three times as much as the manufacturer is getting reimbursed for the medicine.

Last, we need to speed the approval of new medicines as well as generic medicines to the marketplace. Competition is the best medicine to lowering costs over the long term, and we need to build on the work that this Committee passed as part of PDUFA–6 to continue to modernize the Food and Drug Administration to have efficient and safe delivery of new medicines and new generic medicines. Future progress is needed, and patients are waiting for the kind of innovation our sector can deliver.

Thank you very much.

[The prepared statement of Ms. Reilly follows:]

PREPARED STATEMENT OF LORI M. REILLY

Chairman Alexander, Ranking Member Murray, and Members of the Committee, thank you for inviting me to participate in today's hearing. Understanding the role the drug delivery system plays in determining what patients pay for medicines is a critical part of the discussion about what can be done to improve patient access and affordability and I appreciate the opportunity to explore this topic with you in depth.

PhRMA represents the country's leading innovative biopharmaceutical research companies, which are devoted to discovering and developing medicines that enable patients to live longer, healthier, and more productive lives. The biopharmaceutical sector is one of the most research- intensive industries in the U.S.: since 2000, PhRMA member companies have invested more than half a trillion dollars in the search for new treatments and cures, including $65.5 billion in 2016 alone.

MEDICINES HAVE TRANSFORMED THE TREATMENT OF MANY DISEASES, HELPING PATIENTS LIVE LONGER AND HEALTHIER LIVES

We are in a new era of medicine in which breakthrough science is transforming patient care and enabling us to more effectively treat chronic disease, the biggest cost driver in our health care system. Innovative medicines represent significant scientific advancements that revolutionize the treatment and thus the downstream healthcare costs of complex and costly diseases, such as cancer, hepatitis C, HIV/AIDS, and cardiovascular disease. In this new era of medicine, many diseases previously regarded as deadly are now manageable and even curable. Today, more than 7,000 medicines are in development worldwide, of which 80% have the potential to be first in class and 42% are personalized medicines.[1] Prescription medicines produce unparalleled value and savings for the health care system, preventing or slowing the progression of disease, and reducing the need for more intensive medical care. Continued advances in biopharmaceutical innovation represent the best opportunities to improve health outcomes and control future health care costs.

New medicines help contain overall health care spending by preventing costly complications and hospitalizations, and replacing other medical interventions. A 2013 study by IMS Institute for Healthcare Informatics estimated that the U.S. health care system could save $213 billion annually by improving the use of medicines.[2] Similarly, research published in *Health Affairs* found that just an extra $1 spent on medicines for adherent patients with congestive heart failure, high blood pressure, diabetes and high cholesterol can generate $3 to $10 in savings on emergency room visits and inpatient hospitalizations.[3]

Based on the growing body of evidence about medicines' benefits, the Congressional Budget Office (CBO) recognizes reductions in other medical expenditures associated

[1] Long G. The Biopharmaceutical Pipeline: Innovative Therapies in Clinical Development. Analysis Group. 2017; Tufts Center for the Study of Drug Development (CSDD). Personalized Medicine Gains Traction But Still Faces Multiple Challenges. Tufts CSDD Impact Report. 2015; 17(3).

[2] IMS Institute for Healthcare Informatics. Avoidable Costs in U.S. Healthcare: The $200 Billion Opportunity from Using Medicines More Responsibly. June 2013.

[3] Roebuck MC, Lieberman JN, Gemmill-Toyama M, et al. Medication Adherence Leads to Lower Care Use And Costs Despite Increased Drug Spending. *Health Affairs*. 2011; 30(1): 99.

with increased use of prescription medicines in Medicare Part D.[4] Research indicates that the savings may be three to six times greater than estimated by the CBO for seniors with common chronic conditions like diabetes and hypertension,[5] and less prevalent conditions such as Parkinson's disease.[6] More recent research has shown that increased use of medicines among patients is associated with reductions in expenditures from avoided use of inpatient and outpatient services in Medicaid as well. For example, among patients with schizophrenia, improved adherence to antipsychotic medicines yielded annual net savings of up to $3.3 billion, or $1,580 per patient per year, driven by lower hospitalizations, outpatient care, and criminal system involvement.[7] Another study found that if 60% of the children enrolled in Medicaid achieved high adherence to asthma treatment in just 14 states, Medicaid could achieve $57.5 million in savings annually.[8]

The Competitive Market for Prescription Medicines Balances Innovation, Patient Access, and Cost Containment

The competitive market is the engine that drives the innovative biopharmaceutical research and development ecosystem. The dynamics of the private, market-based system in the U.S. promote incentives for continued innovation and patient access to needed medicines while leveraging competition to achieve cost containment. Since 2000, biopharmaceutical companies have brought more than 500 new medicines to the U.S. market, resulting in significant progress against some of the most costly and challenging diseases.[9] Yet, as a result of robust negotiation and competition in the marketplace, spending on medicines is growing at the slowest rate in years.[10]

Government, market analyst, and pharmacy benefit manager data all point to the same conclusion: that after peaking in 2014—an anomaly year in which millions of

[4] Congressional Budget Office. Offsetting Effects of Prescription Drug Use on Medicare's Spending for Medical Services. November 29, 2012.

[5] Roebuck MC. Medical Cost Offsets from Prescription Drug Utilization Among Medicare Beneficiaries. *Journal of Managed Care Pharmacy*. 2014; 20(10): 994-995.

[6] Wei YJ, Palumbo FB, Simoni-Wastila L, et al. Antiparkinson Drug Adherence and its Association With Health Care Utilization and Economic Outcomes in a Medicare Part D Population. *Value in Health*. 2014; 17(2): 196-204.

[7] Predmore ZS, Mattke S, Horvitz-Lennon M. Improving Antipsychotic Adherence among Patients With Schizophrenia: Savings for States. *Psychiatric Services*. 2015; 66:343–345.

[8] Rust G, Zhang S, McRoy L. Potential Savings From Increasing Adherence to Inhaled Corticosteroid Therapy in Medicaid-Enrolled Children. *American Journal of Managed Care*. 2015; 21(3): 173-180.

[9] US Food and Drug Administration. Summary of NDA Approvals & Receipts, 1938 to the Present. http://www.fda.gov/aboutfda/whatwedo/history/productregulation/ summaryofndaapprovalsreceipts1938tothepresent/default.htm; US Food and Drug Administration. New Drugs at FDA: CDER's New Molecular Entities and New Therapeutic Biological Products. 2012 – 2015. https://www.fda.gov/drugs/developmentapprovalprocess/ druginnovation/default.htm

[10] QuintilesIMS Institute. Medicine Use and Spending in the US: A Review of 2016 and Outlook to 2021.April 2017

uninsured patients gained coverage and a record number of new medicines were approved—prescription drug spending growth has fallen substantially. Accounting for discounts and rebates, multiple sources report that spending on prescription medicines grew by just 3% to 5% in 2016.[11] As a result of negotiation and competition in the marketplace, spending on retail and physician-administered medicines continues to represent only 14% of overall health care spending, even though scores of new medicines are approved every year. And at the state level, Medicaid programs spent just 4.9% of their budgets on prescription drugs, including new medicines, in 2016, relative to 26% for hospital care and 18.2% for provider services.[12]

The U.S. biopharmaceutical marketplace promotes innovation and affordability through cost containment that is built into the prescription drug lifecycle. While the price of a medicine may increase or decrease over its lifetime, prices fall dramatically as competition occurs among brand-name medicines, and typically fall even further (up to 80%) with the introduction of generics.[13] For instance, the price of one common statin (atorvastatin, known in the branded form as Lipitor) used to lower cholesterol and prevent cardiovascular disease, dropped by about 92% from 2005 to 2013 when generic alternatives came to market.[14] Meanwhile, the average charge for percutaneous transluminal coronary angioplasty (PTCA)—a surgical procedure to treat cardiovascular disease – increased by almost 66% during that same time period. [15]

The U.S. market is structured to take maximum advantage of savings from brand competition and from generics. Three large, sophisticated pharmacy benefit managers (PBMs) manage over 75% of all prescriptions filled.[16] They use brand competition to obtain discounts from manufacturers and take full advantage of the presence of generics to drive savings. This drives the rapid shift of market share to generics (and, looking forward, to biosimilars), a system with few analogues in other health care sectors. As one example of the growing influence of PBMs, industry leader Express Scripts has publicly stated their success in leveraging substantial rebates for hepatitis C medicines led to those

---

[11] QuintilesIMS Institute. Medicine Use and Spending in the US: A Review of 2016 and Outlook to 2021.April 2017; CVS Health. CVS Health PBM Clients Achieved Lowest Prescription Drug Trend in Four Years, Despite Rising Drug Prices. March 15, 2017. http:// www.prnewswire.com/news-releases/cvs-health-pbm-clients-achieved- lowest-prescription-drug-trend-in-four-years-despite-rising-drug-prices-300423726.html; Express Scripts. 2016 Drug Trend Report. February 2017. https://lab.express-scripts.com/lab/drug-trend-report; Which PBM Best Managed Drug Spending in 2016: How Did OptumRx Compare? Drug Channels. April 25, 2017. http://www.drugchannels.net/2017/04/which-pbm-best-managed-drug-spending-in.html#more.

[12] Prescription drug prerebate expenditures tabulated by The Menges Group using FY2016 CMS State Drug Utilization data files and CMS brand/generic indicators for each National Drug Code. Rebate information obtained from FY2016 CMS-64 reports. Post-rebate expenditures derived through The Menges Group tabulations using above information.

[13] IMS Institute for Healthcare Informatics. Price Declines After Branded Medicines Lose Exclusivity in the US January 2016.

[14] Atorvastatin, known in the branded form as Lipitor 10mg: IMS National Sales Perspective (NSP) Invoice Price in 2005 (Branded Lipitor) and in 2013 (Generic Atorvastatin).

[15] Data adapted from: HCUP Hospital Charge Database 2005 to 2013, Average Hospital Charges.

[16] Fein AJ; Pembroke Consulting, Inc., and Drug Channels Institute. 2014-15 Economic Report on Retail, Mail, and Specialty Pharmacies. January 2015. http://drugchannelsinstitute.com/ files/2014-15-PharmacyIndustry-Overview.pdf

treatments being less expensive in the U.S. than in many other western countries.[17] And the competitive market will continue to generate savings in the years ahead, as more than $140 billion of U.S. brand sales are projected to face generic competition between now and 2021.[18] Competition from biosimiliars is estimated to account for $38 billion of the loss in brand spending.

LIST PRICES FOR MEDICINES DO NOT REFLECT SUBSTANTIAL REBATES AND DISCOUNTS AND PROVIDE AN INCREASINGLY INACCURATE PICTURE OF PRESCRIPTION DRUG COSTS

Much of the public debate about the cost of medicines has focused on list prices, which do not account for the rebates and discounts that PBMs and health plans commonly negotiate with biopharmaceutical companies in exchange for preferred formulary placement on lower cost-sharing tiers. For certain medicines used to treat chronic conditions like asthma, high cholesterol, hepatitis C, and diabetes, these discounts and rebates can reduce list prices by as much as 30% to 70%.[19] Biopharmaceutical companies are also required to provide sizable statutory rebates, discounts, and fees to government programs, which have increased in recent years due to an increase in the Medicaid rebate, closing of the Medicare Part D "donut hole" and expansion of the 340B program. These mandatory payments grew by more than 40% between 2013 and 2015, increasing from $29.6 billion to $41.8 billion.[20]

Excluding rebates and discounts from discussions about the cost of prescription medicines provides an increasingly inaccurate picture of marketplace trends. According to PBMs and industry analysts, list prices for brand medicines have grown by an estimated 9% to 12% annually since 2015, while net prices (which take discounts and rebates into account) have grown by just 2.5% to 3.5%.[21]A recent study from the

---

[17] LaMattina J. For Hepatitis C Drugs, U.S, Prices Are Cheaper Than in Europe. *Forbes*. December 4, 2015. http://www.forbes.com/sites/johnlamattina/2015/12/04/for-hepatitis-c-drugs-u-s-prices-are-cheaper-than-in-europe/#7ced43f564bb

[18] QuintilesIMS Institute. Medicine Use and Spending in the US: A Review of 2016 and Outlook to 2021. April 2017.

[19] QuintilesIMS Institute. Estimate of Medicare Part D Costs After Accounting for Manufacturer Rebates. October 2016; Gronholt-Pedersen J, Skydsgaard N, Neely J. Novo Nordisk Defends U.S. Diabetes Drug Pricing. *Reuters*. November 4, 2016. http://www.reuters.com/ article/us-novo-nordisk-prices-idUSKBN12Z184; Silverman E. What the 'Shocking' Gilead Discounts on its Hepatitis C Drugs Will Mean. *Wall Street Journal*. February 4, 2015. https://blogs.wsj.com/pharmalot/2015/02/04/what-the-shocking-gilead-discounts-on-its-hepatitis-c-drugs-will-mean/Barrett P, Langreth R. The Crazy Math Behind Drug Prices: Intermediaries that Negotiate to Lower Prices May Cause Them To Increase Too. *Bloomberg Businessweek*, June 29, 2017. https:// www.bloomberg.com/ news/articles/2017-06-29/the-crazy-math-behind-drug-prices

[20] Berkeley Research Group. The Pharmaceutical Supply Chain: Gross Drug Expenditures Realized by Stakeholder. January 2017.

[21] QuintilesIMS Institute. Medicine Use and Spending in the US: A Review of 2016 and Outlook to 2021.April 2017; Express Scripts. 2016 Drug Trend Report. February 2017. https:// lab.express-scripts.com/lab/drug-

QuintilesIMS Institute demonstrates that net prices for medicines that have been on the market for at least two years *declined* by an average of 2.5% annually from 2010 to 2016, driven by patent expirations and increased competition from generics.[22] The QuintilesIMS report also notes that over the next five years, net prices for existing medicines will continue to decline between 1% and 4% annually, highlighting the important role rebates and discounts will continue to play in containing prescription medicine spending growth in the future.

Claims from PBMs, payers, and others about the skyrocketing prices of medicines almost always focus solely on list prices, which are not reflective of actual spending trends. When new hepatitis C medicines offering cure rates exceeding 90% entered the market, PBMs claimed that these life-saving treatments and cures would bankrupt the health system and their costs were simply unsustainable. Instead, competition among brand manufacturers quickly drove deep discounts averaging 40% to 65% off the list price.[23] Express Scripts now states that their aggressive negotiations have saved Americans $4 billion, cured more patients with hepatitis C than any time in history, and that the discounted price makes it affordable to treat all patients with the infection.[24]

Prior to the launch of PCSK9 inhibitors, a new type of cholesterol lowering medicine that represents a significant advance in treatment of heart disease, PBMs made alarming claims about their cost, projecting up to $150 billion to $200 billion per year in spending for these medicines.[25] CMS' Office of the Actuary, however, projected a much more modest impact, based on expected competition leading to discounts and continued widespread use of generic statins.[26] The Actuary's refusal to accept these inflated claims proved to be the right approach. In fact, PBMs quickly made deals to cover both of the brand competitors on the market and emphasized that the drugs' cost is "far lower than industry forecasts."[27] New research shows that PBMs have also effectively used strict prior authorization and high cost-sharing requirements to suppress utilization of these

---

trend-report; SSR Health. US Brand Pharmaceutical Net Prices Fell 0.3% in 3Q16. January 18, 2017. http://www.ssrllc.com/publication/us-brand-pharmaceutical-net-prices-fell-0-3-in-3q16/

22 QuintilesIMS Institute. Understanding the Drives of Drug Expenditure in the US. September 2017.

23 What Gilead's Big Hepatitis C Discounts Mean for Biosimilar Pricing. Drug Channels. February 5, 2015. http://www.drugchannels.net/2015/02/what-gileads-big-hepatitis-c-discounts.html

24 Express Scripts. The $4 Billion Return on a Promise Kept. January 27, 2015. http://lab.express-scripts.com/lab/insights/specialty-medications/the-4-billion-return-on-a-promise-kept

25 Shrank W, Lotvin A, Singh S, Brennan T. In the Debate About Cost and Efficacy, PCSK9 Inhibitors May Be The Biggest Challenge Yet. *Health Affairs Blog*. February 17, 2015. http://healthaffairs.org/blog/2015/02/17/in-the-debate-about-cost-and-efficacy-pcsk9-inhibitors-may-be-the-biggest-challenge-yet/

26 Kelly C. U.S. Drug Spending Will Increase 7.6% in 2015, Including PCSK9 Costs – CMS. *The Pink Sheet*, July 2015.

27 Express Scripts. "Express Scripts Includes Innovative Cholesterol-Lowering Drugs on National Preferred Formulary." October 6, 2015. http://www.prnewswire.com/news-releases/express-scripts-includes-innovative-cholesterol-lowering-drugs-on-national-preferred-formulary-300155222.html

medicines, resulting in less than one-third of patients prescribed a PCSK9 inhibitor being able to access therapy.[28]

A Complex Distribution and Payment System Shapes the Prices Patients, Health Plans, and the Government Pay for Medicines

The process by which prescription medicines move from biopharmaceutical manufacturers to patients involves multiple stakeholders and numerous financial transactions. This process has evolved significantly in recent years, as supply chain entities have grown to play a larger role in drug distribution and payment. Wholesalers, pharmacies, plan sponsors, and patients all pay different prices for medicines, and the amount that is ultimately paid is determined by confidential negotiations between stakeholders. Many discounts provided by manufacturers do not flow directly through to the patients taking the medicine, and in some cases the full discounts may also not flow through to employers or plan sponsors.[29]

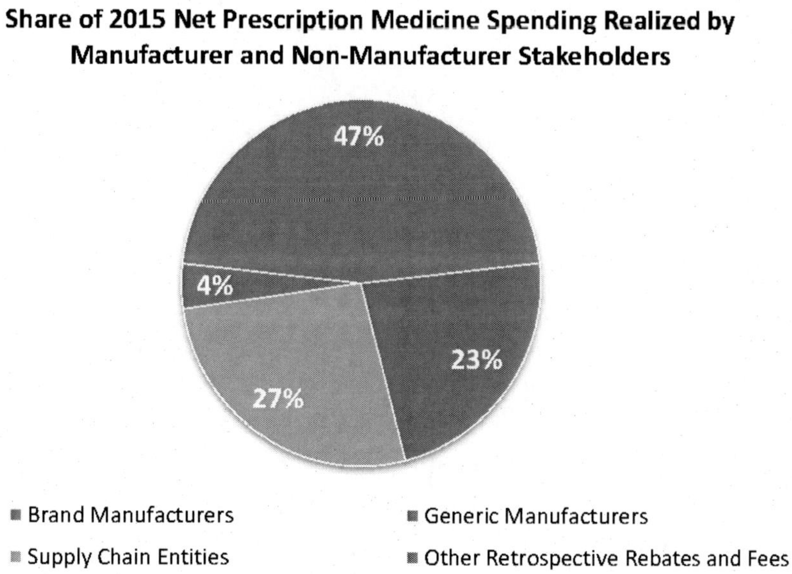

Figure 1.

[28] Navar AM, Taylor B, Mulder H, et al. Association of Prior Authorization and Out-of-Pocket Costs With Patient Access to PCSK9 Inhibitor Therapy. *JAMA Cardiology*. Published online September 27, 2017. doi:10.1001/jamacardio.2017.3451.

[29] Midwestern Business Group on Health. Drawing a Line in the Sand: Employers Must Rethink Pharmacy Benefit Strategies. September 2017. https:// higherlogicdownload.s3.amazonaws.com/MBGH/4f7f512a-e946-4060-9575-b27c65545cb8/UploadedImages/Specialty%20Pharmacy/DMJ_MBGH_Line_in_the_Sand_RV12_9617.pdf

Some manufacturer rebates and discounts are required by law, while others are negotiated between biopharmaceutical companies and powerful commercial payers, many of which cover tens of millions of patients. In recent years, as payers have consolidated and competition between brand medicines has increased, negotiated rebates and discounts have also grown. Multiple data sources indicate that growth in manufacturer rebates and discounts has been substantial and that an increasing share of these discounts and rebates are retained by middlemen involved in distributing and paying for prescription medicines.[30] According to a recent study by the Berkeley Research Group, on average, more than a third of the initial list price of a medicine is rebated back to insurance companies, PBMs and the government, or retained by other stakeholders along the biopharmaceutical supply chain.[31] And the gap between list prices and net prices is growing every year as more of medicine costs are being retained by middlemen in the system.

As shown in Figure 1, accounting for the discounts, rebates and fees paid to PBMs, payers, and the government, brand biopharmaceutical companies realize less than half of total net spending on prescription medicines.[32] Of the $469 billion spent on prescription drugs in the U.S. in 2015, brand manufacturers realized $219 billion; the remainder went to generic manufacturers or was retained as earnings by entities along the supply chain and other stakeholders.[33] The $219 billion realized by the brand biopharmaceutical industry accounts for just 6.8% of the $3.2 trillion spent on health care overall in the U.S. in 2015.[34]

PATIENTS DO NOT DIRECTLY BENEFIT FROM SIGNIFICANT PRICE NEGOTIATIONS HAPPENING IN THE MARKET TODAY

Savings generated from price negotiations between biopharmaceutical companies and payers do not always make their way directly to patients facing high cost-sharing for their medicines. Unlike care received at an in-network hospital or physician's office, health plans base cost-sharing for prescriptions filled in the deductible or with coinsurance on undiscounted list prices, rather than on prices that reflect negotiated rebates and discounts. Enrollment in high deductible health plans and use of coinsurance for

---

[30] QuintilesIMS Institute. Medicine Use and Spending in the US: A Review of 2016 and Outlook to 2021.April 2017; Berkeley Research Group. The Pharmaceutical Supply Chain: Gross Drug Expenditures Realized by Stakeholder. January 2017; Dross D. Will Point-of-Sale Rebates Disrupt the PBM Business? Mercer. July 31, 2017. https://www.mercer.us/our-thinking/healthcare/will-point-of-sale-rebates-disrupt-the-pbm-business.html

[31] Berkeley Research Group. The Pharmaceutical Supply Chain: Gross Drug Expenditures Realized by Stakeholder. January 2017.

[32] *Ibid.*

[33] *Ibid.*

[34] Martin AB, Hartman M, Washington B, et al. National Health Spending: Faster Growth in 2015 As Coverage Expands and Utilization Increases. *Health Affairs*. 2017; 36(1): 166-176.

prescription medicines has grown sharply in recent years, increasingly exposing patients to high out-of-pocket costs based on undiscounted prices, creating scenarios in which medicines appear to be more costly than other health care services. High cost-sharing is a cause for concern, as a substantial body of research clearly demonstrates that increases in out-of-pocket costs are associated with both lower medication adherence and increased abandonment rates, putting patients' ability to stay on needed therapies at risk.[35]

Over the past 10 years, patient cost-sharing has risen substantially faster than health plan costs. For workers with employer-sponsored health insurance, out-of-pocket spending for deductible and coinsurance payments increased by 230% and 89%, respectively, compared to a 56% increase in payments by health plans.[36] Whereas cost-sharing for prescription medicines once consisted almost entirely of copays, use of deductibles and coinsurance has increased rapidly. For example, the share of patient out-of-pocket drug spending represented by coinsurance more than doubled over the past ten years in the commercial market, while the share accounted for by deductibles tripled.[37] The growing use of deductibles and coinsurance for prescription medicines creates affordability challenges for many patients. Patients enrolled in high deductible health plans may be asked to pay thousands of dollars out-of-pocket before any of their prescriptions are covered, while patients with coinsurance are responsible for as much as 30% to 40% of the total cost of their medicines.

Due to the growing gap between list and net prices, patients' cost sharing for medicines is increasingly based on prices that do not reflect plan sponsors' actual costs. For example, market analysts report that negotiated discounts and rebates can lower the net price of insulin by up to 50% to 70%, yet health plans require patients with deductibles to pay the full undiscounted price. As a result, a patient in a high-deductible health plan who pays the list price each month for insulin maybe paying hundreds—or even thousands—more annually than their insurer. Analysis by Amundsen Consulting shows that more than half of patients' out-of-pocket spending for brand medicines is based on the list price of the medicine, even though their health insurer may be receiving a steep discount.[38]

---

[35] IMS Institute for Healthcare Informatics. Emergency and Impact of Pharmacy Deductibles: Implications for Patients in Commercial Health Plans. September 2015; Doshi JA, Li P, Huo H, et al. High Cost Sharing and Specialty Drug Initiation Under Medicare Part D: A Case Study in Patients with Newly Diagnosed Chronic Myeloid Leukemia. *American Journal of Managed Care*. 2016; 22(4 Suppl): S78-S86; Brot-Goldberg ZC, Chandra A, Handel BR, et al. What Does A Deductible Do? The Impact of Cost-Sharing on Health Care Prices, Quantities, and Spending Dynamics. NBER Working Paper 21632, October 2015; Eaddy MT, Cook CL, O'Day K, et al. How Patient Cost-Sharing Trends Affect Adherence and Outcomes. *Pharmacy & Therapeutics*. 2012; 37(1): 45-55.

[36] Claxton G, Levitt L, Long M, et al. Increases in Cost-Sharing Payments Have Far Outpaced Wage Growth. Peterson-Kaiser Health System Tracker. October 4, 2017. https:// www.healthsystemtracker.org/ brief/increases-in-cost-sharing-payments-have-far-outpaced-wage-growth/#item-start

[37] Claxton G, Levitt L, Long M. Payments for Cost Sharing Increasing Rapidly Over Time. Peterson-Kaiser Health System Tracker. April 2016. http://www.healthsystemtracker.org/ insight/examining-high-prescription-drug-spending-for-people-with-employer-sponsored-health-insurance/

[38] Amundsen Consulting. Commercially-Insured Patients Pay Undiscounted List Prices for One In Five Brand Prescriptions, Accounting for Half of Out-of-Pocket Spending on Brand Medicines. March 2017.

Health plans typically use some portion of negotiated rebates to reduce premiums for all enrollees, rather than to directly lower costs for patients facing high cost-sharing due to deductibles and coinsurance. According to one actuarial firm, this results in a system of "reverse insurance," whereby payers require patients with high drug expenditures to pay more out-of- pocket, while rebate savings are spread out among all health plan enrollees in the form of lower premiums.[39] Asking sicker patients with high drug costs to subsidize premiums for healthier enrollees is the exact opposite of how health insurance is supposed to work.

Some patients also end up paying more at the pharmacy counter when they use their insurance, not knowing that their prescriptions would be cheaper if they were paying in cash. Many PBM contracts require pharmacies to charge patients the exact amount negotiated between the PBM and the pharmacy, even if that amount exceeds what the pharmacy would charge to a patient without insurance. Gagclauses in PBM contracts prohibit pharmacists from informing insured patients about the lower cash price, at the risk of the pharmacy being excluded from the PBM's network. In these instances, pharmacies must instead overcharge patients, requiring them to pay the full amount of their copayment, over and above the actual cost of the medication. These overpayments are then "clawed back" from the pharmacy by the PBM.[40]

PBMs Negotiate Lower Medicine Prices for Health Plans and Employers, but Don't Always Pass along All of the Savings

PBMs commonly retain a portion of the rebates they negotiate on behalf of their health plan and employer clients. While the remainder of the rebates are generally passed on to plan sponsors, smaller employers and health plans may not benefit from all of the price concessions the PBM has negotiated with manufacturers, particularly if the PBM decides not to define certain fees or other concessions as "rebates." For example, one benefits consultant has observed that PBMs are increasingly changing the contractual definition of rebates to exclude certain administrative fees, allowing the PBM to retain these payments rather than passing them back to the plan sponsor. These administrative

---

http://www.phrma.org/report/commercially-insured-patients-pay-undiscounted-list-prices-for-one-in-five-brand- prescriptions-accounting-for-half-of-out-of-pocket-spending-brand-medicines

[39] Girod CS, Hart SK, Weltz S. 2017 Milliman Medical Index. May 2017. http:// www.milliman.com/uploadedFiles/insight/Periodicals/mmi/2017-milliman-medical-index.pdf

[40] Hopkins JS. You're Overpaying for Drugs and Your Pharmacist Can't Tell You. *Bloomberg*. February 24, 2017. https://www.bloomberg.com/news/articles/2017-02-24/sworn-to-secrecy-drugstores-stay-silent-as-customers-overpay

fees can be as high as 25% to 30% of the total rebate negotiated with the manufacturer and are often not reported to the plan sponsor by the PBM.[41]

In addition to the rebates they negotiate with biopharmaceutical companies, PBMs are increasingly requiring that if a medicine's list price increases by more than a certain percentage, the manufacturer must provide an additional price protection rebate reimbursing the PBM for all price increases above the threshold. Lack of transparency in contracts between employers and PBMs has led many plan sponsors to question the share of rebate savings being passed through, how much the PBM is retaining for administrative fees, and whether the PBM is disclosing and passing on other price concessions, such as savings from price protection rebates.[42]

Both the portion of the rebate retained by the PBM and the administrative fees they charge their clients are typically based off of a percentage of a medicine's list price. Accordingly, some PBMs may prefer that their formularies include medicines with high list prices and large rebates, rather than medicines with a lower list price. In its most recent report to Congress, the Medicare Payment Advisory Commission discussed incentives that may drive Part D plan sponsors to give formulary preference to medicines with large rebates, rather than lower cost alternatives.[43] These incentives arise because sizable portions of the Part D benefit are not paid for by plan sponsors (e.g., beneficiaries and manufacturers pay for the majority of costs in the coverage gap). Similarly, the Centers for Medicare & Medicaid (CMS) has noted that coverage of medicines with high list prices and large rebates "ease[s] the financial burden borne by Part D plans essentially by shifting costs to the catastrophic phase of the benefit, where plan liability is limited."[44]

Hospital Markups on Medicines Increase Cost-Sharing for Commercially-Insured Patients

The pharmaceutical distribution and payment process differs for medicines administered in a physician office or health care facility vs. those purchased at a pharmacy.

---

[41] Dross D. Will Point-of-Sale Rebates Disrupt the PBM Business? Mercer. July 31, 2017. https://www.mercer.us/our-thinking/healthcare/will-point-of-sale-rebates-disrupt-the-pbm-business.html

[42] Midwestern Business Group on Health. Drawing a Line in the Sand: Employers Must Rethink Pharmacy Benefit Strategies. September 2017. https:// higherlogicdownload.s3.amazonaws.com/MBGH/4f7f512a-e946-4060-9575-b27c65545cb8/UploadedImages/Specialty%20Pharmacy/DMJ_MBGH_Line_in_the_Sand_ RV12_9617.pdf

[43] Medicare Payment Advisory Commission. Status Report on the Medicare Prescription Drug Program (Part D). March 2017. http://medpac.gov/docs/default-source/reports/ mar17_entirereport.pdf

[44] Centers for Medicare & Medicaid. Medicare Part D—Direct and Indirect Remuneration (DIR). January 19, 2017. https://www.cms.gov/Newsroom/MediaReleaseDatabase/Fact-sheets/ 2017-Fact-Sheet-items/2017-01-19-2.html

Providers typically purchase medicines directly, often through a Group Purchasing Organization (GPO). After the physician administers the medicine to the patient, the patient's insurance reimburses the provider for the cost of the medicine as part of the patient's coverage for medical care.

The amount that providers charge for medicines and how much insurers pay varies widely based on where the medicine is administered to the patient. For example, commercial insurers often pay hospital outpatient departments twice as much as physician offices for administering the exact same medicines, including for diseases such as cancer or autoimmune disorders.[45] This is because large hospitals can demand much higher prices from commercial insurers than small physician practices. The Senior Vice President of Oncology and Genetics at UnitedHealthcare described the effect for chemotherapy treatment at high profile cancer centers: "Put simply, the hospitals are saying, 'If you want our beds, you have to take our prices for oncology treatment.'"[46]

The results of hospital markups are astounding. Recent research shows that for twenty medicines administered in hospital outpatient departments, hospitals charge prices that are on average nearly five times higher than their acquisition costs and are reimbursed up to three and a half times their acquisition cost by commercial insurers.[47] For a vast majority of the medicines included in the analysis, this means that the manufacturer—who made the substantial time and R&D investments including clinical trials necessary to develop the treatment—was paid less for the medicine than the hospital.

Hospital markups on prescription medicines have a substantial effect not just on overall healthcare costs, but also on patient affordability. For patients with commercial insurance, coinsurance is the most common form of cost-sharing for provider-administered medicines, which means that the amount the patient must pay is equal to a percentage of the total price the insurer reimburses the provider for the medication. So, when a hospital is paid two or three times the acquisition cost for a medicine, patients are also paying higher coinsurance. As the same United insurance executive quoted above noted "it is immoral to force vulnerable patients to pay triple-digit mark-ups because they have cancer."[48]

---

[45] Magellan RX Management. Medical Pharmacy Trend Report: 2016 Seventh Edition. March 2017.

[46] Newcomer LN. Those Who Pay Have A Say: A View On Oncology Drug Pricing and Reimbursement. *The Oncologist*. 2016; 21(7): 779-81.

[47] The Moran Company. Hospital Charges and Reimbursement for Drugs: Analysis of Markups Relative to Acquisition Cost. October 2017.

[48] Newcomer LN. Those Who Pay Have A Say: A View On Oncology Drug Pricing and Reimbursement. *The Oncologist*. 2016; 21(7): 779-81.

Market Distortions Created by the 340B Program Lead to Higher Health Care Costs

The 340B program, a program originally intended to provide discounts on medicines for safety- net providers, is contributing to higher health care costs and economists suspect that it is also leading to higher list prices for medicines. This program started in 1992, and its basic structure has not been updated since then, despite dramatic changes in the health care system over the past 25 years. The current structure of the program is causing higher health care costs for three main reasons.

First, the 340B discount, which is structured as a percentage discount, creates incentives for hospitals to earn a larger spread from the 340B discounts by prescribing more medicines and higher cost medicines. Economists have noted this may lead prescribing to "shift toward more expensive drugs because profit margins will in general be larger."[49] A 2015 Government Accountability Office study found evidence that 340B was leading to the prescribing of more drugs and more expensive drugs for Medicare patients.[50]

Second, evidence suggests the 340B program shifts care to more expensive and less convenient settings. Government reports suggest that hospitals are taking advantage of guidance that has not been revisited since 1994 which allows hospitals to obtain more 340B discounts by buying community-based physician practices, so that prescriptions written by those physicians then qualify for 340B discounts.[51] As a result, patients are left with fewer community-based provider options and are pushed into higher cost hospital-based settings. Analysis by the IMS Institute for Healthcare Informatics found that average costs for administering cancer drugs are typically twice as high at hospital outpatient departments compared to community-based oncologists, which can lead to "higher patient cost responsibility."[52] Researchers from Memorial Sloan Kettering have noted 340B is helping to drive consolidation of physician practices into hospitals, and that in the absence of reforms "the trend toward consolidation will continue to drive up the cost of commercial insurance…."[53]

Third, the scale of the program as well as its rapid growth may be affecting market prices for prescription drugs. In 2015, roughly 45 percent of all hospitals participated in

---

[49] Conti R, Bach P. Cost Consequences of the 340B Drug Discount Program. *Journal of the American Medical Association*. 2013; 309(19): 1995-1996.

[50] Government Accountability Office. Medicare Part B Drugs: Action Needed to Reduce Financial Incentives to Prescribe 340B Drugs at Participating Hospitals. GAO-15-442, June 2015.

[51] 59 Federal Register 47884.

[52] IMS Institute for Healthcare Informatics. Global Oncology Trend Report: A Review of 2015 and Outlook to 2020. June 2016.

[53] Bach P and Jain RH. Physician's Office and Hospital Outpatient Setting in Oncology: It's About Prices, Not Use. *Journal of Oncology Practice* 2017; 13(1), 4-5.

340B.[54] In an analysis of prescription drug pricing published in the *New England Journal of Medicine,* economists at Harvard University and the University of Chicago concluded that "lawmakers could lower the price of prescription drugs by reforming the federal 340B Drug Pricing Program. […]The scope of the 340B program is currently so vast for drugs that are commonly infused or injected into patients by physicians that their prices are probably driven up for all consumers" (emphasis added).[55] Another study in *JAMA* noted that list prices for drugs are likely higher than they otherwise would be "to offset revenue losses incurred as a larger number of drug sales become eligible for 340B discounts (and thus fewer drugs are sold at full price)."[56] Certain drug classes are disproportionately impacted by the 340B program. Thus, the price distorting impact may be concentrated in certain therapeutic areas, such as medicines for cancer. For example, sales to 340B hospitals account for 33% of *all* Medicare Part B reimbursement for certain types of cancer drugs.[57]

Market-Based Approaches Are the Best Solution for Addressing Health Care Affordability and Controlling Costs

The competitive U.S. health care market provides a sound framework for balancing and supporting patient access, cost containment, and continued progress for patients. Meaningful efforts to address the cost of prescription medicines must include all stakeholders in the supply chain, including biopharmaceutical companies, PBMs, health plans, wholesalers, hospitals, and pharmacies. Policies targeted solely at brand manufacturers—which account for just half of total net spending on prescription medicines and just 6.8% of total U.S. health care spending—are insufficient for addressing broader health care sustainability challenges and risk diminishing the incentives for future innovation.

Strategies for strengthening and enhancing the competitive market include encouraging payers to share negotiated savings with patients at the pharmacy; reforming outdated regulations hindering the adoption of value-based payment arrangements; reforming the 340B drug discount program, which is distorting the market, so that it

---

[54] Medicare Payment Advisory Commission. Report to the Congress: Overview of the 340B Drug Pricing Program. May 2015.

[55] Conti R and Rosenthal M. Pharmaceutical Policy Reform—Balancing Affordability with Incentives for Innovation. *New England Journal of Medicine*. 2016; 374:703-706.

[56] Conti R, Bach P. Cost Consequences of the 340B Drug Discount Program, *Journal of the American Medical Association*. 2013; 309(19): 1995-1996.

[57] Drugs sold to 340B hospitals account for 33% of *all* Part B reimbursement for breast cancer and multiple myeloma drugs. Vandervelde A and Blalock E. Measuring the Relative Size of the 340B Program: 2012-2017. Berkeley Research Group, July 2017.

better serves the purpose for which it was created; and continuing to modernize the Food and Drug Administration (FDA) and assure that there is robust generic and biosimilar competition once a brand medicine loses its exclusivity.

SHARING NEGOTIATED SAVINGS WITH PATIENTS

Changes in insurance coverage for prescription medicines, and the growing use of deductibles and coinsurance in particular, have created affordability challenges for many patients. Health plans should be encouraged to directly pass on more of the savings from negotiated rebates in the form of lower patient out-of-pocket costs, just like they do for other types of health care services. This should be executed in a way that maintains the confidentiality of proprietary pricing information that the Federal Trade Commission has identified as important to the effective functioning of competitive markets. Payers have begun to recognize that using the undiscounted price of a medicine to set cost-sharing is problematic for patients: recent statements from the two largest PBMs note that high deductibles for medicines put patients in a "very difficult position" and indicate that sharing rebate savings directly with patients should be considered as a "best practice."[58] Actuarial research indicates that sharing negotiated savings could save certain commercially insured patients enrolled in plans with high deductibles and coinsurance between $145 and $800 annually, while increasing premiums by 1% or less.[59]

To help patients afford their medicines, biopharmaceutical companies have entered into partnerships with third parties, such as Blink Health and GoodRx, to offer discounted prices directly to patients, outside of their insurance benefit.[60] Encouraging health plans to allow the cost of prescriptions purchased through these third-party programs to count towards patients' deductibles and maximum out-of-pocket spending limits would further reduce patient affordability barriers.

Copay assistance programs offered by biopharmaceutical companies provide another valuable source of assistance for many commercially insured patients who are struggling to afford their out-of-pocket costs, as do manufacturer-sponsored patient assistance programs that help underinsured and uninsured patients obtain the medicines they need for free or nearly free. Recent efforts by health plans to restrict use of copay assistance programs, including no longer counting the full amount patients are asked to pay out-of-

---

[58] Seeking Alpha. Express Scripts Holding (ESRX) Q4 2016 Results – Earnings Call Transcript. February 15, 2017. http://seekingalpha.com/article/4046365-express-scripts-holding-esrx-q4-2016-results-earnings-call-transcript; Seeking Alpha. CVS Health (CVS) Q4 2016 Results – Earnings Call Transcript. February 9, 2017. http://seekingalpha.com/article/ 4044425-cvs-health-cvs-q4-2016-results-earnings-call-transcript?part=single

[59] Bunger A, Gomberg J, Petroske J. Sharing Rebates May Lower Patient Costs and Likely Has Minimal Impact on Premiums. October 12, 2017. http://www.phrma.org/report/point-of-sale-rebate-analysis-in-the-commercial-market

[60] Thomas K. New Online Tools Offer Path to Lower Drug Prices. *New York Times*. February 9, 2016. https://www.nytimes.com/2016/02/10/business/taming-drug-prices-by-pulling-back-the-curtain-online.html

pocket towards their deductibles or out- of-pocket maximums, unfairly penalize patients and threaten their ability to stay on needed medicines.

Reforming Outdated Regulations Hindering the Adoption of Value-Based Payment Arrangements

Changes in the science and pressures for cost containment in the competitive market are driving rapid evolution of payment and care delivery systems, and biopharmaceutical companies are playing a role in this transformation. As therapies become more personalized, and as the health care market moves away from fee-for-service care and toward more integrated care systems, biopharmaceutical companies are increasingly partnering with payers to develop new types of payment arrangements that reward improvements in care and better health outcomes for patients.

Yet while the science and market are moving rapidly, efforts to develop new ways to pay for medicines have been slowed by regulations designed for an earlier era. Such regulations can have the unintended consequence of making it more difficult for payers to prioritize results that matter to patients, and for biopharmaceutical companies to increase the amount of risk they share with payers. For example:

- Ambiguity in FDA rules governing manufacturer communications about their medicines can prevent biopharmaceutical companies from entering into contracts based on the ability of their medicine to reduce hospitalizations or other medical services, since those contracts might be perceived as promoting the medicines for an unapproved indication.
- Lack of clarity in the anti-kickback statute (AKS) can inhibit value-based contracts due to lack of certainty as to whether contracts fit within existing safe harbors and exceptions. By revising the AKS regulations to add a value-based contracting safe harbor, policymakers can facilitate private payers and manufacturers to expand the use of value-based contracts as a solution to health care affordability and controlling drug costs.
- Price reporting rules such as Medicaid Best Price can limit the amount of risk biopharmaceutical companies share with payers within a value based arrangement, because any increased discount beyond the statutory minimum must be offered not only to that payer, but also to all of Medicaid. Exempting value-based arrangements from existing technical and complex Best Price, Average Manufacturer Price, and potentially Average Sales Price requirements to reflect a modern and flexible approach to price reporting would foster expansion of innovative contracting arrangements.

MODERNIZING THE FDA

As the pace of scientific discovery accelerates, it is critical to assure that our regulatory infrastructure keeps up with the science and that FDA regulations are up-to-date, practical, clear and not overly burdensome to foster efficiency, predictability, and the ability of biopharmaceutical companies to innovate and bring new medicines to patients. The Committee's recent action to reauthorize the Prescription Drug User Fee Act creates a solid foundation not only to accelerate approval of new life-saving treatments, but also assure that there is robust generic and biosimilar competition. We thank the Committee for its rapid and bipartisan action.

Accelerating the introduction of new medicines allows the forces of private market competition to keep costs in check and increases the number lifesaving drugs becoming available to patients. Importantly, key provisions of the prescription drug, biosimilar, and generic drug user fee acts will help to eliminate the generic drug application backlog, increase resources to prevent future backlogs, and to streamline the review process and enhance FDA's expertise related to drug-device combination products, an area in which regulatory uncertainties and delays have previously deterred brand and generic manufacturers from investments. Additional opportunities to improve competition include finalizing FDA guidances related to biosimilars and enhancing incentives for generic manufacturers to enter the marketplace where there are no intellectual property or regulatory incentives preventing generic entry but, due to small patient population sizes, there are no brand or generic competitors. Increased competition from generics could be spurred by waiving user fees for eligible products, providing a transferable generic drug priority review voucher, and expediting review of such products and the inspection of their facilities.

Finally, the FDA can further spur efficiency in the market and free up scarce resources through elimination of certain outdated regulations. For example, regulations requiring biopharmaceutical companies to submit postmarketing reports in a format unique to the U.S. are inefficient and burdensome and provide no appreciable benefit compared to the format used globally. A more logical approach for submission of postmarketing reports would be to streamline the formats. Similarly, requiring biopharmaceutical companies to submit all promotional materials to the FDA at the time of dissemination—even if only minor, non- substantive changes have been made to previously submitted pieces—results in submission of thousands of pieces per company per year with no benefit to public health.

REFORMING THE 340B DRUG DISCOUNT PROGRAM

To protect the health care safety net it is critical to ensure that the underlying market works. The 340B program needs both Congressional and administrative updates to help prevent it from continuing to raise costs for consumers and the overall health care system. Stronger rules for hospitals participating in the program will help ensure the program targets the patients and true safety-net facilities it was intended to help. Specific reforms for hospitals participating in the program should include stricter 340B eligibility criteria, limits on contract pharmacy arrangements, requirements that patients see a benefit from the program, a tighter definition of patient eligibility, and limits on which hospital-owned physician practices can participate in 340B.

ASSURING ROBUST COMPETITION AND CONTINUING TO MODERNIZE THE FDA

Economists have reinforced the critical role of boosting competition to address drug cost and access issues. To increase competition:

- Key provisions of the prescription drug, biosimilar, and generic drug user fee acts will spur competition, including policies to eliminate the generic drug application backlog and increased resources to prevent future backlogs, expand FDA's expertise related to drug-device combination products, and reduce the regulatory uncertainty and streamline review of drug-device combination products. Biopharmaceutical companies have stated that current regulatory uncertainties and delays have deterred both generic and brand manufacturers from investments in these areas.
- Reducing the length and increasing the efficiency of drug development will increase competition on both price and clinical effects. Given that the cost of innovator drug development has doubled over the past decade, in part due to increasing FDA requirements, the Prescription Drug User Fee Act includes a range of provisions aimed at reducing uncertainty and creating efficiencies in the both the development and regulatory review of new medicines. Accelerating the introduction of new medicines would allow the forces of private market competition to keep costs in check and increase the number of lifesaving drugs becoming available to patients.
- Enhancing incentives for generic manufacturers to enter the marketplace in areas where there are no intellectual property or regulatory incentives preventing generic entry but due to small population sizes there are no brand or generic

competitors. Increased competition from generics could be spurred by waiving user fees for eligible products, providing a transferable generic drug priority review voucher, and expediting review of such products and the inspection of their facilities.

- Finalizing the various FDA guidances related to biosimilars is necessary to reduce regulatory uncertainties for biosimliar manufacturers and to accelerate the market entry of biosimilars. Biosimilar medicines are an important way to spur competition that will lead to more choices for patients and lower prices for patients and the health care system.

SUSTAINING INCENTIVES FOR INNOVATION IS CRITICAL TO SOLVING FUTURE HEALTH CARE CHALLENGES

Looking ahead, it is clear that medicines offer some of the clearest opportunities to address the challenge of growing health care costs as our population ages. For example, the number of Alzheimer's cases is projected to increase rapidly over the next decade as Baby Boomers begin to reach retirement age, resulting in an enormous human and economic cost. If we can achieve treatment advances that delay Alzheimer's by just five years beginning a decade from now, 2.5 million fewer Americans will be afflicted by the disease and we would avoid $367 billion annually by 2050 in costs for long-term care and similar services for persons with Alzheimer's.[61] Alzheimer's remains a major focus of biopharmaceutical research companies despite high risks; since 1998 there have been 123 unsuccessful attempts to develop a medicine for Alzheimer's, and just four approved medicines.[62] In just the last two years, several promising new therapies failed in mid-and late-stage trials, resulting in the loss of billions of dollars of human, political, and monetary capital.[63]

As with Alzheimer's disease, there is a significant unmet medical need for patients with rare diseases which collectively affect 30 million Americans. But only 5% of these diseases have available treatment options.[64] Given the many diseases where there is significant unmet need, maintaining incentives for the continued development of new medicines will be crucial in addressing the most costly and challenging diseases of our time.

---

[61] Alzheimer's Association. "Changing the Trajectory of Alzheimer's Disease: How a Treatment by 2025 Saves Lives and Dollars." https://www.alz.org/documents_custom/trajectory.pdf

[62] PhRMA. *Researching Alzheimer's Medicines: Setbacks and Stepping Stones.* Summer 2015. Available at: http://phrma.org/sites/default/files/pdf/alzheimers-setbacks-and-stepping-stones.pdf

[63] Ogg JC. The List of Failed Alzheimer's Drug Treatments Keeps Growing. 24/7 Wall Street. September 26, 2017. http://247wallst.com/healthcare-business/2017/09/26/the-list-of-failed-alzheimers-drug-treatments-keeps-growing/

[64] Pharmaceutical Research and Manufacturers of America (PhRMA). Spurring Innovation in Rare Diseases: 2017 update. http://phrma-docs.phrma.org/files/dmfile/Rare-Disease-Udpate_FINAL.pdf.

Yet there is evidence that rising costs in drug development, combined with an increasingly competitive market, have resulted in more uncertainty and lower average returns in recent years. Analysis by a Massachusetts Institute of Technology economist and the IMS Institute finds that increasing market competition has eroded much of the economic profitability of newly launched brand medicines, such that on average financial returns for medicines launched between 2005 and 2009 were insufficient to recoup average R&D and operating costs.[65]

Even drugs that succeed at launch may quickly be supplanted as other new brand competitors enter the market, as occurred with first generation HCV medicines. For example, despite initial success, two protease inhibitors launched in 2011—seen at the time as substantial advances in treatment for HCV—found that they were supplanted by more effective treatments following the introduction of the next generation of medicines in 2013. Thus, despite substantial investment and many years of research and development, competition from newer brands led these medicines to be withdrawn from the market within two years.[66] This underscores the extraordinary risk biopharmaceutical companies confront to bring new treatments to market.

SUMMARY STATEMENT OF LORI M. REILLY

Innovative medicines represent significant scientific advancements that transform the treatment and the downstream healthcare costs of complex and costly diseases. Despite the unparalleled savings and value medicines generate for the health care system, spending on medicines is often inaccurately portrayed as growing rapidly and driving increases in overall health care spending. Discussions about the cost of medicines almost always focus on list prices, which provide a misleading view of actual spending trends because they do not factor in the substantial rebates and discounts that PBMs and health plans negotiate with biopharmaceutical companies or the statutory rebates, discounts, and fees companies are required to provide to government programs. Accounting for these rebates and discounts, net spending on medicines is growing at the slowestrate in years.

A complex distribution system shapes the prices that patients, plan sponsors, and the government pay for medicines. This system has evolved significantly in recent years, and an increasing share of the discounts and rebates negotiated between bio-pharmaceutical companies and payers are retained by middlemen along the pharmaceutical supply chain. Savings generated from price negotiations aren't always passed along directly to patients,

[65] Berndt ER, Nass D, Kleinrock M, Aitken M. Decline in Economic Returns from New Drugs Raises Questions About Sustaining Innovations. *Health Affairs*. 2015; 34(2): 245-252.

[66] Loftus P. Merck Will No Longer Sell its Victrelis Hepatitis C Drug in the US. *Wall Street Journal*, Jan 21, 2015, http://blogs.wsj.com/pharmalot/2015/01/21/merck-will-no-longer-sell-its-victrelis-hepatitis-c-drug-in-the-u-s/

who are increasingly exposed to high out-of-pocket costs for medicines because of the growing use of high deductibles and coinsurance rather than fixed dollar copays.

Unlike for care received at an in-network hospital or physician's office, cost-sharing for prescriptions filled in the deductible or with coinsurance is based on the list price, rather than a price that is reflective of the rebates and discounts negotiated by payers. When a patient's cost sharing is based on a price that does not reflect their health plan's actual costs, that patient can end paying hundreds-or even thousands-more annually for a medicine than their insurer. More than half of patients' out-of-pocket spending for brand medicines is based on the list price, even though their insurers may be receiving a steep discount.

Within the framework of the competitive U.S. health care market, there are several steps that could improve patients' access to medicines, increase affordability for purchasers and patients, and support continued progress for patients. These include encouraging payers to share negotiated savings with patients at the pharmacy counter; reforming outdated regulations hindering the adoption of value-based payment arrangements, reforming the 340B drug discount program to better serve the purpose for which it was created; and continuing to modernize the FDA and ensure robust generic and biosimilar competition.

The CHAIRMAN. Thank you, Ms. Reilly.

Mr. Davis, welcome.

STATEMENT OF CHESTER "CHIP" DAVIS, JR.

Mr. DAVIS. Thank you, Chairman Alexander, Ranking Member Murray, and Members of the Committee. I very much appreciate the invitation to testify here today.

The Association for Accessible Medicines is the Nation's leading trade association for manufacturers of FDA-approved generic prescription drugs. Our members actually manufacture more than 90 percent of all the generic pharmaceuticals dispensed in the United States, providing tens of thousands of jobs in over 150 facilities throughout the country, and manufacture more than 61 billion doses of medication every year here in the United States.

AAM's core mission is to improve the lives of patients by advancing timely access to affordable generic and biosimilar medications.

On behalf of our members, let me begin by thanking the Committee for convening today's hearing to examine the critical challenge of rising drug prices and for your leadership in reauthorizing all the User Fee Programs earlier this year, most particularly for our interest, the Generic and Biosimilar User Fee Programs.

Generic medicines currently represent, as the Chairman said, almost 90 percent—actually 89 percent—of all prescriptions dispensed in the U.S. But, importantly, we account for only 26 percent of all expenditures on prescription drugs, saving patients and payers nearly $5 billion every week. Last year, use of generic medicines saved $253 billion to the U.S. healthcare system. That translates into meaningful patient access.

Generics actually operate currently in a deflationary market, not an inflationary market, and that is an important context. Consider that in the past 12 months, prescriptions of brands have gone down by 7 percent while their revenue has increased slightly. By contrast, generic prescriptions have actually gone up. They're up 2 percent year over year, while revenue has declined by 13 percent.

It is easy to recognize the significant difference between generic and brand name prescription drugs when it comes to prices that we often see at the pharmacy counter. The dramatic difference, however, in how brand and generic drug markets operate is not as widely understood.

When generics enter to provide competition to a brand monopoly, payers typically shift away from the rebate model of reimbursement that you often hear about and rely on distribution channels to effectively lower the price of medicine. Generics, therefore, compete for sales, and because the products are identical, commonly, the only leverage the generic manufacturers have is their ability to lower price and guarantee volume. This creates fierce competition in the marketplace amongst our members, which, in turn, causes prices to decline.

The reality is that the markets for brands and generics are very different, monopolized versus commoditized, and these differences create vastly different incentives for all the stakeholders in the supply chain. This reality was most recently examined and affirmed through a report issued by the University of Southern California Center for Health Policy and Economics entitled "The Flow of Money Through the Pharmaceutical Distribution System." Among the findings was that supply chain stakeholders capture significantly more revenue spent on generics than they do on brands. In fact, for every $100 spent on dispensing a generic medicine in this country, approximately $65 goes to the distribution and reimbursement of those products by members of the supply chain.

In today's market, consolidation in the wholesaler and distributor market and arrangements between pharmacy chains and distributors have left generic manufacturers with a very small number of very large-scale purchasers. Essentially, three purchasers today account for 90 percent of all sales from all generic manufacturers.

Ultimately, a market that has three large-scale purchasers is going to see significant compression and consolidation on the supply side, which is our side. Fewer generic manufacturers running the risk of marketing smaller portfolios can easily translate into less competition, not more, while simultaneously increasing the risk of drug shortages, a scenario none of us want to see happen.

As this Committee has identified and reflected in the title of this hearing, how do these realities affect what patients pay, and what does it mean for them moving forward?

So we all know 30 years ago, Hatch-Waxman created a remarkably strong system designed to balance innovation and access. But that system can only function if there is robust competition amongst buyers and sellers, and that system can only work if generic companies can get the drug samples they need to do the pharmacovigilance and start the FDA application and approval process, which this Committee has spearheaded efforts to accelerate and reform. That system only works when generic medicines have the ability to enter the market when patents and other IP protections are actually supposed to expire, and, ultimately, that system works when public policy doesn't favor one side of the access and innovation equation at the expense of the other.

In closing, we all know that something must be done about prescription drug prices. Given the fact that the new FDA Commissioner, Dr. Scott Gottlieb, has characterized drug cost as a public health concern, AAM respectfully submits that Congress has the opportunity to consider policies that will enhance generic and biosimilar competition. We have provided those in our written testimony, and I look forward to answering your questions as we move forward.

Thank you.

[The prepared statement of Mr. Davis follows:]

Prepared Statement of Chester "Chip" Davis, Jr.

Chairman Alexander, Ranking Member Murray and Members of the Committee,

Thank you for the invitation to testify today. I am Chip Davis, President and CEO of the Association for Accessible Medicines (AAM). AAM is the nation's leading trade association for manufacturers and distributors of FDA-approved generic and biosimilar prescription medicines. Our members provide more than 36,700 jobs at nearly 150 facilities, and manufacture more than 61 billion doses in the United States every year. AAM's core mission is to improve the lives of patients by advancing timely access to affordable generic and biosimilar medications.

I commend you for convening today's hearing to examine the critical challenge of high and rising drug prices.

Generic medicines represent greater than 89% of all prescriptions dispensed in the U.S., but only 26% of expenditures on prescription drugs, saving patients and payers nearly $5 billion every week.[67] Our industry is proud to be able to deliver these savings to the healthcare system.

It is sobering to consider what America's patients would face if there were no FDA-approved generic or biosimilar medicines to provide reliable access to affordable

[67] $253 billion total savings in 2016, equivalent to approximately $5 billion every week. AAM 2017 Generic Drug Access & Savings in the U.S., http://accessiblemeds.org/sites/ default/files/2017-07/2017-AAM-Access-Savings-Report-2017- web2.pdf.

treatments. Generics don't just deliver the most medicine at the lowest cost and greatest savings; generics cushion the significant impact dealt to patients and the healthcare system by high brand name drug prices every day.

Put another way, the availability of low-cost generics offsets the impact of high brand drug prices. Whereas prices for FDA-approved generic medicines are currently declining by over 7% year-over-year, prices for brand drugs, especially biologics and specialty medicines, are increasing at an unsustainable rate. From 2007 to 2016, brand specialty medicines grew to occupy almost 43% of spending. These products treat less than 3% of the population, and can often cost patients thousands of dollars per treatment.

To illustrate this fact, consider that in the past twelve months, prescriptions of brand drugs have decreased by 7%, but their revenue has climbed by 5%. This is a direct result of price increases. By contrast, generic prescriptions increased by 2%, but revenue declined by 13%.[68]

Consider the costs that patients would face in the absence of these levels of generic competition. Last year, use of generic medicines saved $253 billion. It has produced $1.67 trillion in savings over the last ten years. This has produced meaningful and sustained patient access. Without generic medicines, spending on cholesterol drugs would be more than 3.5 times higher, diabetes drugs almost 3 times higher, and spending on breast cancer drugs 8 times higher.[69]

However, the sustainability of a competitive generic market and the availability of generic medicines for patients, uninterrupted by shortages, is in jeopardy. In 1984, Congress enacted the Hatch-Waxman Act which represents a model of successful, bipartisan public policy. Over its more than thirty-year history, the Act has produced a thriving and constantly-changing marketplace by balancing innovation in drug development and accelerating the availability of lower cost generic alternatives. This has important effects on the public health, allowing patients to live longer, healthier lives.

This balance is now threatened by three factors:

- changing and increasingly challenging market and reimbursement frameworks,
- the abuse of laws and regulations by bad actors, and
- a failure of policy to account for the unique challenges facing generic and biosimilar medicines.

In fact, while brand drug innovation has benefited from a series of subsequent laws establishing incentives and development tools, the generic and biosimilar marketplace and patient access has not received an equivalent level of attention. That neglect,

---

68 Morgan Stanley: Major Pharma Rx Chart/North America, September 2017. https:// ny.matrix.ms.com/eqr/ article/webapp/89cddeb4-96d6-11e7-8a10-ce4c0a51e87f?t=1506097268%3A3184%3A22035%3Avmias1106666&m=1&ch=autob#

69 AAM 2017 Generic Drug Access & Savings in the U.S., http://accessiblemeds.org/ sites/default/files/2017-07/2017-AAM-Access-Savings-Report-2017-web2.pdf.

combined with current market and anticompetitive realities, reinforces why this hearing – and the FDA's recent public hearing and the FTC's upcoming public meeting on the same issue – are so important.

Congress must act to support generic and biosimilar competition and supply to ensure continued access for patients. It can do so by:

1. Repealing the misguided Medicaid penalty on generic drugs,
2. Preventing brand abuses designed to block generic and biosimilar competition by passing the bipartisan CREATES Act, and
3. Ensuring that biosimilar medicines have a level and competitive playing field in Medicare.

GENERIC DRUG MARKETS ARE FUNDAMENTALLY DIFFERENT THAN BRANDS

First, it is important to provide context about the generic marketplace. Not only is the FDA approval process different for generics and brand name drugs, but their respective markets and the path by which they reach patients diverge significantly, with important policy implications.

The 1984 Drug Price Competition and Patent Term Restoration Act, commonly referred to as the "Hatch-Waxman" Act, created an abbreviated pathway for generic drugs. This allows manufacturers to rely upon the existing clinical data of the brand product and demonstrate to FDA that their product is the same as the reference product.

Hatch-Waxman also provided numerous lucrative incentives for brand name drug companies, including extensions of patent terms, regulatory exclusivities that guarantee market monopolies regardless of the intellectual property status, and a clear litigation pathway for asserting intellectual property claims against generic manufacturers.

DIFFERENCES IN SUPPLY CHAIN

The balance created by Hatch-Waxman also created a new and different market for generic drugs – separate from brand drugs – that has supported growth in generic utilization and its attendant savings for patients. Although brand manufacturers often criticize pharmacy benefit managers (PBMs) and health plan formulary and rebate practices, the supply chain and pricing models they criticize do not represent the vast majority of prescription drugs distributed in this country. The 89% of prescriptions filled by generic medicines are subject to a different set of economic incentives and arrangements – the result of multiple manufacturers marketing identical products and competing exclusively on price, in a commodity-style market.

When brand manufacturers leverage the pricing power granted by their patents and regulatory exclusivities, PBMs, distributors, and payors rely on formulary management and rebating agreements to control costs.

However, upon generic entry, payors typically shift away from rebate models of reimbursement and rely on distribution channels to effectively lower the price of the medicine. Rather than providing rebates to lower the cost, generic manufacturers must compete for sales to wholesalers. Because the products are virtually identical, the primary leverage manufacturers have is their ability to lower the price and provide the necessary volume. With over 200 generic manufacturers recognized by FDA, competition is fierce and prices decline rapidly. The wholesalers, often in collaborative purchasing agreements with pharmacies across the country, then distribute generic medicines to various retail pharmacies. Generic manufacturers may have to compete even further by negotiating separate payments to pharmacies to stock their product.

The different business model leads to a different type of business planning by generic and biosimilar manufacturers. As part of this, the decisions by which generic and biosimilar manufacturers select which products to develop can take into account multiple variables. Considerations include the complexity in reverse engineering the original product, the state of the intellectual property claimed by the brand manufacturer over the product, the size of the patient population served, the number of likely competitors for that product, the product development and manufacturing capabilities and costs.

Generic drug reimbursement is also different. Rather than relying on per-transaction rebates, PBMs and insurers typically establish a "Maximum Allowable Cost" (MAC) list that sets a specific reimbursement rate for the product, regardless of the generic product cost to the pharmacy. These MAC lists create additional incentives for pharmacies to maximize their dispensing margins by finding the lowest cost source for generic products.

The result is a business model that differs significantly from the brand business model. While brand companies typically market a small number of high margin products, many generic manufacturers market hundreds of products with varying levels of profitability or loss.

Supply Chain Pressures on Generics

These differences in the generic and brand marketplaces create vastly different incentives for the various manufacturers, wholesalers, distributors, pharmacy benefit managers (PBMs), insurers, and retail pharmacies that make up the supply chain. To put it simply, virtually all other actors in the supply chain enjoy significant financial benefits from the manufacture of generic medicines.

This phenomenon was most recently examined by a group of researchers at the USC Leonard D. Schaeffer Center for Health Policy & Economics. That analysis, "The Flow of Money Through the Pharmaceutical Distribution System," identified two items relevant to today's hearing:

- First, for every sale of a brand name drug to a patient, the brand manufacturer captures approximately 76% of that revenue. Comparatively, generic manufacturers keep only half of that percentage. Moreover, generic manufacturers cannot rely on capturing the total volume within the market as the brands do, and therefore individual generic manufacturers are forced to rely on much smaller revenue streams. To put it simply, brand drugs capture a higher percentage of the spend of a higher value market.
- Second, the supply chain captures significantly more of the revenue spent on generic medicines than on brand name drugs. For every $100 spent on dispensing generic medicines in this country, approximately $65 goes to the distribution and reimbursement of those products by the members of the supply chain. PBMs make nearly three times as much on generics as they do on brands. Wholesalers make about eight times more. Pharmacies make over 10 times more for every $100 on generics than brands.[70]

While the analysis demonstrates a series of strong incentives to drive patients to generic medicines, supply chain consolidation may jeopardize that success.

Compared to the fragmented generic drug market, consolidation in the wholesale market and contractual arrangements between pharmacy chains and the wholesalers have left generic manufacturers with only a small number of purchasers. The result is a market where three purchasers account for over 90% of all wholesale revenue.[71]

As these purchasers move more and more towards single-source contracts for generic drugs, it creates a dynamic where it is possible that no more than three generic manufacturers may be able to successfully market any given product. This dynamic risks future competitive success in the generic market as generic drug manufacturers may be forced to maximize economies of scale and consolidate themselves.

[70] Sood, et al., "The Flow of Money Through the Pharmaceutical Distribution System." June 2017. http:// healthpolicy.usc.edu/ documents/ USC%20Schaeffer_Flow%20of%20Money_2017.pdf

[71] Fein, Adam J. Fein. The 2016-2017 Economic Report on Pharmaceutical Wholesalers and Specialty Distributors, September 2016.

COST PRESSURES FOR PATIENTS

Patients thrive because of generic medicines, both in terms of health outcomes and financial savings. For insured patients, over 90% of generic prescriptions are filled for $20 or less out-of-pocket. That is in comparison to just 39% for brands at that price.[72]

Data shows that patients are far less likely to fill a prescription for a high-priced brand drug. In fact, brand name drugs make up 20% of approved claims but account for 40% of all abandoned claims for new patients. Moreover, new patient abandonment rates for generics are three times lower than for branded products.[73] Patient abandonment has a serious effect on patient health – leading to hospitalizations, deaths and extensive health system costs.

This is not to say that the market functions perfectly in providing patients with the lowest cost possible. Many generic medicines are subject to significant markups after they leave the generic manufacturer. As an example, amoxicillin/potassium clavulanate, commonly referred by its branded name Augmentin and used for the treatment of infections, is sold by the generic manufacturer for pennies per pill. However, by the time a patient picks it up at the pharmacy counter, it may have a cash price as high as $60 for 20 pills, or $20 for a fill for patients with commercial insurance.[74]

It is clear the significant benefits for patients of reliable access to affordable generic medicines are at risk. Notwithstanding the economic principle that more suppliers of a good or service creates lower prices for consumers, it is unclear that the new imbalance between 200 generic competitors and a handful of purchasers is sustainable. Some industry analysts have already begun to forecast consolidation among generic manufacturers.

An unfortunate yet foreseeable consequence of fewer generic manufacturers is a significantly increased risk of drug shortages. Evidence suggests that generic drugs are particularly susceptible to drug shortages, potentially related to existing market incentives as well as low reimbursement.[75] Such shortages have a serious effect on patient care. Responding to a series of drug shortages in 2011, Dr. Scott Gottlieb testified before Congress that many such shortages were a direct result of low reimbursement for older, low margin products and that "many hospitals are being forced to ration key medicines and patients to sit on waiting lists for vital drugs."[76]

---

[72] AAM 2017 Generic Drug Access & Savings in the U.S., http://accessiblemeds.org/sites/ default/files/2017-07/2017-AAM-Access-Savings-Report-2017-web2.pdf.

[73] Id.

[74] Data on manufacturer sales from CMS Average Manufacturer Price (AMP) data. Typical pharmacy prices from GoodRx.com.

[75] Stromberg, C. (May 2014). Drug Shortages, Pricing, and Regulatory Activity. National Bureau of Economics Working Paper. http://www.nber.org/chapters/c13102.pdf

[76] Gottlieb, Scott. "Drug Shortages: Why they happen and what they mean" Testimony before the Senate Finance Committee. December 2011. https://www.finance.senate.gov/imo/ media/ doc/Gottlieb%20Testimony1.pdf

THE IMPORTANCE OF RECOGNIZING DIFFERENCES IN POLICYMAKING

It is critical that policymakers take steps to ensure the continued supply of affordable FDA-approved generic medicines. Failure to do so threatens a stable supply of generic medicines.

Congress recently created a new inflation-based penalty in the Medicaid program for generics as part of the Bipartisan Budget Act of 2015.The legislation inappropriately applied a tool crafted for the brand drug market to generic markets, essentially conflating what transpires in a monopolized market with what occurs in a commoditized market with multiple competitors. Under the legislation, generic manufacturers are now subject to additional rebates for products even in the absence of changes in the actual price of the product. This is a direct result of a flawed application of a brand drug scheme that fails to recognize the significant volatility in generic prices.

As a result, manufacturers of affordable generic medicines are now paying millions of dollars in "penalties" on products that have not been subject to a price increase. In many instances, changes in customer mix from one quarter to another have triggered penalties solely due to purchasers getting lower discounts on smaller volume orders – a normal occurrence in a competitive market. These changes do not necessarily reflect any new price being set by the manufacturer, but may merely reflect new purchasing patterns.

These unpredictable, onerous penalties on often low-margin medicines creates significant risk for manufacturers that would consider entering these markets, and makes it more challenging for manufacturers to continue participating in those markets. A recent analysis concluded that the penalty would "increase uncertainty, reduce revenues, encourage manufacturers to exit the market, and discourage the entry of new manufacturers. The predictable effect of discouraging entry into competitive markets is that product availability will be hampered: shortages will be more likely, and the market forces that lead prices to fall will be dampened."[77] Ironically, the analysis also concluded that the penalty "will not only have little effect on generic prices, but it will also have the unanticipated and unintended consequence of increasing the likelihood of shortages for generic medicines."[78]

Accordingly, we urge Congress to repeal this penalty.

---

[77] Manning and Selck, "Penalizing Generic Drugs with the CPI Rebate will Reduce Competition and Increase the Likelihood of Drug Shortages," September 2017. https:// www.accessiblemeds.org/sites/default/files/2017-09/Bates-White-White-Paper-Report-CPI-Penalty-09-12-2017.pdf

[78] Id.

Barriers to Entry

AAM and its members strongly support innovation. The generic and biosimilar marketplaces rely on the existence of a vibrant brand medicine industry. Fortunately, innovation continues to flourish. FDA has already approved more new molecular entities this year than it did in all of 2016. This is good news for all of us.

But the balance between innovation and access requires a clear opportunity for FDA-approved generic or biosimilar entry. Without that competition, there can be no savings for patients or taxpayers. Unfortunately, many brand medicine companies have responded to the threat of competition by deploying new and controversial ways to extend their high monopoly prices.

Challenges to Intellectual Property Law

Recently, one company went so far as to pay a Native American tribe to rent its tribal sovereign immunity by taking ownership of certain brand name drug patents facing a challenge. Allergan, Plc (Allergan), a Dublin, Ireland-based drug company, transferred the patent rights to its blockbuster drug Restasis® to the St. Regis Mohawk tribe in a blatant effort to shield those patents from an administrative review process established by Congress in 2011 and block generic competition.

The deal stands to be a profitable one for Allergan. Restasis® generated $1.4 billion in 2016 sales.[79] For less than 0.1% of the drug's annual sales, Allergan's deal could delay patient access to affordable generic drugs for six more years. This is a supply chain failure that Congress should prevent.

According to press reports, Allergan provided an initial payment of $13.75 million to the St. Regis Mohawk Tribe and $15 million in annual licensing fees. Every day Allergan delays competition, the company takes in over $4 million in revenue due to the lack of generic competition. Allergan will recoup this licensing fee in around four days.

Allergan's transfer of its patents to the St. Regis Mohawk Tribe is an end-run around the legal process established by Congress to challenge questionable patents. If Congress wants to ensure that Americans have access to affordable prescription drugs, it must address schemes like Allergan's to delay generic competition by renting sovereign immunity. The action by Allergan to ensure that patients and payors do not benefit from timely generic competition to Restasis® is an alarming example of the steps that brand name drug companies will take to put profits above the public interest. But it is by no means the only such example. Congress should outlaw these practices and strengthen the IPR system.

---

[79] Annual Report (Form 10-K), at 59 (February 2017) (link)

BARRIERS TO GENERIC AND BIOSIMILAR DEVELOPMENT

As this Committee is aware, many generic and biosimilar manufacturers face significant challenges obtaining the samples needed for generic or biosimilar development. This is a result of the misuse of systems designed to ensure the safety of medicines by certain brand drug companies focused on delaying or prevent competition. Such delays created by misuse, abuse or regulatory failure deserve Congressional attention. In short, if generic and biosimilar development is frustrated, they will never enter the supply chain.

FDA Commissioner Gottlieb has highlighted the abuse of FDA-mandated restricted distribution systems and restricted distribution systems that brand companies create on their own, without any mandate from FDA, to delay or completely prevent generic competition.

This occurs when brand companies, using a Risk Evaluation and Mitigation System (REMS) or their own voluntary "safety" program as an excuse, refuse to sell samples of their products to generic and biosimilar companies so that they can conduct the requisite bioequivalence and other testing. AAM members that have sought to purchase brand products from wholesalers in the supply chain are often informed that the wholesalers' contracts prohibit the sale of the brand product for generic studies. To date, FDA has received more than 150 complaints of specific challenges to obtaining samples.

These abusive practices are directly counter to Congressional intent reflected in both Hatch-Waxman, which seeks to create generic competition as soon as brand monopoly protection has expired, and the Food and Drug Administration Amendments Act, which specifically prohibited the use of REMS to delay generic competition.

FDA has taken steps to limit these kinds of abuses. In 2014, FDA released a draft guidance that attempted to assist prospective generic and biosimilar applicants in their efforts to acquire the samples necessary to conduct bioequivalence testing. Under the guidance, FDA reviews bioequivalence protocols. Following its review and identification of any required changes, FDA sends a letter to the brand sponsor indicating that the proposed testing contains safety protections that provide the same level of patient-protection as those in the applicable brand's safety protocol and that FDA will not consider it a violation of the law for the brand sponsor to provide samples to the designated potential generic or biosimilar applicant. Although well-intentioned, the draft guidance has failed to solve the problem and patients wait in vain for FDA-approved generic and biosimilar versions of these medicines.

Generic applicants are also challenged by brand companies' refusal to negotiate in good faith the creation and implementation of a single-shared REMS system (SSRS). Under current law, if a brand drug is subject to a REMS that contains Elements To Assure Safe Use (ETASU), generic versions cannot be approved unless they are subject to a SSRS to implement the ETASU elements. Moreover, the Federal Food Drug and

Cosmetic Act provides that a generic drug must utilize a shared system along with the brand drug unless FDA waives this requirement for one of the reasons set forth in the statute. In other words, the brand and generic must agree on how to implement the existing safety protocol jointly, unless FDA says otherwise.

The creation of a shared system should be relatively straightforward and simple—generic applicants merely join the existing safety system. Fundamentally, this is the business of generic manufacturers: taking a sole-source product and making it a multi-source product. However, brand companies regularly use a variety of tactics to systematically delay and extend the brand/generic negotiations. This refusal to engage in good faith negotiations can delay the approval of the generic product and force consumers to pay more to fill their prescriptions.

This abuse injures competition. Commissioner Gottlieb recently testified that:

> brand companies often have an incentive to refuse to agree to a single, shared system REMS. By prolonging the negotiations over a single, shared system REMS, they further delay generic drug approval and competition. We see prolonged negotiations and inability to agree on the terms of a single, shared system REMS regularly.[80]

AAM applauds Commissioner Gottlieb's leadership to develop a "Drug Competition Action Plan" to address regulatory issues that are impeding competition, including abuse of restricted distribution and REMS systems. However, AAM is concerned that FDA's enforcement authorities as provided in FDAAA will not be adequate to fully stem the brand abuses that have become so widespread in recent years. For instance, the civil monetary penalties available under FDA's enforcement authority pale in comparison to the revenue available by impeding generic entry. Center for Drug Evaluation and Research (CDER) Director Dr. Janet Woodcock noted that "fines and everything might simply be considered a cost of doing business because there's so much at stake in delaying generic competition."[81] Also, FDA's authority to address the brand abuses using voluntarily imposed restricted distribution system are highly limited.

Brand manufacturers who have recognized the incentives created by REMS-related delays have developed novel distribution schemes that mimic these programs even when the FDA has not recognized any inherent safety risk with the handling or use of the medicine. According to a recent study,[82] 74 drugs are subject to restricted access programs (i.e., drugs that are either subject to REMS or self-imposed restricted distribution programs) with total sales of $22.7 billion in 2016. Of these, 41 drugs are

---

80 Gottlieb, Scott. "Antitrust Concerns and The FDA Approval Process," Testimony before the House Committee on the Judiciary, Subcommittee on Regulatory Reform, Commercial and Antitrust Law, July 2017. https://www.fda.gov/NewsEvents/Testimony/ucm568869.htm

81 Testimony of Dr. Janet Woodcock at "Generic Drug User Fee Amendments: Accelerating Patient Access to Generic Drugs." Senate Committee on Health, Education, Labor and Pensions, January 2016.

82 Alex Brill, REMS and Restricted Distribution Programs: An Estimate of the Market (June 2017), available at http://www.gphaonline.org/media/cms/ Alex_Brill_REMS_Study_June_2017.pdf.

restricted by REMS programs, with $11.5 billion in sales in 2016. The remaining 33 drugs are restricted by the brands in a voluntarily imposed non-REMS program, with $11.2 billion in sales in 2016. And a 2014 study concluded that REMS abuse costs the U.S. healthcare system $5.4 billion annually.[83] Consumers bear $960 million of that cost while Medicare and Medicaid incur $1.8 billion; private insurers bear the remaining $2.4 billion.[84] This estimate is conservative "and should not be construed as the entirety of the lost savings from REMS misuse, either currently or going forward."[85]. AAM and its members are committed to ensuring that all Americans have access to safe, effective and affordable medicines and believe that FDA's REMS programs can and do serve a compelling public good – namely, the safe distribution and use of certain pharmaceuticals that have a higher risk profile. We do not support any policies that would jeopardize patient safety. Any suggestion to the contrary is simply an effort to distract us from the real issue we need to focus on: addressing the use of REMS or non-FDA mandated restrictions on drug supply that are designed to block lower cost generics and biosimilars from coming to market. By refusing to sell their product for research purposes, or restricting its sale to a named patient, brand manufacturers can distort the supply chain to limit competition.

To address this problem once and for all, Congress must pass the CREATES Act, bipartisan legislation introduced by Senators Leahy, Grassley, Klobuchar and Lee, to prevent the misuse of REMS and restricted distribution schemes to delay generic drug competition.

The cost of failure is significant, and will only encourage anti-competitive practices to grow. In the absence of Congressional action, AAM members today must consider the difficulty involved in obtaining branded drugs when determining which generic development programs to pursue. Where access to brand drugs is subject to restricted access programs, some AAM members have determined that generic development was not feasible and decided against initiating these development programs.

This means that patients and taxpayers lose out on opportunities for affordable access to life-saving medicines and our nation's health care system leaves savings on the table.

BIOSIMILAR MEDICINES ARE CRITICAL TO FUTURE SAVINGS

Nowhere is the need for lower-priced alternatives, and the challenges facing them, more real than among high-priced biologic medicines. Biologics, many of which are specialty medicines, are the most rapidly growing segment of increasing brand-name

---

83 Alex Brill, *Lost Prescription Drug Savings from Use of REMS Programs to Delay Generic Market Entry*, at 5 (2014), available at http://www.gphaonline.org/media/cms/ REMS_Studyfinal_July2014.pdf.

84 *Id.*

85 *Id.*

prescription drug costs in the United States, with more than $100 billion in annual spending. And the role of biologic drugs in the health care system is expanding — while only 2 percent of America's patients use biologics, they account for about 40 percent of prescription drug spending in the United States.[86]

These products are often life-saving therapies for serious illnesses, but they come at steep expense to patients, taxpayers and insurers. Many biologics cost tens of thousands of dollars per year per patient — some more than $200,000.

To help bring down prices for patients, Congress designed and approved the Biologics Price Competition and Innovation Act (BPCIA) in 2010 – creating an abbreviated approval pathway for biological products that are demonstrated to be "highly similar" (biosimilar) to or "interchangeable" with an FDA-approved biological product. The BPCIA also gave brand biologic drug manufacturers a 12- year market exclusivity period for their products to ensure a return on investment for new medicines. This period is longer than anywhere else in the world that has a similar abbreviated pathway for biosimilars.

Biosimilar medicines represent a key step forward in reducing high drug prices. They are safe, effective and affordable versions of costly brand biologics. By the year 2025, over 70% of drug approvals are expected to be biological products.[87] Experts estimate that FDA-approved biosimilars could save between $44 billion and $250 billion over the next 10 years.[88] In doing so, they will mean greater access to lifesaving cures for 1.2 million U.S. patients, according to a new analysis. Women, lower income, and elderly patients would particularly benefit from access to biosimilar medicines.

Today, there are 38 biosimilars approved for use in the European Union, but only 7 in the United States. However, more than 66 biosimilar programs are under FDA review for development of 20 different biologic products. The ability of biosimilars to fulfill their potential is threatened by market abuses and policy challenges.

ANTICOMPETITIVE THREATS TO BIOSIMILAR AVAILABILITY

As discussed above, while the abuse of restricted distribution programs continues to impede generic development, the problem of access to samples is likely to be even more acute for biosimilar development. Biosimilars are more complex and difficult to develop than traditional generic drugs. Their development requires multiple lots of the brand product produced over time. If access to the variability that is inherent in brand lot development of biologics is denied, the development of the biosimilar will be greatly delayed and patients will be held hostage to higher prices and fewer options. Plus, unlike

[86] Medicine Use and Spending in the U.S.: A Review of 2016 and Outlook to 2021, April 2017.
[87] U.S. Pharmacist, "Biosimilars: Current Approvals and Pipeline Agents," October 2016 (link).
[88] AAM, "Generic Drug Access & Savings in the U.S.," June 2017 (link).

with small molecule generic drugs, the development of biosimilars is more likely to involve clinical trials requiring even more samples of the reference product. Restricted access to samples at any point during the clinical trial could cause a study to fail. This further highlights the importance of Congressional action on the CREATES Act.

And it now appears that brand manufacturers of biologic drugs are misusing their negotiating leverage to insist on contract terms that effectively block use of biosimilar alternatives by physicians. In a recent lawsuit, one branded company has alleged that another company that manufactures Remicade has misused its negotiating power to force PBMs and purchasers to block access to a biosimilar product. Such actions could threaten the ability of biosimilars to deliver on the promise of savings for patients.

Finally, it is critical to reiterate that biosimilars are just as safe and effective as their reference product. While we understand that physicians must remain directly involved in their patients' treatment, it is also important to recognize that some have sought to create uncertainty around the efficacy and pharmacovigilance standards of biosimilars in comparison to their reference products. These messages are in direct contradiction with the standards established in the BPCIA, and enforced by the FDA. Differentiation between biosimilars and their reference products risks undermining the important provider education that is already being done by FDA. It is also directly in contradiction to the medical evidence found in Europe and other advanced countries that have more experience with biosimilars, and have seen no measurable clinical differences between biosimilars and their reference products.

POLICY BARRIER TO BIOSIMILAR ADOPTION

Biosimilars present a significant opportunity for patient and program savings in the Medicare Part D program. However current law creates barriers to biosimilar access for patients in Part D, who may be forced onto higher priced biologics.

Because of the structure of Medicare Part D, the 50% discount required of brand biologics is counted towards a patient's out of pocket costs – but competing biosimilars are barred from providing such a discount. This creates a perverse incentive for health plans and patients to use a higher-priced brand biologic – moving patients through the coverage gap and into catastrophic coverage faster and with lower out-of-pocket costs compared to a lower-cost biosimilar.

This approach creates substantial barriers for biosimilar manufacturers, as it may be effectively impossible to ever offer sufficient discounts to be included on Part D formularies. The resulting imbalance severely undermines the market potential for biosimilar competition. Ultimately, patients, payers, and Medicare all pay more for brand biologics than they would if the Coverage Gap Discount program were amended to include biosimilars.

Congress should amend the Part D coverage gap discount program to classify biosimilars as "applicable drugs" in the Coverage Gap Discount Program. This change would allow biosimilar manufacturers to pay the 50 percent discounts paid by their brand competitors, and participate on a level playing field to compete for placement on the Part D plan's formulary. It would reduce both patient out-of-pocket costs and save at least $1 billion over the next ten years for the Medicare Part D program.

Additionally, in Part B CMS has chosen to create a coding and reimbursement structure that deeply disincentivizes development of biosimilars. Under current CMS policy, all biosimilars are grouped into an average reimbursement rate, separate from their reference brand product. This allows the brand to maintain control over its reimbursement rate, and allows the company to provide physicians with consistent reimbursement, free from price competition. Meanwhile, the biosimilar products would be forced to compete on price with one-another, despite only ever being compared to the reference product rather than each other.

This policy could significantly limit biosimilar adoption in outpatient settings, which would create a significant barrier to entry for any potential biosimilar competitors. To better incentivize competition in settings reimbursed by Part B, CMS should change this policy to grant individual codes and payment rates to non-interchangeable biosimilars. This would create a market much more conducive to price competition.

Conclusion

AAM and its members commend the Committee for holding today's hearing addressing the challenge of high drug prices through the lens of the pharmaceutical supply chain. Generic and biosimilar medicines are a critical part of the solution for patients and America's health care system. But they are under threat from market imbalances, policies that fail to distinguish their business model from brand drugs, and anti-competitive behavior by other supply chain actors. AAM stands ready to work with you to ensure uninterrupted access to affordable therapies for patients and taxpayers.

Summary Statement of Chester "Chip" Davis, Jr.

Background

- Generic medicines represent greater than 89 percent of all prescriptions dispensed in the U.S., but only 26 percent of expenditures on prescription drugs, saving patients and payers nearly $5 billion every week. Our industry is proud to be able to deliver these savings to the healthcare system.

- In the past twelve months, prescriptions of brand drugs have decreased by 7 percent, but their revenue has climbed by 5 percent. This is a direct result of price increases.
- By contrast, generic prescriptions increased by 2 percent, but revenue declined by 13 percent.
- Without generic medicines, spending on cholesterol drugs would be more than 3.5 times higher, diabetes drugs almost 3 times higher, and spending on breast cancer drugs 8 times higher.
- However, the sustainability of a competitive generic market and the availability of generic medicines for patients, uninterrupted by shortages, is in jeopardy.

Three Factors Threaten Today's Generic and Biosimilar Industry

1. Changing and increasingly challenging market and reimbursement frameworks;
2. The abuse of laws and regulations by bad actors; and
3. A failure of policy to account for the unique challenges facing generic and biosimilar medicines.

Congress Must Act to Support Generic and Biosimilar Competition and Supply to Ensure Continued Access for Patients

It can do so by:

1. Repealing the misguided Medicaid penalty on generic drugs;
2. Preventing brand abuses designed to block generic and biosimilar competition by passing the bipartisan CREATES Act; and
3. Ensuring that biosimilar medicines have a level and competitive playing field in Medicare.

Generic Drug Markets are Fundamentally Different than Brands

- The 89 percent of prescriptions filled by generic medicines are subject to a different set of economic incentives and arrangements—the result of multiple manufacturers marketing identical products and competing exclusively on price, in a commodity-style market.

- Upon generic entry, payors typically shift away from rebate models of reimbursement and rely on distribution channels to effectively lower the price of the medicine.
- The different business model leads to a different type of business planning by generic and biosimilar manufacturers.
- Generic drug reimbursement is also different.
- The result is a business model that differs significantly from the brand business model.
- These differences in the generic and brand marketplaces create vastly different incentives for the various manufacturers, wholesalers, distributors, pharmacy benefit managers (PBMs), insurers, and retail pharmacies that make up the supply chain.
- To put it simply, virtually all other actors in the supply chain enjoy significant financial benefits from the manufacture of generic medicines.
- This is not to say that the market functions perfectly in providing patients with the lowest cost possible. Many generic medicines are subject to significant markups after they leave the generic manufacturer.
- Compared to the fragmented generic drug market, consolidation in the wholesale market and contractual arrangements between pharmacy chains and the wholesalers have left generic manufacturers with only a small number of purchasers.
- The result is a market where three purchasers account for over 90 percent of all wholesale revenue.
- It is unclear that the new imbalance between many generic competitors and a handful of purchasers is sustainable. Some industry analysts have already begun to forecast consolidation among generic manufacturers.
- An unfortunate yet foreseeable consequence of fewer generic manufacturers is a significantly increased risk of drug shortages.
- Evidence suggests that generic drugs are particularly susceptible to drug shortages, potentially related to existing market incentives as well as low reimbursement. Such shortages have a serious effect on patient care.
- It is critical that policymakers take steps to ensure the continued supply of affordable FDA approved generic medicines. Failure to do so threatens a stable supply of generic medicines.

The Chairman. Thank you, Mr. Davis.

Ms. Gallenagh, welcome.

STATEMENT OF ELIZABETH A. GALLENAGH

Ms. Gallenagh. Good morning, Chairman Alexander, Ranking Member Murray, and Members of the Committee. Thank you for the opportunity to participate in today's hearing. I'm Liz Gallenagh, Senior Vice President and General Counsel for the Healthcare Distribution Alliance.

HDA is the national trade association representing primary pharmaceutical wholesale distributors. HDA members include national, regional, and specialty companies. Their expertise streamlines the supply chain to ensure safety and efficiency, serving over 200,000 pharmacy settings across the country while achieving cost savings for our Nation's healthcare system, about $40 billion annually.

The U.S. healthcare supply chain is a complex one. Each day, our 35 primary distributor members, who purchase directly from authorized manufacturers, ship 15 million products daily from about 176 warehouses across the country, a relatively small but highly efficient and effective network. In fact, most pharmaceutical sales in the U.S. flow through our members, nearly 94 percent.

Distributors are unlike any other supply chain participants. Their core business is not manufacturing, and they do not prescribe medicines or dispense to patients. They focus significant resources on the safety and security of the supply chain, and these efforts may, in fact, be the most important service distributors provide. With this Committee's support, several years ago, HDA strongly advocated for the enactment of the Drug Supply Chain Security Act, which sets the framework for unit level traceability of medicines by 2023.

On a daily basis, pharmacies and other providers place orders with HDA distributors for the medicines they need to serve their patients. Without distributors, customers would have to carry weeks of inventory and place daily orders with each and every manufacturer. By working with full line distributors, providers can maintain just-in-time inventories, saving them time, expense, and staff necessary to carry extensive inventories or have large storage facilities.

In addition, primary distributors often provide financial credit terms, pharmacy management systems, and in-store retail support.

With regard to the upstream supply chain, the work of HDA members enables manufacturers to concentrate on developing and producing medicines without the added expense and challenge of getting those medicines to every single dispensing site across the country.

While HDA members are primarily supply chain logistics and operations experts, this is no longer an industry focused solely on moving products from Point A to Point B. Today, they provide a wide array of supporting services that deliver significant value to both ends of the supply chain and ultimately to patients. Some examples of these core services to manufacturers include receiving and accurately processing orders, shipping pharmaceutical products safely, inventory and management, providing manufacturers with ordering and utilization data, and processing returns and chargebacks.

In exchange for these services provided to manufacturers, distributors charge bona fide service fees. These fees are not passed on to the customer and represent a fair market value for a bona fide itemized service actually performed on behalf of the manufacturer that the manufacturer would have to otherwise perform themselves.

The distribution industry is a very high-volume yet very low- profit margin industry with an industry margin just over 1 percent, on average, for 2016. Moreover, a recent Berkeley research group study noted that the distributor profit on overall branded drug cost was just under 1 percent.

Distributors have little impact on overall drug pricing, and, generally, traditional pharmaceutical distributors purchase from manufacturers based on wholesale acquisition cost, or WAC, and charge manufacturers service fees. WAC represents the manufacturer's list price, does not include rebates, prompt payments, or other adjustments in price resulting from proprietary negotiations between the manufacturers and distributors, payer groups, or other customers. Distributors are not privy to how such WAC pricing decisions are made.

On the other side of the equation, distributors typically sell branded drugs to downstream customers based on WACs established solely by manufacturers. They also sell generic drugs to downstream customers based on either WACs or other list prices, or they may also price generic drugs sold to customers in response to the market, for example, when there are more than one generic drug. As such, wholesale distributors do not control the price of prescription drugs, but rather the price is dictated by manufacturers, WAC, or other list prices, as well as market forces, including generic competition.

Primary distributors' goal for the supply chain is a simple one: add efficiency, security, and timely delivery so that providers can concentrate on patient care and ensure that their patients have access to the medications they need. Historically, HDA distributor members have had a positive effect on the supply chain, helping to make the U.S. supply chain one of the safest and most efficient in the world, while taking cost out of the system and having minimal impact on the overall cost of drugs.

Thank you, and I would be happy to answer any questions you may have.

[The prepared statement of Ms. Gallenagh follows:]

Prepared Statement of Elizabeth A. Gallenagh

Chairman alexander, Ranking Member Murray and members of the Committee.

Thank you for the opportunity to participate in today's hearing. I am Liz Gallenagh, Senior Vice President, Government Affairs and General Counsel for the Healthcare

Distribution Alliance (HDA). HDA is the national trade association representing primary pharmaceutical distributors — the vital link between the nation's pharmaceutical manufacturers and more than 200,000 pharmacies, hospitals, long-term care facilities, clinics and others nationwide.

Since 1876, HDA has helped members navigate regulations and innovations to get the right medicines to the right patients at the right time, safely and efficiently. HDA's members include 35 national, regional and specialty primary distribution companies who are not just distributors, but are technology innovators, information management experts, security specialists and efficiency professionals. Their expertise streamlines the supply chain to ensure safety and efficiency, while also achieving cost savings for our nation's healthcare system.

Role in the Supply Chain

The U.S. healthcare supply chain is a complex one and the nation's primary pharmaceutical distributors play a vital role within it. Each day hundreds of thousands of healthcare provider locations must receive needed medicines and other healthcare products from thousands of manufacturers. These manufacturers and providers are served predominantly by 35 HDA primary distributors who operate out of about 176 warehouses and purchase directly from authorized manufacturers...a relatively small, but highly efficient and effective network. In fact, most pharmaceutical sales in the U.S. flow through primary distributors (93.79%).[89]

Every day HDA members work around the clock to safely and efficiently ship 15 million healthcare products (medicines, medical supplies, durable medical equipment, et al.) to pharmacies, hospitals and other healthcare providers in order to keep their shelves stocked with the medications and products they need to treat and serve their patients.

Distributors are unlike any other supply chain participants — their core business is not manufacturing and they do not prescribe medicines or dispense to patients. Their key role is to serve as a conduit for medicines to travel from manufacturer to patient while making sure the supply chain is fully secure and as efficient as possible.

HDA distributor members focus significant resources on the safety and security of the supply chain, and their secure supply chain efforts may in fact be the most important service distributors provide to the overall pharmaceutical delivery system. With this committee's support several years ago, HDA strongly advocated for the enactment of the Drug Supply Chain Security Act (DSCSA), Title II of the Drug Quality Security Act, which sets a framework for unit level traceability of medicines by 2023.

---

[89] *87th Edition HDA Factbook (2016-2017)*

Today, HDA members are in the midst of Phase I implementation efforts and work to collaborate with FDA, state regulatory authorities, and trading partners to build the systems and processes necessary to achieve unit-level traceability of prescription drugs by 2023, as outlined in the law.

RELATIONSHIP WITH PROVIDER CUSTOMERS

On a daily basis, pharmacies, hospitals and other healthcare providers place orders with HDA distributor members for the medicines, supplies and equipment they need to serve their patients. Without pharmaceutical distributors, pharmacies and providers would have to carry weeks of inventory and undertake the time-consuming process of placing individual orders with each and every manufacturer for products needed by the healthcare provider on a daily basis. By working with full-line distributors, providers can maintain just-in-time inventories that saves pharmacies and hospitals the expense and staff necessary to carry extensive inventories or have large storage facilities — both of which would add significantly to their cost of operations.

While distributors provide many services to the pharmacy provider community, the core services are supply chain related — providing on-time and complete shipment of ordered drugs in a safe and efficient manner. In addition, they often provide financial credit, pharmacy management systems, and in-store retail support, among many other services. Traditional distributors serve a broad array of provider types; mostly retail and hospital settings, including chain pharmacy warehouses, mass merchandisers and food chains, and chain pharmacies (39.5%); hospitals, HMOs, clinics and nursing homes (17.2%); independent pharmacies (17.3%); mail order (15.8%). Specialty distributors (and specialty subsidiaries) serve other provider settings such as physician offices, home care, specialty pharmacy, and some retail pharmacy.[90]

RELATIONSHIP WITH MANUFACTURER SUPPLIERS

The work of primary distributors also enables manufacturers to concentrate on developing and producing needed medicines without the added expense and logistical challenges of determining how to get those medicines to the providers and patients across the U.S. However, pharmaceutical distribution has evolved over the last decade from simply managing warehouses and shipping goods. While HDA members are primarily supply chain logistics and operations experts, this is no longer an industry focused solely on moving products from point A to point B. Rather, pharmaceutical distributors provide

[90] 87th Edition HDA Factbook (2016-2017)

a wide array of supporting services that enable the pharmaceutical supply chain to function efficiently and safely, delivering significant value to manufacturers and healthcare providers — and ultimately to patients. Some examples of these core services include: receiving orders and shipping pharmaceutical products in a safe, efficient manner, inventory handling and inventory management, providing manufacturers with data about where, and in which settings, their products are utilized, verifying downstream customer eligibility to purchase products at pricing established under various programs or contracts between such customers and given manufacturers, and processing relevant chargebacks to manufacturers.

In exchange for the variety of distribution and logistics services that primary distributors provide to manufacturers, they charge manufacturers what are referred to as "bona fide service fees" for the provision of these services. These fees, which are not passed on to the customer, represent a fair market value for a bona fide, itemized service actually performed on behalf of the manufacturer that the manufacturer would otherwise perform (or contract for) in the absence of the service arrangement. This model reduces demand volatility — aligning order patterns more closely to actual patient demand and, eliminating artificial demand spikes, allowing for a supply chain that operates more smoothly and predictably.

It should also be noted that without HDA members, each manufacturer would have to ensure that more than 200,000 pharmacy and provider settings receive the medications they need when they need them, employing substantial financial, logistical and staff resources to provide medicines and supplies to hundreds of thousands of dispensing sites. Because distributors provide these logistical, inventory and other service support which manufacturers and pharmacies would otherwise have to perform themselves, the pharmaceutical supply chain is more efficient, reliable and secure, and patients are able to get the medicines they need in a timely fashion, saving our healthcare system approximately $42 billion each year.[91]

PRIMARY WHOLESALE DISTRIBUTORS' ROLE IN DRUG PRICING[92]

The primary pharmaceutical distribution industry is a very high volume, yet very low profit margin industry, with the industry margin just over one percent on average in 2016.

---

[91] The Center for Healthcare Supply Chain Research, *The Role of Distributors in the U.S. Healthcare Industry*, 2011.

[92] HDA's antitrust policy strictly prohibits any discussions which constitute or imply an agreement or understanding between or among its members concerning: 1) prices, discounts, or terms or conditions of sale; 2) profits, profit margins or cost data; 3) market shares, sales territories or markets,; 4) allocation of customers or territories; 5) selection, rejection or termination of customers or suppliers; 6) restricting the territory or markets in which a company may resell products; 7) restricting the customers to whom a company may sell; or 8) any matter which is inconsistent with the proposition that each members company of HDA must exercise its independent business judgment in pricing its services or products, dealing with its customers and suppliers and choosing the markets in which it will compete.

In fact, overall profitability for the primary distribution sector shows little notable change over the past several years, even during recent market volatility.[93] Moreover, in a recent 2017 study, the Berkeley Research Group concluded that the pharmaceutical wholesale distributor profit on overall branded drug costs was just under one percent.[94]

Traditional pharmaceutical wholesale distributors purchase pharmaceuticals from manufacturers based on the Wholesale Acquisition Cost ("WAC"), a publicly available figure reported for each pharmaceutical product by the manufacturer to various compendia such as Medi-Span and RedBook, which publish such prices. WAC represents the manufacturer's list price, and does not include rebates, prompt payment, or other adjustments in price resulting from proprietary negotiations between the manufacturer and wholesaler, downstream payer groups or other customers. Manufacturers (pharmaceutical, biologic, generic, etc.) set the WAC price for their products. Wholesale distributors are not privy to how such WAC pricing decisions are made. Wholesale distributors typically purchase pharmaceuticals from manufacturers based on WAC and they also charge manufacturers distribution fees related to their services, as previously discussed.

Wholesale distributors typically sell branded drugs to downstream customers based on WACs established solely by pharmaceutical manufacturers. Wholesale distributors might also sell generic drugs to downstream customers based on WACs established solely by pharmaceutical manufacturers and published in the various pricing compendia or they may price generic drugs sold to downstream customers in response to the market, which includes supply of competing generic drug and considers the WACs for such generic drug products and competitors to such drug products. As such, wholesale distributors do not control the price of pharmaceuticals rather the price of pharmaceuticals is dictated by published WAC or other list prices determined solely by manufacturers of such products and other market forces, including the WACs of generic drugs that compete with a given generic drug product.

Conclusion

As I noted earlier, primary pharmaceutical distributors have evolved from providing basic inventory management and distribution to now offering a suite of services supporting many different operations of both manufacturers and healthcare providers. Ultimately, these services result in benefits to patients and consumers and have made the U.S. pharmaceutical supply chain one of the safest and most efficient in the world.

---

[93] Data obtained from annual HDMA/HDA industry *Factbook* Publication, compiled and compared across multiple years.

[94] The Pharmaceutical Supply Chain: Gross Drug Expenditures Realized by Stakeholders; 2017; Table 2 http://www.thinkbrg.com/media/publication/863_Vandervelde_PhRMA-January-2017_WEB-FINAL.pdf.

Traditional pharmaceutical wholesale distributors' goal in the pharmaceutical supply chain is a simple one: add efficiency, security and timely delivery of products so providers can concentrate on patient care and ensure their patients have regular access to the medications they need. Historically, HDA distributor members have effectively achieved this goal and have had a positive effect on the supply chain and patients while taking costs out of the pharmaceutical supply chain and having minimal impact on the overall cost of drugs.

Thank you. I would be happy to answer any questions you may have.

SUMMARY STATEMENT OF ELIZABETH A. GALLENAGH

HDA is the national trade association representing primary pharmaceutical distributors—the vital link between the nation's pharmaceutical manufacturers and more than 200,000 pharmacies, hospitals, long-term care facilities, clinics and others nationwide. Since 1876, HDA has helped members navigate regulations and innovations to get the right medicines to the right patients at the right time, safely and efficiently.

Distributors are unlike any other supply chain participants—their core business is not manufacturing and they do not prescribe medicines or dispense to patients. Their key role is to serve as a conduit for medicines to travel from manufacturer to patient while making sure the supply chain is fully secure and as efficient as possible. HDA distributor members focus significant resources on the safety and security of the supply chain, and their secure supply chain efforts may in fact be the most important service distributors provide to the overall pharmaceutical delivery system.

Primary pharmaceutical distributors have evolved from providing basic inventory management and distribution to now offering a suite of services supporting many different operations of both manufacturers and healthcare providers. Ultimately, these services result in benefits to patients and consumers and have made the U.S. pharmaceutical supply chain one of the safest and most efficient in the world.

Traditional pharmaceutical wholesale distributors' goal in the pharmaceutical supply chain is a simple one: add efficiency, security and timely delivery of products so providers can concentrate on patient care and ensure their patients have regular access to the medications they need. Historically, pharmaceutical wholesale distributors have effectively achieved this goal and have had a positive effect on the supply chain and patients while taking costs out of the pharmaceutical supply chain and having minimal impact on the overall cost of drugs.

The Chairman. Thank you, Ms. Gallenagh.

Mr. Merritt, welcome.

STATEMENT OF MARK MERRITT

Mr. MERRITT. Thank you, Mr. Chairman and Members of the Committee, for inviting me to discuss drug pricing and the delivery system drug makers use to bring their products to market.

I'd like to start by providing a brief top line overview of a very complicated subject, an executive summary, if you will, on why there's such anger about drug pricing, especially now; the role supply chains play; and how PBMs use their skill and expertise to reduce overall costs.

There are several reasons why drug pricing has become such a concern in recent years. First is drug makers' recent shift from producing blockbuster drugs like Lipitor, which may have cost $3 a day, to drugs like Sovaldi, which costs $1,000 a day. These are great drugs, but not everybody is prepared to pay $1,000 a day for a new drug even if it is a great drug. All this came on the heels of a decade that saw very little brand inflation, thanks to a wave of competing generics that hit the market at that time.

The second reason for concern were the recent high-profile scandals of three drug makers, specifically Mylan's 400 percent EpiPen price hike and the discovery that two companies, Turing and Valeant, had built entire business models around buying rights to low-cost drugs in order to re-sell them at much higher prices. There were, of course, many hearings on the issues, and I testified at a few of them.

Third is that many health plans have tried to restrain premium increases by raising deductibles in the face of higher costs, not just of drugs but of overall major medical costs. Higher deductibles meant that some patients who had grown accustomed to paying $25 copays, thinking that might actually be the price of the drug, came face to face for the first time with the actual price of drugs, which can run hundreds or even thousands of dollars.

The rise of high-price specialty drugs, the scandals surrounding particular manufacturers, and the emergence of high deductible plans have converged all at one time to raise real visibility on this issue.

I'd like to offer just a few brief thoughts on the drug supply chain. First, supply chains are a routine part of how consumers access not just drugs but almost any product in the marketplace. They're a normal part of American business. They're not something that's unique to prescription drugs or healthcare. They're used all across America.

It should be noted that supply chains have nothing to do with why manufacturers raise prices. Mylan didn't raise EpiPen prices by 400 percent because of supply chain costs. The laws of supply and demand, not supply chains, determine how drug makers and other manufacturers set prices. In its simplest terms, the prescription drug marketplace is like any other, a market of sellers and buyers. Drug makers are the sellers and, like all sellers, set prices according to whatever the market will bear.

Likewise, the buyers want to pay as little as possible. These are the employers, unions, health plans, and government programs that hire PBMs to negotiate price concessions from drug makers. In fact, PBMs do a number of things to reduce cost. PBMs design benefits that encourage patients to use generics and less expensive brands. The PBMs create networks of affordable pharmacies. They reduce cost for consumers. PBMs negotiate rebates and other price concessions from drug companies.

It should be noted that rebates are simply discounts paid after sales have been made instead of at the point of sale. While PBMs have stated publicly that they welcome drug companies to offer alternatives to rebates, including simply lowering a list price of drugs, rebates remain a key way to deliver savings to our clients who determine the amount of rebates each PBM passes through to them.

Ninety percent of rebates are passed through to plan sponsors, and almost half of large employers require 100 percent of rebates to be passed through. Once these are passed through, plans can decide what to do with them. Typically, they're used to reduce premiums, deductibles, copays, but that's up to every plan to do what they want. So the marketplace is evolving on the issue.

It should also be noted that drug makers set and raise prices regardless of rebates they negotiate with PBMs. In fact, Sovaldi's list price was $84,000 and involved no rebate whatsoever until other competitors came to market. Then they were able to bring prices and costs way down, in fact, lower than a lot of price control countries in Europe.

All in all, PBMs reduce drug costs by 30 percent, play a major role in the success of Medicare Part D, and have helped restrain the growth in overall drug spending to 3 percent to 4 percent a year, despite rising list prices.

Finally, there are market-based policy solutions that can reduce costs. I'd like to thank Senators Collins and Franken for their FDA reauthorization amendment to expedite generic approvals, promote competition, and guard against sudden price hikes of decades old drugs. We also urge Congress to work with FDA to accelerate approvals for brand drugs which face limited competition and do whatever possible to bring biosimilars to market faster. These steps would foster competition, which is the key to reducing overall drug prices.

I look forward to answering any questions you might have.

[The prepared statement of Mr. Merritt follows:]

Prepared Statement of Mark Merritt

Introduction

Good morning. My name is Mark Merritt, President and CEO of the Pharmaceutical Care Management Association (PCMA). I appreciate this opportunity to appear before the Committee at this hearing examining the drug supply chain. PCMA is the national association representing America's pharmacy benefit managers (PBMs), which administer prescription drug plans for more than 266 million[95] Americans across dozens of PBMs with health coverage provided through self-insured employers, health insurers, labor unions, Medicare, Medicaid, CHIP, and the Federal Employees Health Benefits Program (FEHBP).

The cost of prescription drugs has understandably garnered a lot of attention, particularly with the recent wave of high priced, high profile specialty drugs like Sovaldi. This development has imposed unique challenges on patients and the employers, unions and government programs that hire PBMs to help make coverage more affordable. By negotiating price concessions from drug companies and recommending strategies that promote generics and more affordable pharmacies, PBMs have played a key role in retraining the rise of overall drug costs to low single-digit increases over the past few years. It is also important to note that prescription drug launch prices and price increases are determined by the same supply-and-demand dynamics of countless other industries that manufacture products and use supply chains to get them to market. Pricing decisions are made unilaterally by manufacturers. There's no correlation between manufacturer price increases and the rebates and discounts they negotiate with PBMs.

At the outset, I want to thank this Committee for its actions to improve generic competition and lower the cost of prescription drugs as part of the Food and Drug Administration (FDA) Reauthorization Act. In addition, I'd like to recognize Senators Collins and Franken for your work on the amendment that addresses clearing the FDA's application backlog as well as expediting generic drug development and promoting competition. Title VIII will help foster a more competitive marketplace to improve the affordability and accessibility of prescription drugs for patients and guard against sudden, astronomical price hikes of decades-old prescription drugs. The HELP Committee has played an important role in fostering the competition that will both reward innovation and maintain affordability. This testimony will outline how PBMs reduce prescription drug costs to provide patients, employers, and public programs with the highest value prescription drug benefits. Additionally, it will suggest a set of policy options to increase competition in the prescription drug marketplace to help reduce costs.

How PBMs Reduce Drug Costs for Payers and Cost-Sharing for Patients

The role of PBMs is to help our clients, including the employers, unions, and health insurers who provide prescription drug benefits, to reduce costs and improve health

[95] PR Newswire, "PBMs Provide Policy Solutions to Increase Competition, Reduce Rx Costs," Feb 04, 2016.

outcomes for consumers. PBMs have a proven track record of delivering high-quality, affordable benefits that address the individual needs of their clients and patients.

PBMs play a crucial role in keeping drug costs down for payers. PBMs operate outside of the "pharmacy supply chain" that physically moves prescription drugs from manufacturers to drug wholesalers to the pharmacy, where they are ultimately dispensed to patients. Rather, PBMs represent insurers and health plans, on the buy side of the economic transaction. In their capacity as benefit managers, PBMs do not take possession of pharmaceuticals, but work on behalf of health care payers to reduce costs.

Given current drug pricing trends, the role of PBMs has become more important than ever. While few plans can afford to offer true "first-dollar" prescription drug coverage, all want to offer the most affordable benefits for consumers. That is why thousands of America's largest, most sophisticated health purchasers – Fortune 500 companies, insurers, state employee programs, state Medicaid programs, unions, and Medicare Part D plans – choose to hire PBMs, even though none are required to.

PBMs typically reduce costs by 30%[96] by, among other things, using their substantial scale and expertise to promote generics and negotiate aggressive rebates, discounts, and other price concessions with manufacturers to reduce premiums and cost-sharing.

The Role and Background of Rebates

Long before PBMs became prominent in the marketplace, the rebate system was created by manufacturers (and in the case of programs like Medicaid and 340B, used by public programs) to reduce the net cost of brand drugs. Most rebates reported by manufacturers are actually paid pursuant to these government discount programs, not to plans administered by PBMs.

As part of manufacturer-PBM negotiations, brand drug manufacturers compete for formulary placement for therapeutically equivalent products by offering rebates for moving market share, which are typically calculated and paid weeks or months after a drug is dispensed. As a result of these negotiations, PBMs can recommend benefit designs that stretch payers' finite dollars and reduce premiums and cost-sharing. These designs include cost-sharing incentives for patients to use the most affordable drugs, which often are generics. The highest cost-sharing is typically reserved for drugs with the least competitive discounts, or in the case of many high-priced, single-source drugs (e.g., cancer therapies), no discount at all. PBMs also support benefit designs that ensure patients do not pay more in cost-sharing than the cost of an actual drug and innovations like electronic prior authorization that reduce physicians' administrative burden.

---

[96] Visante: *Pharmacy Benefit Managers (PBMs): Generating Savings for Plan Sponsors and Consumers*, February 2016.

Rebate savings are used by payers to reduce premiums and out-of-pocket costs for patients. Each payer determines what percentage of rebates is passed through to it, and how much (if any) it wants the PBM to retain as payment for services. While on average payers elect to receive 90% of rebates negotiated by PBMs,[97] an increasing number require PBMs to pass through all of them. About 46% of commercial PBM contracts are negotiated with full pass-through of rebates to payers,[98] and 100% of rebates in the Medicare Part D program are required to be reported to CMS. PBMs are committed to providing rebate transparency and audit rights to their clients.

There is No Connection between the Prices Drugmakers Set and the Rebates They Negotiate with PBMs

A recent study of the top 200 self-administered, patent-protected, brand-name drugs shows no correlation between the launch prices or price increases manufacturers set and the rebates they pay to PBMs.[99] There are many cases of high-priced drugs that carry low rebates and low-priced drugs that carry high rebates. Some high-priced drugs have no rebate at all.

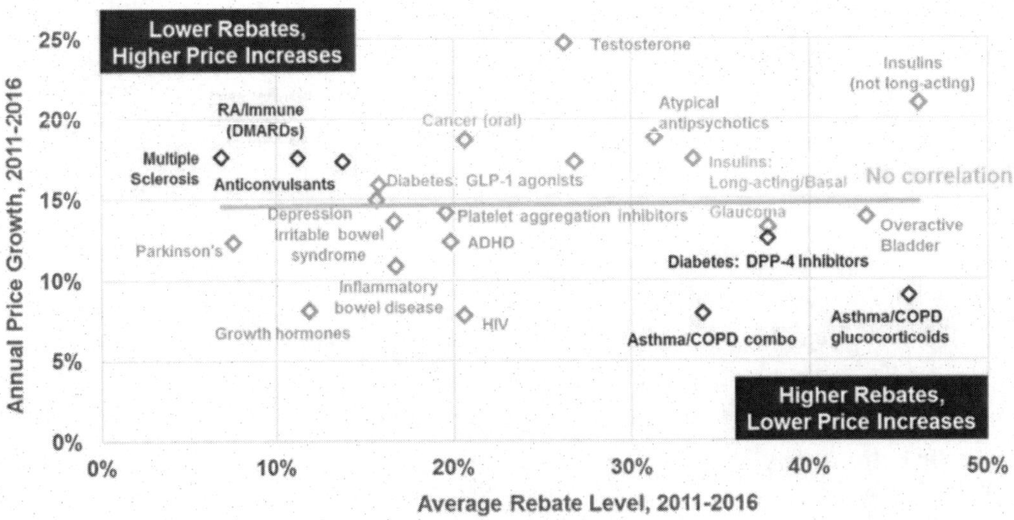

Source: Visante estimates and analysis of SSR Health data, 2017.

[97] Written Testimony of Joanna Shepherd, Ph.D., Emory University for the ERISA Advisory Council Hearing on PBM Compensation and Fee Disclosure, June 19, 2014, Citing J. P. Morgan, "Pharmacy Benefit Management, Takeaways from Our Proprietary PBM Survey," May 21, 2014.

[98] See, Pharmacy Benefit Management Institute, "PBMI Research Report: Trends in Drug Benefit Design," 2016.

[99] Visante, Inc. Increasing Prices Set by Drugmakers; Not Correlated With Rebates, June 2017. Analysis prepared for PCMA

The figure below[100] illustrates the lack of correlation of price changes to rebates, by drug class.

Like manufacturers in other industries, drugmakers set prices according to supply, demand, and the level of competitive alternatives available. Considering the confusion surrounding rebates, PBMs encourage manufacturers to offer payers other ways to reduce net costs.

Hepatitis C Drugs: A Classic Case of Leveraging Competition

The introduction of new therapies for hepatitis C demonstrates how competition in the marketplace can drive significant savings on expensive drugs. In 2013 the first highly effective drug to cure hepatitis C was priced at $84,000 for a cycle of treatment. However, by 2015, after that drug faced competition from additional market entrants, PBMs were able to negotiate a 46% rebate —saving billions.[101] Market competition and the threat of formulary exclusion compelled the manufacturer to agree to this steep rebate. Indeed, after some PBMs excluded the first drug and opted to prefer a competing manufacturer's drug when the competing drug's manufacturer was willing to drop the cost, other PBMs were able to prefer the first drug in their formulary, when the first manufacturer matched the competition. Still other PBMs were then able to keep both on their formulary as the market evolved.

Research on hepatitis C drug costs has subsequently shown that by 2015, when competition had emerged, hepatitis C drug costs negotiated in the U.S. by PBMs for Medicare Part D were usually lower than those in price-controlled European countries and Japan.[102] The case of hepatitis C drugs illustrates clearly the effectiveness of the threat of formulary exclusion to bring manufacturers to the negotiating table.

PBMs Help Commercial Clients Explore Trade Offs to Point-of-Sale (POS) Rebates

POS rebates refer to contract arrangements where negotiated price concessions are estimated before the transaction and then applied immediately at the point of sale. In the commercial market, PBMs already help payers implement POS rebates. Since moving rebates to POS does not reduce overall costs but only redistributes them among different enrollees, payers ask themselves the following questions before choosing this approach:

---

[100] Ibid.

[101] New York Times, "Costly Hepatitis C Drugs for Everyone?" September 2, 2015.

[102] IMS Health, "Comparison of Hepatitis C Treatment Costs Estimates of Net Prices and Usage in the U.S. and Other Major Markets," September 2016.https://www.imshealth.com/files/ web/IMSH%20Institute/ Healthcare%20Briefs/IIHI—Comparison—of—HepatitisC—Treatment—Costs.pdf

- Should rebate savings be used to reduce premiums for all enrollees or out-of-pocket costs for certain ones who take certain drugs?
- Do plans have the administrative and financial capacity to reduce costs at POS even though manufacturers do not pay rebates until months after a drug has been dispensed?
- Do plans understand the limitations of POS rebates? Some high-priced drugs carry no rebates at all and others are so expensive that rebates alone will not guarantee access. A $1,500 drug with a 30% rebate would still cost patients in the deductible $1,050.
- If plans are willing to exchange higher premiums for lower cost-sharing, would it be simpler to just reduce deductibles or co-pays on certain drugs?

Frustration over high drug prices has led some policymakers to explore ways to reduce costs for consumers, including forcing health plans to use rebates to reduce POS costs rather than premiums. However, such policies do not reduce costs; they only shift costs from one group of patients to another.

POS Rebates Do Not Work in Medicare Part D

While plans with POS rebates can be implemented in the commercial market, they have proven unworkable in Medicare Part D and pose risks that could destabilize the program. In fact, POS rebates are already permitted in Part D and have been tried—unsuccessfully—in the past. They lead to significant adverse selection and expose plans to other risks, such as being accused of False Claims Acts violations if they incorrectly estimate the size of rebates. Requiring POS rebates in Part D would dramatically increase costs to the program and taxpayers. According to modeling by the actuarial firm, Milliman, this would result in widespread premium increases and cost taxpayers an additional $20 billion over the next decade.[103]

PBMs Use Direct and Indirect Remuneration (DIR) to Keep Drug Costs and Beneficiary Premiums Low

DIR often refers to negotiated price concessions between pharmacies and health plans or PBMs. However, as coined, DIR is a technical term created by the Centers for Medicare and Medicaid Services (CMS) specific to Medicare Part D that includes both

[103] Milliman, "Value of Direct and Indirect Remuneration (DIR): Impact on Medicare Part D Prescription Drug Plan (PDP) Program Stakeholders," Commissioned by Pharmaceutical Care Management Association, July 2017.https://www.pcmanet.org/wp—content/uploads/ 2017/07/Value-of-PDP-DIR—20170706.pdf

manufacturer rebates and certain incentive payments to pharmacies. These contractual arrangements—even if not specifically labelled DIR—also exist in the commercial market. The vast majority of DIR payments in Part D are PBM-manufacturer negotiated rebates. A much smaller share is made up of incentive payment terms that pharmacies (or their Pharmacy Service Administrative Organizations on their behalf)[104] contractually negotiate with PBMs. Pharmacy DIR payments based on performance metrics hold pharmacies accountable for certain activities such as generic dispensing, cost-effective dispensing, improving medication adherence, and reducing inappropriate drug use.

According to a recent study, the price concessions PBMs negotiate with drug manufacturers and drugstores and report to CMS as DIR are generating significant savings for the federal government and are projected to save enrollees in standalone Part D plans $48.7 billion on their premiums over the next 10 years.[105]

CMS has also found that DIR contributes significantly to keeping Part D premiums low. Earlier this year, CMS released a report that found negotiated DIR price concessions have grown in recent years to moderate beneficiary premiums and reduce costs for the government.[106] The CMS report highlights how negotiated price concessions reduce premiums for Medicare Part D beneficiaries, which also lead to lower costs for the federal government—negotiated price concessions lowered per-beneficiary costs in Part D 28% on average.[107] Stable and affordable premiums have contributed to a 90% satisfaction rate among Part D enrollees.[108]

Policy Recommendations to Improve Competition and Reduce Costs

PCMA supports policies to lower drug costs through increased competition. The policy proposals outlined below to help increase competition in the marketplace include some under HELP Committee jurisdiction and some under Finance or Judiciary Committee jurisdiction.

---

[104] Parties especially noteworthy in the supply chain and key to negotiations between PBMs and pharmacies are large third-party organizations known as pharmacy services administrative organizations (PSAOs). These organizations allow independent pharmacies to pool their collective purchasing power. More than 80 percent of independent pharmacies (18,103 of the 21,511 pharmacies identified by National Council for Prescription Drug Programs data) use PSAOs or other group purchasing organizations to increase their leverage in negotiating their payment terms and conditions with PBMs. The largest PSAOs are controlled by three multi-billion dollar suppliers to pharmacies, providing a further negotiating advantage for independent pharmacies due to the size and sophistication of these parent companies.

[105] Milliman, "Value of Direct and Indirect Remuneration (DIR): Impact on Medicare Part D Prescription Drug Plan (PDP) Program Stakeholders," Commissioned by Pharmaceutical Care Management Association, July 2017.https://www.pcmanet.org/wp-content/uploads/ 2017/07/Value-of-PDP-DIR—20170706.pdf

[106] CMS, "Medicare Part D-Direct and Indirect Remuneration (DIR)" January 19, 2017.https://www.cms.gov/ Newsroom/MediaReleaseDatabase/Fact-sheets/2017-Fact-Sheetitems/2017-01-19-2.html

[107] CMS, Op. Cit.

[108] Morning Consult for Medicare Today, "Ten Years After Implementation, Nearly Nine in 10 Seniors are Satisfied with Part D," July 2016.http://medicaretoday.org/resources/senior-satisfaction-survey/

- Stop anticompetitive product adjustments, i.e., “evergreening.” Drug manufacturers sometimes use tactics such as “product hopping” or “evergreening,” submitting applications to the FDA for approval of a “new” product that is essentially the same as the original product. These product lifecycle management tactics artificially extend drug exclusivity periods and delay the take-up of lower-cost generics.
- Allow for FDA accelerated approval of brand drugs based on increasing competition. Accelerated review is granted to new drug applications that address “unmet need.” The economic need for competition to lower prices should be a criterion of unmet need.
- Revisit and improve biosimilar labeling and naming. Substitutable biosimilars should bear identical names and labels to their innovator analogs. Use of different names will confuse patients and providers and inhibit prescribing of biosimilars.
- Reduce innovator biologic exclusivity to seven years. Seven years of data exclusivity would still provide a sufficient return to manufacturers, while also speeding more affordable biosimilars to market.
- Eliminate use of Risk Evaluation and Mitigation Strategies (REMS) to delay competition. Some manufacturers have used REMS to prevent generic or biosimilar developers from getting sufficient quantities of a drug or biologic to develop a competitor to the innovator product. REMS were never intended for this purpose; this practice should be prohibited.

PCMA also supports enhancing tools in Medicare Part D, Medicaid, and commercial markets to increase competition and affordability. PBMs and health plans can best drive competition among drug manufacturers when they can give plan enrollees a strong incentive to use a competing, higher-value drug. This reduces costs and helps improve adherence among patients. Below are some strategies to strengthen these efforts.

- Create a safe harbor for value-based drug price negotiations from Medicaid Best Price. Today any drug manufacturer must offer state Medicaid programs the lowest price it offers any other payer. This provision is seen as a price floor and is inhibiting creative value-based pricing arrangements.
- Expand drug coverage options for Health Savings Account (HSA)-eligible high-deductible health plans (HDHPs). HDHPs associated with HSAs should have the option of covering prescription drugs with low or no cost-sharing prior to reaching the deductible, especially drugs that qualify for a preventive drug list. This policy can be achieved by expanding the current preventive drug list used by HDHPs.

- Remove Part D's protected classes. Designating "classes of clinical concern" where all or substantially all drugs in a class must be covered allows drug manufacturers to name their price. CMS already applies careful plan formulary coverage checks to assure proper coverage.
- Make biosimilars subject to the 50% Part D coverage gap discount. The ACA did not apply to biosimilars the 50% Part D coverage gap discount. This could have the unintended consequence of encouraging prescribing of more expensive innovator biologics when lower cost biosimilars are available.
- Encourage greater use of generics for Medicare Part D Low Income Subsidy (LIS) enrollees. MedPAC recommended allowing the Secretary of HHS to lower cost-sharing on generics and raise it for brands that have generic competition. Increasing the differential between brands and generics and allowing plans to lower generic cost-sharing would save money for enrollees and Medicare.
- Eliminate the tax deduction for direct-to-consumer (DTC) drug ads that mention a specific product. While DTC drug ads may encourage some people to see a doctor, they drive up unnecessary utilization and the cost of health care.

These are all common-sense ideas that would improve affordability for payers, taxpayers, and consumers, and increase competition.

Conclusion

PBMs evolved because they increase the value of prescription drug benefits. PCMA's member companies harness market forces and competition to corral drugs costs and deliver high-quality benefits and services to their payer clients and enrollees. In its search for solutions to address high drug costs, PCMA encourages the Committee to pursue policies that foster and encourage competition to keep prescription drug costs and pharmacy benefits more affordable for employers, enrollees, taxpayers, and government programs.

PCMA member companies welcome continuing discussion among all stakeholders to create a robust, sustainable market that will continue to deliver needed cures and treatments for patients who suffer through disease and chronic illness. PCMA looks forward to working with this Committee and the rest of Congress to find additional ways to promote savings consistent with high-quality, high-value prescription drug benefits.

Thank you for the opportunity to testify. I am happy to answer any questions.

SUMMARY STATEMENT OF MARK MERRITT

America's pharmacy benefit managers (PBMs) administer prescription drug plans for more than 266 million Americans across dozens of PBMs with health coverage provided through self-insured employers, health insurers, labor unions, Medicare, Medicaid, CHIP, and the Federal Employees Health Benefits Program (FEHBP).

The cost of prescription drugs has understandably garnered a lot of attention. However, despite the rise of list prices on certain brand drugs, PBMs have held the rise of overall drug costs to low single-digit increases over the past few years. It is also important to note that prescription drug launch prices and price increases are determined by the same supply-and-demand dynamics of countless other industries that manufacture products and use supply chains to get them to market. Pricing decisions are made unilaterally by manufacturers. There's no correlation between manufacturer price increases and the rebates and discounts they negotiate with PBMs.

The role of PBMs is to help our clients, including the employers, unions, and health insurers who provide prescription drug benefits, to reduce costs and improve health outcomes for consumers. PBMs have a proven track record of delivering high-quality, affordable benefits that address the individual needs of their clients and patients.

Given current drug pricing trends, the role of PBMs has become more important than ever. While few plans can afford to offer true ''first-dollar'' prescription drug coverage, all want to offer the most affordable benefits for consumers. That is why thousands of America's largest, most sophisticated health purchasers—Fortune 500 companies, insurers, state employee programs, state Medicaid programs, unions, and Medicare Part D plans—choose to hire PBMs, even though none are required to.

PBMs typically reduce costs by 30 percent by, among other things, using their substantial scale and expertise to promote generics and negotiate aggressive rebates, discounts, and other price concessions with manufacturers to reduce premiums and cost-sharing.

PCMA supports policies to lower drug costs through increased competition. The policy proposals outlined below to help increase competition in the marketplace include some under HELP Committee jurisdiction and some under Finance or Judiciary Committee jurisdiction.

- Stop anticompetitive product adjustments, i.e., "evergreening."
- Allow for FDA accelerated approval of brand drugs based on increasing competition.
- Revisit and improve biosimilar labeling and naming.
- Reduce innovator biologic exclusivity to seven years.

- Eliminate use of Risk Evaluation and Mitigation Strategies (REMS) to delay competition.
- Create a safe harbor for value-based drug price negotiations from Medicaid Best Price.
- Expand drug coverage options for Health Savings Account (HSA)-eligible high-deductible health plans (HDHPs).
- Remove Part D's protected classes.
- Make biosimilars subject to the 50 percent Part D coverage gap discount.
- Encourage greater use of generics for Medicare Part D Low Income Subsidy (LIS) enrollees.
- Eliminate the tax deduction for direct-to-consumer (DTC) drug ads that mention a specific product.

These are all common-sense ideas that would improve affordability for payers, taxpayers, and consumers, and increase competition.

The Chairman. Thank you, Mr. Merritt.

Mr. Menighan.

STATEMENT OF THOMAS E. MENIGHAN

Mr. MENIGHAN. Thank you, Chairman Alexander and Ranking Member Murray, for the opportunity to discuss a very important topic for our Nation's patients, families, and pharmacists. It's an honor to be here.

I'm Tom Menighan, American Pharmacists Association CEO. APhA is America's largest, oldest, and most diverse pharmacist organization. We promote patient access and coverage for pharmacists' quality patient care services. Our members contribute to healthcare in a wide variety of settings, including physician offices, specialty and community pharmacies both chain and independent, senior care, ambulatory care, and health systems.

For many years as a practicing community pharmacist and specialty pharmacy owner, I've shared the challenges with patients facing financial choices between food and medicine. Today's topic is of concern to America's 300,000 pharmacists, the professional on the front line, informing patients about medication cost and explaining complex insurance coverage policies.

As the organization representing pharmacists in all practice settings, we support policies that increase patients' access to affordable and cost-effective medicines.

Decisions among the entire supply chain impact patient medication costs, including arrangements among manufacturers, wholesalers, insurers, and PBMs. Pharmacies are where millions of Americans are first confronted with complex pharmaceutical pricing policies or changes in coverage, formularies, prior authorization, deductibles, copayments, many of which they don't know or understand.

Upstream decisions often limit pharmacists' options to impact patients' final drug costs. Instead of helping to address the nearly $300 billion the U.S. spends annually on medication use problems, fixing the problems of medication use, community pharmacists spend much of their day on the phone pursuing appropriate, covered, affordable treatment.

To address this challenge, we support a transparent pricing framework that would eliminate or identify mechanisms like rebates and post point of sale price fees imposed on pharmacies. These policies generally result in higher point of sale prices to consumers and, consequently, higher beneficiary copayments. We also encourage policies that allow any willing pharmacy to enter into contracts with insurers or PBMs to increase patient access and choice, which can improve adherence and health outcomes.

AphA requests the Committee to look beyond the drug price spend in isolation. Policies should consider the relationship between effective medication use and lower medical costs rather than squaring them in siloes. Full value in healthcare will come from integrating these siloes and their related costs and outcomes.

As drugs become more expensive, complex, and personalized, the need to optimize their impact and value should increase. To get the greatest benefit from medications, patients must understand how to use their medications safely and effectively. Empowered pharmacists can assist patients in optimizing the medication use and decreasing patient cost by providing services focused on safe and appropriate use.

For example, pharmacists provide medication management services, especially important for patients who take multiple drugs or have chronic conditions, and we address hospital readmissions by helping patients transition between care settings.

Unfortunately, Medicare does not cover our services. Many of our Nation's seniors are medically underserved, despite 91 percent of Americans living within five miles of a community pharmacy. Pharmacists are a well-trained and underutilized healthcare resource, which can positively affect beneficiaries' care and the entire Medicare program.

We ask your support today for S. 109, the Pharmacy and Medically Underserved Areas Enhancement Act, and urge its swift passage to provide access to underserved seniors. Not only will access increase, but the Act will help improve beneficiary outcomes, particularly those impacted by medications. But we have to be on the team.

Finally, AphA supports a safe and secure supply chain. America's pharmacists and patients should not have to worry about diversion and counterfeits. We believe proposals to legalize importation of non-FDA approved drugs will do more harm than good. Importantly, we have great concern regarding importations' impact on patient safety and continuity of care. We believe it is in direct conflict with recent efforts by Congress to secure the U.S. supply chain and secure and improve patient safety.

In summary, thank you for including pharmacists today, the medication experts, on the patient's healthcare team in this discussion. Ultimately, the most expensive medicine is the one not purchased, not taken, abandoned, or not used correctly by patients. Pharmacists stand ready to help.

I look forward to answering any questions on the positive role we can play and do play in reducing patients' prescription drug costs.

Thank you.

[The prepared statement of Mr. Menighan follows:]

STATEMENT OF THOMAS E. MENIGHAN

Thank you Chairman Alexander and Ranking Member Murray for inviting me to testify today on a very important topic for our nation's patients, families, and their pharmacists: prescription drug prices.[109] It is an honor to be here.

My name it Tom Menighan and I am the Executive Vice President and CEO of the American Pharmacists Association, or APhA.

APhA is America's oldest, largest and most diverse pharmacist organization. APhA was founded in 1852, and represents pharmacists, pharmaceutical scientists, student pharmacists, pharmacy technicians, and other parties invested in improving medication use and advancing patient care. APhA members practice and contribute to providing care in all practice settings, including community pharmacies, hospitals, long-term care facilities, community health centers, physician offices, ambulatory clinics, managed care organizations, hospice settings, and the uniformed services. APhA promotes patient access and coverage for pharmacists' quality patient care services.

I was a practicing community pharmacist and specialty pharmacy owner for many years. Like many other pharmacists, I needed to make careful purchasing decisions to provide patient access to needed medications and negotiate with other members of the supply chain and payers to stay viable. I've also shared the challenges with patients who face financial choices between food and medicine for themselves or loved ones. Today's topic is of major concern to America's 300,000 pharmacists—the health care professional most often at the front lines of informing patients about their medication cost or copay amount and explaining complicated insurance coverage policies.

Pharmacies are where millions of Americans are first exposed to the impact of complex pharmaceutical pricing policies or confronted with changes in coverage, formularies, prior authorization, deductibles and co-payments or co-insurance, many of

[109] The cost of prescription drugs increased by 8.77% in 2016, according to data from the Truveris National Drug Index. Over the past 3 years, annual price increases have increased by an average of 9.98%. *See*, Truveris. Prescription Drug Prices Continue to Climb, Soaring 8.77% in Latest Truveris NDI Report. Press Release. May 10, 2017. Available at: https://www.truveris.com/resources/press-releases/prescription-drug-prices-continue-to-climb- soaring-8.77-in-latest-truveris-ndi-report

which they didn't know existed or understand. My comments today will focus on the following areas – cost versus value, patients' access to medications, and medications' safety and affordability.

COST VERSUS VALUE

As drugs become more and more expensive, complex, and personalized, the need to optimize their impact also increases. In order to get the greatest benefit from medications, patients must understand how to use their medications safely and effectively. Pharmacists have more medication-related education and training than any other health care professional. Pharmacists can and do assist patients in optimizing the impact of medications and decreasing patients' costs by providing services focused on safe and appropriate medication use. For example, pharmacists provide medication management services, which are especially important for patients who have complex care plans, take multiple drugs or have chronic conditions. Additionally, to address hospital readmissions, pharmacists help patients transition between care settings.

Unfortunately, despite the fact that many states and Medicaid programs are turning to pharmacists to increase access to health care and address medication-related costs, Medicare Part B does not cover the services pharmacists can provide. Pharmacists are trained to do more than place medication in a container and while 91% of Americans live within 5 miles of a community pharmacy[110] many of our Nation's seniors are medically underserved. Pharmacists are an underutilized health care resource which can positively affect beneficiaries' care[111] and the entire Medicare program.

APhA strongly believes S.109, the *Pharmacy and Medically Underserved Areas Enhancement Act*, is a bipartisan proposal that will improve patient care, health outcomes, impact of medications,[112] and consequently, the viability of the Medicare program. Introduced by former Health Subcommittee Chair Chuck Grassley (R-IA) and Senators Bob Casey (D-PA), Susan Collins (R-ME), and Sherrod Brown (D-OH), S. 109 has 45 bipartisan cosponsors. Similar legislation obtained 51 cosponsors in the 114th Congress.

The legislation will enable Medicare patients in medically underserved communities to better access health care through state-licensed pharmacists practicing according to their own state's scope of practice. In medically underserved communities, pharmacists

---

[110] NCPDP Pharmacy File, ArcGIS Census Tract File. NACDS Economics Department.

[111] CMS. Evidence Supporting Enhanced Medication Therapy Management. Center for Medicare and Medicaid Innovation. 2016. Available at: https://innovation.cms.gov/Files/x/mtm- evidencebase.pdf

[112] *See* Avalere Health. Exploring Pharmacists' Role in a Changing Healthcare Environment. May 2014. Available at: http://avalere.com/expertise/life-sciences/insights/exploring-pharmacists-role-in-a-changing-healthcare-environment Also, *See* Avalere Health. Developing Trends in Delivery and Reimbursement of Pharmacist Services. October 2015. Available at: http://avalere.com/expertise/managed-care/insights/new-analysis-identifies-factors-that-can- facilitate-broader-reimbursement-o

are often the closest health care professional and accessible outside normal business hours. Helping patients receive the care they need, when they need it, is a common sense and bipartisan solution that will improve outcomes and reduce overall costs.

The importance of medication-related services cannot be overstated, especially in the Medicare program. Medications are the primary method of treating chronic disease and are involved in 80 percent of all treatment regimens. Moreover, the United States spends nearly $300 billion annually on medication-related problems, including nonadherence.[113] Accordingly, not only will S.109 increase beneficiaries' access to health care, it will help improve their outcomes—particularly those impacted by medications. APhA appreciates the support by many Committee members for the *Pharmacy and Medically Underserved Areas Enhancement Act* and urges its swift passage to allow pharmacists to deliver these vital services as providers in medically underserved areas.

We also encourage the Committee, when considering policy changes, to look beyond isolated components of health care to determine cost and value. Because health coverage is frequently analyzed by the benefit type such as inpatient, outpatient, and drug coverage, a patient's overall services, costs and outcomes may never be reviewed comprehensively. Policies cannot continue to consider drug and medical coverage, and their related costs and outcomes, separately if we are to achieve true value in health care. Current coverage and payment policies related to prescription drugs place incentives on the short-term, focusing on cost containment for the product rather than weighing the overall clinical benefit to the patient and the impact to their medical costs. Breaking down the many silos within our health care system will help address that $300 billion dollars spent on medication-related problems—many of which are preventable.[114]

PATIENTS' ACCESS TO MEDICATIONS

As the organization representing pharmacists in all practice settings, APhA has been, and is, a strong supporter of policies which increase patients' access to affordable and cost effective medicines. Decisions along the entire drug supply chain impact patients' medication costs, including arrangements between manufacturers, wholesalers, insurers, and pharmacy benefit managers, or PBMs. Because of these upstream stakeholder policies, for most patients, pharmacists have limited options to impact patients' final drug costs. Moreover, complex coverage and payment policies hinder the full potential of community pharmacists' clinical education and training from being realized as much of their day is spent on the phone trying to find an appropriate treatment that is not only

[113] New England Healthcare Institute. Thinking Outside the Pillbox: A System-Wide Approach to Improving Patient Adherence for Chronic Disease. August 2009. Available at: http:// www.nehi.net/publications/17-thinking-outside-the-pillbox-a-system-wide-approach-to-improving-patient-medication-adherence-for-chronic-disease/view

[114] Ibid.

covered, but the patient can afford. Consequently, APhA supports a transparent pricing framework which would eliminate such mechanisms as hidden discounts, free goods and post point-of-sale price fees imposed on pharmacies.

To address post point-of-sale fees, known as Direct and Indirect Remuneration (DIR) fees, APhA supports S. 413, the *Improving Transparency and Accuracy in Medicare Part D Spending Act*, that would prohibit Medicare Part D plan sponsors and their PBMs from retroactively reducing payment on clean claims submitted by pharmacies under Medicare Part D. The Centers for Medicare and Medicaid Services (CMS) has acknowledged a notable growth in DIR fees, which have more than tripled in recent years.[115] These policies generally result in higher prices at point of sale which result in the beneficiary paying more because cost-sharing is based on sales prices. S. 413 will boost transparency in drug pricing and facilitate better CMS oversight.

An additional problem facing some pharmacies is the inability to enter into contracts with health plans due to the growth in narrow networks. APhA reiterates the need for Part D plans to be required to contract with any pharmacy willing to accept their contractual terms and conditions. Increasing patient choice will not only improve patients' access to benefits and services, but will likely positively impact patient satisfaction and outcomes, such as adherence. A related issue is limited distribution of some medications. As more costly and complex medications are being developed, some manufacturers, clinics, practitioners' offices and pharmacies have entered into contracts that effectively limit the distribution of certain medications. To address these issues, APhA encourages the Committee to examine narrow networks and the limited distribution of certain medications and the impact these mechanisms have on patients and competition.

Drug shortages are another factor that can negatively affect patients in terms of cost and the availability of their treatments. APhA urges the Committee to consider mechanisms to both better control the price of medications in shortage and also to improve tracking and prediction systems used to identify drugs in shortage. APhA also strongly supports the appropriate prosecution of entities that engage in price gouging and profiteering of medically necessary drug products in response to drug shortages.

MEDICATIONS' SAFETY AND AFFORDABILITY

APhA supports congressional efforts to increase patients' access to appropriate, safe, effective, and affordable prescription medications. We are a strong supporter of the user fee acts, like the *FDA Reauthorization Act of 2017 (FDARA)*, which have helped innovative and cost affordable treatments reach patients more quickly. Equally, we have

---

[115] *See,* Wakely Consulting Group analysis of S. 413/H.R. 1038. 2017. Available at: http:// www.ncpa.co/ pdf/wakely-report.pdf

encouraged the development and implementation of a framework by the U.S. Food and Drug Administration (FDA) for determining biologic product interchangeability. APhA opposes practices which circumvent the intent of drug product review laws and negatively impact the pharmacist's ability to substitute medications to safe, effective, lower-cost alternatives. Conversely, APhA supports pharmacists collaborating with prescribers and patients to design cost-effective treatment regimens, identify formulary or generic products as a means to reduce costs, and intervene on behalf of the patient to identify alternate therapies.[116]

Although APhA supports congressional efforts to address patients' medication costs, APhA has significant concerns with turning to drug importation achieve lower prices. We believe proposals to legalize importation of non-FDA approved drugs is not a comprehensive solution to the complex issue of drug pricing, threatens patient safety, disrupts care, and directly conflicts with efforts by Congress and federal agencies to increase the integrity and security of the U.S. drug supply pursuant to the *Drug Supply Chain Security Act (DSCSA)*. Furthermore, APhA is concerned savings, if any, will be short-term and importation will instead result in long-term costs to patients and the health care system.

Because drug importation policies effectively encourage patients to buy medications online from foreign sources, APhA fears patients will be at an even greater risk of taking ineffective or harmful medications, including controlled medications in which they weren't prescribed. The lack of a strong regulatory framework for internet pharmacies in certain foreign countries has led to the large number of illegitimate foreign internet pharmacies. APhA's concerns regarding foreign internet pharmacies are compounded by the large number of illegitimate internet "pharmacies" which have increased and become more sophisticated in recent years, making them difficult to track and permanently stop.

Importantly, broader importation laws will further fragment care and hinder the progress made by Congress to move U.S. health care delivery and payment towards value. Because Canadian pharmacists may only fill prescriptions written by Canadian prescribers, expanded importation policies will encourage Americans to seek care from foreign prescribers and pharmacists, whose systems and standards are not integrated into, or consistent with, U.S. systems or care. Value- based care models and other efforts to produce savings and promote quality, such as outcomes- based reimbursement, will be

---

[116] *See* Brief for the FTC as Amicus Curiae, Mylan Pharmaceuticals, Inc. v. Warner Chilcott plc, et al. U.S. 3d Cir. (2016), describing a typical product-hopping scheme, "A brand-name pharmaceutical company expects generic rivals to win FDA approval to compete with the company's profitable brand-name drug using automatically substitutable AB-rated equivalents. To thwart such substitution, the brand-name company introduces minor changes to the drug's formulation, such as therapeutically insignificant tweaks to dosage levels or to the form of administration (e.g., capsules vs. tablets). Before generic equivalents have a change to enter, the brand-name manufacturer then takes various steps to extinguish demand for the original version... The shift in prescriptions is generally a one-way street: once doctors prescribe a medicine and find that it works, they are generally reluctant to switch users back to the original formulation even if a cheaper generic version of it later becomes available." Available at: https://www.ftc.gov/system/files/ documents/ amicus_briefs/mylan-pharmaceuticals-inc.v.warner-chilcott-plc-et-al./ 151001mylanamicusbrief.pdf

more difficult to measure and optimize if patients are allowed to receive care outside the model's mechanisms to drive results.

As previously noted, obtaining safe and effective medications is only one part of appropriate medication use. It also requires a health practitioner's knowledge of the patient's complete medication profile and an understanding by the patient of how to take the medication, side effects and/or potential interactions — all of which could be negatively affected by importation proposals. APhA believes importation of non-FDA approved drugs could hurt the very patients intended to benefit from importation proposals. Consequently, the risks to patient safety from harmful or ineffective products or avoidable medication errors due to fractured care outweighs any increase in access or cost-savings.

In summary, thank you today for including pharmacists—the medication expert on the patient's health care team—in this discussion. Ultimately, the most expensive medicine is the one not purchased, not taken, or not used correctly by patients. Pharmacists stand ready to help.

I look forward to answering any questions on the positive role pharmacists can and do play in reducing patients' prescription drug costs.

ADDENDUM: APHA HOUSE OF DELEGATES POLICIES RELATED TO DRUG PRICING

2004, 1968 Manufacturers' Pricing Policies. APhA supports pharmaceutical industry adoption of a "transparent pricing" system which would eliminate hidden discounts, free goods, and other subtle economic devices. *(JAPhA NS8:362 July 1968) (JAPhA NS44(5):551 September/October 2004) (Reviewed 2006)(Reviewed 2011)(Reviewed 2016)*

1985 Pharmaceutical Pricing. APhA supports a system of equal opportunity with the same terms, conditions, and prices available for all pharmacies. *(Am Pharm NS25(5):52 May 1985) (Reviewed 2004) (Reviewed 2006)(Reviewed 2011)(Reviewed 2016)*

2004, 1977 Prescription Drug Advertising. APhA does not oppose the dissemination of price information to patients, by advertising or by any other means. *(JAPhA NS17:448 July 1977)(JAPhA NS44(5):551 September/October 2004)(Reviewed 2006)(Reviewed 2011)(Reviewed 2016)*

2016, 1994 Pharmacy Services Benefits in Health Care Reform. A single set of pricing rules, eliminating class-of-trade distinctions, for medications, medication delivery systems, and other equipment so that no payer, patient, or provider is disadvantaged by cost shifting. The right for every American to choose his/her own provider of medications and pharmacists' services and for all pharmacists to participate in the health plans of their choice under equally applied terms and conditions. *(Am Pharm NS34(6):58 June 1994) (Reviewed 2004) (Reviewed 2010) (Reviewed 2011)(JAPhA 56(4); 379 July/August 2016*

2016 Biologic, Biosimilar, and Interchangeable Biologic Drug Products. APhA urges the development of programs and policies that facilitate patient access to and affordability of biologic products. *(JAPhA 56(4); 369 July/August 2016)*

2005, 1977 Government-Financed Reimbursement. APhA supports only those government-operated or -financed, third-party prescription programs which ensures that participating pharmacists receive individualized, equitable compensation for professional services and reimbursement for products provided under the program. *(JAPhA NS17:452 July 1977) (JAPhA NS45(5):558 September/October 2005) (Reviwed 2009(Reviewed 2011)(Reviewed 2012)(Reviewed 2017)*

2012 Drug Supply Shortages and Patient Care. APhA encourages the active investigation and appropriate prosecution of entities that engage in price gouging and profiteering of medically necessary drug products in response to drug shortages. *(JAPhA NS52(4) 457 July/August 2012)(Reviewed 2017)*

2005, 1981 Third-party Reimbursement Legislation

APhA supports enactment of legislation requiring that third-party program reimbursement to pharmacists be at least equal to the pharmacists prevailing charges to the self-paying public for comparable services and products, plus additional documented direct and indirect costs, which are generated by participating in the program.

(Am Pharm NS21(5):40 May 1981) (Reviewed 2005) (Reviewed 2009)(Reviewed 2014)

1967 Drugs Provided Under Social Security Act: Guidelines for Pharmaceutical Service. Since it is probable or likely that APhA may have to consider and act upon some proposals in the area of drug costs before the next annual meeting, we recommend that APhA Board of Trustees be guided by whether the proposals: (a) Permit pharmacists to select and dispense a quality drug product; (b) Establish some mechanism to assist pharmacists in selecting quality, drug products under the cost and other criteria established; (c) Permit the use of any available drug product when unique medical circumstances so require; (d) Establish a reasonable remuneration base for pharmacists rendering services under the program; (e) Guarantee recipients free choice of pharmacy; and (f) Limit the reimbursement for pharmacists' services to those provided by duly licensed pharmacists. *(JAPhA NS7:315 June 1967) (Reviewed 2005) (Reviewed 2009)(Reviewed 2014)*

2017 Pharmacy Performance Networks. APhA supports performance networks that improve patient care and health outcomes, reduce costs, use pharmacists as an integral part of the health care team, and include evidence-based quality measures. *(JAPhA 57(4): 441 July/August 2017)*

[Summary Statement of Thomas E. Menighan]

Thank you Chairman Alexander and Ranking Member Murray for the opportunity to discuss a very important topic for our Nation's patients, families, and their pharmacists.

It is an honor to be here.

I am Tom Menighan, the American Pharmacists Association's (APhA), Executive Vice President and CEO.

APhA is America's oldest, largest and most diverse pharmacist organization. We promote patient access and coverage for pharmacists' quality patient care services. Our members contribute to health care in a wide variety of settings including physician offices, specialty and community pharmacies, senior care facilities, academia and health systems.

I was a practicing community pharmacist and specialty pharmacy owner for many years. I've shared the challenges with patients who face financial choices between food and medicine for themselves or loved ones. Today's topic is of major concern to America's 300,000 pharmacists—the health care professional most often at the front lines of informing patients about their medication cost or copay amount and explaining complicated insurance coverage policies.

As the organization representing pharmacists in all practice settings, APhA is a strong supporter of policies which increase patients' access to affordable and cost effective medicines.

As you know, decisions along the entire drug supply chain impact patients' medication costs, including arrangements among manufacturers, wholesalers, insurers, and pharmacy benefit managers, or PBMs.

Pharmacies are where millions of Americans are first exposed to the impact of complex pharmaceutical pricing policies or confronted with changes in coverage, formularies, prior authorization, deductibles and co-payments, many of which they didn't know or understand. Due to these upstream decisions and policies, for most patients, pharmacists have limited options to impact patients' final drug costs. Instead of helping to address the nearly $300 billion the U.S. spends annually on medication-related problems, community pharmacists spend much of their day on the phone to find an appropriate treatment that is not only covered but the patient can afford.

We support a transparent pricing framework that would eliminate mechanisms like rebates and post point-of-sale price fees imposed on pharmacies. These policies generally result in higher prices at point of sale and consequently, higher beneficiary co-pays. We also encourage policies that allow any willing pharmacy to enter into contracts with insurers or PBMs to increase patient access and choice, which can improve adherence and health outcomes. APhA requests the Committee to look beyond isolated components of health care to determine cost and value. Policies that consider drug and medical coverage, and their related costs and outcomes in separate silos cannot achieve true value in health care.

As drugs become more expensive, complex and personalized, the need to optimize their impact and value also increases. To get the greatest benefit from medications, patients must understand how to use their medications safely and effectively. Empowered pharmacists can assist patients in optimizing the impact of medications and decreasing patients' costs by providing services focused on safe and appropriate medication use.

For example, pharmacists provide medication management services, which are especially important for patients who take multiple drugs or have chronic conditions, and address hospital readmissions by helping patients transition between care settings.

Unfortunately, Medicare Part B does not cover our services. Many of our Nation's seniors are medically underserved, despite 91 percent of Americans living within 5 miles of a community pharmacy. Pharmacists are an underutilized health care resource which can positively affect beneficiaries' care and the entire Medicare program.

We ask your support today for S. 109, the Pharmacy and Medically Underserved Areas Enhancement Act, and urge its swift passage to provide access to underserved seniors. Not only will access increase, it will help improve beneficiary outcomes, particularly those impacted by medications.

Finally, APhA supports a safe and secure supply chain. America's patients and pharmacists should not have to worry about diversion and counterfeits. We believe proposals to legalize importation of non-FDA approved drugs will do more harm than good. Importantly, we have great concern regarding importation's impact on patient safety and continuity of care and believe it is in direct conflict with recent efforts by Congress to secure the U.S. drug supply and improve patient safety.

In summary, thank you today for including pharmacists—the medication expert on the patient's health care team—in this discussion. Ultimately, the most expensive medicine is the one not purchased, not taken, or not used correctly by patients. Pharmacists stand ready to help.

I look forward to answering any questions on the positive role pharmacists can and do play in reducing patients' prescription drug costs.

The Chairman. Thank you very much to all the witnesses. We'll now begin a 5-minute round of questions. I'll begin, and then we'll go to Senator Murray, and then we'll leave and go vote and come back. But we'll continue the hearing so that Senators can ask questions.

Ms. Reilly, did I hear you right? I think you said that three of the pharmacy benefit managers, which Mr. Merritt represents, negotiate rebates for 75 percent of prescriptions sold.

Ms. Reilly. That's correct.

The Chairman. That's about $100 billion of money?

Ms. Reilly. In 2015, over $100 billion was negotiated on behalf of commercial health plans as well as some government mandated——

The Chairman. The rebate is simply—that $100 billion means that the pharmacy benefit managers then—the manufacturers get less money.

Ms. Reilly. Correct.

The Chairman. The pharmacy benefit managers then decide in their negotiations where that $100 billion goes.

Ms. Reilly. Right. So it lowers the net price to the manufacturer. That money either gets sent back to the insurance company, some of which is kept—a portion of which is kept by the pharmacy benefit manager.

The Chairman. Mr. Menighan, you said, I believe, that we don't need rebates. Is that what you said?

Mr. Menighan. No. What I said was that we need——

The Chairman. Do you want to get rid of them?

Mr. Menighan [continuing]. we need more transparency in the system so that we know where they're coming from. At the end of the day when the patient walks up to a pharmacy, and the pharmacy presents them with the cost of the medicine to them, the impact of rebates isn't really felt until after——

The Chairman. Well, Ms. Reilly was saying that people who go into your pharmacies don't really see the direct—or don't necessarily see the direct benefit of the rebate negotiated by the pharmacy benefit managers.

Mr. Menighan. Well, that's fair. They don't.

The Chairman. Senator Murray and I and others of us—we've been working on health insurance, which we find to be very complicated. Where the money goes in prescription drugs is more complicated. I've yet to figure out exactly where it goes.

Why do we need rebates at all? Wouldn't it increase transparency if the drug manufacturers just established a list price and then they negotiated with the pharmacy benefit managers, or to whom-ever else they sold to, a reduction in that price if they wanted to, and then we wouldn't have some mystery about who is getting the benefit of a rebate.

Mr. Menighan. Without commenting on the need for rebates, they're clearly used to drive market share——

The Chairman. Why wouldn't you comment on it?

Mr. Menighan. They're used to drive market share. Oftentimes, in our view, that's not necessarily to the benefit of the patient. When pharmacists are trying to manage medication use——

The Chairman. Well, my question is why do we need rebates.

Ms. Reilly. Well, I would argue——

Mr. Menighan. I don't know why we need rebates.

The Chairman. Mr. Merritt, why do we need rebates? Why don't we just get rid of rebates and let you negotiate directly with the manufacturers, take that $100 billion a year and just reduce the list price? Wouldn't that make it simpler for us to understand where the money goes?

Mr. Merritt. We'd be open to that. I mean, rebates were around before PBMs ever came on the scene, and, usually, rebates are used not just by manufacturers of drugs but other products because they want to keep one high price because their lower volume clients will pay that price. But then as they have bigger volume clients, instead of lowering the price, they'll offer a bigger discount, which is all a rebate is.

Ms. Reilly. I would argue, though, that high rebates are things that both the pharmacy benefit managers and insurance companies like, because they get a big check at the end of the day for those rebates. They then can use those rebate dollars to do what they want to do with them, which is typically to lower premiums.

The Chairman. Right. Well, would you like, Ms. Reilly, to eliminate rebates?

Ms. Reilly. We'd like to see those rebates get passed back to the patient at the point of sale.

The Chairman. Why worry about a big complicated chart that shows how they're being passed back? Why not just eliminate rebates?

Ms. Reilly. Well, I think that's one option, obviously, to have a lower list price. But I will tell you, today, plans and PBMs tend to favor products in terms of the formularies. They prefer to have a product with a high list price and a high rebate because, again, that money flows back to them for them to decide what to do with.

The Chairman. Ms. Gallenagh, what do you think? Do we need rebates at all?

Ms. Gallenagh. Honestly, to be candid, wholesale distributors don't have any role in this rebate.

The Chairman. But you have a nice view of the prescription drug business. Do you think it would be more transparent and easier to follow and the consumers might get a more direct benefit of lower cost if rebates were eliminated?

Ms. Gallenagh. I think it's something to be explored.

The Chairman. That's what we're doing. We're exploring it here, trying to get an—Mr. Davis, what about you?

Mr. Davis. Mr. Chairman, this is a good example of a difference between the branded and the generic market. Historically, the rebate model isn't applied across the entire generic sector. Our work in setting a wholesale acquisition cost is generally directed to the wholesalers. We'll have 20 or 25 generic manufacturers competing for the business of the three wholesalers. That usually leads to sort of an upfront negotiation with them on price, which is what forces the deflationary aspect of the industry.

We are seeing an increased level of involvement between PBMs and brands as branded products come close to patent expiry in an effort to maintain market share that will negatively inhibit a generic getting to market. But, ultimately, the rebate model is not as commonly used on the generic side as it is on the brand side.

The Chairman. Thanks to each of you.

Senator Murray.

Senator Murray. Thank you.

Ms. Reilly, let me start with you. Do you agree that our current system of brand and generic drugs is designed to strike a careful balance between protecting the market share of innovative drugs for a limited period to recoup costs and driving competition to bring prices down after that time? Yes or no?

Ms. Reilly. I do believe that's the intent of our system, yes.

Senator Murray. I do, too. But here's what my concern is. Your member companies are taking some actions now to deliberately disrupt that balance to get the longest market monopoly possible in order to benefit their bottom line, and I'll give you some examples.

AbbVie recently settled in court to extend the market monopoly for Humira to 20 years. Biogen extended its monopoly on the MS drug, Tecfidera, to 15 years by getting additional patents that cover only the drug's dosage amount. Allergan sold its patent for Restasis to the Mohawk Indian tribe to shield it from challenge, protecting a more than 15-year monopoly, and recently settled with a generic challenger to keep it off the market for 7 years.

Are those isolated incidents, or are they part of a larger trend in which companies use the patent system to actually block competition that could actually bring down prices?

Ms. Reilly. Well, those were a lot of examples. Let me try and address each one of them. In the case of patent settlements, companies are given patents by the Patent and Trademark Office, and they believe they have every right to defend those patents in a court of law. In the case of the AbbVie and Amgen patent settlement you mentioned, there was no exchange of money for that patent settlement. The patents on that particular product, according to public records, exceeded actually to 2033, so this product will be coming on the market 10 years prior to when the patents truly expire for that product. I understand there are other companies that are also trying to get on the market to challenge that particular product.

Yes, we have a system, and that system was in part designed by the Hatch-Waxman Act to encourage generic manufacturers to get on the market before our patents actually expire. I think it's a system that's worked incredibly well. In 1984, there were 19 percent of prescriptions that are generic. Today, nearly 90 percent of prescriptions are generic. Patent settlements is one way oftentimes to get products to market well before the patent would actually have expired.

Oftentimes, there are anecdotes pointed out. I would argue that, by and large, patent settlements and the Hatch-Waxman system have served and inured to the benefit of patients in getting those medicines to market sooner than they would have been otherwise.

Senator Murray. Well, Mr. Davis, I'd like you to comment on that, and there also seems—that, as well as I think there's other tactics at play to keep drug prices high. When Congress actually passed the Biologics Price Competition and Innovation Act as part of the ACA, it cleared the path for products to compete with pricey biologics. The CBO estimated that increased competition could save patients and families $7 billion just through 2019. But even though FDA has now approved several of those, we aren't seeing any great savings.

Why is that? Combine it with an answer to the first question.

Mr. Davis. Sure, Senator Murray. Thank you for the question.

I think there are three things that are having an enormous impact on the generic side of the pharmaceutical ecosystem right now that, quite frankly, are threatening its continued viability and sustainability moving forward. One is the market imbalance that I talked about, and, quite frankly, that was created in the market, and it's going to take some time for the market to work that out, where you have essentially three buyers that are in control of 90 percent of the generic drug supply.

The two others, though, are directly related to policy and your question. The second is that there has been a series, both here in Washington and at the state level, of what we would call well-intentioned but misguided policy provisions, for instance, things that look to actually penalize generic manufacturers operating in a deflationary market that are only 26 percent of the total cost but that are not focusing on the increase in cost of branded drugs and specialty drugs year over year. The implementation of a Medicaid rebate penalty on generics passed as part of the 2015 budget agreement is a great example of that, in addition to some bills in places like Maryland and California on the state legislative side.

Directly to your question, the third area is we are absolutely, unequivocally seeing an increased effort on the part of certain branded manufacturers with respect to the amount of anti-competitive behavior designed to keep generics and biosimilars off the market. You mentioned a number of them. I think the reality is, overall, the reason that we're seeing this is because there are companies that are doing the business math and the political math and thinking that they can actually get away with it.

To your question on the biosimilars, interestingly enough, when BPCIA passed as part of the Affordable Care Act, I believe the Federal Government began scoring savings, estimated savings, as early as fiscal year 2014. To your point, the first biosimilar did not get to market until September 2015. Seven have been approved. Only three are on the market. The other four are tied up in litigation.

Senator MURRAY. Thank you, Mr. Chairman. I just think it's really real that in order for competition to bring down costs, we have to make sure the market is actually working. So that's one of the concerns that I have as we move forward.

The CHAIRMAN. In the absence of other Senators, I'll ask a question, and when they come back, I'll defer to them.

With the exception of drugs compounded in pharmacies, each pharmaceutical drug sold in the United States requires a careful review by the Food and Drug Administration before that drug can be sold in the United States. We call that the FDA Gold Standard. There are 4.4 billion prescriptions a year. Most of us, when we go into our local pharmacy or the doctor's office, don't really worry about the safety of those prescriptions because we rely on the FDA Gold Standard.

Sometimes, when the cost of drugs comes up, there are proposals that we should import drugs from other countries and sidestep the careful FDA review and approval of each drug sold in the United States. I'd like to ask each of you, starting with Mr. Menighan and then going across, whether you agree that we should allow drugs approved by other countries to be sold in the United States without careful review and approval of each drug by the Food and Drug Administration.

Mr. Menighan.

Mr. Menighan. The short answer is absolutely not. While AphA appreciates congressional efforts to address patients' medication costs, we don't believe importation is a solution to the complex issue of drug pricing. Broadened importation of non-FDA approved meds threatens patient safety, directly conflicts with congressional efforts to increase the integrity and security of the supply chain and the Drug Supply Chain Security Act, and disrupts continuity of care and value-based payment and delivery. We're concerned that savings, if any, will be short-term, and importation will instead result in long-term cost to patients.

The Chairman. Thank you.

Mr. Merritt.

Mr. Merritt. I'll give the short answer. We oppose that.

The Chairman. Thank you, Mr. Merritt.

Ms. Gallenagh.

Ms. Gallenagh. We would absolutely oppose importation as it would threaten patient safety in this country. We have done a lot of work on the Drug Supply Chain Security Act, and we're currently in the Implementation Phase 1 of that law. One of the things that it requires is serialized product by all manufacturers in this country. There is no global standard for serialization currently. It also involves data exchange for each transaction that happens from the manufacturer to distributor to pharmacy by 2023 at the unit level. There is also no global standard for that data exchange.

We've done a lot of work to try and protect the U.S. supply chain and make it as safe as possible, and we don't think that allowing foreign imports will do anything to keep that level of security.

The Chairman. Senator Collins has returned, and I'm going to turn the chair over to her. But I'd like for Mr. Davis and Ms. Reilly to answer my question about drug importation.

Mr. Davis. Yes, Mr. Chairman. Briefly, we share the concern that you've heard from the other witnesses here today relative to safety. The Secretary of Health and Human Services has the opportunity to certify and legalize importation if they determine, whether it's a Republican or Democratic health official, that it's safe and cost effective. No one has been willing to do that.

I will tell you, also, there's an additional element related to generics from a practical perspective, which is far and away, as a market basket, generics are less expensive in the U.S. market than they are in major developed markets across the world. So it would beg the question: Why would you want to be importing something that's more expensive to begin with?

The Chairman. Ms. Reilly.

Ms. Reilly. I would just add on to what the panelists have said previously. But opening our borders to potentially counterfeit medicines risks the health and safety of Americans. Counterfeiting medicines is a low-penalty, low-risk enterprise, and if we open the borders, we are subjecting Americans to unsafe medicines. So we adamantly oppose.

STATEMENT OF SENATOR COLLINS

Senator COLLINS. [presiding]. Thank you for your response.

First of all, let me say that I love having the gavel in my hand——

[Laughter.]

Senator COLLINS ——even if it's only temporary and because of the need of other Members to go vote. I went and voted early so that I could relieve Senator Alexander so the Chairman could go vote.

Last year, the Senate Aging Committee did an extensive investigation into the spiraling cost increases of certain prescription drugs. It's been mentioned this morning. We looked at Turing, we looked at Valeant, and what we found was a pattern of certain, what I call, hedge fund pharma companies buying the rights to a drug and then, overnight, increasing the cost by as much as literally 5,000 percent in the case of Daraprim.

These were companies that played absolutely no role in the development of the pharmaceutical. So there wasn't any investment in R and D that would justify that kind of increase.

I am particularly pleased that the Chairman is holding this hearing today, because I think that we have a lot of work to do. One of the issues that really troubles me is the lack of transparency in the system. The MAC price is not what most people pay. Prices vary, depending on what pharmaceutical benefit manager negotiated the cost. Prices vary according to, obviously, whether a generic can be substituted.

But there's just a lack of transparency in the entire system, and I'd like to go across the panel and have each of you comment on how we can increase transparency into the pricing, because until we do that, it is going to be very difficult for us to get a handle on whether these cost increases are justified.

Ms. Reilly.

Ms. REILLY. Thank you for the question, and thank you for the work that you've done on issues that you raised, such as the ones with Daraprim, Turing, and Valeant pharmaceuticals. We, too, share the concerns that you raised about the fact that companies can buy and essentially engage in regulatory arbitrage, knowing that the approval through the FDA may take years.

There are a number of solutions that we've talked about as well that we think merit some consideration, whether the FDA can fasttrack reviews of medicines to compete with these products, whether they can list on their websites suppliers and names of companies that may be able to help in producing competing product. So we are thankful for your leadership on that issue and would welcome working with you on that.

The issue of transparency, I think, is a very important one. Oftentimes, when we hear the word, transparency, it means different things to different people. Transparency is important, but it's important if it applies holistically. Oftentimes, the transparency legislation that we've seen wants to focus on one industry, the brand name pharmaceutical industry, and leave out the rest of the supply chain.

As I mentioned in my testimony, brand name pharmaceuticals represent about half of what we spend on total drugs in this country. The rest is subsumed by generic manufacturers, as Chip mentioned, just over 20 percent, but the rest is as a result of supply chain, be it wholesalers, distributors, pharmacy benefit managers, payers, and hospitals.

If we're going to have a discussion on transparency, which we would welcome, we think it's important to have one that holistically involves the entire supply chain, because there are costs, as I mentioned before, in the hospital sector alone where they are increasing their reimbursement two and a half times over what they acquire a pharmaceutical product for. We definitely need to have more transparency into areas like that.

Senator COLLINS. I see two of my Members of the Committee have returned. So rather than going down the line, I'm going to switch to another question that I want to make sure I get in, and, Mr. Merritt, I'm going to direct it to you and Mr. Menighan.

Last night, NBC Nightly News ran a story about an investigation which found that a wide variety of prescription drugs on certain insurance plans are actually cheaper when the consumer pays out of pocket. That makes no sense to me. We also learned that at least in some negotiations, in some contracts, there is a gag order that prevents pharmacists from telling patients that they would be better off paying out of pocket than using their health insurance.

I would like both of you to answer the question of how common is this practice, and how can this occur? How can it occur that a prescription benefit manager, whose very job is to negotiate prices, is negotiating a price that's actually higher than the consumer would pay out of pocket?

Mr. Merritt.

Mr. Merritt. Yes, it's a really good question, and the answer to your question is it's not something that should be going on in the marketplace. It's an outlier behavior. I'm not even sure if it's a PBM or an insurer behavior. But it's not something that we support. We think the person ought to—who goes to the pharmacy ought to pay the lesser amount if it's a cost-sharing or the cost of the drug. So if there's a generic that costs $5 and there's a $20 copay, they should pay $5. They shouldn't pay that. So I agree that it's a practice that we don't support. It's an outlier practice and a practice that we hope goes away.

Mr. Menighan.

Mr. Menighan. Thank you, Senator Collins. First, I should say that I didn't handle an earlier question about rebates. We oppose rebates in all their forms.

With regard to the question that you just asked, pharmacists are incredibly frustrated with their inability to help patients. Providing patient care shouldn't be this difficult. My members feel incredibly frustrated with their lack of connectivity, their lack of communication with plans. Essentially, they have no negotiating power, and they're sort of told what they have to do, and they can take it or leave it. They can either be in a network or not, typically not, and if they're in the network, they're told how to perform. So——

Senator Collins. So is it an outlier——

Mr. Menighan. No, it's not an outlier.

Senator Collins ——or is this a common practice?

Mr. Menighan. It's common.

Senator Collins. Thank you.

Senator Kaine.

STATEMENT OF SENATOR KAINE

Senator Kaine. Thank you, Madam Chair, and thank you to the witnesses for their good testimony. I want to ask a couple of questions.

Mr. Menighan, if I can start with you at the front line with pharmacies and dealing with patients—commonly, I hear, as I travel around Virginia, about how high prices affect financial decisions whether—your last line was great. The most expensive drug is one that somebody doesn't get, often for a financial reason, or if they get, they don't use it correctly. One in four Americans who take prescription drugs report that they have difficulty affording them, and then these high costs lead to lack of access, and that disproportionately affects the most vulnerable people in my population.

Just talk a little about your customers. How do you see this high price challenge affecting your customers?

Mr. Menighan. Well, on the front end, at the first purchase of a medication, oftentimes patients do have to make hard choices, and pharmacists are in a great position to help with those choices if given the latitude to do so. Oftentimes, we spend our time chasing administrivia when, in fact, we should be spending our time coaching patients on effective use of their medicines, which they so desperately need.

Patients won't make lifestyle choices, won't be better nourished, won't increase their activity without long-term coaching and support. When they face these major barriers on the front end, often-times they throw up their hands and say, "I can't do it. It's too hard," and they go back to their old ways, and they don't manage their chronic disease.

At its core, these front line decisions that patients have to make and the limited resources and the lack of transparency that affects pharmacists' ability to understand the reasons behind why PBMs may say this drug is available, this one is not, and the conflict that occurs there when a physician says, "This is the drug that I want for my patient. I think it's best for that patient," the pharmacist says, "I'd like to give that to you, but it's going to cost you $500," and the patient says, "I can't handle that. I give up," pharmacists are really challenged with that.

To the degree that we know the reasons behind those formulary choices, we can be better advocates for our patients. To the degree that we can insert lower-cost options in collaborations with our physician colleagues, we can help our patients. But we need the time to do that and we need the transparency and better understanding of the information behind those decisions that are often made far above us and without any transparency.

Senator Kaine. I would like the record to reflect that Mr. Menighan's use of the phrase, administrivia, suggests a new word that should be included in the Webster's Collegiate Dictionary in the coming year. I've never heard it, and I really like it, and I'm going to use it, steal it, and say I thought of it.

[Laughter.]

Senator Kaine. My next question is for——

Mr. Menighan. It's yours, Senator.

Senator Kaine. My next question is for Mr. Davis.

Mr. Davis, your written testimony has a really nice thing that I love, Congress must act to support generic and biosimilars, and you give us three things. I want to make sure I really get—one, the CREATES Act, I understand. There are two I want to make sure I understand, and I wonder if you could explain.

First, repealing the misguided Medicaid penalty on generic drugs. Describe what that penalty is and why it's misguided.

Mr. Davis. Sure, Senator. Thank you for the question. In the fall of 2015, as part of the budget agreement that I believe was reached in October of that year, a rebate penalty that has long been associated with the branded industry—in Medicaid, you pay a base level rebate if you're a branded product, and then if your price increases exceed medical inflation, there's an additional penalty over and above. That was instituted in the early 1990's through a process in an effort to constrain a monopolist company's ability to take price increases above and beyond the rate of inflation.

Through weekend deliberations around that budget agreement, there was a decision made—there had been a bill introduced in the House and Senate that, quite frankly, had languished for several years, that was ultimately included in an effort because it was allegedly scored at saving about a billion dollars over 10 years. The net effect of that provision, Senator, is that it actually applies in a commoditized market and can impact a generic manufacturer when they don't take a price increase.

So that penalty has now gone into effect beginning earlier this year, and we have heard from our members that in certain instances some 40 percent of their generic portfolio is impacted by this additional penalty in instances when they did not take a price increase.

Senator Kaine. It's a penalty that affects generics in a different way than branded pharmaceuticals?

Mr. Davis. Yes, Senator. We have an added additional expense back to the government that is not tied to when companies actually take a price increase. That's the net effect.

Senator Kaine. Thank you. Then, second, you want to ensure that biosimilar medicines have a level and competitive playing field in Medicare. Could you describe that, as my last question?

Mr. Davis. Sure. Thank you. There's two components to that. One actually is that our members would actually like for biosimilars to be included in the 50 percent discount to the Medicare Part D coverage gap, so, actually, to make sure that there's not sort of an inverse incentive to make sure that a patient actually stays on the higher cost biosimilar—or, excuse me—biologic if it's appropriate to be on the biosimilar, but we actually have to be exposed to the same 50 percent discount in the coverage gap. So that's something that we have supported, and we would urge Congress to consider that at the appropriate option.

Then the last area with respect to that—and, actually, CMS, to their credit, is now looking at several of the reimbursement policies that originally came out relative to how they were going to treat biosimilars. We think there's more opportunity to encourage the marketplace, not distinguish the originator biologic and then group all biosimilars that have never been compared to each other in a separate J code, and we're optimistic that perhaps CMS will continue that evaluation and come up with a different decision. But that's going to be critical to making sure that we have a more conducive environment for biosimilars moving forward.

Senator Kaine. Thank you.

Senator Collins. Senator Cassidy.

STATEMENT OF SENATOR CASSIDY

Senator Cassidy. Thank you. I think a lot about drugs, and I have to admit it turns my head. I'm going to focus on insulin, and then I may come back to something else in a little bit, and I'm going to focus on it in two different areas.

Ms. Reilly, if we speak about some of our insulin products, they're increasing at 20 percent per year. The Wall Street Journal had an article in 2016 about 2015, and at that point, they actually referred to the role of PBMs. But if I look prior to 2015, there were no rebates, appreciably, being given to PBMs, but prices were going up anywhere from 10 percent to 23 percent per year, and this is toward the end of the monopoly. So, presumably, they've recouped their expense of new drug development, but costs are going up 20 percent per year so that, I think, from 2010 to 2015, something goes from $114 to $228. As deductibles have grown, patients can't afford this.

You make a good case that we're investing in development, et cetera, but when costs are going up 20 percent per year on the tail end of a monopoly—presumably those costs have been recouped— Americans with diabetes and all Americans are upset. What do you say about that?

Ms. Reilly. Thank you for asking that question. I think the diabetes marketplace, to your point, is often confusing. Today, it is, I would argue, one, if not the most, competitive marketplaces. On average——

Senator Cassidy. But can we go back to that specific period from, say, 2010 to 2015, or 2011, where people were basically price taking. They were getting 20 percent increases per year, even though, presumably, they had recouped their cost of investment prior to that.

Ms. Reilly. Well, I would argue, Senator Cassidy, that rebates were occurring well before 2010. Today, the average rebate in the diabetes market——

Senator Cassidy. Okay. If I may, in 2014—2013 to 2014, quarter four, year to year, the price list for Novo Nordisk was 22 percent with a rebate of 1.2 percent increase. For Sanofi, it was 23 percent with a rebate change of 5.4 percent, net price increase 20.8 percent and 26.4 percent. I'm not sure I'm seeing that, at least in that period up to 2014.

Ms. Reilly. Right, and I'm not sure what the data is that you're looking at, Senator Cassidy, but what I can tell you is that today, the rebates and discounts publicly reported averaged between 60 percent and 70 percent.

Senator Cassidy. Again, I'm not speaking of today. I'm speaking of that period in the early part of this decade.

Ms. Reilly. Right.

Senator Cassidy. Those drugs have now had a new competitor, and, frankly, when there's new competitors, PBMs drive bigger rebates, and I'll have a question for Mr. Merritt about that in just a second. But if you're an American looking at the insulin price— believe me, there's a guy from Lafayette, Louisiana, who texts me about three times a week, talking about how his daughter cannot afford insulin, and the price increase it's had, coupled with her high deductible premium, and he's a Republican, pro-business, but he's about his daughter's diabetes. So what do we say to her?

Ms. Reilly. I would say a couple of things that are important that have happened. Prior to, I would say, 2012, most patients that took medicine did not have a deductible for their medicine. When they showed up at the pharmacy counter in January, the price that they paid for their medicine was often a copay and a pretty modest one—for diabetes medicine, often $20. From 2012 to 2015, there's been a dramatic increase in the number of patients that today have a deductible——

Senator Cassidy. So you're addressing—if I may, because I have limited time. You're addressing the fact that the individual may not have been seeing the price—but there's still price—somebody's paying. It's either indirectly through the premium or directly through a copay. So somebody is paying.

Ms. Reilly. Well, I would argue, too, though, Senator Cassidy, when companies price their product, they're not just looking to get reimbursed for the prices that they spent on getting that individual product to market. Companies are investing in the next generation of cures and treatments. Those costs also have to be recouped. There's been many advancements in the space of insulin since they first began many years ago, and some of the newer insulins are longer acting. Patients can——

Senator Cassidy. If I may say, though, just to counter that a little bit, there's been more of an emphasis on raising prices on established drugs than on new innovative drugs, and I think that statistic—I don't have that statistic in front of me, but I've read that in the past.

Ms. Reilly. Well, I would say last year, price increases on all drugs was at 2.5 percent. So price increases have certainly moderated over the past few years. While that may have been the case several years ago, we are not seeing the kind of price increases that we had years ago.

Senator Cassidy. Let me go to Mr. Merritt. I'm sorry. I don't mean to be rude. I apologize.

Mr. Merritt, now, I've learned to say what I've been told, not what I know. But this Wall Street Journal article to which I refer with my questions to Ms. Reilly point out that in 2015, actually, insulin prices did moderate. Prior to that, it's kind of like, oh, my gosh, I wish my stocks were doing as well. But in 2015, it actually flattened, but the price increased dramatically because they had to pay high rebates to PBMs. A competitor had entered; the PBM could choose; and so to pay the rebate, they jacked up their price in order to pay for the rebate.

The CEO of Mylan came in to speak to me. She said actually their price was relatively flat, and then a competitor came in. PBMs came and said, "Wait a second. There's now a competitor. We'll only carry you if you give us a big rebate." They had to increase their price in order to pay the rebate. She said it's paradoxical in the world of PBMs. When there is no competitor, your prices are lower and competition increases the price. I've heard that from the CEO of Mylan and from the Wall Street Journal. Your thoughts regarding that?

Mr. Merritt. I would disagree with that. Let's remember Mylan raised the price of EpiPen 400 percent just because it felt like doing it, and——

Senator Cassidy. They would counter and say, "No, we had to do it because there's now a competitor, albeit on the market only for a short time, and we were told that they would not carry my EpiPen, that they would carry the competitor unless we paid the rebate. That's when we increased it."

Mr. Merritt. I don't think that happened. I think the reality is if they'd just lower the price, that would make it great, too, because all we want is the lowest net cost.

Senator Cassidy. So, wait a second. On insulin—again, I'm looking at this Wall Street Journal article dated from October 2016, and they say that at that point, the net price going back to the manufacturer remained flat, even though the price increased dramatically, and they were paying the PBM for this with a delta between their net price and their list price. Are you disagreeing with that, too?

Mr. Merritt. Again, the simplest thing is for them just to lower their prices. Typically, a rebate goes up because the price goes up. If the price goes up, our clients are going to demand that we get more of a discount. That's just how it works. What we want is lower net cost. That can be done in a number of different ways, and to Chairman Alexander's point, rebates are one way things can work, but the simplest thing would just be for prices to go down.

Senator Cassidy. I am way over, but I'll do it for the record and ask you to direct the response directly to the article in the Wall Street Journal which disagrees with that a little bit.

I'm sorry for being way over. I apologize to my colleagues. Senator COLLINS. Senator Hassan.

STATEMENT OF SENATOR HASSAN

Senator Hassan. Thank you, Senator Collins, and I want to add my thanks to Chairman Alexander and Ranking Member Murray for holding this hearing, and thank you all to the witnesses for being here today.

Ms. Reilly, I hear from granite staters all the time who struggle to afford their medications, and they are so frustrated. Drug makers are reaping sky-high profits as patients choose between having their medicine or, for example, heating their homes, choices they have to make too often because of the brazenly anti-competitive behavior that bad actors in the drug industry engage in, most recently, Allergan, who makes the blockbuster dry eye drug, Restasis.

Restasis brought in sales of $1.5 billion last year alone, which is, on average, $4 million per day. Allergan has had a market monopoly on this multibillion dollar drug since its approval in 2002, and, boy, is it working to keep it that way. On September 8th of this year, just 1 week before its patents were set to be subject to a hearing at the U.S. Patent and Trademark Office, Allergan announced it had cut a deal with a Native American tribe in order to shield the Restasis patents from review by exploiting the doctrine of tribal sovereign immunity.

In this outrageous first of its kind deal, which just yesterday, a Federal district court judge called a ploy, Allergan assigned ownership of the Restasis patents over to the tribe. Then it basically leases back the patents from the tribe and continues to sell the blockbuster drug. So Allergan is using tribal sovereign immunity to shield the Restasis patents from review, maintaining its market monopoly, preventing generic competition, and keeping prices and profits high. Meanwhile, patients who need Restasis arc struggling to afford it.

Allergan's behavior here is unacceptable, and if other drug companies follow its lead, the problem is only going to get worse. I'm very concerned about the potentially devastating implications of the deal for our entire patent system, for the delicate balance struck in the Hatch-Waxman Act, and, most importantly, for patients' access to affordable drugs.

Ms. Reilly, your organization has a role to play here. In May 2017, PhRMA approved new membership criteria to—and this is a quote—"tackle the biggest challenges facing patients," and PhRMA expelled 22 member companies, which was seen as a response to public concern over the rising cost of prescription drugs and to remove bad actors.

Ms. Reilly, you are head of Membership for PhRMA. What I want to know, yes or no, is whether you believe Allergan's actions are consistent with the mission of your organization.

Ms. Reilly. First of all, thank you very much for the question. I want to make clear a few things. Today, our member companies are asked to defend their patents, not——

Senator Hassan. Ms. Reilly, I have very limited time and another question to ask. So yes or no, is it consistent?

Ms. Reilly. I believe the IPR process, which is in play here, is a process that needs significant reform. Our companies——

Senator Hassan. That's fine. But to exploit tribal sovereign immunity to avoid competition as opposed to dealing with the patent system, in my view, is unacceptable. I'm sorry, but because I have limited time, I'd like to move on to my next question, which is to Ms. Gallenagh.

I want to discuss with you my serious concerns about the Wash ington Post 60 Minutes report this weekend on a bill from last year that your organization lobbied for aggressively. The DEA had the power to immediately stop distributors from supplying opioids and other prescription drugs to pill mills and other corrupt sources. But according to the DEA Chief Administrative Law Judge, last year's law makes it much harder for the DEA to use that power. Under the new law, the agency must provide substantial evidence that a distributor's actions makes death or serious bodily harm considerably more likely, and the DEA needs to do so before any witnesses are produced or any evidence is admitted at a hearing.

As a result, the judge writes that the law appears—and this is his quote—"completely eliminate the DEA's ability to ever impose an immediate suspension." Yet, Ms. Gallenagh, your organization spokesperson told the Washington Post, quote, "To be clear, this law does not decrease DEA's enforcement against distributors." That's a direct contradiction from what the judge is saying, and it's his job to interpret the law. Doesn't that make your organization's statement pretty misleading?

Ms. Gallenagh. Thank you for the question, Senator. The opioid epidemic, in general, is a very serious concern and a complex issue that we are also very concerned about as distributors, and we work with our supply chain partners daily to try and find solutions to that.

Senator Hassan. Ms. Gallenagh, I understand that. But here's the point. The point is that your organization, which lobbied aggressively for this law last year claimed that it does not decrease the DEA's enforcement against distributors, and the DEA Chief Administrative Law Judge says you're wrong, that the law completely eliminates the DEA's ability to take certain enforcement actions. It's his job to interpret the law. So is the judge wrong, or is your organization statement misleading?

Ms. Gallenagh. In that sense, I believe that the judge's statement was misleading, and I stand behind our organization's defense, and I——

Senator Hassan. I'd suggest you read the judge's article, which has now been published, because what he points out, among other things, is that for all this time when there wasn't a statutory definition of immediate harm that constrained the DEA the way the bill that was passed last year does, over many, many years, the industry didn't challenge the DEA's actions, because the DEA—very often, there's almost no case law on it. So I'd suggest you go read it, because there are a lot of us extraordinarily concerned——

The Chairman [presiding]: We're a minute over.

Senator Hassan. I thank you for your time, thank you, Chairman Alexander.

The Chairman. Thank you, Senator Hassan.

Senator Young.

STATEMENT OF SENATOR YOUNG

Senator Young. Thank you, Chairman.

Ms. Reilly, the congressional Research Service tells us the United States spends more for prescription drugs than other wealthy countries. In Europe, drug prices are set by governments, not by pharmaceutical companies. There's a recent study by McKinsey which indicated, on average, the difference between the price of one drug in the United States and the same drug in France, UK, Germany, Italy, and Spain was 50 percent. So U.S. consumers, by my reading, are subsidizing the world's research and development. I'm not the first one to divine this insight.

Research and Development magazine tells us the U.S. accounted for 46 percent of global life sciences R and D, a vast majority of that going to biopharma. So the challenge is even if Europeans or wealthy countries were to raise their prices and reduce the extent to which they're free riding, that wouldn't automatically lead to a decrease in prices here in the U.S. for our consumers. Instead, a company would be punished by their investors and by their stockholders for lightening the burden on rank and file Americans who are trying to obtain pharmaceuticals.

I guess my question is twofold. The first part should be an easy sort of yes or no, as I would see it. Am I correct that foreign countries' pricing and reimbursement systems actually affect our prescription drug costs?

Ms. Reilly. I would definitely say that the U.S. does bear the burden for the world in terms of supporting research and development. I think the numbers that you gave are much higher than I've seen in terms of the price differential between the United States and other countries. Oftentimes, those rely on list prices which are not the net price paid.

Senator Young. So go back and look at the McKinsey study and see where you disagree with their premises and their findings. Maybe we could engage in a dialog offline about that.

Ms. Reilly. Absolutely.

Senator Young. The second part of the question is since you've acknowledged there is an impact of these foreign reimbursement systems and foreign pricing on the price to U.S. consumers, how might we mitigate to extent to which Americans, our innovators, our consumers, are shouldering the burden of financing the world's medical innovation?

Ms. Reilly. Well, one thing I think is important to make clear is we do have a different system in the United States. We reward innovation, companies that bring their products to market, and we pay more up front, and we pay significantly less on the back end.

Senator Young. So you're giving me a lot of background. Are there strategies we might use as policymakers to change this dynamic or mitigate the extent to which we're shouldering the burden like through free trade agreements, for example?

Ms. Reilly. Absolutely. Stronger trade agreements could go a long way to ensure that other countries are paying more of their fair share. I would note a comment that Mark said, which is with regard to the recent Hep C medicines. PBMs here on record said that patients here were paying less than what was being paid abroad in part because of the considerable market consolidation we have in the PBM market, where you have many PBMs that are buying on behalf of more people than entire foreign countries and the EU.

Senator Young. Are there other strategies we might employ to reduce the price to consumers in the State of Indiana?

Ms. Reilly. Well, I think again, we have to look at what our insurance market system looks like today. I think, oftentimes, we treat pharmaceuticals very different than we treat other aspects of the healthcare system. Based on an individual's biology, if you need a medicine, you're being asked to pay significantly more out of pocket as opposed to if you needed to go into a hospital setting. So I think we do need to examine whether it's fair to say to a patient with rheumatoid arthritis, "You need to pay 40 percent of the price of your medicine," and if I go in the hospital, I need to pay 4 percent of the cost.

Senator Young. So one possibility to lower prices and increase value, as I understand it, is the use of outcome-based contracts increasingly being piloted by pharmaceutical companies and insurers alike. Can you explain how these contracts work in summary fashion and their potential to lower drug costs for patients, and then perhaps elaborate on any policy initiatives we here might engage in that might be standing in the way of moving these pilots to scale?

Ms. Reilly. Sure. Great question. I think there are a number of innovative arrangements that are being produced, the goal of which is to say instead of purchasing medicines historically like we have, which is based on a volume basis, we'll pay for whatever we buy, and a movement toward saying we will pay for those medicines at differential rates, potentially, depending on if they meet the outcome that the payer and the pharmaceutical company can mutually agree to.

There's lots of potential benefits of moving in this direction. First of all, our companies are putting our money where our mouth is. We may be getting paid less or, in some cases, nothing, depending on if our medicine produces, as we believe it should, so it's helpful for the healthcare system with the ability to lower cost, helpful for patients, too, because the goal, again, is also that if patients aren't being helped by them, then their cost sharing should also be lowered by those medicines. They're in their infancy stage in part because there are government rules, like the anti-kickback statute, price reporting, and communications with the FDA that need to be addressed to make these become much bigger than they are today.

Senator Young. I'll follow-up with you and your organization to see if there's specific ways we might be helpful to empower our companies to make use of these contracts.

Ms. Reilly. Absolutely.

Senator Young. Thank you so much.

Ms. Reilly. Appreciate it.

The Chairman. Thank you, Senator Young.

Senator Warren.

Statement of Senator Warren

Senator Warren. Thank you, Mr. Chairman.

The high cost of prescription drugs is a huge problem. Let's talk about the best way to tackle this public health crisis.

Ms. Reilly, your association, which is called PhRMA, represents brand name drug companies, and you said in your testimony that, quote, "the competitive market is the engine that drives the drug industry." So I take it you think that market solutions are the most effective way to deal with the rising price of drugs.

Ms. Reilly. I do believe that markets lower cost, yes.

Senator Warren. Good. I love markets, and I also believe in market-based solutions. So let's talk about one of the best market- based solutions, and that's competition. If the restrictions that prevent purchasers from importing the exact same drugs at lower prices from places like Canada were removed, we'd see some real competition, and we'd see some lower prices.

Another market solution is negotiation. If the Federal Government were allowed to negotiate more competitive drug prices for Medicare beneficiaries, then prices would come down.

Ms. Reilly, you've already said that PhRMA opposes importation of drugs from Canada. Let me ask about letting the Federal Government negotiate with drug companies over Medicare prices— these two market-based solutions.

Ms. Reilly. Well, I would argue price controls are not a market- based solution. When foreign——

Senator Warren. I'm sorry. I didn't ask about price controls. I asked about bringing in drugs that would compete with prices here.

Ms. Reilly. Bringing in drugs from other countries that price control their products is not a market-based way to get the drug prices——

Senator Warren. So you would be in favor of drug importation from any place that's not doing what you call price control?

Ms. Reilly. I would argue that almost every country outside of the U.S. artificially limit prices——

Senator Warren. Oh, so there's no place that we can import from that would satisfy your requirements. How about the Federal Government competing and actually having some competition and saying, "We're going to negotiate prices."

Ms. Reilly. I think there's often a fallacy that because the Federal Government is not setting prices in Medicare that there's not negotiation, and that couldn't be further from the truth. As we've seen in the Medicare Part D program, there's been robust negotiation. Rebates are over 35 percent, on average, in Part D. Premiums have been low.

Senator Warren. Let me just stop you there. I just want to make sure I understand the point of the group that you represent here and lobby for, and that is—is it that the Federal Government ought to be able to negotiate all drug prices?

Ms. Reilly. No, we don't believe the Federal Government is in the best position. We have rapid market consolidation in the pharmacy benefit manager space that exerts significant pressure to the tune of over $100 billion in rebates last year.

Senator Warren. I understand that you have other concerns. But drug competition from Canada, price negotiation, are market solutions. They're not government mandates, and I would have thought that if you believe in market solutions, you would have embraced them.

Ms. Reilly. Well, I don't believe that price controls are market- based solutions, and I also think that you need to look at the downsides that happen in those countries, which is patients don't get the kind of access that they get to therapies here in the United States.

Senator Warren. I realize that you can call it price controls, but this is a real question of whether or not there's any place else for consumers to go to purchase drugs, or whether or not the Federal Government can negotiate on a drug-by-drug basis every time tax-payers are picking up the ticket.

Ms. Reilly. Well, the Congressional Budget Office has looked at this——

Senator Warren. I looked it up, and the organizations who are testifying here today spent a combined total of $30 million lobbying Congress last year. PhRMA, your organization, is responsible for almost three-quarters of that total, and a lot of that money that is spent lobbying Congress is to keep drug prices high. That's what improves profitability for your industry and the companies you represent.

Here's what I think is really wrong about this. You talk about wanting market solutions, but your industry isn't based on competitive markets. It's based on totally artificial taxpayer granted monopolies. Companies invent new drugs, and then the government hands the companies the exclusive right to manufacture and sell those drugs at whatever prices they want for decades. So I just have a little bit of time left. But I want to ask—do you know the average length of a government granted monopoly for top-selling drugs in this country?

Ms. Renilly. Ten to twelve years.

Senator Warren. Yes, 10 to 12 years. The law says five, 5 years of exclusivity, but drug companies game the system. According to a 2015 analysis by researchers at Harvard, companies end up with a monopoly that lasts a medium length of 12 and a half years.

I know that I'm out of time, Mr. Chairman.

Ms. Reilly. Senator Warren, patents are 20 years long, 20 years. That is how long a pharmaceutical patent is. We also have 5 years of data exclusivity.

Senator Warren. I'm sorry. The law says 5 years of exclusivity on the basic drugs.

Ms. Reilly. Absolutely.

Senator Warren. The average—do you think the Harvard study—they don't know how to do it there, to study how much money you're making off these things or how long you have exclusivity?

Ms. Reilly. Senator Warren, I'm simply saying that companies have 5 years of data exclusivity. Immediately after that, a generic company can get to market, and let me tell you, they try very hard to get to market as soon as they can.

Senator Warren. You're saying that the drug companies don't game the system at all to expand their exclusivity to an average of 12 and a half years? It just happens? Please try your story on someone else.

Ms. Reilly. Senator Warren, patents are 20 years long. Exclusivity is a completely different——

Senator Warren. Try this story on someone else who's going to be willing to listen to it. Taxpayers watch——

The Chairman. If you want to——

Senator Warren. ——thank you, Mr. Chairman.

The Chairman. ——you can finish your point.

Senator Warren. No, no. I just wanted to say taxpayers watch when we've granted exclusivity to these companies, and then they watch as the prices go up, and there's not a darned thing for tax- payers to do about it. This is just fundamentally wrong.

The Chairman. Thank you, Senator Warren.

Senator Murkowski.

Statement of Senator Murkowski

Senator Murkowski. Thank you, Mr. Chairman.

Ms. Gallenagh, I want to follow-up just very quickly with the discussion that you were having with Senator Hassan regarding this latest news with the weakening of the

DEA enforcement authorization—a big exposé this weekend through 60 Minutes, Washington Post. You have a drug czar that is now effectively withdrawn from this position. The President himself is saying we need to look into this and to investigate it.

One of our colleagues on the other side of the aisle has already introduced legislation that would repeal it. There have been some that have suggested it needs to be modified.

You've indicated to Senator Hassan that you think that the judge had misinterpreted—or you disagreed with the judge's interpretation, I believe. But do you think that what was passed in 2016 is actually good and sound, or do you believe that, in fact, given what we know today, it might need to be modified or amended in some way?

Ms. Gallenagh. Thank you, Senator. First, let me say Senators Hatch and Whitehouse, who authored that bill in the Senate, worked very closely with the DEA to ensure that the bill did not inhibit the ability to take action against registrants. DEA did not oppose that bill.

Also, regarding the ALJ's article, which was a draft, I understand, ALJ's are not involved in issuing immediate suspension orders. They are recommended by DEA staff. They are issued by an administrator or a deputy administrator, and——

Senator Murkowski. But do you think that something needs to be done to address what clearly has come out to be limitations within DEA's authority that we might need to address through legislation?

Ms. Gallenagh. I think that it should be explored as to what DEA's limited actions were and their limited involvement with collaborating with industry and talking about defining the terms that registrants operate under. We have pages of questions that we have submitted to the agency over the years that have gone unanswered. This bill, from our understanding, is sound, and we supported it. But we are open to talking through those issues more closely with you and with other offices.

Senator Murkowski. I do think that it is an issue that has really risen to perhaps a higher level, given what we are seeing around this country with regards to just the easy availability of these opioids that are just ravishing parts of our country. So this is something that needs to be continued and addressed.

I've listened to the testimony from each of you and have read through your written comments, and I just have to express the frustration that I think the general public feels in just being so limited in their ability to understand why. All they know is that the most expensive part of their healthcare that they can see is what is going on with the cost of their prescription drugs.

Then when we talk about, well, all we need is transparency. But if you look to try to understand it, you've got a manufacturer that sets a list price, but almost nobody pays that. You've got the PBMs that negotiate different prices. You've got the GPOs who might negotiate different prices. You've got one hospital that might charge something different than a hospital across the street. There may be rebates. There may be discounts. There may be other pricing things. There is no way that anyone can follow this.

For the average consumer, if you all are talking transparency, it doesn't mean anything to them. So I look to ways that we might be more transparent that actually could translate to something. We put on the back of any product what the ingredients are and how that's allocated out. When Alaskans get a permanent fund dividend, it actually lists on that voucher, if you will, where all of the associated costs are attributed to.

Are we crazy to think that we could be doing more with actually accounting for the cost so that the consumer could better understand and make it legible? Because right now, it's impossible to understand, and even those of us who are listening to you as supposed experts, it's all Greek, and we're not doing anything to help the consumer.

Maybe it's a rhetorical question here, but I challenge you all to translate how the pricing mechanisms—who gets discounts, who doesn't, why it's fair for one hospital to charge something that the other one doesn't? In no other industry that I can think of do you have this latitude for a discrepancy in pricing and the ability to just set it and be done with it.

I'm over my time. So perhaps if you can respond to me with some concrete examples of the ways that we can be more transparent— because I think that, ultimately, that can help us push down the cost. But right now, it's impossible to discern.

Thank you, Mr. Chairman.

The Chairman. I'd like to ask—the witnesses are welcome to respond to the Senator in writing with concrete examples. I think that would be helpful to her and to all of us.

Senator Murphy.

STATEMENT OF SENATOR MURPHY

Senator Murphy. Thank you very much, Mr. Chairman.

Just to Senator Murkowski's point, I got to be the chairman of Connecticut General Assembly's Health Committee when I was 29 years old because I was the only one who took the time to try to figure out how a drug was priced, what AWP and AMP meant, what the dispensing fee meant. It was the most opaque market that existed in our state's healthcare system, and to this day, I think there are only a couple of state legislators in Connecticut who understand how a drug is priced either in the private market or through Medicaid, and it does behoove us when we talk about transparency to understand that if you just layer transparency on a pricing system today that has a thousand different prices, it's really difficult.

I just have one question, because I know we've got to sneak in Senator Baldwin and myself before the bell here, and it's for Ms. Reilly, so I'll just prepare you for it.

The Trump administration recently announced that it wants to expand association health plans and something called limited duration insurance plans. That was part of last week's Executive Order. The risk here is that you're now going to set up one system of care for healthy people who can get into those plans, which don't require you to price without respect to medical acuity, and one system for sick people, who will then stay in the marketplaces under the Affordable Care Act where insurance plans can't discriminate.

Your CEO said on television last week that the Executive Order was a good idea, because we need to be trying everything that can lower costs for patients. But the fact of the matter is when you review these short-term limited duration plans, by and large, they do not cover prescription drugs. If you look at the best-selling plans that are sold on E-Health, they exclude preexisting conditions, they exclude mental health, exclude substance abuse, they exclude prescription drugs, and maternity expenses.

I looked up the best-selling plan in my home state, which is offered by National General Accident and Health, and it doesn't cover prescription drugs, either. So why is PhRMA taking a position to support the Executive Order when, to the extent that these short-term duration plans become available to more and more Americans, it'll exclude the very product that you sell, in addition to all sorts of other coverages that people desperately need?

Ms. Reilly. Thank you for the question. Let me offer two points, the first of which is our CEO was asked that question before the Executive Order was actually released, so I would note that. The second, I think some of the words that we heard coming out prior to the release of it had to do with how do we increase competition, how do we address some of the consolidation that's happening in the marketplace. I think those are principles that many people espouse.

I think the details in terms of how this ultimately gets worked out—the devil is certainly in the details, and we will be looking anxiously as the various agencies look to implement that, because, again, our goal is to ensure that patients have access to care. That is our primary goal.

Senator Murphy. So let me just ask that more specifically. If the result of the—I understand what the rhetoric is when the President talks about his executive actions. They are often very different than the actual words in the EOs. If the results of this Executive Order is to dramatically expand access to limited duration plans, is that something that PhRMA would support?

Ms. Reilly. Our goal, as I said before, is to ensure patients have access to therapies, including innovative medicines, because so many patients rely on them. So we will be looking in earnest as the agencies work on this to ensure that patients do continue to have access to medicines.

Senator Murphy. I would argue that now would be the time to weigh in and make your feelings known on this.

Thank you, Mr. Chairman.

The Chairman. Thank you, Senator Murphy.

Senator Baldwin.

STATEMENT OF SENATOR BALDWIN

Senator Baldwin. Thank you, Mr. Chairman.

Today, we've heard many competing reasons and even how it's very complex to know why drug prices are high and are increasing. So I continue to believe that we should start from the beginning of the story. I have a bipartisan bill with Senator McCain, and it's pretty simple. It would give us more information as policymakers by establishing basic transparency for drug companies when they increase the price of drugs. That's it.

In fact, California just enacted, with bipartisan support, a new law similarly requiring transparency for drug price increases.

While many changing factors contribute to a price that a patient pays, one factor has remained constant. We now see drug companies systematically increasing list prices of existing drugs every year. According to reports in just the first quarter of 2017, there were 40 increases of drug prices, which is more than the first quarter of 2016.

If, as we have heard today, the list price provides an inaccurate picture, then I'm not sure why we shouldn't just ask drug companies for information to help paint an accurate picture and to explain why we are seeing these prices increase as my bipartisan bill would do.

Mr. Davis, you noted that in the last year, revenues for branded drugs have increased as a direct result of price increases. Can you please briefly elaborate on this and describe what your industry is seeing when it comes to list price increases? I do want to ask another question, so please be brief and concise.

Mr. Davis. Sure. Thank you, Senator, for the question. Just to clarify, are you asking the question relative to the brands or to the generics?

Senator Baldwin. Revenues from branded drugs that you noted in your testimony.

Mr. Davis. Yes. So what we've actually seen—and this is an example of how different the markets operate—is that while we're experiencing a period of unprecedented price deflation in the generics, where actually year over year, the prescriptions are going up, the revenue is going down in our industry. That's the opposite of what we're seeing in the branded side, where the prescriptions are actually going down, and the revenue is continuing to go up.

So there can be a whole host of economic reasons for that. One of them that we submitted in our testimony is we are seeing an increasing level—despite some of the communications about supporting generic and biosimilar competition, we are seeing an increased level of activity—some of it was referenced earlier by Senator Hassan in her comments around outsourcing IP to Native American tribes—lately of these types of behaviors that are making it more challenging for generics to get to the market.

Senator Baldwin. Ms. Reilly, like my colleagues have reflected in their comments and questions, I way too often hear concerns, stories from my constituents, about the impact of drug price increases on their lives. Often, these are tearful discussions, because your health and the ability to treat health conditions is deeply personal. I hear about the insulin list prices that have continued to increase since 2002, about top-selling drugs like Humira that have increased almost every year for 10 years, and about the more than 14 drugs for multiple sclerosis that have increased since 2004 to an annual average of about $83,000.

A woman named Diane from Webster, Wisconsin, talked about a heartbreaking conversation she had with her husband earlier this year where they decided that she would stop taking her MS medication after 23 years because of it reaching $90,000 a year.

At the same time, reports have indicated that most of the big drug companies spend more on marketing than on research and development. A recent Health Affairs study of the 20 top-selling drugs found that earnings from charging high drug prices in the U.S. exceeded global spending in R and D.

Ms. Reilly, last year, your trade association updated its membership criteria to stipulate that branded companies invest in certain amounts of global R and D spending per year to be eligible to join. Given this renewed commitment to R and D, do you support drug companies making their R and D spending and investments more transparent for the public, as my bipartisan bill would do, including when they increase the list price of an existing drug? Yes or no?

Ms. Reilly. Absolutely. Research and development costs—and I think our companies, by and large, make that information public. It is an important part of what we do. I would take issue—our companies spend significantly more on research and development than they do on marketing costs. With regard to transparency——

Senator Baldwin. Do you disagree with the conclusions of the Health Affairs study?

Ms. Reilly. I do, yes. With regard to transparency, again, I think a couple of things are important. One, it needs to be holistic and applied to the entire supply chain. As we talked about here today, we're half or slightly less than half of what we spend on brand name drugs. Lots of other folks in the supply chain also have a piece of this equation, and I think that needs to be explored.

Senator Baldwin. I understand the arguments you've made. However, let's start at the beginning. Let's get transparency throughout, but let's start at the beginning, and the Fair Drug Pricing Act would be a good start in that direction.

Ms. Reilly. I would just say list prices, too, as we've talked about here today, are not indicative of net prices and what are actually paid in the marketplace.

The Chairman. Thank you, Senator Baldwin.

I'm going to need to go vote, so I'm going to thank each of you for coming today. You've been excellent in helping us put a spotlight on drug prices.

We have two Senators who—one or two—who have questions to ask. I'm going to ask Senator Franken to chair in my absence, and he'll ask his questions, and then if other

Senators come back who have not asked their questions, he'll call on them, and then he'll adjourn the hearing. So thank you very much for coming.

Senator Franken, thank you for chairing.

STATEMENT OF SENATOR FRANKEN

Senator Franken. [presiding] Thank you, and as you're leaving, I'd like to thank you and Senator Murray for calling this hearing and also for the important negotiations that you're involved in. So thank you.

I just wanted to do that. Sorry I haven't been here for the whole thing. I've had some other stuff to do, and I ran back so that I could do this, and so if you'll excuse me—actually, I didn't run back. This is just such an exciting hearing.

[Laughter.]

Senator Franken. It seems like from your testimony and some of—mainly from your testimony that, like, every one of you in some way or another is responsible for getting prices down. That's what it seemed like from your testimony. I think Senator Young touched on this, but I want to try to go over it again for myself.

The U.S. spends more on prescription drugs than any industrialized country, in part because drug prices are higher in the U.S. than in any other country. The drug industry pushes back and says that these price comparisons don't take into account the discounts that manufacturers give to insurers and other actors in the system. So to cut through that, I'd like to ask you some questions. Let's use the drug, Advair, which is an asthma inhaler example. It's produced in North Carolina. So it's a drug that's produced in the United States.

Ms. Reilly, what is the list price for Advair in the United States, and how does it compare to the cost in Canada, France, and Germany?

Ms. Reilly. I honestly do not know the list price of Advair off the top of my head, so I'd have to get back to you on that.

Senator Franken. Sure, sure. That's very understandable. I'm going to ask you the price of every drug and see how you do.

[Laughter.]

Senator Franken. No. A Bloomberg news report from 2015 found that the list price, this is the list price, for Advair was $309.60 in the United States. Accounting for, say, a 50 percent discount, then the price would be $154.80, which is still higher than the price in Canada, which, in 2015, was $74.12. The price in Germany was $37.71, and the price in France was just $34.52.

Ms. Reilly, why are prices so much higher in the United States for a drug produced in the United States? This is true for drugs that are produced in the United States and not produced in the United States. Why are they so much higher? I think Americans really want to know this, and I think they want to know this because you guys talked about research. Americans pay for a lot of the basic research, right?

Ms. Reilly. Yes.

Senator Franken. Yes, through NIH.

Ms. Reilly. Our industry, yes.

Senator Franken. But much of it the taxpayer pays directly to the NIH to do the basic research. Most of the research you do is not—in your industry is not basic research.

Ms. Reilly. We do a fair amount of basic research.

Senator Franken. You do a fair amount.

Ms. Reilly. Yes.

Senator Franken. Most of it is not basic research, and I'll give you the figures on that and we'll call that up in a second.

Ms. Reilly. I'm aware.

Senator Franken. These higher prices in the United States support high-level profits and some research and development costs, but we also pay these high prices because of the way our system is structured, the laws we set, and the clout of the drug industry. For example, Congress passed a law that prohibits the Federal Government from negotiating with drug manufacturers for lower prices for Medicare, which is the single largest payer for prescription drugs. In those other countries, you have the government able to bargain with the pharmaceutical companies.

All of you presented yourself as part of the piece that keeps the prices down. Why are the prices so much higher—in this case, assuming a 50 percent discount from the list price—and in a number of cases, twice as high, four times as high as Canada, France, respectively, and more than four times as high as Germany. Why? Americans want to know why.

Ms. Reilly. I'm happy to start. We do have a different system in the U.S. relative to other European countries. We actually compensate companies for the innovation and the value of the medicines that they bring. I would argue in many European countries, the prices are artificially depressed. They tend to also pay more when a medicine goes generic, and they use fewer generics.

In total, our systems are spending—if you compared, on average, how much we spend, yes, they probably do spend a little bit less. I would argue, though, that our country incentivizes new therapies and innovation to come to market, and then after that period of time, when a patent expires and exclusivity is gone, 90 percent of the market—95 percent of the market shifts overnight to low-cost generics.

In that system that we have, we are able to support a broader innovation ecosystem. The fact that we have 90 percent generics here and in most European countries, it's 50 percent to 60 percent, in part, because they don't incentivize their entry. They don't incentivize the dropping of price here. We do so in a way that those additional resources are able to fuel the next generation of therapies for patients.

Senator Franken. I would suggest it is very small comfort for the Minnesotans that I visit around my state who can't pay for their pharmaceuticals, and I would suggest to you that this is a longer discussion. But Americans have to ask, why do Americans pay more, two times as much, four times as much, for our pharmaceuticals, many of which we produce, many of which we've done the basic research for through the NIH. Why do we have to pay—why does the American consumer have to pay more than the Canadian consumer for the same drug, more than the German consumer, more than the French consumer?

Ms. Reilly. Senator, I would also argue——

Senator Franken. Okay, go ahead.

Ms. Reilly. I was going to say there is a case here for the need for stronger trade agreements to ensure that other countries, particularly European countries, are paying more of their fair share.

Senator Franken. So the answer is just to make them pay more.

Ms. Reilly. No. I think them paying more would permit prices here to potentially fall. It would also permit more money to go back into research and development, which over time lowers the cost of therapies, both innovative therapies as well as generics.

Senator Franken. Does anybody else on the panel care to comment?

Mr. Davis. Yes, Senator. If I could just add, just to reinforce a comment previously made, to say that all drugs are more expensive in the United States fails to recognize the distinction Ms. Reilly talked about between brands and generics. It is a carefully—it historically has been a carefully balanced ecosystem created by Hatch-Waxman, where, as a country, we made a decision in the 1980's to actually make the investment for the ability to bring novel therapeutics to market sooner rather than later, and then, ultimately, get a utilization rate and lower cost generics than we have in the rest of the world.

So to the question that was asked earlier, why shouldn't we consider importing generics from Canada, by example, they're more expensive in Canada. So I'm not sure why we would import something that's less expensive here to begin with.

Senator Franken. I'll bet the idea—and I approve of being able to import. I'll bet the idea would be to import the drugs that are cheaper. That's just my guess about what consumers would do, and I almost—I don't know. I used to be in comedy, and I almost think that your answer there was a tad absurd, which is—of course, we're not saying we need the right to import the same drug that's more expensive in the other country. Do you understand kind of the absurdity of saying that?

Mr. Davis. Yes. Senator, my intention in saying that was to look at policy and understand that the markets operate fundamentally differently. The commoditized market in the United States is what drives generic prices lower than they are in other developed markets. That was my only point.

Senator Franken. Thank you. But I do want to say that if you look at the whole universe of drug prices, we pay more, and we pay a lot more, and you're acknowledging that. That's what I'm talking about.

I'll go to Senator Whitehouse.

STATEMENT OF SENATOR WHITEHOUSE

Senator Whitehouse. Let me ask the panel to focus on a very specific issue, which is the question of monopoly. Let's set aside for a second the licensed monopoly that people get when their intellectual property is protected by a patent or a trademark. Let's just set that aside. We're not talking about that particularly approved monopoly. We're talking about other kinds.

Does everybody agree that we have seen circumstances recently in which a drug manufacturer has an effected monopoly with respect to one or more of their products? Does anybody dispute that phenomenon? Everybody agrees with that phenomenon? We've seen it, right? That's not complicated. Yes, everybody agrees.

Let's say that you are a patient, and you have taken a particular drug for many, many years, and it's not under any kind of trademark or patent protection. But somebody who's not even in the pharmaceutical industry, an investor, comes in and sees a monopoly, buys it, and jacks the price up by 500 percent, just because they can. We know that has happened also, don't we? Yes from everybody, no dissent with that, Okay.

So here's the problem that I have, which is that in that circumstance, the question then is: Where do you go? How do people respond to that particular problem? The thesis that I have is that in those circumstances, which we all admit are true, there is a clear monopoly, and, further, we see price manipulation consistent not with any market, but with monopoly power.

My thesis is that there's no place for anybody to go. There's no entity in the U.S. Government that has the authority to say, "Hold it. That's a monopoly. You are extracting monopoly rents," to use the economic term, "and you've got to knock it off." You may be able to get a lawsuit out of the Department of Justice for an antitrust or price fixing type violation, but we haven't seen a lot of that. The FDA nibbles around the edges of this problem. It doesn't have authority to step in at that point.

Shouldn't there be some place in government where it is clear that once a monopoly exists, and there's no doubt about that, and it's clear that monopoly rent extraction is being done, nothing related to market pricing. In that narrow circumstance, shouldn't there be somebody able to act? Let's go right down the line here, starting with Mr. Menighan.

Mr. Menighan. Thank you, Senator. We share your frustration. We often serve as uncompensated insurance agents for those with coverage who have to navigate complex insurance regs and coverage issues and copayments and insurance. We want desperately to be part of the team that helps people navigate the system in a more effective way.

Senator Whitehouse. You concur that right now, there's no place to go? There's no office——

Mr. Menighan. We have relatively few places, other than perhaps compassionate use programs that some companies provide, but not all companies provide that.

Senator Whitehouse. Mr. Merritt.

Mr. Merritt. Yes, it's frustrating. It is part of the marketplace. What we've seen——

Senator Whitehouse. Not part of a legitimate marketplace, though, right? Extracting monopoly rents isn't viewed by any economist as being legitimate economic behavior, is it?

Mr. Merritt. Well, we didn't like it when Mr. Shkreli went and bought up Daraprim and sold it for thousands of percent more, and I testified in the same panel a year or two ago. It's outragcous.

Senator Whitehouse. But other than scolding him here in Congressional Committees, nobody said, "No, you can't do that."

Mr. Merritt. I'll tell you that one thing we did—and I'll let Lori talk about the legality of it—but just something we did in the marketplace. When Daraprim—the price was jacked up—he bought the drug for—was it $13.50, or something like that, and jacked it up to several hundred dollars. If you look at that from a price control perspective, maybe it would be great if he just cut that in half to a few hundred dollars. Or if you looked at—well, maybe he shouldn't charge more than it was originally, $13.00.

What we did was we found a compound pharmacy out in San Diego that would do it for $1, and then we cut his drug off the formulary and said, "Here, everybody can have this drug for $1, but you can't have the Daraprim. It's overpriced." So there are some things we can do in the marketplace, but that's not to say or imply that it's not a challenge. It just takes time to overcome.

Senator Whitehouse. My time is already out. So if you have quick responses, I'll go to Ms. Gallenagh.

Ms. Gallenagh. Thank you, Senator. As you know, HDA members are unique in the supply chain, but we do support anything that supports increased competition in the marketplace.

Senator Whitehouse. Mr. Davis?

Mr. DAVIS. Senator, I think what you've been characterizing is the equivalent of a de facto monopoly.

Senator Whitehouse. Yes.

Mr. Davis. Not one that government licenses, but de facto, and it requires a lot of analysis before individuals like Mr. Shkreli decide to go in there. I do think, moving forward, there is a need to continue focus here. I do think that some of the things that the new FDA commissioner in the announcement of his Drug Competition Action Plan and legislation that this Committee ensured was part of FDARA, which was a listing of Daraprim-like drugs, so there's more visibility and increasing the—in an effort to try to minimize the risk associated with more of those types of circumstances——

Senator Whitehouse. But do you agree that nobody presently has regulatory authority over exorbitant monopoly prices?

Mr. Davis. No, correct. To the credit of the FDA commissioner, I think he's doing what he can within his remit.

Senator Whitehouse. Trying to, but there is no——

Mr. Davis. But does he have all the authority to address that in and of himself? No.

Senator Whitehouse. Ms. Reilly.

Ms. Reilly. I would say companies, like in the instance of Daraprim, took advantage of regulatory arbitrage to dramatically increase a price. I do think there is a lot that the FDA could do.

Senator Whitehouse. But there was no direct regulator on the beat whose responsibility was to look for a clear de facto monopoly and address the excess price extraction.

Ms. Reilly. Right, and to Chip's point, I think there's been a lot more——

Senator Whitehouse. I'm sorry. Right? I just want to make sure I heard you, your answer. You said right?

Ms. Reilly. I would say in that particular case—and we've seen a handful of others that mimic the same pattern—is exactly right.

I think the FDA is trying to do—but more could be done, and we've got lots of ideas on how you could address that.

Senator Whitehouse. Thanks for letting me go over, Chairman Franken.

Senator Franken. Oh, I went way over. I'm even going to ask one more question, just to Mr. Merritt, real quick.

Pay-for-delay, since we're talking about monopolies. Pay-for-delay—a drug company has a patent, and then a generic comes up, the patent runs out, the generic has it, the company has it, and they pay the generic not to bring it to market. What do you think of that practice?

Mr. Merritt. Well, we oppose that practice. It is an interesting economic question, because I've heard both sides on it, and I think—well, Chip can address this better than me. But what generics would say is, ''Well, gosh, it's so hard to break through a patent that at least if I can get a settlement, we'll try to get a generic to market,'' and there's some incentive to do that. But, overall, our industry is on the other side of that issue.

Senator Franken. Thank you.

The hearing record will remain open for 10 days. Members may submit additional information for the record within that time, if they would like. The HELP Committee will meet again tomorrow, October 18th, at 9:30 a.m. for an executive session.

Thank you all for being here today. The Committee will stand adjourned.

ADDITIONAL MATERIAL. RESPONSE BY LORI M. REILLY TO QUESTIONS OF SENATOR ALEXANDER, SENATOR MURRAY, SENATOR BALDWIN, SENATOR BENNET, SENATOR FRANKEN, SENATOR ROBERTS, AND SENATOR WHITEHOUSE

Chairman Alexander

Question 1. What is the role of rebates, and do we need them?

Answer 1. Payers have significant influence over which medications are covered on their formularies and how much patients have to pay out-of-pocket for their prescriptions. In order to increase patients' access to their medicines, biopharmaceutical manufacturers commonly negotiate rebates with payers and PBMs in exchange for formulary inclusion or placement on a lower cost-sharing tier. Rebates allow differential levels of discounting to occur, reflecting the robust levels of competition in the market, which economists believe leads to lower average prices. We believe today's system needs to evolve not to eliminate rebates, but to make sure that rebates make their way back to patients to help lower patient costs.

Question 2. How do rebates affect your industry? Do your members contract and get paid based on the public ''list'' price, or using a ''nct'' pricc that takes into account rebates?

Answer 2. Rebates are used in private negotiations by manufacturers to gain access to payer formularies and determine level of formulary tier placement. Manufacturers pay rebates as a percentage of the current list price (WAC price) at the time the pharmacy dispenses the medicine to the patient. The manufacturer sets the ''list'' price of a medicine, but is actually paid the ''net'' price, which is the amount after rebates and any other discounts and fees have been removed. In recent years, net prices have been growing much more slowly than list prices. Focusing on list prices alone results in a perception that drug prices are growing at unsustainable rates, when the prices manufacturers actually receive are in fact growing at low single digit rates. According to IMS Institute for Healthcare Informatics, brand net prices grew at just 3.5 percent in 2016, after taking into account discounts and rebates.

Question 3. Would you support a policy that would allow supply chain participants to contract for lower prices on the front end rather than after the fact with rebates?

Answer 3. Today's pharmaceutical distribution and payment system is complex, and by almost any measure is very successful. It delivers over six billion prescriptions to patients every year, and generates deep discounts which have held growth in prescription drug costs in check; drug costs grew more slowly than overall health care costs in five out of the last 10 years.

Rebates, by themselves, are not problematic, so long as patients, health plans, and employers are all able to benefit from them so that they lower total costs for the health care system. A system in which all discounts are applied only at the point of sale would likely run the risk of reducing the ability of purchasers with significant market leverage to obtain deeper discounts. Economists at the Federal Trade Commission and Congressional Budget Office (CBO) have argued that such differential levels of discounting tend to result in lower average prices.

However, we do need to make sure that the system is working for patients, and that savings provided by manufacturers find their way to patients and can help reduce patient cost sharing. We are encouraged by signs that the Center for Medicare & Medicaid Services is considering policies to apply rebates to patient cost sharing in Medicare Part D, and believe that will help the market work better. Another way to help the market work better is to remove barriers to alternative payment arrangements (such as when a manufacturer agrees to forgo payment if a medicine does not work as intended). These new types of arrangements offer potential to reward the best value for patients.

Senator Murray

Question 1. In the written testimonies submitted to the committee, there is a lot of blame shifting when it comes to where the fault of high drug prices lays. We can all agree that our complex health system is inefficient, but, for that reason, the blame is shared, and everyone bears responsibility to fix the problem.

Please provide more than one policy proposal, which does not involve any other members of the supply chain, that your industry in particular could implement, either with or without the help of Congress or the Administration, to bring down costs for patients and families, including the reasons why you believe it would bring down costs.

Answer 1. While our current system has worked well in driving innovation for patients and holding down costs, many patients still struggle to access their medicines. Now is the time to have the critical conversation about how to promote and sustain medical innovation and ensure access so that patients and the health care system benefit from the tremendous scientific advancement and progress we are seeing today. In order for this to happen, we believe the entire health care system, including medicines, should be driven by value and that the private marketplace is best equipped to align health improvements with costs moving forward.

America's biopharmaceutical companies are committed to working with policymakers and stakeholders to advance solutions that further enhance the private marketplace, lower costs and drive value for patients, and promote continued medical innovation.

1. Value-Driven Health Care: The market is already moving towards better recognizing and rewarding value and biopharmaceutical companies are working with private health insurers to implement new payment arrangements that recognize improvements in care and better patient outcomes. But outdated laws and regulations are making it challenging to move in this direction and for manufacturers to share appropriate scientifically sound information with payers on the value that medicines provide. Removing these barriers will not only help drive value and efficiency in the health system, but drive more robust competition in the marketplace and reduce costs for patients. As we continue the shift towards rewarding value, better quality measurement and value assessment tools will be critical to holding the health care system accountable and ensuring patient-centered, value-based health care in the private sector.
2. Modernizing Drug Discovery, Development and Approval: To get medicines approved faster while ensuring safety, we need to modernize the U.S. Food and Drug Administration (FDA) with new technologies and expertise to keep up with 21st century science. Modernizing the FDA will bring down the time and cost of developing new medicines, which will bring medicines to patients faster and enhance competition in the market.
3. Engaging and Empowering Consumers: Quality and cost information should be readily available to patients to drive greater market efficiency and better align benefit design with patient preference and need. Insurance companies should also pass on more of the discounts they receive to patients in the form of lower out-of-pocket costs, just like they do for other types of health care services.
4. Addressing Market Distortions and Fostering Competition: Regulations that stand in the way of competition should be revised or eliminated. For example, unnecessary and overly burdensome regulations create market distortions that impede competition by impacting the introduction of new medicines and in some cases generics. Policies are needed to encourage generic entry in circumstances where incentives are lacking, such as in markets with very small population sizes. Additionally, the 340B program is widely understood to distort the market and is in need of significant reform. Addressing market distortions will increase competition, revive the health care market and improve affordable access to medicines for patients.

The market-based U.S. health care system has worked well over time, but more can be done to help it work even better. As we move towards value-driven health care, we can build a sustainable, patient-centered, and science-driven health care system that stems the growth of chronic disease and harnesses today's hopes to discover tomorrow's cures.

The complete platform of PhRMA's ideas can be viewed in more detail here: http://phrma.org/sites/default/files/policy-solutions.pdf.

Question 2. Patients and families are right to expect—and deserve—more transparency from the prescription drug supply chain. Recently, experts and lawmakers have started asking questions about the work of Pharmacy Benefit Managers, or ''PBMs,'' that negotiate on behalf of insurers and employers for rebates, off the list prices for drugs, in addition to other services like developing pharmacy networks and drug formularies. The details of that work and who really benefits are largely kept confidential.

Question 2(a). Do patients at the pharmacy counter always benefit from the discounts PBMs secure from drug manufacturers? If no, what policy solutions do you propose to address that gap for your industry? For others in the supply chain?

Answer 2. Patients typically do not benefit directly from discounts and rebates negotiated between biopharmaceutical manufacturers and payers. Instead, payers typically use manufacturer rebates in part to reduce premiums for all of their covered members, rather than to directly reduce the cost that an individual patient has to pay at the point of sale. This increases patient cost sharing unnecessarily.

Answer 2(a). Patients should benefit from negotiated savings in the form of lower out-of-pocket costs at the pharmacy, just as they do for other types of healthcare services. It has been reported that for certain medicines—including those used to treat diabetes, asthma, high cholesterol, and hepatitis C, rebates can reduce list prices by as much as 30 percent to 70 percent. If a larger share of these rebates were shared with patients at the point of sale it could dramatically lower cost sharing for some patients.

Question 2(b). When PBMs negotiate with drug companies, is the goal to secure the largest rebate, or to secure the lowest prices for patients? Put another way, if drug company A company offered a drug for a list price of $100 with a rebate of $50, and drug company B offered the drug for $40 dollars with no discount, which drug would get preferred placement on the PBM's formulary?

Answer 2.(b) PBMs market their role as negotiating for the lowest possible prices for their clients. Typically decisions about placement of medicines on formularies are based on multiple factors, including price. Since administrative fees and the size of the rebate retained by PBMs are commonly based off of a percentage of a medicine's list price, PBMs may have financial incentives to include medicines with high list prices and large rebates on their formularies. In this example, the PBM may earn more on the drug offered by company A, which may impact which medicine receives preferred placement on their formulary.

Question 2(c). We've heard that drug companies will sometimes make deals with PBMs by offering big rebates on an exciting and expensive new product in exchange for favorable placement on the formulary for the rest of that company's drugs, even if those products aren't the least expensive options for patients. Given that PBM contracts are not public, and these examples cannot be verified, can you clarify whether these ''book of business'' deals exist? Or is every PBM contract, price, and rebate negotiated on a product-by-product basis only?

Answer 2(c). Manufacturers may approach rebate negotiations in a variety of ways. PhRMA does not have any source of information about specific types of deals or negotiations, and cannot comment on individual company pricing decisions or offer insight into this question.

Question 2(d). Pharmaceutical companies often say they need to raise drug prices in order to compete by offering larger rebates to PBMs. If that is true, what explains price increases for drugs that don't face direct competition?

Answer 2(d). Manufacturers base pricing decisions on a range of factors including affordability, access, and reinvestment needs for R&D to develop tomorrow's innovative medicines. PhRMA does not have any source of information about specific types of negotiations, and cannot comment on individual company pricing decisions or offer insight into this question.

Question 3. The hearing record shows that we both agree that the US drug market represents a careful balance between protecting innovative products from competition for a limited time, and fostering a robust and competitive generics market to drive costs down for consumers after that time. If this balance works correctly, market forces will help keep costs low.

Innovative products are protected from competition by both exclusivity periods granted by the FDA, and patents. While exclusivity periods are fixed terms that run from the date of drug approval, twenty-year patent protections begin from the date the patent is granted, which could be well before drug approval, or well after. I fully support a robust patent system that protects innovation, however, as I made clear in the hearing, I do not support perpetual market monopolies that eliminate proper market forces and keep drug prices high.

While there are several high profile examples of new patents on drugs sought by companies solely to keep competition off the market, an analysis conducted by researchers at University of California Hastings College of the Law found that this is a widespread practice in the pharmaceutical industry. Examining patents in the FDA Orange Book, the authors found that between 2005-2015, at least 74 percent of the drugs associated with new patents each year were existing approved drugs.

Question 3(a). Please explain how new patents on drugs already on the market and nearing the end of a previous patents' life can improve the innovation and affordability of that drug.

Answer 3. Patents are issued by the U.S. Patent and Trademark Office (PTO) under the Patent Act (title 35 of the U.S. Code). Under that Act, the PTO is to issue (or grant) patents for inventions that are new, useful, and non-obvious, and that meet the other requirements relating to disclosures in an application. A patent discloses the invention and then includes claims for what is actually protected by the patent. The PTO grants patents only after a thorough review of a filed application and its claims by patent examiners that are specialists in the relevant technical area. The examiner raises issues about whether the claimed invention is entitled to patent protection based on the patentability requirements referenced earlier. There is interaction between the inventor and the examiner referred to as the patent prosecution process. If the applicant demonstrates to the examiner that the application meets all of the requirements for a patent, the PTO grants the patent.

Answer 3(a). Once the patent is granted, the owner has the exclusive right to make, use, sell, offer for sale, or import the patented invention described in the claims during the patent term. The basic term of protection is 20 years from filing, although the Patent Act provides for limited extensions to the term to compensate for PTO or regulatory approval process delays.

In the pharmaceutical industry, patents are available for various types of inventions, and include patents that claim the active drug substance, the drug product (including formulations, dosage forms and combinations), and new methods of using a drug, as well as patents that claim manufacturing processes.

Contrary to recent assertions by Feldman and Wang,[117] IP protections do not impede competition in the U.S.; rather, they drive companies to innovate by providing a degree of assurance that companies may earn a return on an otherwise risky and costly investment in R&D. Specifically, IP protections can foster the entry of new competitors to market during the term of the patent. For example, in less than a year after market entry of the first in a new class of hepatitis C treatments, there were multiple competitors on the market that competed on both price and clinical effects which resulted in robust competition in the marketplace. The competition was so fierce that Express Scripts, the U.S.' largest PBM, now touts that hepatitis C treatment is less expensive here than in other western countries thanks to aggressive market negotiation. The study doesn't provide any data about generic entry or pricing to support the contention that so-called ''evergreening'' is inhibiting competition.

In addition, innovation doesn't stop once a product first receives approval as there may be additional patented innovations that occur post-approval that benefit patients. Specific benefits that might come from additional innovation include:

- Knowing the appropriate dosing for using a medication in pediatric populations is necessary to ensure the safe and effective use of medicines in this vulnerable patient population.
- Additional R&D, which may include lengthy and costly Phase III trials, may result in expanded uses of existing medicines and new formulations of such medicines. These innovations may include new dosing regimens and reduced

[117] Feldman, Robin and Connie Wang. 'May Your Drug Price Be Ever Green.' Oct 31 2017. SSRN. https://papers.ssrn.com/sol3/papers.cfm/abstract-id=3061567

side effects, both of which may increase patient compliance with treatment. In turn, these innovations may result in improved health outcomes and a reduction in unnecessary hospitalizations.

- Ongoing innovation increases brand-to-brand competition, spurs continued innovation, and provides payers with increased leverage in negotiating rebates and other discounts.

Question 1(b). Please provide an estimate of the amount of money spent by your member companies in 2016 defending patents on their products that were granted after the completion of such product's phase III trial supporting the first FDA approval.

Answer 1(b). PhRMA does not collect or track this particular information, and it is not publicly available.

Question 1(c). Please provide the total number of patents granted to PhRMA member companies in 2016.

Answer 1(c). PhRMA does not collect or track information on patents granted to companies by PTO.

Question 1(d). Please provide the number of patents granted to PhRMA member companies in 2016 that were not for new molecular entities or new indications.

Answer 1(d). PhRMA does not collect or track information on patents granted to companies by PTO.

Senator Baldwin

Ms. Reilly, in your testimony on October 17, you explained that higher drug prices in the United States are needed to support an "innovation ecosystem." Compared to lower prices in Europe and Canada, you argued that higher prices here provide companies the financial resources to "fuel the next generation of therapies for patients." You said that your member companies spend significantly more on research and development than marketing and that they do a great deal of basic research to develop new therapies. However, as the first chart (Table 1) from Professor William Lazonick's paper[118] makes clear, PhRMA's members in the S&P 500 are spending significantly more buying back their own stock and issuing dividends than they are on research and development. To me, this suggests that R&D isn't as important to your members as boosting the stock price.

The second chart (Table 4) provides a key piece of the puzzle. Pharmaceutical executives receive an inordinate amount of their compensation in the form of stock-based based pay. This seems to explain the broad trend of price increases that squeeze consumers—because the decision makers at your member companies are incentivized to

[118] Lazonick, William. 'US Pharma's Financialized Business Model'. Jul 13 2017. Institute for New Economic Thinking.

do so by boards and shareholders who elect to pay executives in stock. I would appreciate answers to the following questions:

Question 1(a). How do buybacks and dividends help the pharmaceutical industry develop “the next generation of drug therapies?”

Answer 1(a). Since 2000, PhRMA members alone have invested over three-quarters of a trillion dollars in the search for and development of new therapies, $600 billion of that in the United States—more R&D than any other sector, including the federal government. The incredible complexity of drug discovery and development requires a wider R&D ecosystem made up of patient organizations, academia, large and small industry players and government agencies bringing their expertise together. Whatever the business strategies of our members, it cannot be justly or fairly denied that our companies provide the lion’s share—by far—of the resources and conduct the vast majority of the research by which new advances in treatment and of the therapies yet to come are made within that R&D ecosystem.

Stock buybacks and dividends are well-established business strategies often demanded by investors that return capital to investors, and make up part of an investor’s total return on a stock. Investors can use those returns to fund other investments. If returns from high-risk biopharmaceutical investments are deemed too low, they will invest those returns elsewhere. [Meaning less of the investment capital needed to fund new biotech startup companies, engage in high-risk drug discovery, and develop the next generation of drug therapies.]

In an era when many publicly traded companies of all sectors offer buybacks and/or dividends to their shareholder investors, and given competitive capital markets, buybacks/dividends may be a sound strategy to maintain investor interest in the biopharmaceutical industry.

Question 1(b). Do you recognize that pharmaceutical companies could spend billions less on buybacks and dividends and instead lower their drug prices by the same amount and still generate the same operating revenue?

Answer 1(b). PhRMA is committed to advancing public policies in the United States and around the world that support innovative medical research, yield progress for patients today, and provide hope for the treatments and cures of tomorrow. We have no advocacy role related to individual member company business strategies.

Question 1(c). How does spending billions more on buybacks and dividends help promote ‘‘value-driven health care’’ which is part of your organization’s mission statement?

Answer 1(c). PhRMA is committed to advancing public policies in the United States and around the world that support innovative medical research, yield progress for patients today, and provide hope for the treatments and cures of tomorrow. We have no advocacy role related to individual member company business strategies.

Question 1(d). Does PhRMA believe its members should maximize shareholder value?

Answer 1(d). PhRMA represents the country's leading innovative biopharmaceutical research companies, which are devoted to discovering and developing medicines that enable patients to live longer, healthier, and more productive lives. PhRMA is committed to advancing public policies in the United States and around the world that support innovative medical research, yield progress for patients today, and provide hope for the treatments and cures of tomorrow.

Question 1(e). Do you believe that a pharmaceutical executive who receives over 90 percent of their compensation in the form of stock will make increasing the stock price their top priority?

Answer 1(e). PhRMA's mission is to conduct effective advocacy for public policies that encourage the discovery of important, new medicines for patients by biopharmaceutical research companies. We have no involvement in business, operational, or human resource decisions of our member companies, including those related to employee compensation.

Question 1(f). Why do you believe we are seeing this trend of pharmaceutical corporations providing a higher than average percentage of total direct compensation to their executives in the form of stock, as illustrated in Table 2?

Answer 1(f). PhRMA's mission is to conduct effective advocacy for public policies that encourage the discovery of important, new medicines for patients by biopharmaceutical research companies. We have no involvement in business, operational, or human resource decisions of our member companies, including those related to employee compensation.

As the table points out, the executive compensation practices in question are used throughout the corporate world, in keeping with policies in the tax code. It is my understanding that current tax reform legislation in the House of Representatives contains a provision that would eliminate the section of the tax code that encourages stock options as a key performance-based compensation tool.

Question 1(g). Given the connection illustrated here between stock-based executive pay, stock prices, and drug price increases, do you think that the pharmaceutical industry should reconsider how their executives are compensated?

Answer 1(g). PhRMA represents the country's leading innovative biopharmaceutical research companies, which are devoted to discovering and developing medicines that enable patients to live longer, healthier, and more productive lives.

We are committed to advancing public policies in the United States and around the world that support innovative medical research, yield progress for patients today and provide hope for the treatments and cures of tomorrow. We have no involvement in human resource decisions at our member companies, including those related to employee compensation.

Senator Bennet

Question 1. In your testimony, each of you indicated that there is some role for value-based arrangements that health plans can set up with drug manufacturers for outcomes-based reimbursement. However, there are still relatively few of these arrangements in place.

I recently sent a letter with Senators Cassidy, Warner, and Young to request a GAO study on value-based arrangements. We asked GAO to assess the savings potential for consumers and the government in outcomes-based arrangements.

What do you expect we will find in this study?

Answer 1. As GAO looks at outcomes-based arrangements, I would anticipate that they will probably find that outcomes-based arrangements have reduced costs for consumers and health plans, and that there is some evidence that these arrangements have reduced costs for the government. In addition, I expect that you will find that there are significant legal and regulatory barriers that limit the proliferation of these and other value-based contracts, and modernizing key regulations would increase the benefits and wide-spread adoption of value-based arrangements.

Outcomes-based arrangements can reduce costs for patients by allowing the payer to give the medicine improved formulary placement, and thus reducing coinsurance or utilization management for patients.[119] A recent Commonwealth Fund study highlighted two medicines for which outcomes-based contracts resulted in better formulary placement and lower cost sharing for patients. As stated by the Commonwealth Fund, one medicine "was given preferred formulary status, meaning that patients were responsible for lower copayment" and another medicine received preferred formulary status in some cases.[120] GAO's study will likely identify other cases where outcomes-based contracts reduced cost sharing or otherwise improved patient access to medicines.

Outcomes-based arrangements can also improve outcomes for patients and reduce medical costs for private payers and the government. These benefits were recognized by a recent survey of representatives from 45 health plans representing 183 million covered lives. Of the payers surveyed that had participated in an outcomes-based arrangement, 38 percent had experienced and improvement in patient outcomes and 33 percent had experienced cost savings as a result of the outcomes-based arrangement.[121]

These benefits are not surprising. The Congressional Budget Office has recognized that, improved use of medicines reduces spending reduces on medical services such as

---

[119] Note that utilization management can increase costs for patients if they are forced to try multiple medicines before accessing a medicine that works for them, or through other costs from not managing their disease.

[120] Seely E and Kesselheim A. "Outcomes-Based Pharmaceutical Contracts: An Answer to High U.S. Drug Spending?" Commonwealth Fund. Issue Brief. September 2017.

[121] Avalere Health. Payer Perspectives on Outcomes-Based Contracting: Avalere Policy 360. May 22, 2017.

hospitalizations and emergency room visits.[122] Value-based arrangements can support improved use of medicines by allowing payers to provide broader access to medicines, as discussed earlier. They can also support development of data about which patients benefits most from innovative medicines in the real world. Both of these changes can support better use of medicines and lead to reduce spending on medical services.

Outcomes-based arrangements may also reduce the cost of prescription medicines, as manufacturers provide additional rebates for patients who do not meet the agreed to outcomes targets. These arrangements may also encourage payer and manufacturer negotiations to focus on the value of medicines instead of the difference between list and net prices.

Outcomes-based contracts in Medicare Advantage or Medicare Part D plans can lead to savings for the Federal government. Under Part D's competitive, market-based structure, innovator companies contract directly with Part D plans and Medicare Advantage (or MA-PD) plans. To the extent that outcomes-based arrangements improve use of medicines, they can reduce MA plan spending, which could reduce MA plan bids. In addition, if outcomes-based arrangements reduce plans' cost of providing Part D benefits, this could reduce plans' risk and thus permit lower plan bids, reducing the government's costs. Outcomes-based arrangements could also reduce reinsurance costs by increasing rebates paid by innovator companies.

Outcomes-based arrangements in Medicaid can also reduce government costs. Though the operational hurdles to such arrangements are substantial, manufacturers can enter into outcomes-based arrangements directly with states through supplemental rebate agreements. In addition, to the extent that manufacturers enter into outcomes-based arrangements with Medicaid Managed Care plans, that can also reduce plan costs and the premiums that these plans charge to states.

Question 1. What impediments exist to creating outcomes-based reimbursements?

Answer 1. PhRMA identified the top barriers to outcomes-based contracts in a member survey released earlier this year. The top barriers identified in our member survey were:

- Concern or uncertainty about how the contract might affect price reporting metrics (e.g., Medicaid Best Price, Average Sales Price, Average Manufacturer Price) Concern about potentially implicating the federal anti-kickback statute (which generally prohibits providing something of value in return for Medicare or Medicaid business) or uncertainty about how to structure the arrangement to ensure compliance with the anti-kickback statute, and

---

[122] Congressional Budget Office (CBO). Offsetting Effects of Prescription Drug Use on Medi- care's Spending for Medical Services. 2012. Available at: https://www.cbo.gov/sites/default/ files/112th-congress-2011-2012/reports/MedicalOffsets-One-col.pdf

- Concern or uncertainty about FDA regulations concerning clinical or economic outcomes claims.[123]
- Operational barriers, including inability to measure outcomes and payer access to medical and pharmacy data.

Additional information about each of these barriers is provided below.

Price Reporting Metrics

By law, drug manufacturers must calculate and report to the federal government various drug pricing metrics that affect the drug's payment rate or the manufacturer rebate in certain government programs. In reporting these metrics, manufacturers must adhere to a complex set of government price-reporting rules for calculating Average Sales Price in Medicare Part B and Best Price in Medicaid. These highly technical price-reporting rules were established long before the introduction of new approaches to contracting. While the price-reporting rules do permit biopharmaceutical companies to make reasonable assumptions, to the extent there is ambiguity about how to capture innovative contracting methods, this can create uncertainty for biopharmaceutical companies. Value-based contracts in the private market necessitate a more modern and flexible approach to price reporting.

Anti-Kickback Statute

Concern about potentially implicating the federal anti-kickback statute or uncertainty about how to structure the arrangement to ensure compliance with the anti-kickback statute was also identified as a substantial barrier across contract types. The anti-kickback statute is broadly written. While it was designed to achieve the important goal of deterring health care fraud, it may also inadvertently thwart beneficial innovative programs that present low risk of fraud and abuse and could lead to better patient outcomes and significant savings for our health care system. Legislative exceptions and regulatory safe harbors were created to protect beneficial arrangements under the anti-kickback statute; however, the key safe harbor regulations for manufacturers were developed over twenty years ago, and did not anticipate the market's shift to value-based payment and contracting. Value-based contracts should have clear protection under the anti-kickback statute.

---

[123] Pharmaceutical Research and Manufacturers of America. Barriers to Value-Based Contracts for Innovative Medicines: PhRMA Member Survey Results. March 2017.

FDA Regulation of Manufacturer Communications

In January, the FDA released a series of new draft guidance documents, including guidance on communications with payers and formulary committees.[124] This guidance provides helpful clarify for the biopharmaceutical industry. While the draft guidance makes clear that FDA "does not regulate the terms of contracts between firms and payors," it does address many of the communications that may take place in the contracting negotiations. To that extent, the draft guidance provides come clarity to manufacturers and may reduce the level of concern around the barrier posed by FDA regulations. However, the guidance does not answer all questions or provide sufficient latitude for communications about medically accepted unapproved uses of approved medications, so further change is needed.

Operational Challenges

Prioritization of these challenges by survey respondents supports ongoing efforts to improve measurement of health outcomes, including development of patient centric and patient reported outcomes. It also suggests an ongoing need to improve data systems to reduce the burden of outcome measurement. Many organizations are working to address these challenges and do the important work of building a system that can support expansion of value-based contracting for biopharmaceuticals and broader development of a value-driven healthcare system.

Senator Franken

Question 1. The pharmaceutical industry has an opportunity to leverage amazing new treatments to improve the health of millions of people. Three million people in the United States have Hepatitis C, and your industry has developed new treatments that could save many of these peoples' lives. For example, there are three new Hepatitis C drugs that have a 90 percent cure rate. But right now, treatment costs an average of $84,000 per course of treatment. Even with discounts offered to state Medicaid programs, the annual cost to Medicaid for these drugs is still between $20,000 and $30,000 annually, which is still too high for many states to provide care to all in need. The price of treatment is out of reach for many Americans, and we have learned that this is largely due to drug companies setting prices not based on what it cost the company to develop the drug, but

---

[124] Food and Drug Administration. "Draft Guidance: Drug and Device Manufacturer Communications With Payors, Formulary Committees, and Similar Entities—Questions and Answers." January 2017.

more based on ''what the market will bear.'' The more drug corporations set prices with the goal of maximizing revenue, the more millions of Americans will not be able to access urgently needed medicines.

What measures would you support to ensure that everyone who needs a medicine is able to get it—without busting personal and state budgets?

Answer 1. New medicines are transforming care for patients fighting debilitating diseases like cancer, hepatitis C, high cholesterol and more. Yet, in the midst of all this progress, medicine costs in the US are growing at the slowest rate in years and spending on retail and physician-administered medicines continues to represent only 14 percent of overall health care spending, even as scores of new medicines—including cures for hepatitis C—reach patients year after year.[125] 9,[126] Despite claims that hepatitis C medicines are bankrupting state Medicaid programs, spending on the new generation of hepatitis C medicines represented less than 3.5 percent of national Medicaid prescription drug spending net of rebates in 2015 and less than 2 percent of total annual Medicaid spending.[127]

One reason our current marketplace for medicines has been successful in controlling costs is that health insurers and pharmacy benefit managers are powerful, sophisticated purchasers who use their leverage to negotiate discounts and rebates off the "list prices" of medicines on behalf of payers. Today, the top 3 PBMs have considerable negotiating power, accounting for three-quarters of the market.[128] As one example of the growing influence of PBMs, industry leader Express Scripts has publicly stated their success in negotiating substantial rebates for hepatitis C medicines has made it affordable to treat everyone with the disease.[129] Moreover, owing to the success of this competitive market dynamic, negotiated prices here in the US are typically lower than in most European countries.[130] In Medicaid, robust negotiation of supplemental rebates on top of federally

---

[125] Medicare & Medicaid Services (CMS), Office of the Actuary, National Health Statistics Group, data. The Nation's Health Dollar ($3.2 Trillion), Calendar Year 2015, Where it Went.https://www.cms.gov/Research-Statistics-Data-and-Systems/Statistics-Trends-and-Reports/NationalHealthExpendData/Downloads/PieChartSourcesExpenditures2015.pdf. Accessed May 2017.

[126] Altarum Institute. A 10-Year Projection of The Prescription Drug Share of National Health Expenditures, Including Nonretail. http://altarum.org/publications/a-10-year-projection-of-the- prescription-drug-share-of-national-health-expenditures-including. May 2017.

[127] The Menges Group analysis of FY2015 CMS 64 reports and State Drug Utilization data files. Rebate information was obtained from CMS-64 reports, and post-rebate expenditures de- rived through Menges Group tabulations using above information.

[128] AJ Fein; Pembroke Consulting, Inc. Drug Channels Institute. The 2017 economic report on U.S. pharmacies and pharmacy benefit managers. http://drugchannelsinstitute.com/prod- ucts/industry-report/pharmacy.January 2017.

[129] LaMattina J. For Hepatitis C Drugs, U.S, Prices Are Cheaper Than in Europe. Forbes. De- cember 4, 2015. http://www.forbes.com/sites/johnlamattina/2015/12/04/for-hepatitis-c-drugs- u-s-prices-are-cheaper-than-in-europe/7ced43f564bb.

[130] IMS Health, "Comparison of Hepatitis C Treatment Costs," September 2016 https://www.imshealth.com/files/web/IMSH20Institute/Healthcare20Briefs/IIHI-Comparison-of- HepatitisC-Treatment-Costs.pdf.

mandated rebates for medicines reduced prices of hepatitis C medicines by 40 to 65 percent.[131]

But in order for these medicines to be effective, patients need access to treatment. Many patients are struggling to access the medicine they need. This is due to several factors that are unrelated to the "price" of a medicine, including the growth of high deductible health care plans,[132] and insurance designs that subject patients to four or more cost sharing tiers for prescription medicines (often with coinsurance).[133] Both of these growing trends force patients to pay cost sharing based on the full list price of a medicine through deductibles or with coinsurance, even if their insurer receives a significant discount from the manufacturer. In fact more than half of commercially insured patients' out-of-pocket spending for brand medicines is based on the full list price.[134] We believe insurance companies should pass on more of the discounts they receive to patients in the form of lower out-of-pocket costs, just like they do for other health care services.

Question 1. How do you propose that we curb the profit incentives that drove up the price of Hepatitis C drugs and left millions without access to treatment so that this pricing model is not replicated across all of the new specialty drugs that are now in the pipeline?

Answer 1. The market for hepatitis C medicines provides an illustration of how the market-based system in the US drives innovation and medical advances while leveraging competition to control costs.

Just six years ago, the only available treatment for hepatitis C was associated with debilitating flu-like side effects and cured just half of patients. The rapid pace by which new medicines emerged to meet this substantial unmet need over the past few years was driven by market-based incentives which encouraged competing biopharmaceutical companies to make the risky and costly investments in research and development needed to bring new medicines to market. Within a year of the introduction of the first major breakthrough hepatitis C treatment, this competitive dynamic resulted in multiple market entrants which enabled payers to leverage deep discounts for these medicines in exchange for favorable formulary placement. In fact, today publicly reported discounts range from 40-65 percent and payers tout their aggressive negotiating tactics have made it affordable to treat everyone with the disease. But what is truly remarkable is in the span of just 6 years a cure has been developed for a deadly and costly disease, which researchers now

---

[131] Drug Channels, What Gilead's Big Hepatitis C Discounts Mean for Biosimilar Pricing, Feb- ruary 2015, http://www.drugchannels.net/2015/02/what-gileads-big-hepatitis-c-discounts.html/more.

[132] Kaiser/HRET 2017 Employer Health Benefits Survey. Available here: https://www.kff.org/health-costs/report/2017-employer-health-benefits-survey/

[133] Kaiser/HRET 2017 Employer Health Benefits Survey. Available here: https://www.kff.org/ health-costs/report/2017-employer-health-benefits-survey/

[134] PhRMA, "Commercially-Insured Patients Pay Undiscounted List Prices for One in Five Brand Prescriptions, Accounting for Half of Out-of-Pocket Spending on Brand Medicines," 2017. Analysis by Amundsen consulting. Available at: http://www.phrma.org/report/ commercially-insured-patients-pay-undiscounted-list-prices-for-one-in-five-brand-prescriptions-accounting-for- half-of-out-of-pocket-spending-brand-medicines

project will be rare by 2036 with today's more effective treatments and current screening guidelines.[135]

While our current system has worked well in driving innovation for patients and holding down costs, many patients still struggle to access their medicines. Now is the time to have the critical conversation about how to promote and sustain medical innovation and ensure access so that patients and the health care system benefit from the tremendous scientific advancement and progress we are seeing today. In order for this to happen, we believe the entire health care system, including medicines, should be driven by value and that the private marketplace is best equipped to align health improvements with costs moving forward.

America's biopharmaceutical companies are committed to working with policymakers and stakeholders to advance solutions that further enhance the private marketplace, lower costs and drive value for patients, and promote continued medical innovation. We support moving in this direction through the following core themes, described earlier.

- Value-Driven Health Care
- Modernizing Drug Discovery, Development and Approval
- Engaging and Empowering Consumers
- Addressing Market Distortions and Fostering Competition

The market-based U.S. health care system has worked well over time, but more can be done to help it work even better. As we move towards value-driven health care, we can build a sustainable, patient-centered, and science-driven health care system that stems the growth of chronic disease and harnesses today's hopes to discover tomorrow's cures.

Senator Roberts

Question 1. When the Biologics Price Competition and Innovation Act passed in 2010, the Congressional Budget Office projected $7 billion in savings to the federal government from 2010-2019.

Do you think we can achieve this projected savings over the next two years?

Answer 1. The inclusion of the provisions related to biologics and biosimilars within the Affordable Care Act was very important to future of biopharmaceutical innovation. While we can't speculate on how CBO previously derived its estimates, some of the more

[135] Kabiri M, Jazwinski AB, Roberts MS, Schaefer AJ, Chhatwal J. The Changing Burden of Hepatitis C Virus Infection in the United States: Model Based Predictions. Annals of Internal Medicine. 2014; 161(3): 170.

recent non-government estimates such as Quintiles IMS suggests about $37 billion in biologic sales will be subject to biosimilar competition between now and 2021.

Question 1. What have been the main delays for biosimilars?

Answer 1. I believe that the earlier estimates were potentially overly optimistic given the substantial costs and scientific and regulatory uncertainties associated with developing biologic medicines. In addition, the earlier CBO estimates did not adequately consider the substantial time required for the FDA to develop the range of guidances necessary to inform the review and approval of biosimilar medicines. To date the FDA has not finalized all of the necessary guidances. As of October 2017,the agency has approved seven biosimilars.

Question 1. Does Congress need to clarify parts of the biosimilars law, and can that be done without causing further delay and uncertainty about the pathway for these products, pushing savings even further into the future?

Answer 1. At this time, I do not think there is anythıng that needs to be clarified in the statute. I believe the FDA has the appropriate authorities to develop the necessary guidance to inform the development, review, and approval of these products, as evidenced by the approval of seven biosimilars since passage of BPCIA.

Question 2. In 2015, Express Scripts and Imprimis partnered to offer a compounded alternative to Daraprim in an effort to provide a lower-cost option since no approved generic was on the market. Do you believe compounded drugs should be considered a substitutable alternative for FDA approved drugs when there is not a patient medical need?

Answer 2. The FDA has identified a number of approaches to fostering competition when there are small patient populations and no IP or regulatory exclusivities serving as a barrier to entry. The new FDA Commissioner has taken a number of steps, as has Congress, in facilitating the entry of additional competitors in these circumstances, which I believe will help avoid this occurrence in the future.

As the FDA has identified a number of potential concerns with compounded drugs, PhRMA does not view compounding as the optimal approach to addressing this type of situation. According to the FDA, there can be health risks associated with compounded drugs that do not meet federal quality standards. Compounded drugs made using poor quality practices may be sub-orsuper-potent, contaminated, or otherwise adulterated. Additional health risks include the possibility that patients will use ineffective compounded drugs instead of FDA-approved drugs that have been shown to be safe and effective.

Question 3. Would striking the non-interference clause save the government, or patients, money? What impact could it have on access to new innovative therapies?

Answer 3. Medicare Part D is a highly successful program, providing access to affordable prescription drug coverage for seniors and disabled individuals while keeping costs low. Despite numerous claims that repealing the non-interference provision would save money, CBO has repeatedly said government negotiation would have a "negligible" impact on federal spending unless the government also limited seniors' access to needed prescription medications. Furthermore, large, powerful Part D plans already negotiate discounts and rebates directly with biopharmaceutical companies and many brand-name prescription drugs carry substantial rebates,"[136] often as much as 20-30 percent. These negotiations result in significant cost savings for seniors and taxpayers. According to CBO, total Part D costs are 45 percent, or $349 billion, lower than initial ten-year projections.[137] Therefore, undermining this competitive feature of Part D could have real consequences, including reduced access, less choice and higher premiums for America's seniors and people living with disabilities who rely on Medicare Part D coverage to access needed medicines.

There are real concerns that if the non-interference clause were removed from Medicare law, the only way for the government to negotiate lower prices would be by imposing access or coverage restrictions on medicines in Medicare. For instance, other federal programs that utilize restrictive formularies, like the Veterans' Affairs program, limit access to innovative medicines. A recent study by Xcenda found that of 25 newly FDA-approved first-in-class therapies, Part D plans covered an average of 81 percent, compared to just 12 percent under the VA.[138] In addition, recent research shows that imposing VA-style pricing in Part D would reduce life expectancy of Medicare beneficiaries by nearly 2 years, significantly shrink the drug development pipeline by as much as 25 percent, and result in the loss of trillions of dollars in consumer welfare.[139]

Senator Whitehouse

Question 1. During the hearing, we discussed "de facto" monopolies of prescription drugs, or monopolies that occur outside of the patent and exclusivity protections granted to new drugs. You all acknowledged that we have seen instances of industry outsiders taking advantage of these de facto monopolies and dramatically increasing the prices of drugs. Addressing this unfair price manipulation in a targeted way will require the proper identification of de facto monopolies. How can we ensure de facto monopolies are correctly identified?

Answer 1. The Turing Daraprim situation was caused when a small company was able to corner the market in an older, off-patent drug that treats a serious condition in a

---

[136] 2017 Medicare Trustees Report, p. 143, footnote 66.

[137] See CBO Medicare Baselines available at www.cbo.gov

[138] Comparing Drug Coverage: Medicare Part D vs Veterans Affairs Program. Xcenda, August 26, 2016. http://www.xcenda.com/Insights-Library/Archive/Xcenda-Original-Research-Stark-Contrast-in-Part-D-vs-VA-Coverage-of-Newly-Approved-Drugs/.

[139] Moreno, G, van Eijndhoven, E, Benner, J, et al. (2017). The Long-Term Impact of Price Controls in Medicare Part D. Forum for Health Economics and Policy, January 2017, doi:10.1515/fhep-2016-0011.

small patient population. This situation is an exception not the rule. In this case, there is a lack of a market incentive for a generic entry.

The FDA has already taken steps to avoid this type of situation by publishing a list of products that meet the criteria of a small patient population yet has no competitors and no patent or exclusivity barriers to entry of competitors be they brand, generic, or biosimilars. In addition, the FDA has stated an intent to expedite the review of potential competitors and take other steps to foster the entry of additional competitors. PhRMA believes the FDA has taken sufficient steps to identify situations that could be taken advantage of by unscrupulous actors.

RESPONSE BY CHESTER "CHIP" DAVIS TO QUESTIONS OF SENATOR ALEXANDER, SENATOR MURRAY, SENATOR BENNET, SENATOR ROBERTS, AND SENATOR WHITEHOUSE

Chairman Alexander

Question 1. What is the role of rebates, and do we need them? *Question 2.* How do rebates affect your industry? Do your members contract and get paid based on the public "list price, or using a "net" price that takes into account rebates?

Question 3. Would you support a policy that would allow supply chain participants to contract for lower prices on the front end rather than after the fact with rebates?

Answer 1. In response to brand manufacturer pricing power granted by their patents and regulatory exclusivities, PBMs and payors rely on formulary management and rebating agreements to control costs.

Answer 2. However, upon generic entry, payors typically shift away from rebate models of reimbursement and rely on distribution channels to effectively lower the price of the medicine. Rather than providing rebates to lower the cost, generic manufacturers must compete for sales to wholesalers. Because the products are identical, the primary leverage generic manufacturers have is their ability to lower the price and provide the necessary volume. Rebates are simply not a factor in our industry.

Generic drugs currently allow supply chain participants to contract for lower prices on the front end. With over 200 generic manufacturers recognized by FDA, competition is fierce and prices decline rapidly. The wholesalers, often in collaborative purchasing agreements with pharmacies across the country, then distribute generic medicines to various retail pharmacies. Generic manufacturers may have to compete even further by negotiating separate payments to pharmacies to stock their product.

These differences in the generic and brand marketplaces create vastly different incentives for the various manufacturers, wholesalers, distributors, pharmacy benefit managers (PBMs), insurers, and retail pharmacies that make up the supply chain. To put it simply, virtually all other actors in the supply chain enjoy significant financial benefits from the manufacture of generic medicines.[140] Ultimately, generic manufacturers do not pay rebates on individual sales of their products like brands do. Wholesalers force generic manufacturers to compete with one another on the front-end price.

However, compared to the fragmented generic drug market, consolidation in the wholesale market and contractual arrangements between pharmacy chains and the wholesalers have left generic manufacturers with only a small number of purchasers. The result is a market where three purchasers account for over 90 percent of all wholesale revenue.[141]

Answer 3. The current state of the market puts these savings generics offer at risk. As these purchasers move more and more toward single-source contracts for generic drugs, it creates a dynamic where it is possible that no more than three generic manufacturers may be able to successfully market any given product. This risks future competitive success in the generic market as generic drug manufacturers may be forced to maximize economies of scale and consolidate themselves. AAM has no position on the viability or utility of rebates or whether the supply chain would be better served negotiating savings on the front-end rather than relying on this contracting agreement. We would however call your Committee's attention to supply chain consolidation and its impact on our industry.

Senator Murray

Question 1. In the written testimonies submitted to the committee, there is a lot of blame shifting when it comes to where the fault of high drug prices lays. We can all agree that our complex health system is inefficient, but, for that reason, the blame is shared, and everyone bears responsibility to fix the problem.

Please provide more than one policy proposal, which does not involve any other members of the supply chain, that your industry in particular could implement, either with or without the help of Congress or the Administration, to bring down costs for patients and families, including the reasons why you believe it would bring down costs.

Answer 1. AAM strongly supports regulatory and reimbursement environments that allow generic and biosimilar medicines to compete in open markets. These have produced robust competition with a proven track record of savings for the U.S. health care system—$253 billion in 2016, and $1.67 trillion over the preceding decade. Medicare and Medicaid alone saved $77 billion and $37.9 billion, respectively.

---

[140] Sood, et al., "The Flow of Money Through the Pharmaceutical Distribution System." June 2017. http://healthpolicy.usc.edu/documents/USCpercent20Schaeffer-Flow percent20of percent20Money-2017.pdf

[141] Fein, Adam J. Fein. The 2016–2017 Economic Report on Pharmaceutical Wholesalers and Specialty Distributors, September 2016.

We believe there are a range of opportunities for Congress and the Administration to further the development of competitive markets, further delivering savings to patients, payers and governments.

Electronic Labeling

In 2014, the FDA released a proposed rule[142] establishing guidelines for the use of electronic labeling for pharmaceuticals. Electronic labeling, or e-labeling, would replace paper Prescribing Information package inserts for prescription drugs received by physicians, pharmacists, and other healthcare professionals.

Prescription drug labeling, or Prescribing Information, contains the information necessary for the safe and effective use of a drug product and is intended for use by healthcare professionals. The labeling is submitted to FDA as part of a manufacturer's drug application and is subject to agency approval, updated periodically to include the most current information about the product. Manufacturers provide this information in the form of paper package inserts for prescription drugs received by healthcare professionals.

Eliminating the paper labeling requirements would reduce the cost of manufacturing, while simultaneously providing health care professionals with the most up-to-date safety information. A final rule would significantly reduce costs for manufacturers, allowing them to maintain deflationary trends currently seen in the generics market of about 8 percent per year. We encourage the Committee to work with FDA to modernize pharmaceutical labeling procedures.

Increasing Generic Utilization in Medicare

The nonpartisan Medicare Payment Advisory Commission (MedPAC) has estimated that "nearly 70 percent of Medicare's total spending for Part D plans was on behalf of the 30 percent of Part D enrollees who receive the LIS." Despite having greater health needs requiring more prescriptions, these high-cost beneficiaries routinely miss opportunities to take advantage of lower cost generic drugs. However, Part D plans have limited ability to modify drug copayments for LIS enrollees. Thus, brand-name drug copays for LIS enrollees do not differ significantly from generic drug copays— meaning LIS enrollees do not have an incentive to choose the generic drug when one is available.

Compared with other Part D beneficiaries, Low-Income Subsidy (LIS) not only fill more prescriptions but fill more expensive prescriptions. This is why MedPAC has

[142] "Electronic Distribution of Prescribing Information for Human Prescription Drugs, Including Biological Products," 79 Fed. Reg. 75,506 (Dec. 18, 2014).

recommended changes to Medicare Part D cost-sharing policies for LIS enrollees to improve generic utilization—changes that have been echoed by a range of nonpartisan experts. The Congressional Budget Office (CBO) has estimated that similar proposals could save the Federal Government $17.7 billion over 10 years[143], while ensuring that these beneficiaries continue to have access to high-quality prescription drugs.

AAM encourages Congress to consider legislation directing the Centers for Medicare and Medicaid Services (CMS) to modify the Medicare Part D LIS copayment structure to encourage the use of generic medicines by these beneficiaries. This policy would build on the cost and access successes that both private and public purchasers have achieved as they have moved to more aggressively utilize generic drugs, while assuring beneficiary access to life-saving medications.

Ensure Access to Biosimilar Medicines in Medicare

Nowhere is the need for lower-priced alternatives, and the challenges facing them, more real than among high-priced biologic medicines. Biologics, many of which are specialty medicines, are the most rapidly growing segment of increasing brand-name prescription drug costs in the United States, with more than $100 billion in annual spending. The role of biologic drugs in the health care system is expanding—while only 2 percent of America's patients use biologics, they account for about 40 percent of prescription drug spending in the United States.[144]

To help bring down prices for patients, Congress designed and approved the Biologics Price Competition and Innovation Act (BPCIA) in 2010—creating an abbreviated approval pathway for biological products that are demonstrated to be "highly similar" (biosimilar) to or "interchangeable" with an FDA-approved biological product.

Biosimilar medicines represent a key step forward in reducing high drug prices. They are safe, effective and affordable versions of costly brand biologics. Experts estimate that FDA-approved biosimilars could save between $44 billion and $250 billion over the next 10 years.[145] In doing so, they will mean greater access to life-saving cures for 1.2 million U.S. patients, according to a new analysis. Women, lower income, and elderly patients would particularly benefit from access to biosimilar medicines.

However current law creates barriers to biosimilar access for patients in Part D, who may be forced onto higher priced biologics. Because of the structure of Medicare Part D, the 50 percent discount required of brand biologics is counted toward a patient's out of pocket costs—but competing biosimilars are barred from providing such a discount. This

[143] Proposals for Health Care Programs—CBO's Estimate of the President's Fiscal Year 2016 Budget (March 12, 2015)

[144] Medicine Use and Spending in the U.S.: A Review of 2016 and Outlook to 20, April 2017.

[145] AAM, "Generic Drug Access & Savings in the U.S.," June 2017 (*link.*)

creates a perverse incentive for health plans and patients to use a higher-priced brand biologic—moving patients through the coverage gap and into catastrophic coverage faster and with lower out-of-pocket costs compared to a lower-cost biosimilar.

This approach creates substantial barriers for biosimilar manufacturers, as it may be effectively impossible to ever offer sufficient discounts to be included on Part D formularies. The resulting imbalance severely undermines the market potential for biosimilar competition. Ultimately, patients, payers, and Medicare all pay more for brand biologics than they would if the Coverage Gap Discount program were amended to include biosimilars.

AAM encourages Congress to pass legislation to classify biosimilars as "applicable drugs" in the Coverage Gap Discount Program. This change would require biosimilar manufacturers to pay the 50 percent discounts paid by their brand competitors, and participate on a level playing field to compete for placement on Part D plans' formularies. It would reduce both patient out-of-pocket costs and save at least $1 billion over the next 10 years for the Medicare Part D program.

Senator Bennet

Question 1. In your testimony, each of you indicated that there is some role for value-based arrangements that health plans can set up with drug manufacturers for outcomes-based reimbursement. However, there are still relatively few of these arrangements in place.

I recently sent a letter with Senators Cassidy, Warner, and Young to request a GAO study on value-based arrangements. We asked GAO to assess the savings potential for consumers and the government in outcomes-based arrangements.

What do you expect we will find in this study?

What impediments exist to creating outcomes-based reimbursements?

Answer 1. AAM strongly supports efforts to ensure value in prescription drug purchasing. In fact, generic drugs are the best "value-based" purchasing model—a proven approach to delivering value and savings to patients and payers, including Medicare and Medicaid. In the last 10 years, generic competition has produced $1.67 trillion in savings for the U.S. health care system.

As policymakers consider new approaches such as "value-based" or "outcomes-based" arrangements, it is important to note that the level of price concessions that seem to be part of such arrangements do not compare to the savings associated with generic medicines—which can drop as low as 20 percent of the brand drug price within a year of the loss of brand drug market exclusivity. For that reason, greater flexibility in brand contracting will not likely significantly alter the generics landscape or the central role of generic drugs in delivering FDA-approved medicines to patients at lower costs.

However, policymakers should carefully consider whether such arrangements will truly result in lower prices and reduced costs. As part of such scrutiny, policymakers should examine whether brand drug manufacturers may abuse their market power to delay or impede generic entry.

Senator Roberts

Question 1. When the Biologics Price Competition and Innovation Act passed in 2010, the Congressional Budget Office projected $7 billion in savings to the Federal Government from 2010–2019. Do you think we can achieve this projected savings over the next 2 years? What have been the main delays for biosimilars? Does Congress need to clarify parts of the biosimilars law, and can that be done without causing further delay and uncertainty about the pathway for these products, pushing savings even further into the future?

Answer 1. Biosimilars can offer more savings to patients, payers, and the Federal Government when more products come to market.

FDA-approved biosimilar medicines represent a key step forward in reducing high drug prices. They are safe, effective and more affordable versions of costly brand biologics. Experts estimate that FDA-approved biosimilars could save between $54 billion and $250 billion over the next 10 years.[146] In doing so, the cost savings will lead to greater access to lifesaving cures for 1.2 million U.S. patients. Women, lower income, and elderly patients would particularly benefit from access to biosimilar medicines.

Currently seven products have been approved by the FDA, but only three have been able to come to market due to legal road-blocks initiated by the innovator company(s). Additionally, the three products that have come to market have faced market road-blocks initiated by the innovator company(s). AAM believes that we can achieve the projected savings if biosimilars are able to overcome barriers created by innovator companies, such as unscrupulous marketing tactics to impede competition. Education is another important aspect of the conversation. Recently, FDA unveiled a new education campaign to help educate prescribers and to help dismiss the myths perpetuated by the innovator companies. However current law also creates barriers to biosimilar access for patients in Part D, who may be forced onto higher priced biologics. Because of the structure of Medicare Part D, the 50 percent discount required of brand biologics is counted toward a patient's out of pocket costs—but competing biosimilars are barred from providing such a discount. This creates a perverse incentive for health plans and patients to use a higher-priced brand biologic—moving patients through the coverage gap and into catastrophic coverage faster and with lower out-of-pocket costs compared to a lower-cost biosimilar.

---

[146] AAM, "Generic Drug Access & Savings in the U.S.," June 2017 (*link*).

This approach creates substantial barriers for biosimilar manufacturers, as it may be effectively impossible to ever offer sufficient discounts to be included on Part D formularies. The resulting imbalance severely undermines the market potential for biosimilar competition. Ultimately, patients, payers, and Medicare all pay more for brand biologics than they would if the Coverage Gap Discount program were amended to include biosimilars. AAM encourages Congress to pass legislation to classify biosimilars as "applicable drugs" in the Coverage Gap Discount Program.

Question 2. In 2015, Express Scripts and Imprimis partnered to offer a compounded alternative to Daraprim in an effort to provide a lower-cost option since no approved generic was on the market. Do you believe compounded drugs should considered a substitutable alternative for FDA approved drugs when there is not a patient medical need?

Answer 2. We believe the key distinction between outsourcing facilities, which provide stock supplies of compounded drugs, and traditional compounders, who tailor products to individual patients, is the prescription. This point has been repeatedly made by the FDA and Commissioner Gottlieb in recent public statements. The prescription requirement is critical to ensure product quality, create oversight accountability, and maintain incentives for outsourcing facilities to invest in quality systems. Outsourcing facilities should not be allowed to compound approved products and must be held to Good Manufacturing Practices (cGMP) as prescribed by DQSA and the FDA. Widespread compounding like that envisioned by Imprimis threatens the underpinnings of FDA's "gold standard" approval.

Senator Whitehouse

Question 1. During the hearing, we discussed "de facto" monopolies of prescription drugs, or monopolies that occur outside of the patent and exclusivity protections granted to new drugs. You all acknowledged that we have seen instances of industry outsiders taking advantage of these de facto monopolies and dramatically increasing the prices of drugs. Addressing this unfair price manipulation in a targeted way will require the proper identification of de facto monopolies. How can we ensure de facto monopolies are correctly identified?

Answer 1. We understand that many older, off-patent products have provided complex problems for policymakers. The FDA has also recognized this problem and begun exploring ways to help create market-based solutions for instances when brand companies abuse their monopolies for these products, including recently publishing a list of such products for public consumption. AAM supported this legislation and is working collaboratively with FDA to implement it.

A generic company considers a range of factors when determining whether to pursue development of a generic version of an approved drug. AAM's assessment of FDA's "List of Off-Patent, Off-Exclusivity Drugs without an Approved Generic" revealed that the list contains 264 products, and consists of 83 products that are often deemed inappropriate development candidates due to their product type and the capital investment required (e.g., radio-pharmaceuticals, amino acid/electrolyte replacements). Of the remaining 181 potential products, 144 products have low volume sales, which reduces the attractiveness of developing the product. Generic companies evaluate potential product candidates with low sales; however, the drugs often treat small patient populations or are no longer the standard of care. Ultimately any manufacturer that abuses one of these "de facto monopolies" is effectively relying on regulatory arbitrage to delay competition from reaching the market. However, it is important to remember that any specific restrictions on product pricing will likely ultimately completely deter generic entry, which has been shown to be the most effective method of reducing brand prices.

Question 2. While we want to make sure people can afford their medications, it strikes me that patient assistance programs that reduce out-of-pocket costs for patients also serve to help companies maintain their market share, even when there is a lower-cost drug available that is just as effective. What effect do patient assistance programs have on costs to patients and to the overall health care system? How could Congress help ensure patient assistance programs don't mean wasteful spending of our health care dollars, while still preserving patient access?

Answer 2. We agree that copay coupons and patient assistance programs designed to protect brand market share may skew functioning markets, and push additional cost back onto the health system exclusively to the benefit of the brand manufacturer.

However, in instances where manufacturers work with payers to ensure that programs are designed in way that lower patient out- of-pocket costs without pushing additional cost on the system, those programs should be encouraged.

RESPONSE BY MARK MERRITT TO QUESTIONS FROM SENATOR ALEXANDER, SENATOR MURRAY, SENATOR BENNET, SENATOR CASSIDY, SENATOR HASSAN, SENATOR ISAKSON, SENATOR ROBERTS, SENATOR WARREN, AND SENATOR WHITEHOUSE

Senator Alexander

Question 1. What is the role of rebates, and do we need them?

Answer 1. After settling a 1996 class-action lawsuit by retail pharmacies alleging that manufacturers were illegally discounting their products more to health insurers, drug manufacturers turned to rebates as a way to grant price concessions to drug purchasers who demonstrated they could move market share. Previously, manufacturers had offered hospitals and managed care plans discounted list prices up front, but under the settlement, manufacturers abandoned that practice. By calculating the market share a given organization had moved to a manufacturer's drug and paying rebates after the insurer or PBM presented data demonstrating their enrollees' use of a given product, manufacturers could recognize PBMs' and health plans' abilities to influence patients' choice of drugs and still comply with their court settlement. As part of today's manufacturer-PBM negotiations, brand drug manufacturers compete by offering rebates for market-share influencing formulary placement, typically for therapeutically equivalent products. As a result of these negotiations, PBMs can recommend benefit designs that reduce the net cost of drugs and stretch payers' finite dollars to reduce premiums and cost-sharing. Without rebates, payers and patients would pay considerably more for brand drugs and health coverage costs would be higher. Unless manufacturers devise a different legal way of bringing down net drug costs (or decide to lower their prices significantly), rebates are needed.

Question 2. How do rebates affect your industry? Do your members contract and get paid based on the public "list" price, or using a "net" price that takes into account rebates?

Answer 2. PCMA is not privy to contract negotiations of its members' business. PBMs typically respond to payer requests for proposals, which lay out the payer's terms and conditions. Each payer determines what percentage of rebates it wants the PBM to pass through to it, and how much (if any) it wants the PBM to retain as payment for services. While on average payers elect to receive 90 percent of rebates negotiated by PBMs, an increasing number require PBMs to pass through all of them. About 46 percent of commercial PBM contracts are negotiated with full pass-through of rebates to payers, and 100 percent of rebates in the Medicare Part D program are required to be reinvested for subsequent year benefits. PBMs are committed to providing rebate transparency and audit rights to their clients.

Question 3. Would you support a policy that would allow supply chain participants to contract for lower prices on the front end rather than after the fact with rebates?

Answer 3. Yes. PBMs work to obtain the lowest net cost from manufacturers and are open to other means besides rebates to achieve it.

Senator Murray

Question 1. In the written testimonies submitted to the committee, there is a lot of blame shifting when it comes to where the fault of high drug prices lays. We can all agree that our complex health system is inefficient, but, for that reason, the blame is shared, and everyone bears responsibility to fix the problem.

Please provide more than one policy proposal, which does not involve any other members of the supply chain, that your industry in particular could implement, either with or without the help of Congress or the Administration, to bring down costs for patients and families, including the reasons why you believe it would bring down costs.

Answer 1. Because PBMs negotiate with manufacturers and with pharmacies to bring down the cost of prescription drugs, there is little PBMs could do on their own without involving other actors in the drug supply chain. PCMA has a wide range of policy proposals to bring down the cost of drugs, which we will send along with this document.

Question 2. Patients and families are right to expec —and deserve—more transparency from the prescription drug supply chain. Recently, experts and lawmakers have started asking questions about the work of Pharmacy Benefit Managers, or "PBMs," that negotiate on behalf of insurers and employers for rebates, off the list prices for drugs, in addition to other services like developing pharmacy networks and drug formularies. The details of that work and who really benefits are largely kept confidential.

Question 2(a)1. Do patients at the pharmacy counter always benefit from the discounts PBMs secure from drug manufacturers? If no, what policy solutions do you propose to address that gap for your industry? For others in the supply chain?

Answer 2,2(a). There is not a simple answer to this question. In general, rebate savings are used by payers to reduce premiums and out-of-pocket costs for patients. A PBM acts as a third-party administrator under contract to the payer. The amount of rebates passed back to a payer is established by the contract between the payer and the PBM. The allocation of rebates the payer receives is up to the payer, which establishes the benefit designs in its health plans. As we understand it, such contract terms vary widely among PBMs and payers.

Question 2(b). When PBMs negotiate with drug companies, is the goal to secure the largest rebate, or to secure the lowest prices for patients? Put another way, if drug company A company offered a drug for a list price of $100 with a rebate of $50, and drug company B offered the drug for $40 dollars with no discount, which drug would get preferred placement on the PBM's formulary?

Answer 2(b). PBMs negotiate with drug manufacturers to achieve the lowest net cost of drugs for the client payer.

Question 2(c). We've heard that drug companies will sometimes make deals with PBMs by offering big rebates on an exciting and expensive new product in exchange for favorable placement on the formulary for the rest of that company's drugs, even if those products aren't the least expensive options for patients. Given that PBM contracts are not public, and these examples cannot be verified, can you clarify whether these "book of business" deals exist? Or is every PBM contract, price, and rebate negotiated on a product-by-product basis only?

Answer 2(c). In its role as a trade association, PCMA does not and, for antitrust reasons cannot, have access to our member companies' proprietary contracts with other entities. Therefore, we do not know the answer to the question.

Question 2(d). Pharmaceutical companies often say they need to raise drug prices in order to compete by offering larger rebates to PBMs. If that is true, what explains price increases for drugs that don't face direct competition?

Answer 2(d). The premise of the question is untrue. Manufacturers alone decide prescription drug launch prices and price increases according to the same supply and-demand dynamics of countless other industries that manufacture products. The launch prices of new drugs and price increases of existing drugs bear no correlation to the rebates and discounts manufacturers negotiate with PBMs. There are high-priced drugs with low rebates and lower-priced drugs with high rebates. It all depends on how much direct competition a given drug faces in the market. Indeed, research shows that the size of negotiated rebates is strongly correlated with the extent to which specific drugs face marketplace competition. Please see attached analyses for more information.

Senator Bennet

Question 1. In your testimony, each of you indicated that there is some role for value-based arrangements that health plans can set up with drug manufacturers for outcomes-based reimbursement. However, there are still relatively few of these arrangements in place.

I recently sent a letter with Senators Cassidy, Warner, and Young to request a GAO study on value-based arrangements. We asked GAO to assess the savings potential for consumers and the government in outcomes-based arrangements.

What do you expect we will find in this study?

Answer 1. It is impossible to speculate without knowing the exact questions asked of GAO, or the data and assumptions that GAO may use to answer the questions. PCMA agrees that out-comes-based arrangements are still in their infancy.

Question 1(a). What impediments exist to creating outcomes-based reimbursements?

Answer 1(a). The Medicaid Best Price Law and elements of the Federal Anti-Kickback Statute may inhibit the formation of value-based agreements.

Senator Cassidy

Question 1. In determining Direct & Indirect Remunerations, should Part D plan sponsors utilize quality and performance measures that are applicable to the services provided by retail and specialty pharmacies?

Answer 1. In its role as a trade association, PCMA is not privy to the contracts our members negotiate. In general, PBMs try to work with pharmacies to lower costs, improve quality, and provide value to patients and payers. PBMs implemented value-based payment incentives with pharmacies, reflecting the trend in every other part of the health system toward basing payment on value, rather than volume, of services.

Question 2. An analysis commissioned by the Coalition of Affordable Prescription Drugs (CAPD) (http:// www.affordableprescriptiondrugs.org/ app/uploads/2017/06/ow-pbm-med-d-report-june-2017-final–1.pdf) found that in 2014 PBMs saved the Medicare Part D program $31.7 billion due to negotiated price reductions. CMS, however, reported that such savings only totaled $17.4 billion (https://www.cms.gov/Newsroom/MediaReleaseDatabase/Fact-sheets/2017-Fact-Sheet-items/201701–19–2.html)—can you please discuss the difference in these two reported amounts?

Answer 2. The respective authors of the studies would be in a much better position to answer this question.

Question 3. In your testimony, you stated PBMs pass through 90 percent of rebates to your customers. Please provide detailed information supporting this statement for those members that participate in the Medicare Part D program.

Answer 3. As a matter of CMS policy, under Part D bidding and medical loss ratio regulatory constructs, every Part D Plan (PDP) and MA-PD must file detailed information with CMS on Part D rebates in its bids. Because that information is proprietary, PCMA does not know what portion of rebates is passed along to beneficiaries but notes that under rules and guidance, plans treat rebates like all other revenue received, so Part D plans must allocate at least 85 percent of all funds to clinical—in contrast to administrative activities.

With respect to the figure in PCMA's testimony, Adam Fein calculated and reported the 90 percent figure in his blog "Drug Channels" on January 14, 2016, in a piece entitled, "Solving the Mystery of Employer-PBM Rebate Pass-Through." It reads, "we estimate that on average, PBMs pass back to employers more than 90 percent of total rebate dollars, regardless of form, received from brand-name pharmaceutical manufacturers."

Additionally, a J. P. Morgan survey of human resources executives at 50 large employers across the United States illustrates current pricing arrangements in PBM contracts. Across all respondents, PBMs on average retained approximately 10 percent of manufacturer rebates,

Question 4. What is PCMA position on "gag clauses" that impose restrictions on pharmacies from informing consumers about lower priced pharmaceutical options? Do PCMA members impose these clauses?

Answer 4. PCMA is not privy to member company contracts with pharmacies. However, our understanding is that PBMs may negotiate terms with pharmacies that prevent pharmacies from suggesting drugs that would deviate from the lowest net price.

However, regardless of any terms of any contract between PBMs and pharmacies, PCMA believes that the patient should always pay the lowest cost-sharing possible for a given drug.

Senator Hassan

Question 1. In general, what portion of the annual revenue and profits for PBMs is derived from the sale of pharmaceuticals through mail-order and specialty pharmacies that they own and operate?

Answer 1. PBMs typically operate as separate enterprises from both mail order and specialty pharmacies, even when under common ownership. Given the widely varying ownership and organizational structures within the PBM industry, it is not possible for PCMA to derive that figure.

Question 1(a). Do you know of any nationwide mail-order only pharmacies that are in an individual PBM network, but not owned by that PBM?

Answer 1(a). In short, no. In its role as a trade association, PCMA is not a party to the contracts our member companies negotiate with pharmacies or other entities, nor do we see those contracts. We cannot answer this question as we lack specific information on the extent or make-up of our member company pharmacy networks.

Question 1(b). In your written testimony, you state that PBMs operate outside of the pharmacy supply chain. Please explain how it is that PBMs do not participate in the "pharmacy supply chain" when each of the biggest three PBMs own their own mail-order pharmacy.

Answer 1(b). Because PBMs never take physical possession of drugs, PCMA considers them to be outside the pharmaceutical supply chain. To the extent that an enterprise also owns mail-order and specialty pharmacies, then PCMA would consider those enterprises to be in the physical supply chain as pharmacies. However, we see the PBM as a fiscal intermediary and outside the supply chain.

Question 2. Have there been quantitative studies that show that rebates are required to make the pharmaceutical market function according to normal laws of economics? Can you provide this evidence?

Answer 2. PCMA believes that rebates per se are not necessary to create a competitive market for branded prescription drugs. The current rebate system was created by drug manufacturers to comply with a decades-old court settlement. Because PBMs work to find the lowest net cost of drugs for their clients, PCMA would support other market-based methods to manage cost.

Question 2(a). If manufacturers of undifferentiated products (e.g. insulin) were required to set a single retail price for their product (with no opportunity for rebates) how would they set those prices?

Answer 2(a). Because drug manufacturers set prices, PCMA is unable to shed any light on this question.

Question 2(b). In your view, would it be more or less transparent for consumers and regulators if manufacturers were required to set a single retail price for their product (with no opportunity for rebates)?

Answer 2(b). PCMA strongly opposes any government action to impose a pricing regime or schedule for prescription drugs. PCMA notes that manufacturers do not sell drugs directly to patients— manufacturers tend to use wholesalers, which supply pharmacies, which ultimately dispense (and sell) drugs to patients. Thus, prices to patients would still likely vary, even if manufacturers set a price for each drug that could not be discounted. As stated above, PCMA would be open to market-based methods other than rebates to help manage the cost of prescription drugs.

Senator Isakson

Question 1. This past January, the Centers for Medicare and Medicaid Services (CMS) released a report showing how PBMs' manipulation of rebates, discounts and other Direct and Indirect Fees (called DIR fees) caused beneficiaries to pay more at the counter and, more importantly, drove claims through the Part D structure in a way that caused claims to be paid in the "catastrophic" coverage level, where Medicare pays more and the PBMs pay less. Should Congress require disclosure and transparency of the fees, rebates, DIR fees, and other remuneration that PBMs collect so that we and America's seniors can better understand how their dollars are being handled by your members?

Answer 1. The CBO examined a similar question—the disclosure of negotiated drug rebates—and found that public disclosure of drug rebates would have increased costs for the Medicare program by "facilitate(ing) tacit collusion" among manufacturers of drugs with very few competitors, which would raise costs. PCMA believes the terms of PBM and pharmacy contracts should not be disclosed for the same reasons—that disclosure results in higher costs from tacit collusion. In fact, CMS found earlier this year that under the current proprietary DIR system, "(h)igher DIR leads to lower bids and, therefore, puts downward pressure on beneficiary premiums."[147]

Question 2. I have heard that PBMs use a methodology known as "Maximum Allowable Price (MAC)" pricing to establish the amount long-term care pharmacies are paid for the cost of acquiring most generic drugs. The concern my constituents shared is that MAC pricing allows PBMs to change payment rates every day, as long as those changes are based on actual and identifiable market-place changes.

---

[147] CMS, "Medicare Part D-Direct and Indirect Remuneration (DIR)" January 19, 2017.https:// www.cms.gov/ Newsroom/MediaReleaseData base/ Fact-sheets/2017-Fact-Sheet-items/ 2017–01– 19–2.html

Answer 2. Because there are typically multiple manufacturers of "MACed" generic drugs, generic drugs are a commoditized market, like soy beans or gasoline. The prices of generic drugs can thus fluctuate rapidly. Because MAC pricing relies on pricing data in the market, MAC prices may change frequently, reflecting a dynamic market.

Question 3. Claims processing fees of $0.25 to $1.00, charged to LTC pharmacies, are a growing concern that I have been hearing about from my state. Most of those concerns revolve around that fact that most claims are processed on a computer-to-computer basis. Can you tell me the reasoning behind PBMs charging these fees to pharmacies when the PBMs are supposed to be reimbursing those very same pharmacies?

Answer 3. We are not privy to our companies' negotiated contracts, but we understand that pharmacies agree to certain fees in their contractual arrangements with PBMs. These fees are not unlike those paid by retailers to credit card companies in exchange for the risk of consumer fraud and for immediate payment for purchases, or the fees that banks charge consumers for ready access to cash through ATMs. Specifically, the fees help support access to the PBM's IT systems, which allow pharmacies to fill prescriptions, determine patient eligibility and cost-sharing, and have claims adjudicated at point of sale by nearly any benefit plan. This system essentially assists in streamlining the process for pharmacies, which would otherwise have to contract with individual employers and plans in order to provide services to their enrollees. Additionally, these fees also support maintaining help lines, benefit manuals, and other services provided to the pharmacy by the PBM.

Senator Roberts

Question 1. Would striking the non-interference clause save the government, or patients, money? What impact could it have on access to new innovative therapies?

Answer 1. The CBO has found that striking Part D's noninterference clause would not result in any further savings beyond those already negotiated by PBMs, unless the government also took steps to restrict the availability of drugs in Part D. Without excluding many drugs and establishing a restricted formulary, the Federal Government would get no greater savings than Part D plans currently do. It seems unlikely that Medicare beneficiaries would be satisfied with a single, very narrow formulary. PCMA cannot speculate on how drug manufacturers would respond to the incentives involved in such a policy change.

Question 2. What obstacles exist for small, innovative, often single product companies to have their treatment included on a formulary? It is my understanding that there are significant challenges for small companies when it comes to getting insurance companies to adequately cover innovative medicines targeting very specific disease states that represent a significant advance for the patient's overall health and reduce the need for other healthcare services. Can you share some instances where small companies and their medicines don't receive equal consideration under a coverage policy, and how it could have significant impacts for patient access to the most appropriate treatment option? When you negotiate, is it on each drug individually, or if a company has more than one drug, do you negotiate across all their products?

Answer 2. PBMs rely on Pharmacy and Therapeutics committees (P&T committees) to advise them on drugs they must include in their formularies. P&T committees, which typically meet quarterly, largely comprise independent clinicians who assess the most current drug therapies. To the extent that a therapy is truly a break-through and must be covered, P&T committees recommend coverage. The furor over pricing of the breakthrough hepatitis C drug Sovaldi illustrates this point—until its competition hit the market, PBMs had to recommend coverage and include it on their formularies, even at its very high price. Beyond that, however, in its role as a trade association, PCMA is not a party to the terms of the negotiations of its member companies with manufacturers. We therefore cannot more specifically answer this set of questions.

Question 3. In your written testimony, you mention support for "innovations like electronic prior authorization (ePA)". Would you expand on your support for ePA as well as on how PCMA sees ePA and these types of innovation positively affecting the drug delivery system?

Answer 3. PCMA believes that the use of ePA can lower administrative costs and in general smooth the process for all parties involved in a prior authorization transaction, especially patients.

Question 4. We have seen increased adoption of ePA by EHRs, payers and pharmacies over the years, specifically in the commercial markets. Are there any barriers your members see to that trend continuing in the commercial market or in public programs such as Medicare and Medicaid?

Answer 4. As PCMA understands it, not all physicians are technologically equipped to handle ePA, and the technology currently in the hands of providers may not have 100 percent, real-time formulary access.

Senator Warren

Competition among Mail-Order Pharmacies

Pharmacy benefit managers (PBMs) manage prescription drug benefits on behalf of plan sponsors, including employers and insurers. In this role, PBMs negotiate prices for covered drugs with drug manufacturers and maintain networks of pharmacies where plan beneficiaries can use their insurance coverage to fill their prescriptions. PBMs also operate their own mail-order pharmacies, and many insurance plans are designed to encourage use of mail-order pharmacies for the filling of certain prescriptions.

Some independent and specialty pharmacies have alleged that PBMs engage in abusive, anti-competitive practices to deny pharmacies access to their networks and instead steer customers toward PBM-owned mail-order pharmacies.[148] 1 Pharmacies argue that PBMs identify minor offenses and use them as a justification for canceling contracts in order to direct more customers to the PBM-owned mail-order service. For instance, several specialty pharmacies suing Express Scripts, one of the Nation's largest PBMs, have alleged that Express Scripts looks for "minor issues concerning [. . .] compliance with the terms of their provider contracts," which are then "trumped up into material breaches" and used to justify termination from the pharmacy network.[149] PillPack, a specialty mail-order pharmacy with a presence in Massachusetts, raised similar concerns last year when it alleged that Express Scripts had accused the pharmacy of contract violations in order to exclude a competitor to Express Scripts' own mail-order pharmacy from its network.[150]

Question 1(a). How many of PCMA's members own or operate mail-order pharmacies?

Answer 1(a). It is our understanding that PCMA members generally offer both mail-service and specialty pharmacy benefits, which also operate through mail and rapid consumer delivery services. Most PCMA members handle major aspects of mail-service and specialty pharmacy operations even if they do not own the actual facility that fulfills the prescription. Additionally, the majority of PCMA members own mail-order prescription fulfillment facilities as well as specialty pharmacies.

Question 1(b). What share of PCMA members that own or operate mail-order pharmacies maintain pharmacy networks that include other, independent mail-order pharmacies?

Answer 1(b). In its role as a trade association, PCMA is not a party to the contracts our member companies negotiate with pharmacies or other entities, nor do we see those contracts. We cannot answer this question, as we lack specific information on the extent or make-up of our member company pharmacy networks.

Question 1(c). Independent pharmacies, including mail-order pharmacies, are regulated by state and Federal standards that govern licensing, accreditation, and other credentialing requirements. Do PCMA members typically impose additional licensing and accreditation conditions that go beyond state and Federal requirements on pharmacies participating in their networks? If so, what purpose do these additional requirements serve?

---

148 Katie Thomas, "Specialty Pharmacies Say Benefit Managers Are Squeezing Them Out," *The New York Times* (October 26, 2017) (online at: https://www.nytimes.com/2017/01/09/ business/specialty-pharmacies-say-benefit-managers-aresqueezing-them-out.html-r=0).

149 Mary Anne Pazanowski, "Express Scripts, Pharmacies Collide over Network Cutes," *Bloomberg BNA* (March 2, 2017) (online at:https://www.bna.com/express-scripts-pharmacies-n57982084674/).

150 Curt Woodward, "PillPack Ends Spat with Huge Prescription Benefits Company," *The Boston Globe* (April 29, 2016) (online at: http://www.bostonglobe.com/business/ 2016/04/29/pillpack-patches-contract-spat-with-huge-benefitscompanhy/ dDS6AKjGmqfnh0lSSfM08H/story.html'event=event12).

Answer 1(c). As stated above, PCMA is not a party to the contracts our member companies negotiate with pharmacies or other entities, nor do we see those contracts. It is our understanding that PBMs may require or prefer network pharmacies to earn accreditation beyond state licensing. Requiring accreditation is common in many other areas of health care network formation, such as physician groups or hospitals.

Accreditation provides greater certainty with respect to pharmacy quality and service than state licensing alone would indicate. Accreditation assesses capabilities including, for example, having plans to rapidly recover business continuity from a natural disaster, a program for compliance with health records privacy laws, and proper training for all pharmacy staff in carrying out their duties, which state licensure alone does not require. These are just a few examples of many.

Question 1(d). Under what circumstances do PCMA members typically audit pharmacies participating in their networks?

Answer 1(d). As stated above, PCMA does not have access to its member companies' pharmacy contracts, but it is our understanding that such contracts typically include audit rights. Medicare Part D plans, by law, are themselves audited by CMS every 3 years. To ensure they meet CMS standards, they would need consistently to audit pharmacies that serve enrollees. PCMA assumes that private payers may have similar requirements as Medicare. In addition, to ensure that pharmacies are complying with their contracts and not defrauding payers, PBMs would have to audit them periodically.

PBMs' Impact on Drug Prices

PBMs argue that their role in the drug supply chain helps constrain the growth of prescription drug prices. For instance, in your written testimony submitted to the Senate Committee on Health, Education, Labor, and Pensions, you stated: "By negotiating price concessions from drug companies and recommending strategies that promote generics and more affordable pharmacies, PBMs have played a key role in restraining the rise of overall drug costs to low single-digit increases over the past few years."

While PBMs generate revenue from contracts with clients that have an interest in reducing the overall cost of prescription drugs purchased by plan beneficiaries, PBMs also own and operate their own pharmacies. As a consequence, PBMs also generate revenue from the sale of prescription drugs. A 2005 investigation by the Federal Trade Commission examined potential conflicts of interest in this dual role and found "strong evidence that in 2002 and 2003, PBM's ownership of mail-order pharmacies generally did not disadvantage plan sponsors" and that there was no evidence of PBMs using various methods to steer pharmacy customers toward more expensive drugs in order to increase profits.[151] The FTC concluded that "competition in this industry can afford plan sponsors with sufficient tools to safeguard their interests."

However, since the FTC's analysis was conducted, competitive dynamics in the pharmacy market have continued to shift. In particular, the pharmacy benefit manager industry has seen substantial consolidation. Some observers have alleged that consolidation, as well as mergers between pharmacies and PBMs, "creates a conflict of interest" and "could push up drug prices."[152]

Question 2(a). In your testimony, you stated that "PCMA's member companies harness market forces and competition to corral drug costs and deliver high-quality benefits and services to their payer clients and enrollees." How has consolidation in the PBM industry impacted market competition and PBMs' ability to "corral drug costs"?

Answer 2(a). There are dozens of PBMs in the U.S. that offer a wide range of services and options to payers, allowing these payers to meet their unique program needs. While it is true that three PBMs together have a large share of the market, the market remains dynamic and competitive. PBMs that are substantially smaller than those with the majority of the market have had success in winning significant employer business, including large employer accounts. The smaller PBMs compete by trying to differentiate themselves from larger PBMs by emphasizing different services, such as individualized account management support, and offering customized PBM offerings.

Competition and innovation in the PBM industry are driving change. In just the past year we've seen:

- Public speculation of a merger of a major PBM/pharmacy chain with a large insurer
- The creation of a joint venture by Walgreens and Prime Therapeutics
- Anthem announce it is starting a pharmacy benefit manager function in 2020 when its current PBM contract expires
- Rite-Aid's acquisition of Envision Rx
- The merger of Optum and Catamaran
- The acquisition of LDI by Diplomat

Additionally, the giant consumer retail purchasing and delivery service Amazon is taking material steps to possibly enter the PBM industry.[153] This market activity involving PBMs, payers, and pharmacies indicates dynamic industries in flux, but one constant is

---

[151] Federal Trade Commission, *Pharmacy Benefit Managers: Ownership of Mail- Order Pharmacies* (August 2005) (online at: https://www.ftc.gov/reports/pharmacy-benefit-managers-ownership-mail-order-pharmacies-Federal-trade-commission-report).

[152] Brian S. Feldman, "Big Pharmacies Are Dismantling the Industry that Keeps US Drug Prices Even Sort-Of under Control," *Quartz* (March 17, 2016) (online at: https://qz.com/636823/ big-pharmacies-are-dismantling-the-industry-that-keeps-us-drug-costs-even-sort-of-under-control/).

[153] https://www.cnbc.com/2017/05/16/amazon-selling-drugs-pharamaceuticals.html

competition. As recently as 2012, the FTC has maintained that the PBM industry is competitive.[154]

Question 2(b). What practices do PCMA members employ to safe- guard against conflicts of interest between their pharmacy businesses and their contracts to negotiate drug prices on behalf of plan sponsors?

Answer 2(b). PCMA notes that the FTC in 2005 found no conflicts of interest with business entities owning both a PBM and a mail-order pharmacy, and we believe that existing market conditions make that finding still applicable. Further, it is our understanding that standard terms of contracts and accreditation typically require disclosure of any conflicts of interest.

Senator Whitehouse

Question 1. During the hearing, we discussed "de facto" monopolies of prescription drugs, or monopolies that occur outside of the patent and exclusivity protections granted to new drugs. You all acknowledged that we have seen instances of industry outsiders taking advantage of these de facto monopolies and dramatically increasing the prices of drugs. Addressing this unfair price manipulation in a targeted way will require the proper identification of de facto monopolies. How can we ensure de facto monopolies are correctly identified?

Answer 1. PCMA supported the work of Senators Collins and McCaskill in introducing the "Making Pharmaceutical Markets More Competitive Act" as an important first step toward creating a more competitive generic drug marketplace. PCMA was pleased this concept was later offered as an amendment by Senators Collins and Franken to the Food and Drug Administration Reauthorization Act of 2017. Specifically, the FDA will now be required to publish a list of generic drugs where there are three or fewer competitors in the market and to expedite the review of generic drug applications where competition is limited. PCMA believes policies such as these can curb the kinds of outrageous actions such as recently seen with price spikes of Daraprim.

Question 2. While we want to make sure people can afford their medications, it strikes me that patient assistance programs that reduce out-of-pocket costs for patients also serve to help companies maintain their market share, even when there is a lower-cost drug available that is just as effective. What effect do patient assistance programs have on costs to patients and to the overall health care system? How could Congress help ensure patient assistance programs don't mean wasteful spending of our health care dollars, while still preserving patient access?

---

[154] Federal Trade Commission, "Statement of the Federal Trade Commission Concerning the Proposed Acquisition of Medco Health Solutions by Express Scripts, Inc." FTC File No. 111– 0210. April 2, 2012.

Answer 2. Some schemes masquerading as patient assistance programs are really marketing schemes. Such programs will tend to help patients purchase only one drug and may not be means tested. Drug copay coupons are the most common form of this activity.

Considered illegal in Federal health programs, copay coupons are banned in Medicare and Medicaid, but are still allowed in the commercial market in most instances. Drug companies rely on financial subsidy programs to increase product uptake among insured patients, to encourage patients to ignore similarly effective, but more affordable options to treat their conditions. By targeting drugs with sub-optimal formulary placement, drug manufacturers use these programs to rapidly increase product utilization outside the boundaries of traditional insurance processes.

PCMA supports programs that facilitate patient access to specialty and high-cost drugs when appropriate. We do not, however, support programs that undermine formulary design. Payer costs rise unjustifiably when enrollees choose expensive drugs over equally effective, more affordable options, and since the use of copay coupons reduces the utilization of these more affordable options, restrictions on copay coupon use can be part of a solution to help slow the rising cost of prescription drug coverage.

PCMA supports applying anti-kickback statute to coupons used in coverage purchased through health care exchanges to prevent their use in these plans, as is the case in Medicare and Medicaid.

RESPONSE BY THOMAS E. MENIGHAN TO QUESTIONS OF SENATOR ALEXANDER, SENATOR MURRAY, SENATOR BENNET, SENATOR CASSIDY, AND SENATOR WHITEHOUSE

Chairman Alexander

Question 1. What is the role of rebates, and do we need them?

Answer 1. During the October hearing, rebates were discussed in the context of those provided by manufacturers to pharmacy benefit managers (PBMs). Generally, APhA opposes rebates given from the manufacturer to the PBM because it sets up a framework that artificially raises point-of-sale prices, which can increase patients' costs and speed up the rate at which they reach the Part D coverage gap. In addition, because pharmacies do not receive any benefit from these rebates, they are unable to pass on savings to patients. With regard to manufacturers' pricing policies, APhA supports pharmaceutical industry adoption of a "transparent pricing" system which would eliminate hidden discounts, free goods, and other subtle economic devices. The lack of a transparent pricing framework negatively impacts the ability of CMS to oversee the Part D program.

Question 2. How do rebates affect your industry? Do your members contract and get paid based on the public "list" price, or using a "net" price that takes into account rebates.

Answer 2. Savings from rebates given from manufacturers to PBMs are not passed on to pharmacies and APhA is not aware of such rebates' savings being passed onto patients. Due to a lack of transparency, it is difficult to determine the extent to which patients benefit from these rebates, if at all. In fact, rebates between manufacturers and PBMs can inflate the point-of-sale price of prescription medication.

Pharmacies purchase their drugs from wholesale distributors. That purchase price is generally based on the volume of purchases the pharmacy or chain or health system can achieve. The more volume purchased, the lower the price, just as in any supply chain in America. But these differences are generally narrow, and totally disconnected from the pricing offered by a PBM to a pharmacy to participate in a network. Simply, the contract price between a PBM and a pharmacy for medications is not based on what that pharmacy actually pays for the medications. Consequently, the amount reimbursed to the pharmacy by the PBM may be less than the pharmacy's cost to acquire the medication. In addition, it is not clear if the value PBMs give a drug in their formularies and benefit design incorporates the price the pharmacist pays to obtain it. Our member pharmacists have indicated they are experiencing more and more products with a negative payment, in which the payer's reimbursement does not cover the cost of providing the medication.

With regard to contracting and list pricing, there is no standard contract between pharmacists and insurers, PBMs and other payers. Therefore, there is no one set of "list" or "net" pricing used. Pricing offered by PBMs is reported by our members to lag when prices rise and excel when prices fall. Many payer contract prices, as well as terms and conditions are 'take it or leave it', and do not provide an opportunity for meaningful negotiation between parties.

Question 3. Would you support a policy that would allow supply chain participants to contract for lower prices on the front end rather than after the fact with rebates?

Answer 3. Currently, pharmacy chains, or pharmacies in buying groups, aggregate buying power to negotiate with suppliers (typically wholesalers) for small discounts on prices charged to wholesalers from manufacturers. Much of the wholesale industry trade with brand name manufacturers is pass through, with fees paid by manufacturers to wholesalers to distribute their products.

APhA would need to see details regarding the referenced policy. APhA would not support a policy that enables more members of the supply chain to retroactively clawback money from pharmacies. Regulations regarding Direct and Indirect Remuneration (DIR) were established to make transparent the rebates secured by PBMs from manufacturers. These rebates, as noted earlier, are not connected in any way to the prices paid by pharmacies to their suppliers for these medications. However, PBMs have taken their required reporting of rebates to CMS as an opportunity to "recover" their disclosed rebates from pharmacies, who do not benefit from the rebates in the first place.

APhA strongly opposes fees imposed by Medicare Part D plan sponsors and their PBMs that retroactively reduce the payments PBMs earlier approved and paid to pharmacies. These pharmacies have already paid the prices charged to them by their suppliers and have dispensed these medicines to Medicare beneficiaries. DIR disclosure was originally designed to capture rebates and other mechanisms not included at the point-of-sale. However, the DIR disclosure by PBMs to CMS are now being used beyond their original purpose to retroactively adjust pharmacies payment months after the sale, sometimes below the price paid by the pharmacy. Because point-of-sale prices paid by beneficiaries is calculated based on the contracted price before DIR is extracted, DIR fees charged to pharmacies do not positively impact what patients pay but rather, increase the point-of-sale price. This can result in the beneficiary paying more because the patient's cost-sharing may be based on sales prices.

Senator Murray

Question 1. In the written testimonies submitted to the committee, there is a lot of blame shifting when it comes to where the fault of high drug prices lays. We can all agree that our complex health system is inefficient, but, for that reason, the blame is shared, and everyone bears responsibility to fix the problem.

Please provide more than one policy proposal, which does not involve any other members of the supply chain, that your industry in particular could implement, either with or without the help of Congress or the Administration, to bring down costs for patients and families, including the reasons why you believe it would bring down costs.

Answer 2. To efficiently use resources, meaning both dollars and clinicians, APhA suggests several reforms that enhance patient access and outcomes while improving transparency in the pharmacy marketplace:

1. Pass the *Pharmacy and Medically Underserved Areas Enhancement Act* (H.R. 592/S. 109). This bill, with strong bipartisan support would enable medically underserved Medicare beneficiaries to better access health care through pharmacist-provided care services. As the medication expert on the care team, pharmacists possess knowledge and expertise to optimize the impact of medications, patient care, and health outcomes and consequently, the viability of the Medicare program. The importance of medication-related services cannot be overstated, especially in the Medicare program. Medications are the primary method of treating chronic disease and are involved in 80 percent of all treatment regimens. Moreover, the United States spends nearly $300 billion annually on medication-related problems, including nonadherence. Accordingly, not only will S.109 increase beneficiaries' access to health care, it will help improve their

outcomes—particularly those impacted by medications. APhA appreciates the support by many Committee members for the Pharmacy and Medically Underserved Areas Enhancement Act and urges its swift passage to allow pharmacists to deliver these vital services as providers in medically underserved areas. APhA also requests the Committee's consideration of policies that include pharmacists as an eligible provider or clinician, such as in advanced payment models (APMs). These models often refer to Part B's named providers, which disincentivizes the optimal use of the entire patient care team, including pharmacists, to deliver effective and quality care efficiently.

2. We also encourage the Committee, when considering drug policy changes, to look beyond isolated components of health care to determine drug cost and value. Because health coverage is frequently analyzed in a silo by the benefit type such as inpatient, outpatient, and drug coverage, a patient's overall services, costs and outcomes may never be reviewed comprehensively. Policies cannot continue to consider drug and medical coverage, and their related costs and outcomes, separately if we are to achieve true value in health care. Current coverage and payment policies related to prescription drugs place incentives on the short-term, focusing on cost containment for the product rather than weighing the overall clinical benefit to the patient and the impact to their medical costs. Breaking down the many silos within our health care system will help address that $300 billion dollars spent on medication-related problems—many of which are preventable.
3. Suboptimal health information technology (HIT) systems continue to be a barrier to the exchange of pertinent health information necessary for optimal coordination of care in various practice settings. For example, unless pharmacists are part of an integrated system or practice, pharmacists are frequently blocked from the electronic exchange of relevant clinical and billing information with other health care providers, insurers, etc. Such restrictions impede the ability of patients, the health care system and payers like Medicare, to benefit from coordinated, team-based care. Pharmacists are the most accessible health care professional and may be the only one in many communities. We encourage the Committee to look at mechanisms and incentives to facilitate pharmacists' ability to access and exchange information through Electronic Health Records (EHRs)—essential to team-based coordinated care.

Senator Bennet

Question 1. In your testimony, each of you indicated that there is some role for value-based arrangements that health plans can set up with drug manufacturers for outcomes-based reimbursement. However, there are still relatively few of these arrangements in place.

I recently sent a letter with Senators Cassidy, Warner, and Young to request a GAO study on value-based arrangements. We asked GAO to assess the savings potential for consumers and the government in outcomes-based arrangements.

What do you expect we will find in this study?

Answer 1. There are a number of publicly disclosed value-based purchasing arrangements between pharmaceutical manufacturers and payers. While we anticipate the GAO study will not focus on pharmacists, if it did, we would expect the GAO would find most, if not all, of these arrangements fail to reimburse pharmacists for the services they provide to improve medication outcomes, thus impeding real value.

Question 2. What impediments exist to creating outcomes-based reimbursements?

Answer 2. Numerous studies have shown that medication management and other pharmacist-provided services improve medication outcomes for patients, yet, pharmacists are often not reimbursed for these services under Medicare, or from private payers. Any value-based arrangements need to include and adequately reimburse pharmacists for the value of the services they provide.

As noted above, the health care system cannot continue to cover and evaluate the drug and medical benefit separately. New Medicare payment and delivery models, such as ACOs, focus on coordinated care and value, but do not include drug coverage.

Question 3. We have seen reports that in some cases, patients who fill prescriptions are charged a copay that is higher than the cash price of the drug and may not be given the chance to choose the less costly option.

What have you heard from pharmacists on how widespread this practice may be?

Answer 3. We have heard from our members that this is a common practice of PBMs. A June 2016 survey of 600 pharmacists by the National Community Pharmacists Association confirms this position. The findings from the survey stated, "Sometimes PBM corporations impose "gag clauses" that prohibit community pharmacists from volunteering the fact that a medication may be less expensive if purchased at the "cash price" rather than through the insurance plan. In other words, the patient has to affirmatively ask about pricing. Most pharmacists (41 percent) said they encountered these restrictions at least 10 times during the past month."[155] While it may be difficult to measure the prevalence of such restrictions, it is also difficult for pharmacists to remember which plan restricts, and which one allows these disclosures. Prohibitions of "gag clauses" would make the system more transparent.

[155] See, http://www.ncpa.co/pdf/dir—fee—pharamcy—survey—june—2016.pdf

Senator Cassidy

Question 1. In determining Direct & Indirect Remunerations, do you believe Part D plan sponsors should utilize quality and performance measures that are applicable to the services provided by retail and specialty pharmacies?

Answer 1. It is important to clarify that pharmacists services are not covered under Medicare Part B, and Part D does not cover most pharmacist-provided services with the exception of medication therapy management (MTM) and immunizations. However, pharmacists are willing to engage in value-based delivery and payment systems and have the outcomes of their services be measured. Therefore, APhA encourages Medicare statutes and policy be amended to treat pharmacists like other health care practitioners which lays needed groundwork to improve access and quality. In addition, we reiterate the need to measure outcomes, quality and cost comprehensively rather than separately in each Medicare program (e.g. Parts A, B, D).

APhA supports the Improving Transparency and Accuracy in Medicare Part D Drug Spending Act, S. 413, which prohibits Medicare Part D plan sponsors/PBMs from retroactively reducing payment on clean claims submitted by pharmacies under Medicare Part D, which would:

- Lower Medicare costs for taxpayers. Virtually all catastrophic costs in Part D are borne by the government. These costs are fueled by pharmacy DIR fees, which have more than tripled in recent years.
- Boost transparency in drug pricing. Prohibiting these pharmacy fees will make Medicare Plan Finder more accurate and facilitate better CMS oversight.
- Give seniors reduced cost-sharing and greater budget predictability. Beneficiaries who use their drug plan to fill prescriptions are negatively impacted by pharmacy DIR fees. This is because retroactive fees lead to inflated drug costs that are the basis for beneficiary cost-sharing amounts.
- Preserve access to independent community pharmacies. Locally owned pharmacies provide enhanced patient care, and are often located in underserved rural and inner-city areas. The number of U.S. independent community pharmacies has declined the past five years and a recent study estimated 3 million rural residents are at risk of losing the only pharmacy in their community with the next nearest pharmacy over 10 miles away, a trend exacerbated by DIR.

Question 2. What role do you believe retail and specialty pharmacies should play in combating the opioid abuse epidemic?

Answer 2. Pharmacists Role/Pharmacists' Care Services. As the medication experts on the patient's health care team, pharmacists play an important role in preventing prescription drug misuse and abuse. Pharmacists are involved in pain management programs that include medication tapering services, work in medication assisted treatment programs, and furnish naloxone where authorized. Depending on state authority, pharmacists working under collaborative practice agreements can initiate, monitor, modify, and discontinue medication therapy, including opioids, and order and interpret laboratory tests in collaboration with other members of the health care team. Pharmacists see the patient's complete medication profile and can help bridge the communication gap between health care providers by coordinating and providing medication-related services. Pharmacists are part of the team helping patients with legitimate pain management needs achieve treatment goals. Pharmacies often serve as an access point for patients to receive care and to dispose of their medications through take-back receptacles.

In addition, pharmacists are required by DEA regulations to ensure that prescriptions for controlled substances are issued for a legitimate medical purpose by a practitioner acting in the usual course of professional practice (See United States Drug Enforcement Administration, Practitioner's Manual, 2006:30 "Federal courts have long recognized that it is not possible to expand on the phrase 'legitimate medical purpose in the usual course of professional practice' in a way that will provide definitive guidelines to address all the varied situations physicians may encounter"). [Pharmacist's corresponding responsibility]

Medication Assisted Treatment (MAT). Pharmacists' roles in the provision of medication-assisted treatment continues to grow, however, their ability to help patients is stunted because they are not eligible to obtain a DATA-waiver. Currently, 48 states and the District of Columbia allow pharmacists to enter into collaborative practice agreements[156] with physicians and other prescribers to provide advanced care to patients, which may include components of MAT. APhA is aware of at least six states that allow pharmacists to prescribe Schedule III, IV and V controlled substances under a collaborative practice agreement. The Comprehensive Addiction and Recovery Act (CARA) of 2016 expanded the law to allow nurse practitioners and physicians assistants to obtain a DATA waiver and provided SAMHSA with authority to modify eligibility requirements to obtain DATA waiver. Pharmacist involvement in MAT for opioid use disorders helps improve access and outcomes, while reducing the risk of relapse.[157],[158] Pharmacists' capabilities are recognized by the Food & Drug Administration (FDA)[159]

---

[156] Collaborative practice agreements create a formal practice relationship between a pharmacist and another health care provider and specify what patient care services—beyond the pharmacist's typical scope of practice- can be per

[157] DiPaula, B.A. & Menachery, E. (Mar/Apr 2015). Physician-pharmacist collaborative care model for buprenorphine-maintained opioid-dependent patients, Journal of the American Pharmacists Association, 55(2), 187-192.

[158] Raisch, W. (2002). Opioid Dependence Treatment, Including Buprenorphine/Naloxone, Pharmacology & Pharmacy, 36(2), 312-321.

[159] Food & Drug Administration, Information for Pharmacist. SUBOXONE (buprenorphine HCl/ naloxone HCl dihydrate, sublingual tablet) and SUBUTEX (buprenorphine HCl, sublingual tablet), available at: http://www.fda.gov/downloads/Drugs/DrugSafety/

and in SAMSHA's 2015 Federal Guidelines for Opioid Treatment Programs.[160] The pharmacy community is united and has taken a cohesive position regarding the need to allow pharmacists to obtain a DATA waiver.[161] Allowing pharmacists to obtain a DATA-waiver will increase access to MAT and address treatment gaps that become more apparent as the opioid epidemic evolves.

Senator Whitehouse

Question 1. During the hearing, we discussed "de facto" monopolies of prescription drugs, or monopolies that occur outside of the patent and exclusivity protections granted to new drugs. You all acknowledged that we have seen instances of industry outsiders taking advantage of these de facto monopolies and dramatically increasing the prices of drugs. Addressing this unfair price manipulation in a targeted way will require the proper identification of de facto monopolies. How can we ensure de facto monopolies are correctly identified?

Answer 1. APhA recognizes the difficulty in identifying patterns indicative of a de facto monopoly. We encourage Congress to require research regarding factors that can be used to better predict when a de facto monopoly may occur. Such research should incorporate members of the supply chain, including pharmacists, and also include recommendations regarding steps that FTC, FDA, and other government agencies may take to prevent price increases. In addition, APhA notes that stakeholders have indicated manufacturers are using Risk Evaluation and Mitigation Strategy (REMS) Programs inappropriately to delay generic drug development and marketing. APhA recommends research include reviewing REMS programs and whether they are serving as barrier to generic drug development and supporting de facto monopolies.

Question 2. While we want to make sure people can afford their medications, it strikes me that patient assistance programs that reduce out-of-pocket costs for patients also serve to help companies maintain their market share, even when there is a lower-cost drug available that is just as effective. What effect do patient assistance programs have on costs to patients and to the overall health care system? How could Congress help ensure

---

PostmarketDrugSafety%InformationforPatientsandProviders/UCM191533.pdf(last accessed November 16, 2015).

160 Substance Abuse and Mental Health Services Administration (SAMHSA), U.S. Department of Health and Human Services, (March 2015), Federal Guidelines for Opioid Treatment Programs, available at: http://store.samhsa.gov/shin/content/PEP15-FEDGUIDEOTP/ PEP15- FEDGUIDEOTP.pdf, last accessed: May 18, 2016.

161 See Joint Statement for the Record: American Pharmacists Association (APhA), Academy of Managed Care Pharmacy (AMCP), American Society of Consultant Pharmacists (ASCP), American Society of Health-System Pharmacists (ASHP), College of Psychiatric and Neurologic Pharmacists (CPNP), National Association of State Pharmacy Associations (NASPA) and National Community Pharmacists Association (NCPA), available at: http://www.pharmacist.com/sites/default/files/files/ Joint20Statement20for20the20 Record20on2020MAT20to20Energy20and20Commerce20Hearing- 10-25-2017.pdf

patient assistance programs don't mean wasteful spending of our health care dollars, while still preserving patient access?

Answer 2. Patient assistance programs may be created for a variety of purposes, including helping patients to access medications. The components and requirements of these programs vary. In some circumstances, pharmacists act as an intermediary to identify patient assistance programs for patients to help maintain their access to needed medications. Because patient assistance programs vary substantially and change, APhA and our members do not have the resources to perform a review of current programs in attempt to determine their value and impact on patients and the overall health care system. APhA encourages research be conducted to better answer Senator Whitehouse's question.

With regards to transfer incentives which may be provided via patient assistance programs, APhA advocates for the elimination of coupons, rebates, discounts, and other incentives provided to patients that promote the transfer of prescriptions between competitors.

[Whereupon, at 12:10 p.m., the hearing was adjourned.]

INDEX

D

N

O

P

Q

R

S

T

U

V

W